Interconnecting Cisco Network Devices Part I (ICND1) Foundation Learning Guide

Anthony Sequeira CCIE #15626

Cisco Press

800 East 96th Street

Indianapolis, IN 46240

Interconnecting Cisco Network Devices Part I (ICND1) Foundation Learning Guide

Anthony Sequeira

Copyright© 2013 Cisco Systems, Inc.

Published by:
Cisco Press
800 East 96th Street
Indianapolis, IN 46240 USA

Printed in the United States of America 1 2 3 4 5 6 7 8 9 0

First Printing June 2013

Library of Congress Cataloging-in-Publication Number: 2013938764

ISBN-13: 978-1-58714-376-2

ISBN-10: 1-58714-376-3

Warning and Disclaimer

Trademark Acknowledgments

Corporate and Government Sales

The publisher offers excellent discounts on this book when ordered in quantity for bulk purchases or special sales, which may include electronic versions and/or custom covers and content particular to your business, training goals, marketing focus, and branding interests. For more information, please contact U.S. Corporate and Government Sales 1-800-382-3419.

corpsales@pearsontechgroup.com

For sales outside of the U.S., please contact: International Sales international@pearsoned.com.

Feedback Information

At Cisco Press, our goal is to create in-depth technical books of the highest quality and value. Each book is crafted with care and precision, undergoing rigorous development that involves the unique expertise of members from the professional technical community.

Readers' feedback is a natural continuation of this process. If you have any comments regarding how we could improve the quality of this book, or otherwise alter it to better suit your needs, you can contact us through e-mail at feedback@ciscopress.com. Please make sure to include the book title and ISBN in your message.

We greatly appreciate your assistance.

Publisher: Paul Boger	**Associate Publisher:** Dave Dusthimer
Business Operation Manager, Cisco Press: Jan Cornelssen	**Executive Editor:** Brett Bartow
Development Editor: Eleanor C. Bru	**Copy Editor:** John Edwards
Technical Editors: Narbik Kocharians, Ryan Lindfield	**Editorial Assistant:** Vanessa Evans
Managing Editor: Sandra Schroeder	**Project Editor:** Mandie Frank
Proofreader: Sheri Cain	**Indexer:** Erika Millen
Cover Designer: Mark Shirar	**Composition:** Trina Wurst

CISCO.

Americas Headquarters
Cisco Systems, Inc.
San Jose, CA

Asia Pacific Headquarters
Cisco Systems (USA) Pte. Ltd.
Singapore

Europe Headquarters
Cisco Systems International BV
Amsterdam, The Netherlands

Cisco has more than 200 offices worldwide. Addresses, phone numbers, and fax numbers are listed on the Cisco Website at **www.cisco.com/go/offices.**

CCDE, CCENT, Cisco Eos, Cisco HealthPresence, the Cisco logo, Cisco Lumin, Cisco Nexus, Cisco StadiumVision, Cisco TelePresence, Cisco WebEx, DCE, and Welcome to the Human Network are trademarks; Changing the Way We Work, Live, Play, and Learn and Cisco Store are service marks; and Access Registrar, Aironet, AsyncOS, Bringing the Meeting To You, Catalyst, CCDA, CCDP, CCIE, CCIP, CCNA, CCNP, CCSP, CCVP, Cisco, the Cisco Certified Internetwork Expert logo, Cisco IOS, Cisco Press, Cisco Systems, Cisco Systems Capital, the Cisco Systems logo, Cisco Unity, Collaboration Without Limitation, EtherFast, EtherSwitch, Event Center, Fast Step, Follow Me Browsing, FormShare, GigaDrive, HomeLink, Internet Quotient, IOS, iPhone, iQuick Study, IronPort, the IronPort logo, LightStream, Linksys, MediaTone, MeetingPlace, MeetingPlace Chime Sound, MGX, Networkers, Networking Academy, Network Registrar, PCNow, PIX, PowerPanels, ProConnect, ScriptShare, SenderBase, SMARTnet, Spectrum Expert, StackWise, The Fastest Way to Increase Your Internet Quotient, TransPath, WebEx, and the WebEx logo are registered trademarks of Cisco Systems, Inc. and/or its affiliates in the United States and certain other countries.

All other trademarks mentioned in this document or website are the property of their respective owners. The use of the word partner does not imply a partnership relationship between Cisco and any other company. (0812R)

About the Author

Anthony Sequeira, CCIE No. 15626, is a seasoned trainer and author regarding all levels and tracks of Cisco certification. Anthony formally began his career in the information technology industry in 1994 with IBM in Tampa, Florida. He quickly formed his own computer consultancy, Computer Solutions, and then discovered his true passion—teaching and writing about Microsoft and Cisco technologies.

Anthony joined Mastering Computers in 1996 and lectured to massive audiences around the world about the latest in computer technologies. Mastering Computers became the revolutionary online training company, KnowledgeNet, and Anthony trained there for many years.

Anthony is currently pursuing his second CCIE in the area of security and then his third Cisco Data Center! When not writing for Cisco Press, Anthony is a full-time instructor for the next-generation of KnowledgeNet, StormWind.com.

Anthony is an avid tennis player, is a private pilot, and enjoys getting beaten up by women and children at his and his daughter's martial arts school, www.sparta.fm.

About the Technical Reviewers

Narbik Kocharians, CCSI, CCIE No. 12410, (R&S, Security, SP) who has over 36 years of experience in the industry, is a Triple CCIE. He has designed, implemented, and supported numerous enterprise networks. Some of the international companies that Narbik has worked for are IBM, Carlton United Breweries, Australian Cable and Wireless, BP, and AMOCO. In the United States, he has worked for 20th Century Insurance, Home Savings of America, Verizon, TTI, Trinet Inc, Andersen Networking and Consulting, and many more. Narbik has been a dedicated CCIE instructor for over 12 years. In 2012, he was awarded the Sirius Top Quality Instructor Award.

Narbik Kocharians established his own school, Micronics Networking & Training, Inc. (www.micronicstraining.com) in 2006, where he teaches Cisco authorized courses from CCNA to CCIE in R&S, Security, SP, and Data Center.

Ryan Lindfield is a Certified Cisco Systems Instructor (CCSI) and consultant, based in Tampa, FL. His first position in 1996 was the systems administrator of Gorilla, a video game developer for Mattel and Disney. In 2001, he became an independent contractor, handling system, network, and security contracts for a wide range of customers, including commercial business (IBM), service providers (Verizon), government contractors (L3), and government entities (TSA). In 2003, he became associated with Boson as technical instructor and developer. Topics of expertise include routing and switching, offensive and defensive security, data center technologies, and IPv6. In 2008, with the help of his wife and fellow Cisco instructor, Desiree Lindfield, he launched Westchase Technologies, providing consulting and educational services for clients globally. On a typical day, he can be found providing authorized training for Computer Data, Global Knowledge, and Boson. When not in the classroom, he spends time designing, troubleshooting, and securing customer networks. He is a frequent attendee of Cisco Live, Blackhat, and Defcon conferences. Ryan holds the following certifications: CCNP, CCNP-Data Center, CCNP-Security, HP MASE Networking, VCP, CISSP, CEH, CHFI, GCFA, OSWP, CPTE, LPI-2, and a variety of Microsoft and CompTIA certifications.

Dedication

This book is dedicated to my amazingly talented daughter, Bella Joy Sequeira. Remember that you can do and become anything that you really put your mind to!

Acknowledgments

As always, thanks to my friend, fantasy baseball nemesis, and tequila-drinking partner, Brett Bartow of Cisco Press. Thanks also to Ellie Bru and everyone else at Cisco Press who worked so tirelessly to make this book a reality!

Thanks also to my friends Ryan Lindfield and Narbik Kocharians, who were kind enough to lend their technical editing services to this text. You guys helped this product tremendously!

Finally, thanks to everyone at StormWind.com for the time and the resources to make this book, and the videos for each chapter, a reality.

Contents at a Glance

Contents

Icons

 Router

 Switch

 Multilayer Switch

 Cisco ASA

 Database

 Cisco CallManager

 IP Phone

 Access Server

 VPN Concentrator

 PIX Firewall

 Router with Firewall

 ATM Switch

 CSU/DSU

 Web Server

 Server

 Hub

 Mac

 PC

 Laptop

 100BaseT Hub

 Repeater

 Bridge

 IP Telephony Router

 uBR910 Cable DSU

 Access Point

 Modem

 Host

 Printer

 Headquarters

 Branch Office

 Home Office

 Ethernet Connection

Serial Line Connection

Network Cloud

Command Syntax Conventions

The conventions used to present command syntax in this book are the same conventions used in the IOS Command Reference. The Command Reference describes these conventions as follows:

- Boldface indicates commands and keywords that are entered literally, as shown. In actual configuration examples and output (not general command syntax), boldface indicates commands that are manually input by the user (such as a show command).

- Italics indicate arguments for which you supply actual values.

- Vertical bars (|) separate alternative, mutually exclusive elements.

- Square brackets [ ] indicate optional elements.

- Braces { } indicate a required choice.

- Braces within brackets [{ }] indicate a required choice within an optional element.

Introduction

This book was written to allow students to gain a comprehensive foundation in the many different technologies that are found in modern internetworks today. From the most critical network devices to their configuration and troubleshooting, this text provides students with numerous examples, illustrations, and real-world scenarios to gain confidence in the vast world of computer networking.

Goals and Methods

The goal of this book is simple: to provide the reader with a strong foundation in each aspect of computer networking covered in the ICND1 Version 2 blueprint from Cisco Systems.

To accomplish this goal, great pains were taken to reorganize, simplify, and elaborate on specific content from previous editions of this text. Review questions were added for each technology to endure mastery. In addition, two new sections were added to each chapter: Additional Resources and Production Network Simulation Questions. The Additional Resources sections each contain a link to a video created by the author. These videos both complement and supplement the material from the chapter. We hope you enjoy them! The Production Network Simulation Questions help bring the material to life and also challenge the reader with a more "real-world" review.

Who Should Read This Book

Three primary audiences were identified for this text:

- The network engineer needing to review key technologies that are important in today's networks.

- The reader who is interested in learning about computer networking and who might lack any previous experience in the subject.

- The reader who is interested in obtaining the Cisco CCNA Certification.

How This Book Is Organized

Although you could read this book from cover to cover, it is designed to be flexible and allow you to easily move between chapters and sections of chapters to cover only the material you need. If you intend to read all the chapters, the order in which they are presented is an excellent sequence.

Chapters 1 through 20 cover the following topics:

- Chapter 1, "The Functions of Networking": What are the key devices that make up a network today? And for that matter, what is so important about a computer network anyway? These questions and more are explored in this first chapter.

- Chapter 2, "The OSI and TCP/IP Models": While most students shudder at the thought of learning these important networking models, this chapter makes this pursuit simple—and perhaps even enjoyable!

- Chapter 3, "LANs and Ethernet": The local-area network and the Ethernet connections that help build it are some of the most important aspects to learn in modern networking. This chapter details these important technologies for the reader.

- Chapter 4, "Operating Cisco IOS Software": This chapter covers the basics of using the software that powers the majority of Cisco devices today.

- Chapter 5, "Switch Technologies": Switch technologies replaced the need for hubs in our network environments and, as such, are a critical component in the modern network. This chapter explores the inner workings of these important devices.

- Chapter 6, "VLANS and Trunks": VLANs permit the creation of broadcast domains (IP subnets) in the local-area network and are of critical importance. So are the trunk links that carry VLAN traffic from Cisco device to Cisco device. This chapter ensures that the reader is well versed in these important technologies.

- Chapter 7, "The TCP/IP Internet Layer": One of the key layers in the OSI model for any network engineer to master is the Internet layer. This chapter is dedicated to this important concept.

- Chapter 8, "IP Addressing and Subnets": What is one topic that many fear in the CCNA curriculum? The mastery of IP addressing—including subnetting. This chapter dispels these fears and provides simple instructions for creating the best IP addressing schemes for your small network.

- Chapter 9, "The TCP/IP Transport Layer": The transport layer of the OSI model is often misunderstood. This chapter ensures that readers can describe the importance and operation of this key layer.

- Chapter 10, "The Functions of Routing": Why is routing so important? How does it work? This chapter is a must-read for anyone who requires more information about these critical network devices called routers.

- Chapter 11, "The Packet Delivery Process": Everything that must occur when you type www.ciscopress.com in your web browser and press Enter is absolutely amazing. This chapter details the processes that occur when two systems communicate on a typical network today.

- Chapter 12, "Configuring a Cisco Router": In Chapter 10, you learn all about the functions that a router must perform, and how the device does it. In this chapter, you learn the basics of configuring a Cisco router to perform its important jobs!

- Chapter 13, "Static Routing": Static routes are extremely important in your network infrastructure. This chapter ensures that you can create them with accuracy and ease in your Cisco-based network.

- Chapter 14, "Dynamic Routing Protocols": There are many different implementations of routing protocols. This chapter sheds light on the different protocols and their differences.

- Chapter 15, "OSPF": OSPF is the most popular interior gateway protocol in use on the planet today. This chapter is dedicated to this important protocol and provides the reader with a strong foundation in this complex routing protocol.

- Chapter 16, "DHCP and NAT": How can we dynamically provide our workstations with their correct IP address information? What are we to do about the exhaustion of TCP/IP addresses today? These critical questions are answered in this chapter.

- Chapter 17, "Securing the Network": To be a CCNA, you must understand the basic concepts involved with network security. This chapter provides that knowledge!

- Chapter 18, "Managing Traffic with Access Control Lists": Access control lists are fundamental constructs in Cisco devices. If you want to master Cisco networking, you must be knowledgeable about these components.

- Chapter 19, "Introducing WAN Technologies": There are a wide variety of methods in use today for sending data long distances in the network. This chapter is dedicated to these various options and provides an overview of WANs for further more in-depth study.

- Chapter 20, "Introducing IPv6": The future of the TCP/IP protocol is here! And it is here to stay (at least for a while). This chapter educates the reader on IP version 6 and even gets him or her configuring this protocol in a dynamically routed network environment!

Chapter 1

The Functions of Networking

This chapter includes the following sections:

- Chapter Objectives

- What Is a Network?

- Physical Components of a Network

- Interpreting a Network Diagram

- Network User Applications

- Impact of User Applications on the Network

- Characteristics of a Network

- Physical Versus Logical Topologies

- Connections to the Internet

- Chapter Summary

- Additional Resources

- Review Questions

- Production Network Simulation Question 1-1

When you are planning, building, or supporting a network, the tasks and components can sometimes be overwhelming. It reminds me of when I would watch my father design, then build, and then support a new home. When I was very young, these looked like truly impossible feats. I believed my father possessed superhuman skills! It was not until later in life that I understood exactly how he did it. He took this amazingly complex overall task and made it much simpler by breaking it down into many subtasks or modules.

It turns out, this is exactly how we can approach networking and the functions of a network. We can break down this very complex area into many different modules and layers. This book presents several "blueprints" that will serve us well in this endeavor. Chapter 2, "The OSI and TCP/IP Models," covers these blueprints specifically, but before we get there, we need to discuss what a network really is and why it is so important to organizations and individuals today.

In this chapter, we also learn that the key to understanding computer networks lies in understanding the foundations of network communications. You see, the key to building a complex network involves gaining an understanding of the physical and logical components of a simple network. To become proficient in networking, you must gain knowledge of why networks are built and the protocols used in modern network designs. This chapter explores the basics of computer networking and provides a solid foundation on which to build a comprehensive knowledge of networking technology.

Chapter Objectives

Upon completing this chapter, you will understand the basic functions of computer networking and be able to describe many different network components and their functions. These abilities include meeting these objectives:

- Define a network and describe examples of networks

- Identify common network components by function

- Interpret network diagrams

- Describe the impact of user applications on the network

- List the characteristics of a network

- Compare and contrast logical and physical topologies

What Is a Network?

A *network* is a connected collection of devices and end systems, such as computers and servers, that can communicate with each other over a particular media. Today, we tend to take this for granted, and we forget that it was not that long ago when the office was connected by what we now call *Sneakernet*. This meant that we would copy files to a disk media and then carry these files to the person who needed them (while wearing sneakers [shoes], of course).

Today, sneakers are seldom the media used to carry our important data, and that is a good thing because more and more companies spread their employees out all over the globe. Today, the media might be copper wires, fiber-optic connections, or even radio waves through the air. Networks carry data in many types of environments, including homes, small businesses, and large enterprises. Large enterprise networks can have a number of locations that need to communicate with each other frequently. Network locations are based on where workers are situated. Common categories for enterprise network locations include

- **Main office:** A main office is a site where everyone is connected through a network and where most corporate information is located. A main office can have hundreds or even thousands of people who depend on network access to do their jobs. A main office might use several connected networks, which can span many floors in an office building or cover a campus that contains several buildings. Oftentimes, the main office is referred to as corporate headquarters, or simply, headquarters.

- **Remote locations:** A variety of remote locations use networks to connect to the main office or to each other. An example of a remote location might be a facility for storing backups from the main office.

- **Branch offices:** In branch offices, smaller groups of people work and communicate with each other through a network. Although some corporate information can be stored at a branch office, it is more likely that branch offices have local network resources, such as printers, but must access information directly from the main office. As you will learn in this course, oftentimes Virtual Private Network (VPN) connections can be created to provide the branch office with secure network connectivity to the main office over an Internet connection. The company might alternatively invest in completely private wide-area network (WAN) connections called leased lines.

- **Home offices:** When individuals work from home, the location is called a home office. Home-office workers often require on-demand connections to the main office or branch offices to access information or to use network resources such as file servers. Once again, Internet-based VPNs are often used for these connections. Home office users are also commonly referred to as *teleworkers* or *telecommuters*.

- **Mobile users:** Mobile users connect to the main office network. The location of the mobile users determines their network access requirements, and this location is often a hotel or conference center, or even a highway rest stop. Once again, Virtual Private Networks are often a critical ingredient in providing mobile users with the network access they require. Mobile user support is one of the fastest-growing areas of networking today, as more and more employees have come to expect this level of network access using a wide variety of devices including mobile smart phones, iPads, and other portable devices. This has led to a new area of computer networking termed Bring Your Own Device (BYOD). As you might expect, this leads to tremendous challenges in connectivity and security. If you are interested in more information about BYOD and Cisco solutions to this growing networking field, visit www.cisco.com/go/byod.

Note   This book has just started and we are already seeing plenty of acronyms. Remember that in addition to an excellent networking terminology glossary, this text also contains a handy reference of networking acronyms.

You can use a network in your home office to communicate through the Internet to locate information, place orders for merchandise, and send messages to friends. You can also have a small office that is set up with a network that connects other computers and printers in the office. Similarly, you might work in a large enterprise with many computers, printers, storage devices, and servers that are used to communicate and store information from many departments over large geographic areas. The great news is that all these network locations share many common components.

Figure 1-1 shows some of the common locations of networks we will discuss in this section that can be used to connect users to business applications. Notice that more and more, thanks to advances in VPN technologies, the Internet can function as the glue that binds the various network locations together.

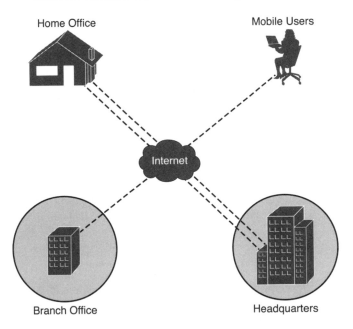

Figure 1-1   *Typical Network Locations*

Physical Components of a Network

There are four major categories of physical components in a typical computer network that we are responsible for at the CCENT/CCNA level:

■ **Endpoints:** Computers and mobile devices are just some of the components that serve as endpoints in modern networks. These devices send and receive data. Endpoints in the network are also printers and servers.

- **Interconnections:** The interconnections consist of components that provide a means for data to travel from one point to another point in the network. This category includes components such as

  - Network interface cards (NICs) that translate computer data into a format that can be transmitted over the local network.

  - Network media such as cables or wireless radio frequencies that provide the means by which signals are transmitted from one networked device to another.

  - Connectors that provide the actual connection points for the media.

- **Switches:** Switches are devices that provide network attachment to the end systems and provide intelligent switching of the data within the local network. As you will learn, these devices operate at Layer 2 of the Open Systems Interconnection (OSI) model and work with Layer 2 addresses called Media Access Control (MAC) addresses.

- **Routers:** Routers interconnect networks and choose the best paths between these networks. These devices operate at Layer 3 of the OSI model and work with Layer 3 addresses called IP addresses.

> **Note**   In this book, you learn much about many of these devices. For example, in Chapter 5, "Switch Technologies," you learn much more about Cisco switches.

Figure 1-2 shows some of these common physical components of the typical network.

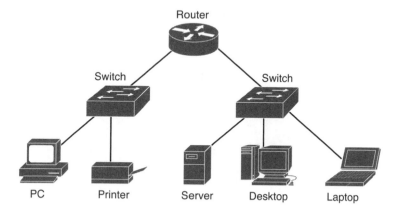

Figure 1-2   *Typical Physical Components of a Network*

Interpreting a Network Diagram

Documentation is one of the most important areas for a modern network administrator. As networking becomes more and more complex, involving a vast number of new and emerging technologies such as wireless, Voice over IP (VoIP), and Video over IP, the network documentation proves critical to maintain and operate the equipment successfully. A key ingredient in the network documentation is network diagrams.

The network diagram captures network-related information. The amount of information and the detail differ from organization to organization. A series of lines and icons commonly represent the network topology. Cisco developed icons to consistently represent its equipment (as well as other vendor equipment) in network diagrams. Of course you will see these symbols used consistently throughout this text. The icons that you should master for the CCENT (and CCNA) certification are depicted in Figure 1-3.

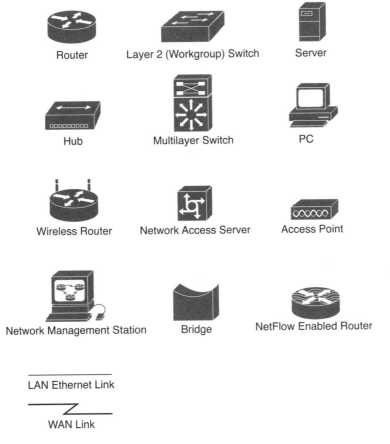

Figure 1-3 *Icons Found in Many Network Diagrams*

Other information can be included in the network diagram as space allows. For example, it is common to identify the interface on a device in the S0/0/0 format for a serial interface, Fa0/0 for a Fast Ethernet interface, or Gi0/1 for a Gigabit Ethernet interface. Realize that the 0/0/0 designation identifies the module, the slot, and the port identifier. This equates to the location in the Cisco device. It is also common to include the network address of the segment in the 192.168.1.0/24 format. Figure 1-4 provides an example of a typical network diagram. In the example, 192.168.1.0 indicates the network address and /24 indicates the subnet mask, and .1 and .2 at the device ends indicate IP addresses on interfaces (.1 corresponds to 192.168.1.1).

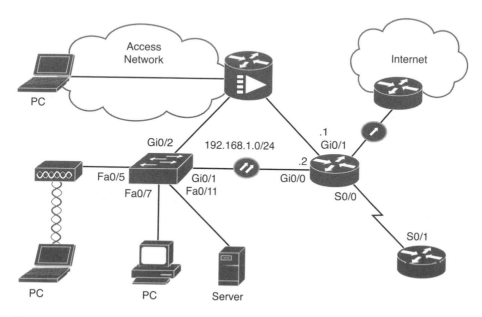

Figure 1-4 *Typical Network Diagram*

Network User Applications

The key to utilizing multiple resources in a data network is having applications that are aware of these communication mechanisms. Although many applications are available for users in a network environment, some applications are common to nearly all users.

The most common network user applications today include the following:

- **Email:** Email is a valuable application for most network users. Users can communicate information (messages and files) electronically in a timely manner, to not only other users in the same network, but also to other users outside the network (suppliers, information resources, and customers, for example). Examples of email programs include Microsoft Outlook and the web-based Gmail by Google.

- **Web browser:** A web browser enables access to the Internet through a common interface. The Internet provides a wealth of information and has become vital to the productivity of both home and business users. Communicating with suppliers and customers, handling orders and fulfillment, and locating information are now routinely done electronically over the Internet, which saves time and increases overall productivity. The most commonly used browsers are Internet Explorer, Safari, Firefox, and Chrome.

- **Instant messaging:** Instant messaging started in the personal user-to-user space; however, it soon provided considerable benefit in the corporate world. Now many instant-messaging applications, such as those provided by Microsoft and Google, provide data encryption and logging, features essential for corporate use.

- **Collaboration:** Working together as individuals or groups is greatly facilitated when the collaborators are on a network. Individuals creating separate parts of an annual report or a business plan, for example, can either transmit their data files to a central resource for compilation or use a workgroup software application to create and modify the entire document, without any exchange of paper. One of the best-known traditional collaboration software programs is Lotus Notes. Lotus Notes is still around today, but renamed IBM Notes. Today, collaboration tools are being built in to just about every major category of network application.

- **Database:** This type of application enables users on a network to store information in central locations (such as storage devices) so that others on the network can easily retrieve selected information in the formats that are most useful to them. Some of the most common databases used in enterprises today are Oracle and Microsoft SQL (Structured Query Language) Server. A hugely popular new application called SharePoint from Microsoft actually relies on Microsoft's own database product—SQL Server.

Impact of User Applications on the Network

The key to user applications is that they enable users to be connected to one another through the various types of software. As a business begins to rely on these applications as part of the day-to-day business process, the network that the applications operate in becomes a critical part of the business. A special relationship exists between these applications and the network. The applications can affect network performance, and network performance can affect applications. Therefore, you need to understand some common interactions between user applications and the network.

Historically, when the interaction between the network and the applications that ran on the network was considered, bandwidth was the main concern. Batch applications such as File Transfer Protocol (FTP), Trivial File Transfer Protocol (TFTP), and inventory updates, which simply used the network to transfer bulk data between systems, would be initiated by a user and then run to completion by the software with no further direct human interaction. As long as the time the application took to complete did not become too excessive, no one really cared about network performance. So while bandwidth was the single big concern with these applications, this concern was mitigated by the nature of how these applications function. I can recall many times going to sleep for the evening during a large network file transfer and waking up happy to see that the transfer had actually completed by morning.

Interactive applications, such as Enterprise Resource Planning (ERP) software, perform tasks, such as inventory inquiries and database updates that require more human interaction. The user requests some type of information from the server and then waits for a reply. With these types of applications, bandwidth becomes even more important because users are intolerant of slow responses. However, application response is not solely dependent on the bandwidth of the network; the server and storage devices also play a part. However, in cases where the network bandwidth becomes a problem, other features such as quality of service (QoS) can alleviate some bandwidth limitations by giving the traffic from interactive applications preference over batch applications.

Another type of application that can be affected heavily by the network is a real-time application. Like interactive applications, real-time applications such as Voice over IP (VoIP) and video applications involve human interaction. Because of the amount of information that is transmitted with video, bandwidth is critical. Interestingly, in the case of VoIP, bandwidth is not as important because packets are very small, but these VoIP applications are extremely latency sensitive. *Latency* refers to delay as the packet moves through the data network. In fact, variations in the amount of latency (*jitter*) can affect the VoIP applications dramatically. Not only is proper bandwidth mandatory, but QoS is also mandatory with many of these real-time applications. VoIP and video applications often must be given the highest priority.

In today's environment, the end user is bombarded with ads indicating how much money can be saved by converting to VoIP and how installation is as easy as dropping a VoIP router into the network. Although this is often true in the home network, it can result in disaster in a small office network. Applications that used to work start to run so slowly that they are unusable, for example, when someone is on the phone, and voice quality is poor. This type of implementation does not provide enough bandwidth to the Internet, nor does it provide a proper QoS scheme.

Of course the great news is that all these issues can be overcome with proper network design and implementation.

Table 1-1 summarizes the different categories of applications that are typical, as well as their characteristics.

Table 1-1   *Typical Network Application Categories*

Application Category	Examples	Characteristics
Batch applications	FTP, TFTP, inventory updates	No direct human interaction; bandwidth important, but not critical
Interactive applications	Inventory inquiry, database update	Human-to-machine interaction; human waiting for response; response time thus important but not critical, unless wait becomes excessive
Real-time applications	VoIP, video	Human-to-human interaction; end-to-end latency critical; bandwidth amounts critical in the case of video

Characteristics of a Network

Many characteristics are commonly used to describe and compare various network designs. When you are determining how to build a network, each of these characteristics must be considered along with the applications that will be running on the network. The key to building the best network is to achieve a balance of these characteristics. Also, always strive to meet the needs of an organization. For example, if the business must have the highest level of availability for its e-commerce services (think Amazon.com), you must ensure that your network meets this requirement head on.

Networks can be described and compared according to network performance and structure, as follows:

- **Speed:** Speed is a measure of how fast data is transmitted over the network. A more precise term would be *data rate*.

- **Cost:** Cost indicates the general cost of components, installation, and maintenance of the network. There are many ways to elaborate on cost. For example, what is the initial investment (capital expenditures) versus the ongoing expenditures (operating expenses)?

- **Security:** Security indicates how secure the network is, including the data that is transmitted over the network. Security encompasses two major domains—internal to the network and external to the network. Many organizations focus on external security, guarding against attacks from outside their organization. Companies cannot forget internal security mechanisms to guard against those within the organization.

- **Availability:** Availability is a measure of the probability that the network will be available for use when required. For networks that are meant to be used 24 hours a day, 7 days a week, 365 days a year, availability is calculated by dividing the time it is actually available by the total time in a year and then multiplying by 100 to get a percentage.

   For example, if a network is unavailable for 15 minutes a year because of network outages, its percentage availability can be calculated as follows:

   ([Number of minutes in a year – downtime] / [Number of minutes in a year]) * 100 = Percentage availability

   ([525600 – 15] / [525600]) * 100 = 99.9971

   For many companies, success in the area of availability is to achieve *five nines*. That is 99.999 percent uptime. Believe it or not, for certain organizations, that would be considered a failure!

- **Scalability:** Scalability indicates how well the network can accommodate more users and data transmission requirements. If a network is designed and optimized for just the current requirements, it can be very expensive and difficult to meet new needs when the network grows.

- **Reliability:** Reliability indicates the dependability of the components (routers, switches, PCs, and so on) that make up the network. Reliability is often measured as a probability of failure, or mean time between failures (MTBF). As you might guess, reliability is often confused with availability. I like to consider reliability as more of a measure of how well the network is meeting the needs of the organization, while availability is a measure of just how often it is there.

- **Topology:** Networks have two types of topologies: the physical topology and the logical topology. The physical topology is the arrangement of the cables, network devices, and end systems (personal computers [PC] and servers) in the network. The logical topology is the path that the data signals take through the physical topology. The logical topology is often much more abstract and less detailed than the physical topology. For example, a cloud might represent a large section of the logical topology to indicate that the traffic moves through a section of the network where details of the exact pathing are not required. Because topologies are so critical in describing a network, this chapter elaborates on physical and logical topologies in the next section.

These characteristics and attributes provide a means to compare different networking solutions. Increasingly, features such as security, availability, scalability, and reliability have become the focus of many network designs because of the importance of the network to the business process. Remember, it is worth repeating, we should construct a network that meets the needs of the business. We should not implement new technologies for the sake of just implementing new cool stuff.

Physical Versus Logical Topologies

Building a reliable and scalable network depends partially on the physical and logical topology. Topology defines the interconnection method used between devices, including the layout of the cabling and the primary and backup paths used in data transmissions. As previously mentioned, each type of network has both a physical and a logical topology.

Physical Topologies

The physical topology of a network refers to the physical layout of the devices and cabling. You must match the appropriate physical topology to the type of cabling that will be installed. Therefore, understanding the type of cabling used is important to understanding each type of physical topology. Here are the three primary categories of physical topologies:

- **Bus:** Computers and other network devices are cabled together in a line.

- **Ring:** Computers and other network devices are cabled together with the last device connected to the first to form a circle, or ring. This category includes both ring and dual-ring topologies.

- **Star:** A central cabling device connects the computers and other network devices. This category includes both star and extended-star topologies.

Figure 1-5 shows some common physical topologies used in networking.

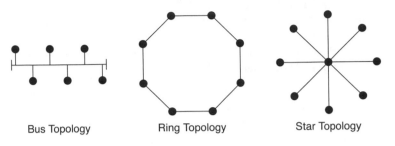

Bus Topology   Ring Topology   Star Topology

Figure 1-5   *Common Physical Topologies*

Logical Topologies

The logical topology of a network refers to the logical paths that the signals use to travel from one point on the network to another—that is, the way in which data accesses the network media and transmits packets across it.

The physical and logical topologies of a network can be the same. For example, in a network physically shaped as a linear bus, the data travels along the length of the cable. Therefore, the network has both a physical bus topology and a logical bus topology.

On the other hand, a network can have quite different physical and logical topologies. For example, a physical topology in the shape of a star, in which cable segments connect all computers to a central hub, can have a logical ring topology. Remember that in a ring, the data travels from one computer to the next, and inside the hub, the wiring connections are such that the signal actually travels around in a circle from one port to the next, creating a logical ring. Therefore, you cannot always predict how data travels in a network simply by observing its physical layout.

A star topology is by far the most common implementation of local-area networks (LAN) today. Specifically, it is the extended star that we see most today. Ethernet uses a logical bus topology in either a physical bus or a physical star. An Ethernet hub is an example of a physical star topology with a logical bus topology.

Figure 1-6 shows some common logical topologies used in networking today and in the past.

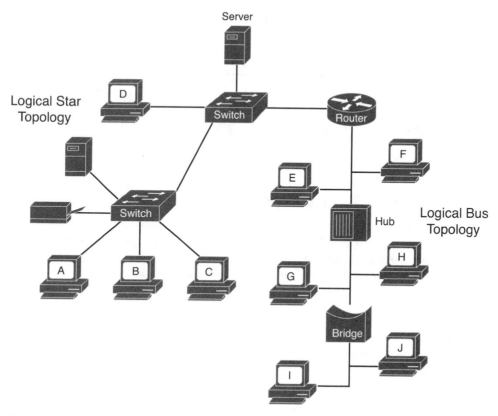

Figure 1-6   *Common Logical Topologies*

Bus Topology

The bus topology is commonly referred to as a linear bus; all the devices on a bus topology are effectively connected by one single cable.

As illustrated in Figure 1-7, in a bus topology, a cable proceeds from one computer to the next like a bus line going through a city. The main cable segment must end with a terminator that absorbs the signal when it reaches the end of the line or wire. If no terminator exists, the electrical signal representing the data bounces back at the end of the wire, causing errors in the network. An example of a physical bus topology is a Thicknet Ethernet cable running through the length of a building with devices taped into it, though this is an antiquated connection method that is no longer used. An example of a logical bus topology is an Ethernet hub.

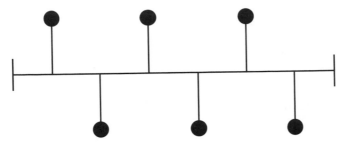

Figure 1-7   *Bus Topology*

Star and Extended-Star Topologies

The star topology is the most common physical topology in Ethernet LANs. When a star network is expanded to include an additional network device that is connected to the main network devices, the topology is referred to as an extended-star topology. The following sections describe both the star and extended-star topologies.

Star Topology

When installed, the star topology resembles spokes in a bicycle wheel. It is made up of a central connection point that is a device, such as a hub, switch, or router, where all the cabling segments actually meet. Each device on the network is connected to the central device with its own cable.

Although a physical star topology costs more to implement than the physical bus topology, the advantages of a physical star topology make it worth the additional cost. Each device is connected to the central device with its own wire, so if that cable has a problem, only that one device is affected and the rest of the network remains operational. This benefit is important and is the reason why almost every newly designed Ethernet LAN has a physical star topology. Figure 1-8 depicts a star topology with all transmissions going through a single point.

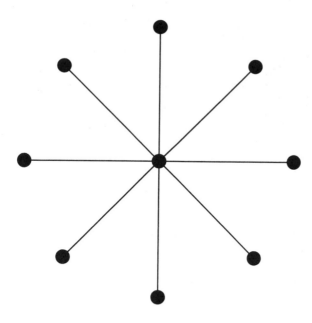

Figure 1-8 *Star Topology*

Extended-Star Topology

A common deployment of an extended-star topology is in a hierarchical design such as a WAN or an enterprise or a campus LAN. Figure 1-9 shows the topology of an extended star.

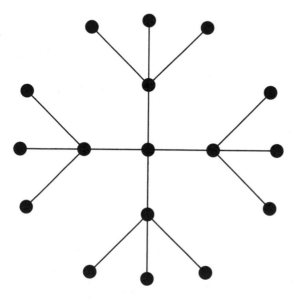

Figure 1-9 *Extended-Star Topology*

The problem with the pure extended-star topology is that if the central node point fails, large portions of the network can become isolated. For this reason, most extended-star topologies employ a redundant connection to a separate set of connection devices to prevent isolation in the event of a device failure.

Ring Topologies

As the name implies, in a ring topology, all the devices on a network are connected in the form of a ring or circle. Unlike the physical bus topology, a ring type of topology has no beginning or end that needs to be terminated. Data is transmitted in a way that is different from the logical bus topology. In one implementation, a "token" travels around the ring, stopping at each device. If a device wants to transmit data, it adds that data and the destination address to the token. The token then continues around the ring until it finds the destination device, which takes the data out of the token. The advantage of using this type of method is that no collisions of data packets occur. Two types of ring topology exist: single-ring and dual-ring.

Single-Ring Topology

In a single-ring topology, all the devices on the network share a single cable, and the data travels in one direction only. Each device waits its turn to send data over the network. The single ring, however, is susceptible to a single failure, stopping the entire ring from functioning. Figure 1-10 shows the traffic flow in a single-ring topology.

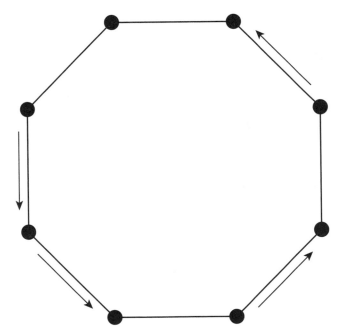

Figure 1-10   *Traffic Flow in a Single-Ring Topology*

Dual-Ring Topology

In a dual-ring topology, two rings allow data to be sent in both directions. This setup creates redundancy (fault tolerance), meaning that if one ring fails, data can be transmitted on the other ring. Figure 1-11 shows the traffic flow in a typical dual-ring topology. Dual-ring topologies are found in fiber-optic WAN technologies as an example.

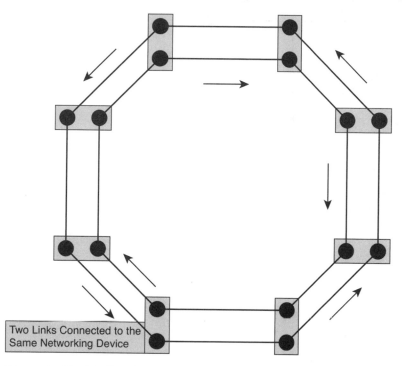

Two Links Connected to the Same Networking Device

Figure 1-11   *Traffic Flow in a Dual-Ring Topology*

Mesh and Partial-Mesh Topologies

Another type of topology that is similar to the star topology is the mesh topology. The mesh topology provides redundancy between devices in a star topology. A network can be fully meshed or partially meshed depending on the level of redundancy needed. This type of topology helps improve network availability and reliability. However, it increases cost and can limit scalability, so you need to exercise care when meshing.

Full-Mesh Topology

The full-mesh topology connects all devices (or nodes) to one another for redundancy and fault tolerance. Implementing a full-mesh topology is expensive and difficult. This method is the most resistant to failures because the failure of any single link does not affect reachability in the network.

Figure 1-12 shows the connections in a full-mesh topology.

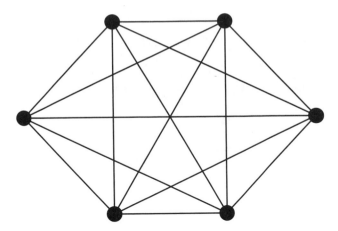

Figure 1-12   *Full-Mesh Topology*

Partial-Mesh Topology

In a partial-mesh topology, at least one device maintains multiple connections to all other devices, without having all other devices fully meshed. This method trades off the cost of meshing all devices by allowing the network designer to choose which nodes are the most critical and appropriately interconnect them.

Figure 1-13 shows an example of a partial-mesh topology.

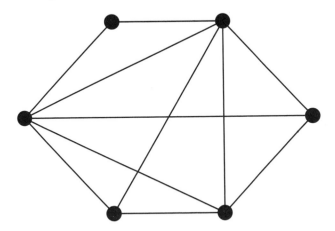

Figure 1-13   *Partial-Mesh Topology*

Connections to the Internet

Another key component for most business users today is a connection to the Internet. An Internet connection is a WAN connection, but small- to medium-sized computer networks can use various methods and topologies to interconnect to the Internet.

You have three common methods of connecting the small office to the Internet. Digital subscriber line (DSL) uses the existing telephone lines as the infrastructure to carry the signal. Cable uses the cable television (CATV) infrastructure. Serial uses the classic digital local loops.

In the case of DSL and cable, the incoming lines are terminated into a modem that converts the incoming digital encoding into a digital format for the router to process. In the case of serial, this is done by channel service unit (CSU)/digital service unit (DSU). In all three cases (DSL, cable, and serial), the digital output is sent to a router that is part of the customer premises equipment (CPE). Figure 1-14 shows the equipment placement for these different connection methods.

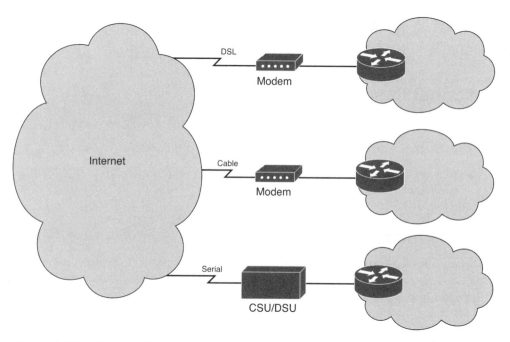

Figure 1-14   *Common Internet Connection Methods*

Chapter Summary

A network is a connected collection of devices that can communicate with each other. Networks in homes, small businesses, or large enterprises allow users to share resources such as data and applications (email, web access, messaging, collaboration, and databases), peripherals, storage devices, and backup devices. Networks carry data (or data packets) following rules and standards called protocols, each with its own specialized function. Networks can be evaluated in terms of both performance and structure, using measures such as speed, cost, security, availability, scalability, reliability, and topology.

It is critically important to document your network and ensure that this documentation is updated and current. There are many tools available to assist in the creation of documentation, and Cisco provides standard icons to represent almost all network objects.

Networks consist of a physical and a logical topology. The logical topology is an abstracted view of the flow of communications. For example, we might say that data flows from Site A to Site B and then on to Site C. A physical topology is a detailing of exactly how the information flows from device to device (often called hop to hop). There are many common types of physical topologies, and this chapter explored several, including the bus, star, and various mesh topologies.

Just as there is variety in the types of networks, types of network devices, and types of network topologies, there is also tremendous variety today in how connections to the Internet are made. These include broadband (cable and DSL) options as well as satellite, cellular, and serial leased lines.

Additional Resources

- Cisco.com Routers Home Page, Cisco Systems: http://cisco.com/go/routers

- Cisco.com Switches Home Page, Cisco Systems: http://cisco.com/go/switches

- Introducing Routers and Switches Video, AJS Networking: http://ajsnetworking.com/rands

Review Questions

Use the questions here to review what you learned in this chapter. The correct answers and solutions are found in Appendix A, "Answers to Chapter Review Questions." This appendix also includes the answers to the Production Network Simulation Questions that follow these Review Questions.

1. Which of the following statements about networks are accurate? (Choose three.)

   a. Networks transmit data in many kinds of environments, including homes, small businesses, and large enterprises.

   b. A main office can have hundreds or even thousands of people who depend on network access to do their jobs.

   c. A network is a connected collection of devices that can communicate with each other.

   d. A main office usually has one large network to connect all users.

   e. The purpose of a network is to create a means to provide all workers with access to all information and components that are accessible by the network.

   f. Remote locations cannot connect to a main office through a network.

2. What is the purpose of a router?

    a. To interconnect networks and choose the best paths between them

    b. To provide the connection points for the media

    c. To serve as the endpoint in the network, sending and receiving data

    d. To provide the means by which the signals are transmitted from one networked device to another

3. What is the purpose of a switch?

    a. To connect separate networks and filter the traffic over those networks so that the data is transmitted through the most efficient route

    b. To choose the path over which data is sent to its destination

    c. To serve as the endpoint in the network, sending and receiving data

    d. To provide network attachment to the end systems and intelligent switching of the data within the local network

4. What is the purpose of network interconnections?

    a. To connect separate networks and filter the traffic over those networks so that the data is transmitted through the most efficient route

    b. To choose the path over which data is sent to its destination

    c. To provide a means for data to travel from one point to another in the network

    d. To provide network attachment to the end systems and intelligent switching of the data within the local network

5. Which of the following are common network applications? (Choose three.)

    a. Email

    b. Collaboration

    c. Graphics creation

    d. Databases

    e. Word processing

    f. Spreadsheets

6. Match each network characteristic to its definition.

___ 1. Speed

___ 2. Cost

___ 3. Security

___ 4. Availability

___ 5. Scalability

___ 6. Reliability

___ 7. Topology

a. Indicates how easily users can access the network

b. Indicates how dependable the network is

c. Indicates the protection level of the network itself and the data that is transmitted

d. Indicates how fast data is transmitted over the network

e. Indicates how well the network can accommodate more users or data transmission requirements

f. Indicates the structure of the network

g. Indicates the general price of components, installation, and maintenance of the network

7. Which physical topology is often used in switched networks today?

a. Dual-ring

b. Star

c. Extended-star

d. Bus

8. Which statement about logical topologies is accurate?

a. A logical topology defines the way in which the computers, printers, network devices, and other devices are connected.

b. A logical topology depends solely on the type of computers to be included in the network.

c. A logical topology describes the paths that the signals travel from one point on a network to another.

d. A network cannot have different logical and physical topologies.

9. Match each topology type to its correct description.

___1. All the network devices connect directly to each other in a linear fashion.

___2. All the network devices are directly connected to one central point, with no other connections between them.

___3. All the devices on a network are connected in the form of a circle.

___4. Each device has a connection to all the other devices.

___5. At least one device maintains multiple connections to other devices.

___6. This design adds redundancy to the network.

a. Star

b. Bus

c. Full-mesh

d. Ring

e. Partial-mesh

f. Dual-ring

10. Which type of network application is the most impacted by end-to-end latency?

a. Batch applications

b. Interactive applications

c. Real-time applications

d. Web-based applications

Production Network Simulation Question 1-1

Your boss has informed you that you are responsible for designing and configuring the network for a new small branch office opening in your organization. He has already decided that he wants to use Gigabit Ethernet links because a friend told him that is the best thing to do when building a new network. Your boss has informed you there are fourteen PCs and two Mac Pros that are to be connected, and that all these devices will need very fast Internet access.

What are two categories of networking devices you will need? Also provide your boss with a short description of why each is required.

Chapter 2

The OSI and TCP/IP Models

This chapter includes the following sections:

- Chapter Objectives

- Understanding the Host-to-Host Communications Model

- The OSI Reference Model

- Data Communications Process

- Peer-to-Peer Communication

- The TCP/IP Protocol Stack

- OSI Model Versus TCP/IP Stack

- Chapter Summary

- Additional Resources

- Review Questions

- Production Network Simulation Question 2-1

Remember, mastering a complex topic is going to require that we break it up into smaller pieces to make things more manageable. This chapter presents two very powerful "blueprints" that we can follow when it comes to computer networking mastery. The OSI and TCP/IP models prove to be critical for an understanding of the complexities of internetworking. These "host-to-host communication models" were created to help define how network processes function, including the various components of networks and the transmission of data. Understanding the structure and purpose of the most commonly used protocol stack—TCP/IP—is central to understanding how one host communicates with another. This chapter introduces the OSI and TCP/IP models and describes the functions of the layers of each model.

Chapter Objectives

Upon completing this chapter, you will be able to describe the OSI and TCP/IP models and their various component parts. You will also be able to describe the importance of these networking models, a feat that has historically been difficult for many students of networking. These abilities include meeting these objectives:

- Understand the concept of the host-to-host communications model

- Describe the layers of the OSI model

- Describe the process of encapsulation and deencapsulation

- Understand the manner in which systems use the OSI layers

- Describe the layers of the TCP/IP model

- Compare and contrast the OSI and TCP/IP models

Understanding the Host-to-Host Communications Model

The Open Systems Interconnection (OSI) reference model was created to help define how network processes function in general, including the various components of networks and transmission of data. Understanding the structure and purpose of the OSI model is central to understanding how one host communicates with another. This section introduces the OSI model and describes each of its layers. Remember that this is a reference model to provide a framework for building protocols and to help people understand the process around network communications and not a communications standard in itself.

Note   This section is a discussion of the OSI reference model and not the OSI protocol.

No matter what type of connectivity, operating system, or network services interconnect computers and computer networks, the fact still remains that for these devices to communicate, some rules must exist. Like any system of communication, rules govern how the communication takes place. Also, some medium for the communication to take place over exists. For example, a language has rules for the formation of sentences using basic words. This language can be used for verbal communication, using air as the medium, or written communication, using paper as the medium.

Most languages have rules that specify how words are put together and then how they are spoken or written. In many western languages, words are written from left to right, but in some eastern languages, words are written from right to left or even top to bottom. To be able to effectively communicate, you must understand how to read the words and in what order to read them.

Many of the computers and operating systems within an organization are manufactured by different companies and use different types of programs to operate; however, if these systems are going to communicate with one another, they must use a common set of rules for data communications. The rules that define how systems talk to one another are called *protocols*.

Many internetworking protocols can be used to establish communications paths between systems, and each of these protocols provides very similar functions. To provide a way to establish some common and open rules for building a data communications protocol, the International Organization for Standardization (ISO) created the OSI reference model.

The OSI Reference Model

The OSI reference model is the primary model for network communications. The early development of local-area networks (LAN), metropolitan-area networks (MAN), and wide-area networks (WAN) was chaotic in many ways. The early 1980s saw tremendous increases in the number and sizes of networks. As companies realized that they could save money and gain productivity by using networking technology, they added networks and expanded existing networks as rapidly as new network technologies and products were introduced.

By the mid-1980s, companies began to experience difficulties from all the expansions they had made. It became more difficult for networks using different specifications and implementations to communicate with each other. The companies realized that they need-ed to move away from proprietary networking systems, those systems that are privately developed, owned, and controlled.

Note   In the computer industry, proprietary is the opposite of open. Proprietary means that one company or a small group of companies controls all usage of the technology. Open means that free usage of the technology is available to the public.

To address the problem of networks being incompatible and unable to communicate with each other, the ISO researched different network schemes. As a result of this research, the ISO created a model that would help vendors create networks that would be compatible with, and operate with, other networks.

The OSI reference model, released in 1984, was the descriptive scheme that the ISO cre-ated. It provided vendors with a set of standards that ensured greater compatibility and interoperability between the various types of network technologies produced by compa-nies around the world. Although other models exist, most network vendors today relate their products to the OSI reference model, especially when they want to educate custom-ers on the use of their products. The OSI model is considered the best tool available for teaching people about sending and receiving data on a network.

It is quite ironic that both instructors and students alike will groan when the subject of the OSI model is brought up. When used correctly, this model really does prove to be the best way to both teach and learn about networking. One of the reasons this is true is that the OSI model allows us to focus on portions of this vastly complex topic. To use the house building analogy once again, it is like focusing on the electrical as opposed to the plumbing and framing.

The OSI reference model has seven layers, as shown in Figure 2-1, each illustrating a particular network function. This separation of networking functions is called *layering*. The OSI reference model defines the network functions that occur at each layer. More importantly, the OSI reference model facilitates an understanding of how information travels throughout a network. In addition, the OSI reference model describes how data travels from application programs (for example, spreadsheets), through a network medium, to an application program located in another computer, even if the sender and receiver are connected using different network media.

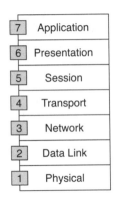

Figure 2-1 *OSI Reference Model*

Dividing the network into these seven layers provides these advantages:

- **Reduces complexity:** It breaks network communication into smaller, simpler parts.

- **Standardizes interfaces:** It standardizes network components to allow multiple vendor development and support.

- **Facilitates modular engineering:** It allows different types of network hardware and software to communicate with each other.

- **Ensures interoperable technology:** It prevents changes in one layer from affecting the other layers, allowing quicker development.

- **Accelerates evolution:** It provides effective updates and improvements to individual components without affecting other components or having to rewrite the entire protocol.

- **Simplifies teaching and learning:** It breaks network communication into smaller components to make learning easier. Yes, I know this might be difficult for you to believe right now!

Note   It is important that you memorize the seven layers of the OSI model. There are two common mnemonic devices to aid you in this endeavor. From the top of the model down, you can use the popular mnemonic All People Seem to Need Data Processing. Or, if you prefer, you can start from the bottom and work your way up with Please Do Not Throw Sausage Pizza Away.

The practice of moving information between computers is divided into seven techniques in the OSI reference model.

Each OSI layer contains a set of functions performed by programs to enable data to travel from a source to a destination on a network. The following sections provide brief descriptions of each layer in the OSI reference model.

Layer 7: The Application Layer

The application layer is the OSI layer that is closest to the end user of the network. This layer provides network services to the user's applications. It differs from the other layers in that it does not provide services to any other OSI layer, but only to applications outside the OSI reference model. The application layer establishes the availability of intended communication partners and synchronizes and establishes agreement on procedures for error recovery and control of data integrity. Examples of services that operate at this layer include Hypertext Transfer Protocol (HTTP) and Simple Mail Transfer Protocol (SMTP). As you probably know, these services facilitate web browser and email applications, respectively. This layer was certainly named appropriately and therefore is easy to memorize its function.

Layer 6: The Presentation Layer

The presentation layer ensures that the information that the application layer of one system sends out is readable by the application layer of another system. For example, a device using a network application communicates with another device, one using extended binary coded decimal interchange code (EBCDIC) and the other using American Standard Code for Information Interchange (ASCII) to represent the same characters. If necessary, the presentation layer might be able to translate between multiple data formats by using a common format. The easy way to memorize the function of this layer is to think about it presenting data in an understandable format to the application layer.

Layer 5: The Session Layer

The session layer establishes, manages, and terminates sessions between two communicating hosts. It provides its services to the presentation layer. The session layer also synchronizes dialogue between the presentation layers of the two hosts and manages their data exchange. For example, web servers have many users, so many communication processes are open at a given time. Therefore, keeping track of which user communicates on which path is important. In addition to session regulation, the session layer offers provisions for efficient data transfer, class of service, and exception reporting of session layer, presentation layer, and application layer problems. With the session layer in charge of managing sessions, memorization is certainly simple once again.

Layer 4: The Transport Layer

The transport layer segments data from the sending host's system and reassembles the data into a data stream on the receiving host's system. For example, business users in large corporations often transfer large files from field locations to a corporate site. Reliable delivery of the files is important, so the transport layer breaks down large files into smaller segments that are less likely to incur transmission problems.

The boundary between the transport layer and the session layer can be thought of as the boundary between application protocols and data-flow protocols. Whereas the application, presentation, and session layers are concerned with application issues, the lower four layers are concerned with data-transport issues. It is the lower four layers where we make our money as Cisco network engineers!

The transport layer attempts to provide a data-transport service that shields the upper layers from transport implementation details. Specifically, issues such as reliability of transport between two hosts are the concern of the transport layer. In providing communication service, the transport layer establishes, maintains, and properly terminates virtual circuits. Transport error detection and recovery and information flow control provide reliable service.

At the transport layer, we begin to have addressing that is critical for networking functions. While the application, presentation, and session layers are not concerned with network addressing, this changes dramatically beginning at the transport layer. For example, at the transport layer, port numbers can be used to determine what particular network service the data is destined for. You will learn more about port numbers and how these are used in Chapter 9, "The TCP/IP Transport Layer." Because the transport layer is so important to us and so complex, we gave it an entire chapter of its own.

Layer 3: The Network Layer

The network layer provides connectivity and path selection between two host systems that might be located on geographically separated networks. The growth of the Internet has increased the number of users accessing information from sites around the world, and the network layer manages this connectivity. Thought of in these terms of the public Internet, I guess we can consider it one of the busiest layers! The addressing that is used at the network layer is called IP addressing. This addressing is a critical component used to direct data from one device to another, or even from one device to many devices. IP addresses are covered in much more detail in Chapter 8, "IP Addressing and Subnets," and Chapter 20, "Introducing IPv6."

Layer 2: The Data Link Layer

The data link layer defines how data is formatted for transmission and how access to the network is controlled. This layer is responsible for defining how devices on a common media communicate with one another, including addressing and control signaling between devices. The addressing found at the data link layer is called Media Access Control, or MAC, addressing. This addressing is covered in much more detail in Chapter 3, "LANs and Ethernet."

Layer 1: The Physical Layer

The physical layer defines the electrical, mechanical, procedural, and functional specifications for activating, maintaining, and deactivating the physical link between end systems. Characteristics such as voltage levels, timing of voltage changes, physical data rates, maximum transmission distances, physical connectors, and other similar attributes are defined by physical layer specifications. When my father would build those houses I mentioned in Chapter 1, he would hire an electrician who would love this layer.

> **Note**   It is important to also master the OSI model by layer references. For example, know that the network layer is often simply called Layer 3, while the data link layer is termed Layer 2, and so on.

The Data Communications Process

All communications on a network originate at a source and are sent to a destination. A networking protocol using all or some of the layers listed in the OSI reference model moves data between devices. Recall that Layer 7 is the part of the protocol that communicates with the application, and Layer 1 is the part of a protocol that communicates with the media. A data frame is able to travel across a computer network because of the layers of the protocol. The process of moving data from one device in a network is accomplished by passing information from applications down the protocol stack, adding an appropriate header at each layer of the model. This method of passing data down the stack and adding headers and trailers is called *encapsulation*. After the data is encapsulated and passed across the network, the receiving device removes the information added, using the messages in the header as directions as to how to pass the data up the stack to the appropriate application.

Data encapsulation is an important concept to networks. It is the function of like layers on each device, called *peer layers*, to communicate critical parameters such as addressing and control information.

Although encapsulation seems like an abstract concept, it is actually quite simple. Imagine that you want to send a coffee mug to a friend in another city. In my case, it would be a Boston Red Sox mug to one of my New York Yankees fan friends. How will the mug get there? Basically, it will be transported on the road or through the air. You cannot go outside and set the mug on the road or throw it up in the air and expect it to get there. You need a service to pick it up and deliver it. So, you call your favorite parcel carrier and give it the mug. But, that is not all. Here is the complete process:

1. Pack the mug in a box.

2. Place an address label on the box so that the carrier knows where to deliver it.

3. Give the box to a parcel carrier.

4. The carrier drives it down the road toward its final destination.

This process is similar to the encapsulation method that protocol stacks use to send data across networks. After the package arrives, your friend has to reverse the process. He takes the package from the carrier, reads the label to see who it is from, and finally opens the box and removes the mug. The reverse of the encapsulation process is known as deencapsulation. The next sections describe the encapsulation and deencapsulation processes in more detail using our network data instead of sports mugs.

Encapsulation

As indicated in the previous section, encapsulation on a data network is similar to the process of sending that mug. However, instead of sending a coffee mug to a friend, you send information from an application from one device to another. The information sent on a network is referred to as data or data packets.

Encapsulation wraps data with the necessary protocol information before network transit. Therefore, as the data moves down through the layers of the OSI reference model, each OSI layer adds a header (and a trailer, if applicable) to the data before passing it down to a lower layer. The headers and trailers contain control information for the network devices and receiver to ensure proper delivery of the data and to ensure that the receiver can correctly interpret the data.

Figure 2-2 illustrates how encapsulation occurs. It shows the manner in which data travels through the layers. These steps occur to encapsulate data:

1. The user data is sent from an application to the application layer.

2. The application layer adds the application layer header (Layer 7 header) to the user data. The Layer 7 header and the original user data become the data that is passed down to the presentation layer.

3. The presentation layer adds the presentation layer header (Layer 6 header) to the data. This then becomes the data that is passed down to the session layer.

4. The session layer adds the session layer header (Layer 5 header) to the data. This then becomes the data that is passed down to the transport layer.

5. The transport layer adds the transport layer header (Layer 4 header) to the data. This then becomes the data that is passed down to the network layer.

6. The network layer adds the network layer header (Layer 3 header) to the data. This then becomes the data that is passed down to the data link layer.

7. The data link layer adds the data link layer header and trailer (Layer 2 header and trailer) to the data. A Layer 2 trailer is usually the frame check sequence (FCS), which is used by the receiver to detect whether the data is in error. This then becomes the data that is passed down to the physical layer.

8. The physical layer then transmits the bits onto the network media as defined by the media type.

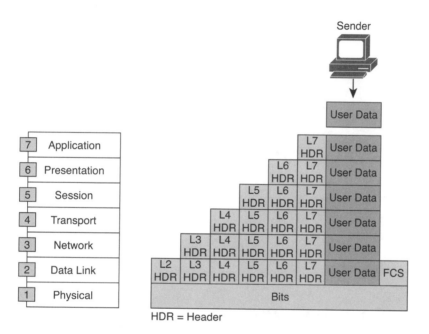

Figure 2-2   *Data Encapsulation*

Deencapsulation

When the remote device receives a sequence of bits, the physical layer at the remote device passes the bits to the data link layer for manipulation. The data link layer performs the following process, referred to as deencapsulation:

1. It checks the data-link trailer (the FCS) to see whether the data is in error.

2. If the data is in error, it is discarded.

3. If the data is not in error, the data link layer reads and interprets the control information in the data-link header.

4. It strips the data-link header and trailer and then passes the remaining data up to the network layer based on the control information in the data-link header.

Each subsequent layer performs a similar deencapsulation process, as shown in Figure 2-3.

Think of deencapsulation as the process of reading the address on a package to see whether it is for you and then opening and removing the contents of the package if it is addressed to you.

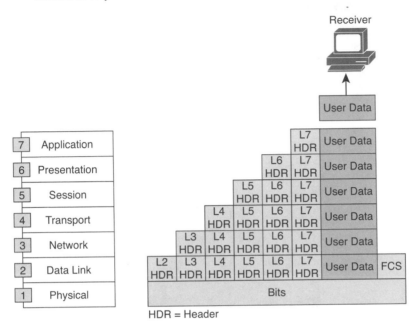

Figure 2-3 *Deencapsulation*

Peer-to-Peer Communication

For data to travel from the source to the destination, each layer of the OSI reference model at the source must communicate with its peer layer at the destination. This form of communication is referred to as *peer-to-peer communication*. During this process, the protocols at each layer exchange information, called *protocol data units (PDU)*, between peer layers, as shown in Figure 2-4.

Data packets on a network originate at a source and then travel to a destination. Each layer depends on the service function of the OSI layer below it. To provide this service, the lower layer uses encapsulation to put the PDU from the upper layer into its data field. It then adds whatever headers the layer needs to perform its function. As the data moves down through Layers 7 through 5 of the OSI reference model, additional headers are added. The grouping of data at the Layer 4 PDU is called a *segment*.

The network layer provides a service to the transport layer, and the transport layer presents data to the internetwork subsystem. The network layer moves the data through the internetwork by encapsulating the data and attaching a header to create a *datagram* (the Layer 3 PDU). The header contains information required to complete the transfer, such as source and destination logical addresses. A more common term than datagram for the network layer PDU is a *packet*.

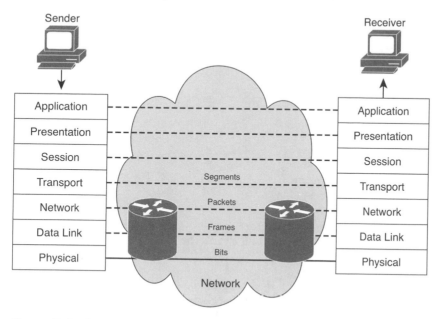

Figure 2-4   *Peer-to-Peer Communication*

The data link layer provides a service to the network layer by encapsulating the network layer datagram in a *frame* (the Layer 2 protocol data unit [PDU]). The frame header contains the physical addresses required to complete the data-link functions, and the trailer contains the frame check sequence (FCS). The FCS is used to ensure that there are no errors in the frame.

The physical layer provides a service to the data link layer, encoding the data-link frame into a pattern of 1s and 0s (bits) for transmission on the medium (usually a wire) at Layer 1. The Layer 1 PDU is indeed called the *bit*.

Network devices such as hubs, switches, and routers work at the lower three layers. Hubs are at Layer 1, switches are at Layer 2, and routers are at Layer 3. A switch that can both route and switch is called a Layer 3 switch, or a multilayer switch.

The TCP/IP Protocol Stack

The TCP/IP suite is a layered model similar to the OSI reference model. Its name is actually a combination of two individual protocols, Transmission Control Protocol (TCP) and Internet Protocol (IP). These are just two of the many protocols in the TCP/IP suite of protocols. TCP/IP is divided into layers, each of which performs specific functions in the data communication process.

Both the OSI model and the TCP/IP stack were developed by different organizations at approximately the same time as a means to organize and communicate the components that guide the transmission of data.

Although the OSI reference model is universally recognized, the historical and technical open standard of the Internet is the TCP/IP protocol stack. The TCP/IP protocol model, shown in Figure 2-5, varies slightly from the OSI reference model.

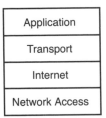

Figure 2-5   *TCP/IP Protocol Stack*

Notice that the TCP/IP protocol stack has four layers. The functions of each layer are described in the following list:

- **Application layer:** The application layer handles high-level protocols, including issues of representation, encoding, and dialog control. The TCP/IP model combines all application-related issues into one layer and ensures that this data is properly packaged for the next layer. Note that this layer encompasses the functions of the session, presentation, and application layers from the OSI model.

- **Transport layer:** The transport layer deals with QoS issues of reliability, flow control, and error correction. One of its protocols, TCP, provides reliable network communications. Notice that this layer coordinates to the transport layer of the OSI model.

- **Internet layer:** The purpose of the Internet layer is to send source datagrams from any network on the internetwork and have them arrive at the destination, regardless of the path they took to get there. This layer coordinates with the network layer of the OSI model.

- **Network access layer:** The name of this layer is broad and somewhat confusing. It is also called the host-to-network layer. It includes the LAN and WAN protocols and all the details in the OSI physical and data link layers.

OSI Model Versus TCP/IP Stack

Both similarities and differences exist between the TCP/IP protocol stack and the OSI reference model. Figure 2-6 offers a side-by-side comparison of the two models.

Similarities between the TCP/IP protocol stack and the OSI reference model include the following:

- Both have application layers, though they include different services.

- Both have comparable transport and network layers.

- Both assume packet-switched technology, not circuit-switched. (Analog telephone calls are an example of circuit-switched technology.)

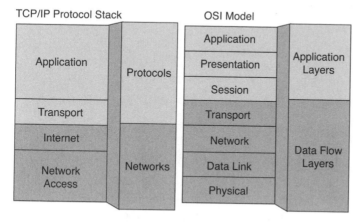

Figure 2-6   *OSI Model Versus TCP/IP*

The differences that exist between the TCP/IP protocol stack and the OSI reference model include the following:

- TCP/IP combines the presentation and session layers into its application layer.

- TCP/IP combines the OSI data link and physical layers into the network access layer.

TCP/IP protocols are the standards around which the Internet developed, so the TCP/IP protocol stack gains credibility just because of its protocols. In contrast, networks are not typically built on the OSI reference model, even though the OSI reference model is still used today as a guide.

Chapter Summary

In this chapter, you learned the details surrounding the OSI and TCP/IP models. You learned the layers of these models and their functions. You also learned why these models are so important, and you can now compare and contrast the two models.

This chapter also presented the way in which end systems use these models and the processes of encapsulation and deencapsulation.

Additional Resources

■ OSI Model, Wikipedia: http://en.wikipedia.org/wiki/OSI_model

■ Troubleshooting with the OSI Model Video, AJS Networking: http://ajsnetworking. com/osi

Review Questions

Use the questions here to review what you learned in this chapter. The correct answers and solutions are found in Appendix A, "Answers to Chapter Review Questions."

1. Which of the following statements about the purpose of the OSI model are accurate? (Choose two.)

   a. The OSI model defines the network functions that occur at each layer.

   b. The OSI model facilitates an understanding of how information travels throughout a network.

   c. The OSI model ensures reliable data delivery through its layered approach.

   d. The OSI model allows changes in one layer to affect the other layers.

2. Match each OSI layer to its function.

   ___ 1. Physical

   ___ 2. Data link

   ___ 3. Network

   ___ 4. Transport

   ___ 5. Session

   ___ 6. Presentation

   ___ 7. Application

   a. Provides connectivity and path selection between two host systems that might be located on geographically separated networks

   b. Ensures that the information sent at the application layer of one system is readable by the application layer of another system

   c. Defines how data is formatted for transmission and how access to the network is controlled

   d. Segments data from the system of the sending host and reassembles the data into a data stream on the system of the receiving host

   e. Defines the electrical, mechanical, procedural, and functional specifications for activating, maintaining, and deactivating the physical link between end systems

   f. Provides network services to the applications of the user, such as email, file transfer, and terminal emulation

g. Establishes, manages, and terminates sessions between two communicating hosts and also synchronizes dialogue between the presentation layers of the two hosts and manages their data exchange

3. Arrange the steps of the data encapsulation process in the correct order.

___1. Step 1

___2. Step 2

___3. Step 3

___4. Step 4

___5. Step 5

___6. Step 6

___7. Step 7

___8. Step 8

a. The presentation layer adds the presentation layer header (Layer 6 header) to the data. This then becomes the data that is passed down to the session layer.

b. The session layer adds the session layer header (Layer 5 header) to the data. This then becomes the data that is passed down to the transport layer.

c. The application layer adds the application layer header (Layer 7 header) to the user data. The Layer 7 header and the original user data become the data that is passed down to the presentation layer.

d. The network layer adds the network layer header (Layer 3 header) to the data. This then becomes the data that is passed down to the data link layer.

e. The transport layer adds the transport layer header (Layer 4 header) to the data. This then becomes the data that is passed down to the network layer.

f. The user data is sent from an application to the application layer.

g. The data link layer adds the data link layer header and trailer (Layer 2 header and trailer) to the data. A Layer 2 trailer is usually the frame check sequence, which is used by the receiver to detect whether the data is in error. This then becomes the data that is passed down to the physical layer.

h. The physical layer then transmits the bits onto the network media.

4. At which layer does deencapsulation first occur?

a. Application

b. Data link

c. Network

d. Transport

5. Match each layer with the function it performs in peer-to-peer communication.

___1. Network layer

___2. Data link layer

___3. Physical layer

a. Encapsulates the network layer packet in a frame

b. Moves the data through the internetwork by encapsulating the data and attaching a header to create a packet

c. Encodes the data-link frame into a pattern of 1s and 0s (bits) for transmission on the medium (usually a wire)

6. What is the function of a network routing protocol?

a. Uses sets of rules that tell the services of a network what to do

b. Ensures reliable delivery of data

c. Moves data to its destination in the most efficient manner

d. Is a set of functions that determine how data is defined

7. Match each TCP/IP stack layer to its function.

___1. Provides applications for file transfer, network troubleshooting, and Internet activities, and supports the network

___2. Segments data for transmission on the network.

___3. Defines the electrical, mechanical, procedural, and functional specifications for activating, maintaining, and deactivating the physical link between end systems

___4. Provides routing of data from the source to a destination by defining the packet and addressing scheme, moving data between the data link and transport layers, routing packets of data to remote hosts, and performing fragmentation and reassembly of data packets

a. Network Access

b. Internet layer

c. Transport layer

d. Application layer

8. Which layer of the TCP/IP stack maps directly to the OSI stack?

a. Network layer

b. Transport layer

c. Application layer

d. Data link layer

9. What is a PDU referred to as at the transport layer?

    a. Frame

    b. Packet

    c. Bits

    d. Segment

10. What is the second layer from the bottom in the TCP/IP model?

    a. Network

    b. Data link

    c. Internet

    d. Transport

Production Network Simulation Question 2-1

One of your fellow engineers just told you that he was informed by a superior that the recent problems with network performance are a result of network layer issues. Your fellow engineer wants to know what this means. Specifically, tell him what classic network device exists at this layer, and what type of addressing it deals with.

Chapter 3

LANs and Ethernet

This chapter includes the following sections:

- Chapter Objectives

- Understanding LANs

- Connecting to an Ethernet LAN

- Chapter Summary

- Additional Resources

- Review Questions

- Production Network Simulation Question 3-1

Local-area networks (LAN) tend to spoil us as network users. These collections of high-speed network equipment allow us to achieve remarkable speeds in accessing network data and information. LANs are a relatively low-cost means of sharing expensive resources. LANs allow multiple users in a relatively small geographic area to exchange files and messages and to access shared resources such as file servers. LANs have rapidly evolved into support systems that are critical to communications within an organization. This chapter will ensure that you are comfortable describing these important network structures.

This chapter also describes different Ethernet media options (copper and fiber), which are presented together with a description of the most common connectors and cable types. Ethernet frame structure is introduced, and important fields are described. MAC addresses and their function are also elaborated on.

Chapter Objectives

Upon completing this chapter, you will be able to describe LAN networks. You will also be able to describe common Ethernet technologies typically found within these important areas of the overall network. These abilities include meeting these objectives:

- Define a LAN

- Identify the components of a LAN

- Describe the types of Ethernet LAN connection media

- Describe the fields of an Ethernet frame

- Define the structure and function of MAC addresses

Understanding LANs

A local-area network is a common type of network found in home offices, small businesses, and large enterprises. Understanding how a LAN functions, including network components, frames, Ethernet addresses, and operational characteristics, is important for an overall knowledge of networking technologies.

This section describes LANs and provides fundamental knowledge about LAN characteristics, components, and functions. It also describes the basic operations of an Ethernet LAN and how frames are transmitted over it.

The Definition of a LAN

A LAN is a network of computers and other components located relatively close together in a limited area. LANs can vary widely in their size. A LAN might consist of only two computers in a home office or small business, or it might include hundreds of computers in a large corporate office or multiple buildings. Figure 3-1 shows some examples of LANs.

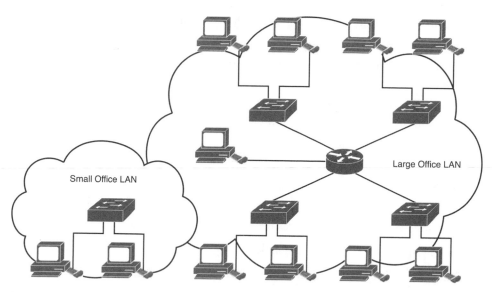

Figure 3-1   *Examples of LANs*

A small home business or a small office environment could use a small LAN to connect two or more computers and to connect the computers to one or more shared peripheral devices such as printers. A large corporate office could use multiple LANs to accommodate hundreds of computers and shared peripheral devices, for departments such as finance or operations, spanning many floors in an office complex.

Components of a LAN

Every LAN has specific components, including hardware, interconnections, and software. Figure 3-2 highlights some typical hardware components of a LAN.

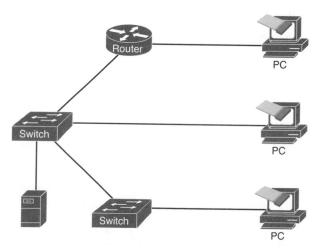

Figure 3-2   *Typical Components of a LAN*

Regardless of the size of the LAN, it requires these fundamental components for its operation:

- **Computers:** Computers serve as the endpoints in the network, sending and receiving data.

- **Interconnections:** Interconnections enable data to travel from one point to another in the network. Interconnections include these components:

  - **NICs:** Network interface cards (NIC) translate the data produced by the computer into a format that can be transmitted over the LAN.

  - **Network media:** Network media, such as cables or wireless media, transmit signals from one device on the LAN to another.

- **Network devices:** A LAN requires the following network devices:

  - **Hubs:** Hubs provide aggregation devices operating at Layer 1 of the OSI reference model. However, hubs have been replaced in this function by switches, and it is very rare to see hubs in any LAN these days.

  - **Ethernet switches:** Ethernet switches form the aggregation point for LANs. Ethernet switches operate at Layer 2 of the OSI reference model and provide intelligent distribution of frames within the LAN.

  - **Routers:** Routers, sometimes called gateways, provide a means to connect LAN segments. Routers operate at Layer 3 of the OSI reference model.

- **Protocols:** Protocols govern the way data is transmitted over a LAN and include the following:

  - Ethernet protocols

  - Internet Protocol (IP)

  - Internet Protocol version 6 (IPv6)

  - Address Resolution Protocol (ARP) and Reverse Address Resolution Protocol (RARP)

  - Dynamic Host Configuration Protocol (DHCP)

Functions of a LAN

LANs provide network users with communication and resource-sharing functions, including the following:

- **Data and applications:** When users are connected through a network, they can share files and even software application programs. This makes data more easily available and promotes more efficient collaboration on work projects.

- **Resources:** The resources that can be shared include both input devices, such as cameras, and output devices, such as printers.

■ **Communication path to other networks:** If a resource is not available locally, the LAN, through a gateway, can provide connectivity to remote resources—for example, access to the web.

How Big Is a LAN?

A LAN can be configured in a variety of sizes, depending on the requirements of the environment in which it operates.

LANs can be of various sizes to fit different work requirements, including the following:

■ **Small office/home office (SOHO):** The SOHO environment typically has only a few computers and some peripherals such as printers.

■ **Enterprise:** The enterprise environment might include many separate LANs in a large office building or in different buildings on a corporate campus. In the enterprise environment, each LAN might contain hundreds of computers and peripherals..

Figure 3-3 demonstrates the dramatic differences that can exist with the size of LANs.

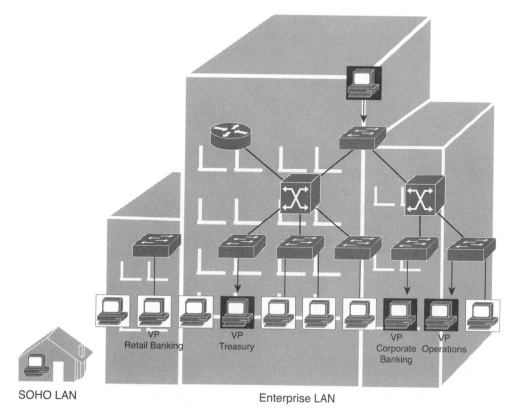

Figure 3-3 *Different LAN Sizes*

Ethernet

Ethernet is the most common type of LAN. It was originally developed in the 1970s by Digital Equipment Corporation (DEC), Intel, and Xerox (DIX) and was called DIX Ethernet. It later came to be called thick Ethernet (because of the thickness of the cable used in this type of network), and it transmitted data at 10 megabits per second (Mbps). The standard for Ethernet was updated in the 1980s to add more capability, and the new version of Ethernet was referred to as Ethernet Version 2 (also called Ethernet II).

The Institute of Electrical and Electronics Engineers (IEEE) is a professional organization that defines network standards. IEEE standards are the predominant LAN standards in the world today. In the mid-1980s, an IEEE workgroup defined new standards for Ethernet-like networks. The set of standards they created was called Ethernet 802.3 and was based on the carrier sense multiple access with collision detection (CSMA/CD) process. Ethernet 802.3 specified the physical layer (Layer 1) and the MAC portion of the data link layer (Layer 2). Today, this set of standards is most often referred to as simply "Ethernet."

Ethernet LAN Standards

Ethernet LAN standards specify cabling and signaling at both the physical and data link layers of the OSI reference model. This topic describes Ethernet LAN standards at the data link layer.

Figure 3-4 shows how LAN protocols map to the OSI reference model.

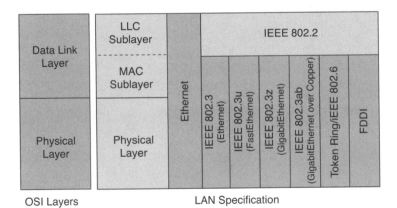

Figure 3-4 *Ethernet and the OSI Model*

The IEEE divides the OSI data link layer into two separate sublayers:

- **Logical link control (LLC):** Transitions up to the network layer
- **MAC:** Transitions down to the physical layer

LLC Sublayer

The IEEE created the LLC sublayer to allow part of the data link layer to function independently from existing technologies. This layer provides versatility in services to the network layer protocols that are above it, while communicating effectively with the variety of MAC and Layer 1 technologies below it. The LLC, as a sublayer, participates in the encapsulation process.

An LLC header tells the data link layer what to do with a packet when it receives a frame. For example, a host receives a frame and then looks in the LLC header to understand that the packet is destined for the IP protocol at the network layer.

The original Ethernet header (prior to IEEE 802.2 and 802.3) did not use an LLC header. Instead, it used a type field in the Ethernet header to identify the Layer 3 protocol being carried in the Ethernet frame.

MAC Sublayer

The MAC sublayer deals with physical media access. The IEEE 802.3 MAC specification defines MAC addresses, which uniquely identify multiple devices at the data link layer. The MAC sublayer maintains a table of MAC addresses (physical addresses) of devices. To participate on the network, each device must have a unique MAC address.

The Role of CSMA/CD in Ethernet

Ethernet signals are transmitted to every station connected to the LAN, using a special set of rules to determine which station can "talk" at any particular time. This topic describes that set of rules.

Ethernet LANs manage the signals on a network by CSMA/CD, which is an important aspect of Ethernet. Figure 3-5 illustrates the CSMA/CD process.

In an Ethernet LAN, before transmitting, a computer first listens to the network media. If the media is idle, the computer sends its data. After a transmission has been sent, the computers on the network compete for the next available idle time to send another frame. This competition for idle time means that no one station has an advantage over another on the network.

Stations on a CSMA/CD LAN can access the network at any time. Before sending data, CSMA/CD stations listen to the network to determine whether it is already in use. If it is, the CSMA/CD stations wait. If the network is not in use, the stations transmit. A collision occurs when two stations listen for network traffic, hear none, and transmit simultaneously (see Figure 3-5). In this case, both transmissions are damaged, and the stations must retransmit at some later time. CSMA/CD stations must be able to detect collisions to know that they must retransmit.

When a station transmits, the signal is referred to as a carrier. The NIC senses the carrier and consequently refrains from broadcasting a signal. If no carrier exists, a waiting station knows that it is free to transmit. This is the "carrier sense" part of the protocol.

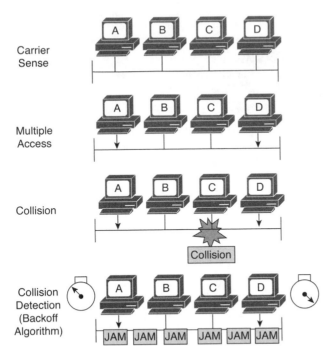

Figure 3-5   *CSMA/CD Process*

The extent of the network segment over which collisions occur is referred to as the collision domain. The size of the collision domain has an impact on efficiency and therefore on data throughput. In today's LANs, switches have replaced hubs. The reason this occurs is that switches create tiny collision domains containing just one device. This eliminates the potential for collisions. This process is often called "microsegmentation" of the network.

In the CSMA/CD process, priorities are not assigned to particular stations, so all stations on the network have equal access. This is the "multiple access" part of the protocol. If two or more stations attempt a transmission simultaneously, a collision occurs. The stations are alerted of the collision, and they execute a backoff algorithm that randomly schedules retransmission of the frame. This scenario prevents the machines from repeatedly attempting to transmit at the same time. Collisions are normally resolved in microseconds. This is the "collision detection" part of the protocol.

While collisions are resolved quickly, it is still advantageous to eliminate them entirely from the network. This allows much more efficient communications. This is accomplished through the use of switches as described earlier.

Ethernet Frames

Bits that are transmitted over an Ethernet LAN are organized into frames. In Ethernet terminology, the "container" into which data is placed for transmission is called a *frame*. The frame contains header information, trailer information, and the actual data that is being transmitted.

Figure 3-6 illustrates all the fields that are in a MAC layer of the Ethernet frame, which include the following:

- **Preamble:** This field consists of 7 bytes of alternating 1s and 0s, which synchronize the signals of the communicating computers.

- **Start-of-frame (SOF) delimiter:** This field contains bits that signal the receiving computer that the transmission of the actual frame is about to start and that any data following is part of the packet.

- **Destination address:** This field contains the address of the NIC on the local network to which the packet is being sent.

- **Source address:** This field contains the address of the NIC of the sending computer.

- **Type/length:** In Ethernet II, this field contains a code that identifies the network layer protocol. In 802.3, this field specifies the length of the data field. The protocol information is contained in 802.2 fields, which are at the LLC layer. The newer 802.3 specifications have allowed the use of Ethertype protocol identifiers when not using the 802.2 field.

- **Data and pad:** This field contains the data that is received from the network layer on the transmitting computer. This data is then sent to the same protocol on the destination computer. If the data is too short, an adapter adds a string of extraneous bits to "pad" the field to its minimum length of 46 bytes.

- **Frame check sequence (FCS):** This field includes a checking mechanism to ensure that the packet of data has been transmitted without corruption.

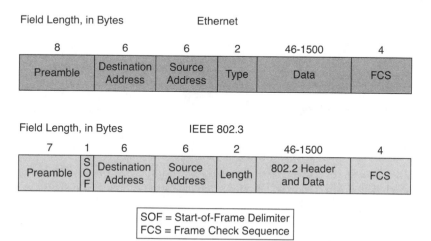

Figure 3-6 *Ethernet Frames*

Ethernet Frame Addressing

Communications in a network occur in three ways: unicast, broadcast, and multicast. Ethernet frames are addressed accordingly. Figure 3-7 shows forms of Ethernet communications.

The three major types of network communications are as follows:

- **Unicast:** Communication in which a frame is sent from one host and addressed to one specific destination. In a unicast transmission, you have just one sender and one receiver. Unicast transmission is the predominant form of transmission on LANs and within the Internet.

- **Broadcast:** Communication in which a frame is sent from one address to all other addresses. In this case, you have just one sender, but the information is sent to all connected receivers. Broadcast transmission is essential when sending the same message to all devices on the LAN.

- **Multicast:** Communication in which information is sent to a specific group of devices or clients. Unlike broadcast transmission, in multicast transmission, clients must be members of a multicast group to receive the information.

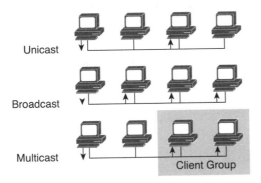

Figure 3-7 *Ethernet Communications*

Ethernet Addresses

The address used in an Ethernet LAN, which is associated with the network adapter, is the means by which data is directed to the proper receiving location. Figure 3-8 shows the format of an Ethernet MAC address.

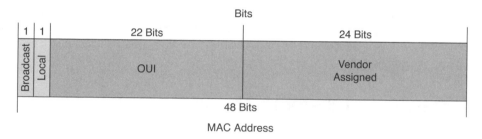

Figure 3-8 *Ethernet MAC Address*

The address that is on the NIC is the MAC address, often referred to as the burned-in address (BIA), and some vendors allow the modification of this address to meet local needs. A 48-bit Ethernet MAC address has two components:

- **24-bit Organizational Unique Identifier (OUI):** The letter O identifies the manufacturer of the NIC. The IEEE regulates the assignment of OUI numbers. Within the OUI, the two following bits have meaning only when used in the destination address:

  - **Broadcast or multicast bit:** This indicates to the receiving interface that the frame is destined for all or a group of end stations on the LAN segment.

  - **Locally administered address bit:** Normally the combination of OUI and a 24-bit station address is universally unique; however, if the address is modified locally, this bit should be set.

- **24-bit vendor-assigned end station address:** This uniquely identifies the Ethernet hardware.

MAC Addresses and Binary-Hexadecimal Numbers

The MAC address plays a specific role in the function of an Ethernet LAN. The MAC sublayer of the OSI data link layer handles physical addressing issues, and the physical address is a number in hexadecimal format that is actually burned into the NIC. This address is referred to as the MAC address, and it is expressed as groups of hexadecimal digits that are organized in pairs or quads, such as the following: 00:00:0c:43:2e:08 or 0000:0c43:2e08. Figure 3-9 shows the MAC address format compared to the MAC frame.

Figure 3-9 *Hexadecimal MAC Address*

Each device on a LAN must have a unique MAC address to participate in the network. The MAC address identifies the location of a specific computer on a LAN. Unlike other kinds of addresses used in networks, the MAC address should *not* be changed unless you have some specific need.

Connecting to an Ethernet LAN

In addition to understanding the components of an Ethernet LAN and the standards that govern its architecture, you need to understand the connection components of an Ethernet LAN. This section describes the connection components of an Ethernet LAN, including network interface cards (NIC) and cable.

Ethernet Network Interface Cards

A NIC is a printed circuit board that provides network communication capabilities to and from a personal computer on a network. Figure 3-10 shows an example of a NIC.

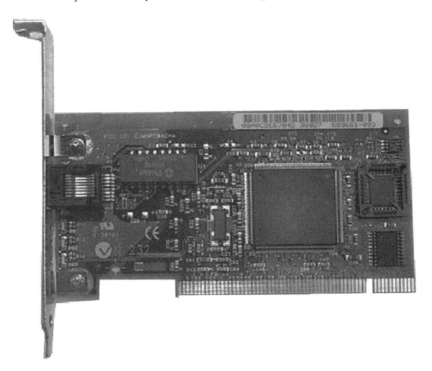

Figure 3-10   *Network Interface Card*

Also called a LAN adapter, the NIC plugs into a motherboard and provides a port for connecting to the network. The NIC constitutes the computer interface with the LAN.

The NIC communicates with the network through a serial connection, and with the computer through a parallel connection. When a NIC is installed in a computer, it requires an interrupt request line (IRQ), an input/output (I/O) address, a memory space within the operating system (such as DOS or Windows), and drivers (software) that allow it to perform its function. An IRQ is a signal that informs a central processing unit (CPU) that an event needing its attention has occurred. An IRQ is sent over a hardware line to the microprocessor. An example of an interrupt request being issued is when a key is pressed on a keyboard, and the CPU must move the character from the keyboard to RAM. An I/O address is a location in memory used by an auxiliary device to enter data into or retrieve data from a computer.

The MAC address is burned onto each NIC by the manufacturer, providing a unique, physical network address.

Ethernet Media and Connection Requirements

Distance and time dictate the type of Ethernet connections required. This section describes the cable and connector specifications used to support Ethernet implementations.

The cable and connector specifications used to support Ethernet implementations are derived from the EIA/TIA standards body. The categories of cabling defined for Ethernet are derived from the EIA/TIA-568 (SP-2840) Commercial Building Telecommunications Wiring Standards. EIA/TIA specifies an RJ-45 connector for unshielded twisted-pair (UTP) cable.

The important difference to note is the media used for 10-Mbps Ethernet versus 100-Mbps Fast Ethernet. In networks today, where you see a mix of 10- and 100-Mbps requirements, you must be aware of the need to change over to UTP Category 5 to support Fast Ethernet.

Connection Media

Several types of connection media can be used in an Ethernet LAN implementation. Figure 3-11 shows typical connection types.

The most common type of connection media is the RJ-45 connector and jack illustrated in Figure 3-11. The letters RJ stand for registered jack, and the number "45" refers to a specific physical connector that has eight conductors.

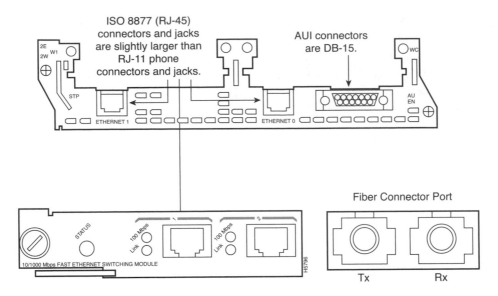

Figure 3-11 *Connection Types*

A Gigabit Interface Converter (GBIC), shown in Figure 3-12, is a hot-swappable I/O device that plugs into a Gigabit Ethernet port. A key benefit of using a GBIC is that it is interchangeable, allowing you the flexibility to deploy other 1000BASE-X technology without having to change the physical interface or model on the router or switch. GBICs support UTP (copper) and fiber-optic media for Gigabit Ethernet transmission.

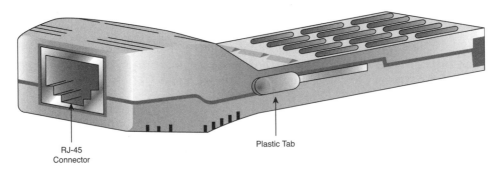

Figure 3-12 *1000BASE-T GBIC*

Typically, GBICs are used in the LAN for uplinks and are normally used for the backbone. GBICs are also seen in remote networks.

The fiber-optic GBIC, shown in Figure 3-13, is a transceiver that converts serial electric currents to optical signals and converts optical signals to digital electric currents.

Figure 3-13   *Fiber GBIC*

Optical GBICs include these types:

- Short wavelength (1000BASE-SX)

- Long wavelength/long haul (1000BASE-LX/LH)

- Extended distance (1000BASE-ZX)

Unshielded Twisted-Pair Cable

Twisted-pair is a copper wire–based cable that can be either shielded or unshielded. UTP cable is frequently used in LANs. Figure 3-14 shows an example of a UTP cable.

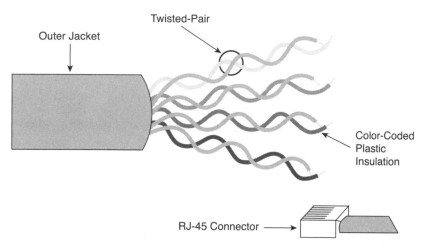

Figure 3-14   *UTP Cable*

UTP cable is a four-pair wire. Each of the eight individual copper wires in UTP cable is covered by an insulating material. In addition, the wires in each pair are twisted around each other. The advantage of UTP cable is its ability to cancel interference, because the twisted wire pairs limit signal degradation from electromagnetic interference (EMI) and radio frequency interference (RFI). To further reduce crosstalk between the pairs in UTP cable, the number of twists in the wire pairs varies. Both UTP and shielded twisted-pair (STP) cable must follow precise specifications regarding how many twists or braids are permitted per meter.

UTP cable is used in a variety of types of networks. When used as a network medium, UTP cable has four pairs of either 22- or 24-gauge copper wire. UTP used as a network medium has an impedance of 100 ohms, differentiating it from other types of twisted-pair wiring, such as that used for telephone wiring. Because UTP cable has an external diameter of approximately 0.43 cm, or 0.17 inches, its small size can be advantageous during installation. Also, because UTP can be used with most major network architectures, it continues to grow in popularity.

Here are the categories of UTP cable:

- **Category 1:** Used for telephone communications; not suitable for transmitting data

- **Category 2:** Capable of transmitting data at speeds of up to 4 Mbps

- **Category 3:** Used in 10BASE-T networks; can transmit data at speeds up to 10 Mbps

- **Category 4:** Used in Token Ring networks; can transmit data at speeds up to 16 Mbps

- **Category 5:** Capable of transmitting data at speeds up to 100 Mbps

- **Category 5e:** Used in networks running at speeds up to 1000 Mbps (1 Gbps)

- **Category 6:** Consists of four pairs of 24-gauge copper wires, which can transmit data at speeds of up to 1000 Mbps

- **Category 6a:** Used in networks running at speeds up to 10 Gbps

The most commonly used categories in LAN environments today are Categories 1 (used primarily for telephony), 5, 5e, and 6.

UTP Implementation

For a UTP implementation in a LAN, you must determine the EIA/TIA type of cable needed and also whether to use a straight-through or crossover cable. This topic describes the characteristics and uses of straight-through and crossover cables, as well as the types of connectors used when UTP is implemented in a LAN. Figure 3-15 shows an RJ-45 connector.

Figure 3-15   *RJ-45 Connector*

If you look at the RJ-45 transparent-end connector, you can see eight colored wires, twisted into four pairs. Four of the wires (two pairs) carry the positive or true voltage and are considered "tip" (T1 through T4); the other four wires carry the inverse of false voltage grounded and are called "ring" (R1 through R4). *Tip* and *ring* are terms that originated in the early days of the telephone. Today, these terms refer to the positive and negative wires in a pair. The wires in the first pair in a cable or a connector are designated as T1 and R1, the second pair as T2 and R2, and so on.

The RJ-45 plug is the male component, crimped at the end of the cable. As you look at the male connector from the front, the pin locations are numbered from 8 on the left to 1 on the right.

The jack is the female component in a network device, wall, cubicle partition outlet, or patch panel.

In addition to identifying the correct EIA/TIA category of cable to use for a connecting device (depending on which standard is being used by the jack on the network device), you need to determine which of the following to use:

- A straight-through cable (either T568A or T568B at each end)

- A crossover cable (T568A at one end; T568B at the other)

In Figure 3-16, the RJ-45 connectors on both ends of the cable show all the wires in the same order. If the two RJ-45 ends of a cable are held side by side in the same orientation, the colored wires (or strips or pins) can be seen at each connector end. If the order of the colored wires is the same at each end, the cable type is straight-through.

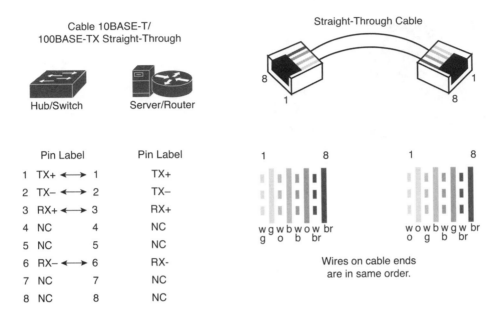

Figure 3-16 *Straight-Through Cable*

With crossover cables, the RJ-45 connectors on both ends show that some of the wires on one side of the cable are crossed to a different pin on the other side of the cable. Specifically, for Ethernet, pin 1 at one RJ-45 end should be connected to pin 3 at the other end. Pin 2 at one end should be connected to pin 6 at the other end, as shown in the Figure 3-17.

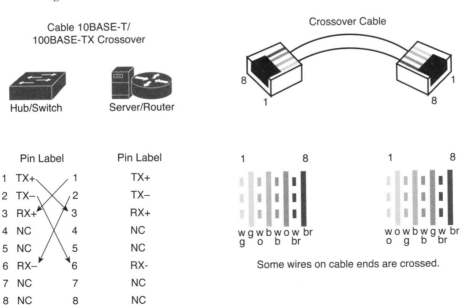

Figure 3-17 *Crossover Cable*

Figure 3-18 shows the guidelines for choosing which type of cable to use when intercon-necting Cisco devices. In addition to verifying the category specification on the cable, you must determine when to use a straight-through or crossover cable.

Use straight-through cables for the following cabling:

- Switch to router

- Switch to PC or server

- Hub to PC or server

Use crossover cables for the following cabling:

- Switch to switch

- Switch to hub

- Hub to hub

- Router to router

- Router Ethernet port to PC NIC

- PC to PC

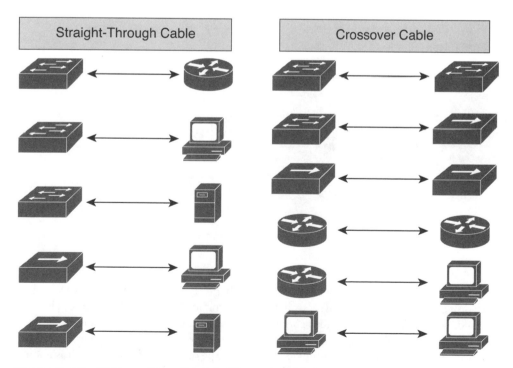

Figure 3-18   *When to Use a Straight-Through Cable Versus a Crossover Cable*

Auto-MDIX

After reading the previous section, you might be concerned about when you are cabling your network, you might make a critical mistake! Imagine, just one wrong type of cable, and your entire LAN might fail to access key resources. Fortunately, there is great news because of a new technology called Auto-MDIX. Auto-MDIX stands for automatic medium-dependent interface crossover, a feature that lets the interface automatically discover whether the wrong cable is installed. A switch that supports the Auto-MDIX feature detects the wrong cable and causes the switch to swap the pair it uses for transmitting and receiving. This solves the cabling problem, and the switch is able to communicate just fine regardless of the fact that you connected the "wrong" cable. Obviously, this new technology is very desirable and is making its way to more and more Cisco devices all the time.

Optical Fiber

An optical fiber is a flexible, transparent fiber that is made of very pure glass (silica) and is not much bigger in diameter than a human hair. It acts as a waveguide, or "light pipe," to transmit light between the two ends of the fiber. Optical fibers are widely used in fiber-optic communications, which permit transmission over longer distances and at higher bandwidths (data rates) than other forms of communication. Fibers are used instead of metal wires because signals travel along them with less loss and with immunity to electromagnetic interference. Figure 3-19 shows an example of optical fiber.

Optical Fiber (Single Mode)

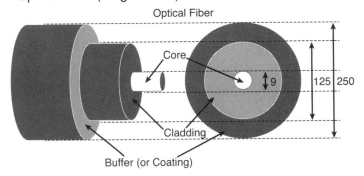

Dimensions are in μm (10⁻⁶ meters)

Figure 3-19   *Optical Fiber*

The two fundamental components that allow a fiber to confine light are the core and the cladding. Most of the light travels from the beginning to the end inside the core. The cladding around the core provides confinement. The diameters of the core and cladding are shown in this illustration, but the core diameter can vary for different fiber types. In this case, the core diameter of 9 μm is very small—the diameter of a human hair is about 50 μm. The outer diameter of the cladding is a standard size of 125 μm. Standardizing the size means that component manufacturers can make connectors for all fiber-optic cables.

The third element in this picture is the buffer (coating), which has nothing to do with the confinement of the light in the fiber. Its purpose is to protect the glass from scratches and moisture. The fiber-optic cable can be easily scratched and broken, like a glass pane. If the fiber is scratched, the scratch could propagate and break the fiber. Another important aspect is the need to keep the fiber dry.

The most significant difference between single-mode fiber (SMF) and multimode fiber (MMF) is in the ability of the fiber to send light for a long distance at high bit rates. In general, MMF is used for shorter distances at a lower bit rate than SMF. For long-distance communications, SMF is preferred. There are many variations of fiber for both MMF and SMF. Figure 3-20 shows the two fiber types.

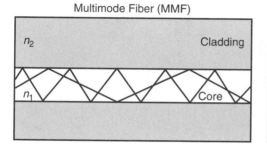 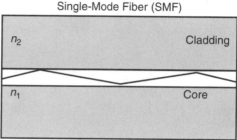

Figure 3-20   *Fiber-Optic Types*

The most significant physical difference is in the size of the core. The glass in the two fibers is the same, and the index of refraction change is similar. The core diameter can make a major difference. The diameter of the fiber cladding is universal for matching fiber ends.

The effect of having different-size cores in fiber is that the two fiber types will support different ways for the light to get through the fiber. The left image illustrates MMF. MMF supports multiple ways for the light from one source to travel through the fiber (the source of the designation "multimode"). Each path can be thought of as a mode.

For SMF, the possible ways for light to get through the fiber have been reduced to one, a "single mode." It is not exactly one, but that is a useful approximation. Table 3-1 summarizes the characteristics of MMF and SMF.

Table 3-1   *Summarizing MMF and SMF Characteristics*

MMF Characteristics	SMF Characteristics
LED transmitter usually used	Larger transmitter usually used
Lower bandwidth and speed	Higher bandwidth and speed
Shorter distances	Longer distances
Less expensive	More expensive

An optical fiber connector terminates the end of an optical fiber. A variety of optical fiber connectors are available. The main differences among the types of connectors are dimensions and methods of mechanical coupling. Generally, organizations standardize on one kind of connector, depending on the equipment that they commonly use, or they standardize per type of fiber (one for MMF, one for SMF). Taking into account all the generations of connectors, about 70 connector types are in use today. Figure 3-21 shows some common connector types.

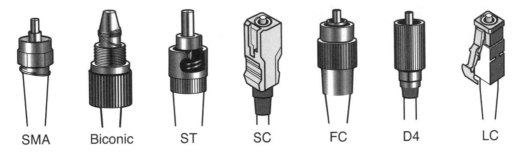

SMA   Biconic   ST   SC   FC   D4   LC

Figure 3-21   *Common Fiber-Optic Connector Types*

There are three types of connectors:

- Threaded

- Bayonet

- Push-pull

These materials are used for connectors:

- Metal

- Plastic sleeve

Most common connectors are classified as these types:

- **ST:** Typical for patch panels (for their durability)

- **FC:** Typical used by service providers for patch panels

- **SC:** Typical for enterprise equipment

- **LC:** Typical for enterprise equipment, commonly used on Small Form-Factor Pluggable (SFP) modules

In data communications and telecommunications applications today, small-form-factor connectors (for example, LCs) are replacing the traditional connectors (for example, SCs), mainly to pack more connectors on the faceplate and thus reduce system footprints.

Chapter Summary

LANs are a critical component in computer networks today. While these structures come in many different sizes, they are always used to carry data at speeds as fast as possible over short geographic distances.

Ethernet is the most common type of LAN used today. Standards unique to Ethernet specify Ethernet LAN cabling and signaling at both the physical and data link layers of the OSI reference model. Bits that are transmitted over an Ethernet LAN are organized into frames. Ethernet LANs manage the signals on a network using a process called CSMA/CD.

A NIC or LAN adapter plugs into a motherboard and provides an interface for connecting to the network. The MAC address is burned onto each NIC by the manufacturer, providing a unique, physical network address that permits the device to participate in the network.

The cable and connector specifications used to support Ethernet implementations are derived from the EIA/TIA standards body. The categories of cabling defined for Ethernet are derived from the EIA/TIA-568 (SP2840) Commercial Building Telecommunications Wiring Standards. Several connection media are used for Ethernet, with RJ-45 and GBIC being the most common.

A GBIC is a hot-swappable I/O device that plugs into a Gigabit Ethernet port on a network device to provide a physical interface.

UTP cable is a four-pair wire. Each of the eight individual copper wires in UTP cable is covered by an insulating material, and the wires in each pair are twisted around each other. A crossover cable connects between similar devices like router to router, PC to PC, or switch to switch. A straight-through cable connects between dissimilar devices like switch to router or PC to switch.

This chapter also examined fiber-optic media. Optical fiber is a flexible, transparent fiber that is made of very pure glass (silica) and is not much bigger than a human hair. It acts as a waveguide, or "light pipe," to transmit light between the two ends of the fiber. Optical fibers are widely used in fiber-optic communications, which permit transmission over longer distances and at higher bandwidths (data rates) than other forms of communication.

Additional Resources

- Gigabit Ethernet, Wikipedia: http://en.wikipedia.org/wiki/Gigabit_Ethernet
- How Fiber Optics Work, How Stuff Works: http://computer.howstuffworks.com/fiber-optic.htm

Review Questions

Use the questions here to review what you learned in this chapter. The correct answers and solutions are found in Appendix A, "Answers to Chapter Review Questions."

1. What organization is responsible for Ethernet standards?

   a. ISO

   b. IEEE

   c. EIA

   d. IEC

2. What are the characteristics of Ethernet 802.3? (Choose three.)

   a. Based on the CSMA/CD process

   b. Is a standard that has been replaced by Ethernet II

   c. Specifies the physical layer (Layer 1)

   d. Developed in the mid-1970s

   e. Specifies the MAC portion of the data link layer (Layer 2)

   f. Also referred to as thick Ethernet

3. Which statement about an Ethernet address is accurate?

   a. The address used in an Ethernet LAN directs data to the proper receiving location.

   b. The source address is the 4-byte hexadecimal address of the NIC on the computer that is generating the data packet.

   c. The destination address is the 8-byte hexadecimal address of the NIC on the LAN to which a data packet is being sent.

   d. Both the destination and source addresses consist of a 6-byte hexadecimal number.

4. Which statement about MAC addresses is accurate?

   a. A MAC address is a number in hexadecimal format that is physically located on the NIC.

   b. A MAC address is represented by binary digits that are organized in pairs.

   c. It is not necessary for a device to have a unique MAC address to participate in the network.

   d. The MAC address can never be changed.

5. Which statement about NICs is accurate?

   a. The NIC plugs into a USB port and provides a port for connecting to the network.

   b. The NIC communicates with the network through a serial connection and communicates with the computer through a parallel connection.

   c. The NIC communicates with the network through a parallel connection and communicates with the computer through a serial connection.

   d. A NIC is also referred to as a switch adapter.

6. Which minimum category of UTP is required for Ethernet 1000BASE-T?

    a. Category 3

    b. Category 4

    c. Category 5

    d. Category 5e

7. Match the UTP categories to the environments in which they are most commonly used.

    ___1. Category 1

    ___2. Category 2

    ___3. Category 3

    ___4. Category 4

    ___5. Category 5

    ___6. Category 5e

    ___7. Category 6

    ___8. Category 6e

    a. Capable of transmitting data at speeds up to 100 Mbps

    b. Used in networks running at speeds up to 1000 Mbps (1 Gbps)

    c. Consists of four pairs of 24-gauge copper wires, which can transmit data at speeds up to 1000 Mbps

    d. Used for telephone communications; not suitable for transmitting data

    e. Used in Token Ring networks; can transmit data at speeds up to 16 Mbps

    f. Capable of transmitting data at speeds up to 4 Mbps

    g. Used in 10BASE-T networks; can transmit data at speeds up to 10 Mbps

    h. Used in networks running at speeds up to 10 Gbps

8. Which type of UTP cable would you use to connect a router to a PC to have the devices pass user data?

    a. Straight-through

    b. Crossover

    c. Rollover

    d. None of these options are correct.

9. Which type of UTP cable would you use to connect a switch to another switch?

    a. Straight-through

    b. Crossover

    c. Rollover

    d. None of these options are correct.

10. What type of optical fiber provides higher speeds and bandwidths?

   a. MMF

   b. SMF

   c. MNF

   d. GMF

Production Network Simulation Question 3-1

Your colleague has come to you desperate for help. He needs to know what type of Ethernet cable he needs to use in each of these segments he is responsible for:

   1. The PC to the switch

   2. The switch to another switch

   3. The switch to a router

   4. The router to another router

None of these devices support the Auto-MDIX feature, so provide him with the correct cable type for each instance.

Chapter 4

Operating Cisco IOS Software

This chapter includes the following sections:

- Chapter Objectives

- Cisco IOS Software Features and Functions

- Cisco IOS CLI Functions

- Configuring Network Devices

- External Configuration Sources

- Entering the EXEC Modes

- Help in the CLI

- Managing Cisco IOS Configuration

- Improving the User Experience in the CLI

- Chapter Summary

- Additional Resources

- Review Questions

- Production Network Simulation Question 4-1

What good would your computer be without any software installed within it? It would be a very complex and expensive paperweight! Just as your computer runs software such as an OS (operating system), so does your Cisco router and switches. Cisco IOS Software is a feature-rich network system software that provides network intelligence to meet most of today's networking demands. This chapter describes Cisco IOS Software and the basic Cisco IOS command-line interface (CLI) functions and operations. The chapter also describes how to navigate the Cisco IOS CLI configuration modes, how to use embedded keyboard help, how to manage configurations, and how to use additional Cisco IOS features to improve the user experience in the CLI. For those readers who are tired of all the theory in computer networking that we have dealt with thus far, this chapter is for you!

Chapter Objectives

Upon completing this chapter, you will be able to describe the features and functionality of Cisco IOS Software. You will also be able to navigate the CLI and take advantage of many features designed to improve your user experience. These abilities include meeting these objectives:

- List the features and functions of Cisco IOS Software

- Define the functions and use of the Cisco IOS CLI

- Describe the user EXEC mode

- Describe privileged EXEC mode

- Enter EXEC mode

- Explain the role of CLI error messages

- Describe how to manage Cisco IOS configurations

- Describe how to improve the user experience in the Cisco IOS CLI

Cisco IOS Software Features and Functions

Like a computer, a switch or router cannot function without an operating system. Without an operating system, the hardware does not have any capabilities. Cisco IOS Software is the system software in Cisco devices. It is the core technology that extends across most of the Cisco product lines. Cisco IOS Software is used for most Cisco devices, regardless of the size and type of the device. It is used for routers, LAN switches, small wireless access points, large routers with numerous interfaces, and many other devices.

Note   Cisco also makes additional versions of the IOS for enterprise- and Internet service provider (ISP)–grade equipment. Also, Cisco has created a Next Generation Operating System (NX-OS) for its storage-area network (SAN) and data center (DC) equipment. While these operating systems are not covered at the CCENT level, I certainly want you to be aware of them.

The Cisco IOS Software operational details vary on different internetworking devices, depending on the purpose and feature set on the device.

The services that are provided by Cisco IOS Software are generally accessed using the CLI. The CLI is accessed through a console connection, a modem connection, or a Telnet or Secure Shell (SSH) session. Regardless of which connection method is used, access to the Cisco IOS CLI is generally referred to as an EXEC session. The look and feel of the CLI is similar among different device types, although features that are accessible through the CLI vary, based on the version of Cisco IOS Software and the type of device.

While features will vary, Cisco IOS Software typically enables the following network services in Cisco products:

- Features to carry the chosen network protocols and functions

- Connectivity that enables high-speed traffic between devices

- Security controls that monitor access and prohibit unauthorized network use

- Scalability that adds interfaces and capability as needed for network growth

- Reliability that ensures dependable access to networked resources

Cisco IOS CLI Functions

Cisco IOS Software uses a CLI through the console as its traditional environment to enter commands. Cisco IOS Software is designed as a modal operating system. The term *modal* describes a system where there are various modes of operation, each having its own domain of operation. The CLI uses a hierarchical structure for the modes.

To enter commands into the CLI, type or copy and paste the entries within one of the several console command modes. Each command mode is indicated with a distinctive prompt. The term *prompt* is used because the system is prompting you to make an entry. By default, every prompt begins with the device name. Following the name, the remainder of the prompt indicates the mode. As commands are used and modes are changed, the prompt changes to reflect the current context. Pressing the Enter key instructs the device to parse and execute the command.

The typical interface to a Cisco IOS device is through a console connection or a Telnet connection to the CLI. Figure 4-1 shows an administrator configuring a router and switch through a console connection. The type of cable used to connect the administrator's PC to the console port of the Cisco device is called a rollover cable.

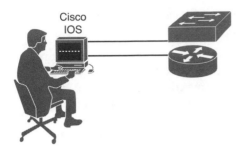

Figure 4-1   *Administrator Connecting to the CLI*

As a security feature, Cisco IOS Software separates EXEC sessions into two access levels:

- **User EXEC:** Allows a person to access only a limited number of basic monitoring commands.

- **Privileged EXEC:** Allows a person to access all device commands, such as those used for configuration and management, and can be password protected to allow only authorized users to access the device.

Note   Cisco actually creates 16 security levels for you on its devices, but it only populates the two listed above by default. These 16 levels are numbered 0 through 15. Level 1 is user EXEC and level 15 is Privileged EXEC. The other security levels can be used by administrators to enact what is called Role-Based Access Control (RBAC). This permits many different levels of administrative control over the device.

Configuring Network Devices

The Cisco IOS CLI is used to communicate the configuration details that implement the network requirements of an organization. This topic describes the initial steps for starting and configuring a Cisco network device.

When a Cisco IOS device is started for the first time, its initial configuration with default settings is sufficient for it to operate at Layer 2. When a Cisco router is started for the first time, however, the device does not have sufficient information in its initial configuration to operate at Layer 3, because the device management requires IP address information on its router interfaces, at a minimum. However, when an "unconfigured" Cisco device starts for the first time, with no "startup configuration" settings, the IOS will prompt you for basic configuration information using an interactive dialog mode called setup mode.

This basic configuration sets up the device with the following information:

- Protocol addressing and parameter settings, such as configuring the IP address and subnet mask on an interface

- Options for administration and management, such as setting up passwords

Changes to these minimal or default configurations to meet particular network requirements constitute many of the tasks of a network administrator. Figure 4-2 shows the basic startup steps for a Cisco router or switch.

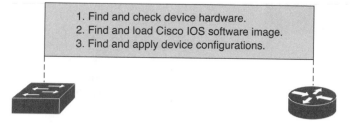

Figure 4-2 *Switch and Router Startup Steps*

When a Cisco device starts up, the following three main operations are performed on the networking device:

1. The device performs hardware-checking routines. A term often used to describe this initial set of routines is power-on self-test (POST).

2. After the hardware has been shown to be in good working order, the device performs system startup routines. These initiate the switch or device operating system IOS software.

3. After the operating system is loaded, the device tries to find and apply software configuration settings (later to be stored in the startup config file) that establish the details needed for network operation.

Typically, a sequence of fallback routines provides software startup alternatives, if needed.

External Configuration Sources

A Cisco device can be configured from sources that are external to the device. Figure 4-3 illustrates just some of the sources from which a Cisco device can obtain configuration settings.

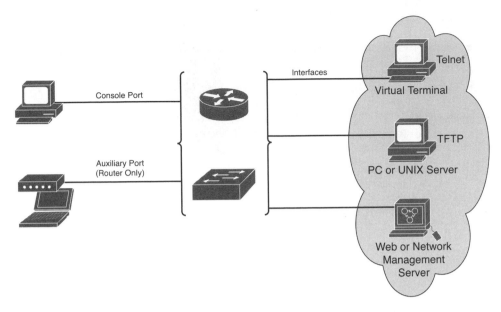

Figure 4-3 *Sources for Router Configurations*

You can access a device directly or from a remote location without being physically connected to the device. You can connect directly by using a console cable connection to the console (CON) port, or you can connect from a remote location by dialing into a modem connected to the auxiliary (AUX) port on the device. After a Cisco device is properly configured, you can also make an over-the-network connection, through Telnet (to VTY ports). In general, the console port is recommended for initial configuration because it displays device startup messages, whereas the auxiliary port does not provide this information. A Cisco IOS device can be configured through the following connections:

- **Console terminal:** Upon initial installation, you can configure networking devices from the console terminal, which is connected through the console port. You will need the following items to configure a Cisco device from the console port:

  - RJ-45–to–RJ-45 rollover cable

  - Personal computer (PC) or equivalent with "terminal" communications software configured with the following settings:

    - Speed: 9600 bits per second

    - Data bits: 8

    - Parity: None

    - Stop bit: 1

    - Flow control: None

- **Remote terminal:** To support a remote device, a modem connection to the auxiliary port of the device allows a remote device to be configured from a remote terminal. However, the auxiliary port of the device must first be configured for communication with the external modem. You need the following items to connect remotely to the auxiliary port on a Cisco device:

  - Straight-through serial cable

  - 14.4-kilobits-per-second (kbps) modem

  - PC or equivalent with suitable communications software

  After initial startup and after an initial basic configuration, you access and configure the device in the following ways:

- Establish a terminal (vty) session using Telnet.

- Configure the device through the current connection, or download a previously written startup config file from a Trivial File Transfer Protocol (TFTP) server on the network.

- Download a configuration file using a network management software application such as Cisco Prime.

Note   Not all network devices have all the ports shown in Figure 4-3. For example, some Cisco small office/home office (SOHO) devices do not have an auxiliary port.

Entering the EXEC Modes

As described earlier in this chapter, Cisco IOS Software supports two EXEC command modes: user EXEC mode and privileged EXEC mode. The following procedure outlines how to enable and enter the different EXEC modes on a Cisco switch or device:

1. Log in to the device initially with a username and password (if login is configured for CON, AUX, or VTY connections). This brings the device to a user EXEC mode prompt. A prompt displays to signify the user EXEC mode. The right-facing arrow (>) in the prompt indicates that the device or switch is at the user EXEC level. Enter **exit** to close the session from the user EXEC mode.

2. Enter the **?** command at the user EXEC-level prompt to display command options available in the user EXEC mode. The **?** command in privileged EXEC mode reveals many more command options than it does at the user EXEC level. This feature is referred to as context-sensitive help.

User EXEC mode does not contain any commands that might control the operation of the device or switch. For example, user EXEC mode does not allow reloading or configuring of the device or switch.

Critical commands, such as **configuration** and **management**, require you to be in privileged EXEC (enable) mode.

To change to privileged EXEC mode from user EXEC mode, enter the **enable** command at the hostname> prompt. If an enable password or an enable secret password is configured, the switch or device will then prompt you for the required password.

Note   If both an enable password and a secret password are set, the secret password is the one that is required.

When the correct enable password is entered, the switch or device prompt changes from hostname> to hostname#, indicating that the user is now at the privileged EXEC mode level. Entering the ? command at the privileged EXEC level will reveal many more command options than those available at the user EXEC mode level.

To return to the user EXEC level, enter the **disable** command at the hostname# prompt.

Example 4-1 demonstrates the commands and router prompts described here.

Example 4-1   *Using the CLI of the Cisco Router*

```
R1 con0 is now available

Press RETURN to get started.

R1> exit

R1 con0 is now available

Press RETURN to get started.

R1> ?
Exec commands:
  access-enable     Create a temporary Access-List entry
  access-profile    Apply user-profile to interface
  clear             Reset functions
  connect           Open a terminal connection
  crypto            Encryption related commands.
  disable           Turn off privileged commands
<output omitted>
R1> enable
Password:
R1# ?
Exec commands:
  access-enable     Create a temporary Access-List entry
```

```
    access-profile    Apply user-profile to interface
    access-template   Create a temporary Access-List entry
    archive           manage archive files
    audio-prompt      load ivr prompt
    auto              Exec level Automation
    beep              Blocks Extensible Exchange Protocol commands
    bfe               For manual emergency modes setting
    calendar          Manage the hardware calendar
    call              Voice call
    call-home         Call-Home commands
    cd                Change current directory
    clear             Reset functions
    clock             Manage the system clock
    cns               CNS agents
    configure         Enter configuration mode
<output omitted>
R1# disable
R1>
```

> **Note** For security reasons, a Cisco network device will not echo, or show on the screen, the password that is entered. However, if a network device is configured over a modem link, or if Telnet is used, the password is sent over the connection in plain text. Telnet by itself does not offer a method to secure packets that contain passwords or commands. Secure Shell (SSH) Protocol, which runs on most Cisco devices, allows communication securely over insecure channels and provides strong authentication. SSH can be seen in this context as an encrypted form of Telnet.

Help in the CLI

Cisco devices use Cisco IOS Software with extensive command-line input help facilities, including context-sensitive help. This topic describes the CLI help that is available on Cisco devices.

The Cisco IOS CLI on Cisco devices offers the following types of help:

- **Word help:** Enter the character sequence of an incomplete command followed immediately by a question mark. Do not include a space before the question mark. The device will display a list of available commands that start with the characters that you entered. For example, enter the **sh?** command to get a list of commands that begin with the character sequence sh.

■ **Command syntax help:** Enter the **?** command to get command syntax help to see how to complete a command. Enter a question mark in place of a keyword or argument. Include a space before the question mark. The network device will then display a list of available command options, with <cr> standing for carriage return. For example, enter **show ?** to get a list of the various command options supported by the **show** command.

Special Ctrl and Esc key sequences, the Tab key, the up-arrow and down-arrow keys, and many others can reduce the need to reenter or type entire command strings. Cisco IOS Software provides several commands, keys, and characters to recall or complete command entries from a command history buffer that keeps the last several commands that you entered. These commands can be reused instead of reentered, if appropriate.

Console error messages help identify problems with an incorrect command entry. Error messages that might be encountered while using the CLI are shown in Table 4-1.

Table 4-1   *CLI Error Messages*

Error Message	Meaning	How to Get Help
% Ambiguous command: "show con"	You did not enter enough characters for your device to recognize the command.	Reenter the command followed by a question mark (?), *without* a space between the command and the question mark.
		The possible keywords that you can enter with the command are displayed.
Incomplete command	You did not enter all the keywords or values required by this command.	Reenter the command followed by a question mark (?), *with* a space between the command and the question mark.
Invalid input detected at '^' marker	You entered the command incorrectly. The caret (^) marks the point of the error.	Enter a question mark (?) to display all the commands or parameters that are available.

The command history buffer stores the commands that have been most recently entered. To see these commands, enter the Cisco IOS **show history** command.

You can use context-sensitive help to determine the syntax of a particular command. For example, if the device clock needs to be set but the clock command syntax is not known, the context-sensitive help provides a means to check the syntax for setting the clock.

If the word *clock* is entered but misspelled, the system performs a symbolic translation of the misspelled command as parsed by Cisco IOS Software. If no CLI command matches the string input, an error message is returned. If there is no Cisco IOS command that begins with the misspelled letters, by default, the device will interpret the misspelled command as a host name and attempt to resolve the host name to an IP address, and then try to telnet to that host.

Context-sensitive help will supply the entire command, even if you enter just the first part of the command, such as **cl?**.

If you enter the **clock** command but an error message indicating that the command is incomplete is displayed, enter the question mark command (**?**) (preceded by a space) to determine what arguments are required for completing the command sequence. In the **clock ?** example, the help output shows that the keyword **set** is required after **clock**.

If you now enter the **clock set** command and then press Enter, but another error message displays indicating that the command is still incomplete, press Ctrl-P (or the up-arrow key) to repeat the command entry. Then, add a space and enter the question mark command (**?**) to display a list of command arguments that are available at that point in the CLI for the given command.

After the last command recall, the administrator can use the question mark command (**?**) to reveal the additional arguments, which involve entering the current time using hours, minutes, and seconds.

After entering the current time, if you still see the Cisco IOS Software error message indicating that the command entered is incomplete, recall the command, add a space, and enter the question mark (**?**) to display a list of command arguments that are available at that point for the given command. In the example, enter the day, month, and year using the correct syntax, and then press Enter to execute the command.

Syntax checking uses the caret symbol (^) as an error-location indicator. The caret symbol appears at the point in the command string where an incorrect command, keyword, or argument has been entered. The error-location indicator and interactive help system provide a way to easily find and correct syntax errors. In the clock example, the caret symbol (^) indicates that the month was entered incorrectly. The parser is expecting the month to be spelled out.

Enhanced Editing Commands

The Cisco IOS CLI includes an enhanced editing mode that provides a set of editing key functions. Although the enhanced line-editing mode is automatically enabled, you can disable it. You should disable enhanced line editing if there are scripts that do not interact well when enhanced line editing is enabled. Use the **terminal editing** EXEC command to turn on advanced line-editing features and the **terminal no editing** EXEC command to disable advanced line-editing features.

Most commands are "undone," or turned off, by reentering the command with the word **no** in front of it. The **terminal** commands are one of the odd exceptions to the "no" rule. Notice that terminal editing is turned off by entering **terminal no editing** (instead of "no terminal editing").

One of the advanced line-editing features is to provide horizontal scrolling for commands that extend beyond a single line on the screen. When the cursor reaches the right margin, the command line shifts ten spaces to the left. The first ten characters of the line can no longer be seen, but you can scroll back to check the syntax at the beginning of the command.

The command entry extends beyond one line, and you can only see the end of the command string:

```
SwitchX> $ value for customers, employees, and partners.
```

The dollar sign ($) indicates that the line has been scrolled to the left. To scroll back, press Ctrl-B or the left-arrow key repeatedly until you are at the beginning of the command entry. You can also press Ctrl-A to return directly to the beginning of the line.

The key sequences are shortcuts or hot keys provided by the CLI. Use these key sequences to move the cursor around on the command line for corrections or changes. Table 4-2 describes each of the shortcuts.

Table 4-2   *Command-Line Editing Keys*

Command-Line Editing Key Sequence	Description
Ctrl-A	Moves the cursor to the beginning of the command line
Ctrl-E	Moves the cursor to the end of the command line
Esc-B	Moves the cursor back one word
Esc-F	Moves the cursor forward one word
Ctrl-B	Moves the cursor back one character
Ctrl-F	Moves the cursor forward one character
Ctrl-D	Deletes a single character to the left of the cursor
Backspace	Removes one character to the left of the cursor
Ctrl-R	Redisplays the current command line
Ctrl-U	Erases a line
Ctrl-W	Erases a word to the left of the cursor
Ctrl-Z	Ends configuration mode and returns directly to the privileged EXEC mode hostname# prompt
Tab	Completes a partially entered command if enough characters have been entered to make it unambiguous

Note   The Esc key is not functional on all terminals.

Command History

The Cisco CLI provides a history or record of commands that have been entered. This feature, called the *command history buffer*, is particularly useful in helping recall long or complex commands or entries.

With the command history feature, you can complete the following tasks:

- Display the contents of the command buffer.

- Set the command history buffer size.

- Recall previously entered commands stored in the history buffer. There is a buffer for the EXEC mode and another buffer for the configuration mode.

By default, command history is enabled, and the system records the last ten command lines in its history buffer.

To change the number of command lines that the system will record and recall during the current terminal session only, use the **terminal history** command at the user EXEC mode prompt.

To recall commands in the history buffer beginning with the most recent command, press Ctrl-P or the up-arrow key. Repeat the key sequence to recall successively older commands.

To return to more recent commands in the history buffer, after recalling older commands by pressing Ctrl-P or the up-arrow key, press Ctrl-N or the down-arrow key. Repeat the key sequence to recall successively more recent commands.

On most computers, there are additional select and copy facilities available. You can copy a previous command string, paste or insert it as the current command entry, and then press Enter.

Managing Cisco IOS Configuration

A Cisco router has the following four primary types of memory:

- **RAM:** Stores routing tables and the fast-switching cache. RAM holds the current running configuration file, the currently loaded IOS, and so on.

- **NVRAM:** Used for writable permanent storage of the startup configuration settings.

- **Flash:** Provides permanent storage of the Cisco IOS Software image file, backup configurations, and any other files through memory cards.

- **ROM:** Provides the POST routine and also provides a mini-IOS that can be used for troubleshooting and emergencies, such as when the stored IOS in flash is corrupted. The mini-IOS provided by ROM can also be for password recovery.

  ROM cannot be modified or copied to by device administrators.

The **show startup-config** command displays the saved startup configuration settings stored in NVRAM. The **show running-config** command displays the current configuration settings currently running in RAM. Figure 4-4 shows the location of the running and startup configuration files, along with where the setup utility copies the configuration.

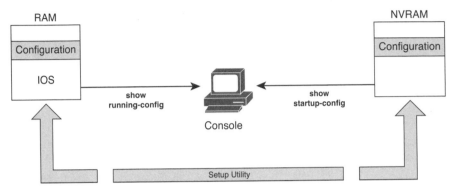

Figure 4-4 *Location of Configuration Files*

The **show running-config** command displays the current running configuration in RAM.

When you issue the **show running-config** command on a router, you will initially see "Building configuration...." This output indicates that the running configuration is being built from the active configuration settings currently running and currently stored in RAM.

After the running configuration is built from RAM, the "Current configuration:" message appears, indicating that this is the current running configuration that is currently running in RAM.

The first line of the **show startup-config** command output indicates the amount of NVRAM used to store the configuration. For example, "Using 1359 out of 32762 bytes" indicates that the total size of the NVRAM is 32,762 bytes and the current configuration stored in NVRAM takes up 1359 bytes.

You can copy configuration files from the router or switch to a file server using FTP, SCP, HTTP, TFTP, and others. For example, you can copy configuration files to back up a current configuration file to a server before changing its contents, thereby allowing the original configuration file to be restored from the server. The protocol that is used depends on which type of server is used.

You can copy configuration files from an external server to the running configuration in RAM or to the startup configuration file in NVRAM of the router or switch for one of the following reasons:

- To restore a backed-up configuration file.

- To use the configuration file for another router or switch. For example, you might add another router or switch to the network and want it to have a configuration similar to the original router or switch. By copying the file to the network server and making the changes to reflect the configuration requirements of the new router or switch, you can save time.

■ To load the same configuration commands onto all the routers or switches in the network so that all the routers or switches have similar configurations.

In addition to using the setup utility or the CLI to load or create a configuration, there are several other sources for configurations that you can use.

You can use the Cisco IOS **copy** command to move configurations from one component or device to another. The syntax of the **copy** command requires that the first argument indicate the source (where the configuration is to be copied from), followed by the destination (where the configuration is to be copied to). For example, in the **copy running-config tftp:** command, the running configuration in RAM is copied to a TFTP server.

Use the **copy running-config startup-config** command after a configuration change is made in RAM and must be saved to the startup configuration file in NVRAM. Similarly, copy the startup configuration file in NVRAM back into RAM with the **copy startup-config running-config** command. Notice that you can abbreviate the commands.

Similar commands exist for copying between a TFTP server and either NVRAM or RAM. Use the **configure terminal** command to interactively create configurations in RAM from the console or remote terminal. Use the **erase startup-config** command to delete the saved startup configuration file in NVRAM.

When a configuration is copied into RAM from any source, the configuration merges with the existing configuration in RAM. New configuration parameters are added, and changes to existing parameters overwrite the old parameters. Configuration commands that exist in RAM for which there is no corresponding command in NVRAM remain unaffected.

Copying the running configuration from RAM into the startup configuration file in NVRAM overwrites the startup configuration file in NVRAM.

After the commands to configure the router or switch have been entered, you must save the running configuration to NVRAM with the **copy running-config startup-config** command. If the configuration is not saved to NVRAM and the router or switch is reloaded, the configuration will be lost and the router or switch will revert to the last configuration saved in NVRAM.

You can use the TFTP servers to store configurations in a central place, allowing centralized management and updating. Regardless of the size of the network, there should always be a copy of the current running configuration online as a backup.

The **copy running-config tftp:** command allows the current configuration to be uploaded and saved to a TFTP server. The IP address or name of the TFTP server and the destination filename must be supplied. During the copying process, a series of exclamation marks shows the progress of the upload.

The **copy tftp: running-config** command downloads a configuration file from the TFTP server to the running configuration of the RAM. Again, the address or name of the TFTP server and the source and destination filenames must be supplied. In this case, because you are copying the file to the running configuration, the destination filename should be running-config. This is a merge process, not an overwrite process.

Figure 4-5 summarizes this important information.

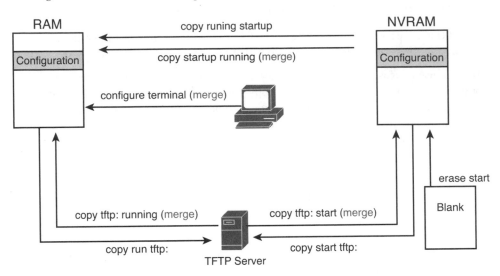

Figure 4-5 *Managing Configuration Files*

Improving the User Experience in the CLI

When you use **show** commands (for example, **show running-config**), Cisco IOS Software automatically pauses its display of the output after a specified number of lines and displays "--More--" text. It then waits for user input to continue with the display. You must press the spacebar to display a set of subsequent lines or press Enter to display a single line.

You can use the **terminal length** command, followed by a number, to control the number of lines that are displayed without pause. A value of 0 prevents the router from pausing between screens of output. By default, the value is set to 24.

Another very useful feature that improves the user experience in the CLI is filtering of **show** outputs. Using filtering, you can display only the parts of **show** outputs that you are interested in. You can filter outputs by providing the pipe (l) character after a **show** command, followed by a filtering parameter and a filtering expression.

Table 4-3 describes filtering parameters that are available for output filtering.

Table 4-3 show *Command Output Modifiers*

Parameter	Description
begin	Shows all the output lines from a certain point, starting with the line that matches the filtering expression
exclude	Excludes all output lines that match the filtering expression

Parameter	Description
include	Includes all output lines that match the filtering expression
section	Shows the entire section that starts with the filtering expression

Note You can use output filters in combination with any **show** command. The **show running-config** command mentioned above is used for the sake of simplicity only.

Chapter Summary

Cisco IOS Software provides network services to Cisco products to perform various internetworking functions. The Cisco IOS CLI uses a hierarchy of commands in its command-mode structure. Two basic configuration modes are user EXEC and privileged EXEC mode.

Context-sensitive help and console error messages are available in the Cisco IOS CLI to help you configure Cisco devices. You can use hot keys and shortcuts, command history, and output filters to improve the CLI user experience.

Two general configurations that are used by Cisco routers and switches are the running configuration and the startup configuration. The **copy** command allows saving and backing up these important configuration files.

Additional Resources

- Cisco IOS, Wikipedia: http://en.wikipedia.org/wiki/Cisco_IOS

- Operating Cisco IOS Software Video, AJS Networking: http://ajsnetworking.com/ios

Review Questions

Use the questions here to review what you learned in this chapter. The correct answers and solutions are found in Appendix A, "Answers to Chapter Review Questions."

1. When a Cisco device starts up, which of the following does it run to check its hardware?

   a. Flash

   b. RAM

   c. POST

   d. TFTP

2. When a Catalyst switch or Cisco router starts up, what is the first operation performed?

   a. The device performs system startup routines.

   b. The device performs hardware-checking routines.

   c. The device attempts to locate other devices on the network.

   d. The device tries to find and apply software configuration settings.

3. Upon initial installation of a Cisco switch or router, the network administrator typically configures the networking devices from a _____.

   a. CD-ROM

   b. TFTP server

   c. Console terminal

   d. Modem connection

4. If a network administrator is supporting a remote device, the preferred method is to use a modem connection to the _____ of the device for remote configuration.

   a. LAN port

   b. Uplink port

   c. Console port

   d. Auxiliary port

5. Which access level allows a person to access all router commands and can be password protected to allow only authorized individuals to access the router?

   a. User EXEC level

   b. Setup EXEC level

   c. Enable EXEC level

   d. Privileged EXEC level

6. How do you instruct a Cisco device to parse and execute an entered command?

   a. Press the Send key.

   b. Press the Enter key.

   c. Add a space at the end of the command.

   d. Wait 5 seconds after you enter a command.

7. Which CLI prompt indicates that you are working in privileged EXEC mode?

   a. hostname#

   b. hostname>

   c. hostname-exec>

   d. hostname-config

8. Which command would you enter in privileged EXEC mode to list the command options?

   a. ?

   b. init

   c. help

   d. login

9. What command do you use to save your configuration so that it can persist after a reboot of the device?

   a. copy running-config startup-config

   b. save

   c. backup

   d. copy startup-config running-config

10. What command can you run to see all the configuration of EIGRP on the device?

    a. show run | eigrp

    b. show eigrp all

    c. show run | section eigrp

    d. show run | begin router eigrp 100

Production Network Simulation Question 4-1

Your peer has the following configuration in RAM on Router CO1:

```
hostname CO1
!
interface fastethernet0/0
ip address 10.10.10.1 255.255.255.0
no shutdown
!
interface fastethernet0/1
shutdown
!
interface serial0/0
ip address 192.168.1.1 255.255.255.0
no shutdown
```

He is going to perform the command **copy tftp: running-config.**

The configuration he is copying from the TFTP server is as follows:

```
hostname BO1
!
interface fastethernet0/1
ip address 172.16.1.101 255.255.255.0
no shutdown
```

What is the configuration in RAM that results?

Chapter 5

Switch Technologies

This chapter includes the following sections:

- Chapter Objectives

- The Need for Switches

- Switch Characteristics

- Starting and Configuring a Switch

- Switching Operation

- Troubleshooting Common Switch Media Issues

- Chapter Summary

- Additional Resources

- Review Questions

- Production Network Simulation Question 5-1

For many years, hubs were used to connect multiple devices together in the local-area network. These devices operated at Layer 1 and were called "bit spitters" by network engineers. Sadly, these devices made no intelligent forwarding decisions. They simply took in bits on a port and sent these bits out all other ports on the device. Obviously, these devices led to collisions of frames on the network. To use the terminology you will learn in this chapter, these devices created one large collision domain consisting of many devices. A collision domain defines the devices that can experience a frame collision, and with hubs placing many devices in such a domain, these devices would help create frequent collisions. This chapter speaks to the next-generation replacement technology for hubs, Cisco Catalyst switches. You will learn the basic characteristics of these devices, find out how they function, configure their basic settings, and even learn to troubleshoot the most common problems with these devices.

Chapter Objectives

Upon completing this chapter, you will be able to describe modern switching technologies and configure basic parameters on a switch. These abilities include meeting these objectives:

- Describe the need for switches in modern networks

- Define a collision domain versus a broadcast domain

- Detail the characteristics of a modern switch

- Explain the steps of a typical switch installation

- Describe the function of common LEDs on switches

- Connect to the console port of a switch

- Apply a basic configuration to the switch

- Explain the internal switching operations of a switch

- Troubleshoot common media and port issues with switches

The Need for Switches

As soon as we want to connect three or more local devices together, we need to use a dedicated network device to enable communication between hosts.

In the earliest of networks, where network devices had few Ethernet segments, the end host devices had to compete for the same bandwidth, with only one device being able to transmit data at a time. The network segments that share the same bandwidth are known as *collision domains*, because when two or more devices within that segment try to communicate at the same time, collisions can occur.

Today, it is common to use switches as network devices operating at the data link layer (Layer 2) of the Open Systems Interconnection (OSI) model to divide a network into segments and reduce the number of devices that are competing for bandwidth. Each new segment results in a new collision domain. More bandwidth is available to the devices on a segment, and collisions in the network are eliminated.

As shown in Figure 5-1, each switch port connects to a single PC or server. Each switch port represents a unique collision domain, while all ports on the switch represent a unique broadcast domain.

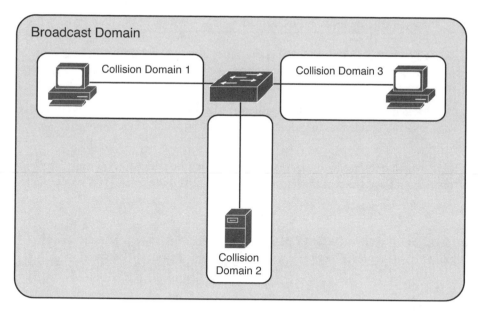

Figure 5-1 *Switch Creating Multiple Collision Domains*

Note   The fancy term for placing a single device in its own collision domain with switches is called *microsegmentation* of the network.

Ethernet switches selectively forward individual frames from a receiving port to the port where the destination node is connected. This selective forwarding process can be thought of as establishing a momentary point-to-point connection between the transmitting and receiving nodes. The connection is made only long enough to forward a single frame. During this instant, the two nodes have a full-bandwidth connection between them and represent a logical point-to-point connection. This is also known as full-duplex communication.

The switch builds and maintains a table, called a MAC table, which matches a destination MAC address with the port that is used to connect to that destination. For each incoming frame, the destination MAC address in the frame header is compared to the list of addresses in the MAC table. Switches then use MAC addresses as they decide how to forward frames.

Here are the steps used by a switch to process unicast frames on an Ethernet LAN:

1. When a unicast frame is received on a port, the switch compares the destination MAC address to the MAC addresses contained in its tables.

2. If the switch determines that the destination MAC address of the frame resides on the same network segment as the source, it does not forward the frame. This process is called *filtering*, and by performing this process, switches can significantly reduce the amount of traffic going between network segments by eliminating the unnecessary frames.

3. If the switch determines that the destination MAC address of the frame is not in the same network segment as the source, it forwards the frame to the appropriate segment.

4. If the switch does not have an entry for the destination address, it transmits the frame out all ports except the port on which it received the frame. This process is called *flooding*.

Note   It is critical that a CCENT/CCNA candidate understand this process thoroughly. You should be able to describe filtering, forwarding, and flooding in detail.

Switch Characteristics

As you learned in the previous section, switches have become a fundamental part of most networks. The introduction of full-duplex communications (having a connection that can carry transmitted and received signals at the same time) has helped enable 1-Gbps Ethernet and beyond.

Here are some important characteristics of switches:

High port density: Switches have high port densities: 24- and 48-port switches operate at speeds of 100 Mbps, 1 Gbps, and 10 Gbps. Large-enterprise switches can support hundreds of ports.

Large frame buffers: The ability to store more received frames before having to start dropping them is useful, particularly when there might be congested ports to servers or other parts of the network.

Port speed: Depending on the cost of a switch, it might be possible to support a mixture of speeds. Ports of 100 Mbps are expected, but switches offering ports supporting 1 or 10 Gbps are more common.

Fast internal switching: Having fast internal switching allows many speeds: 100 Mbps, 1 Gbps, and 10 Gbps. The method that is used can be a fast internal bus or shared memory, which affects the overall performance of the switch.

Low per-port cost: Switches provide high port density at a lower cost. For this reason, LAN switches can accommodate network designs featuring fewer users per segment, therefore increasing the average available bandwidth per user.

Starting and Configuring a Switch

Before you start a Cisco Catalyst switch, the physical installation must meet operational conditions. After the switch is turned on and startup is complete, the initial software settings can be configured. Verifying that the switch startup has been completed without error is the first step in deploying a Catalyst switch. The switch must start successfully and have a default configuration to operate on the network. This section presents an overview of switch installation and describes how to verify the initial operation and configuration.

Switch Installation

Physical installation and startup of a Catalyst switch requires completion of these steps:

1. Before performing physical installation, verify the following: switch power requirements and switch operating environment condition requirements (operational temperature and humidity).

2. Use the appropriate installation procedures for rack mounting, wall mounting, or table or shelf mounting.

3. Before starting the switch, verify that network cable connections are secure.

4. Attach the power cable plug to the power supply socket of the switch. The switch will start. Some Catalyst switches, including the Cisco Catalyst 2960 Series, do not have Power buttons.

5. Observe the boot sequence: When the switch is on, the power-on self-test (POST) begins. During POST, the switch LEDs blink while a series of tests determine that the switch is functioning properly. The Cisco IOS Software output text is displayed on the console.

When all startup procedures are finished, the switch is ready to configure.

Switch LED Indicators

The front panel of a switch has several lights, called *LEDs*, to help monitor system activity and performance. LED indicators provide only a quick view of the status of the switch. For a more detailed view, Cisco IOS commands are used.

The front of the switch features these LEDs:

System LED: Indicates whether the system is receiving power and functioning correctly.

Remote Power Supply LED: Indicates whether the remote power supply is in use.

Port Mode LEDs: Indicate the current state of the Mode button, which is used to switch between different modes. The modes are used to determine how the Port Status LEDs are interpreted.

Port Status LEDs: Have different meanings, depending on the current value of the Mode LED.

For more details about LED indicators and their functions, refer to the Cisco Switch Hardware Installation Guide. It is recommended that you refer to the model-specific documentation. The reference for the Catalyst 2960 switches can be found at www.cisco.com/en/US/docs/switches/lan/catalyst2960/hardware/installation/guide/higover.html.

Figure 5-2 shows the LED locations on the Catalyst 2960 switch.

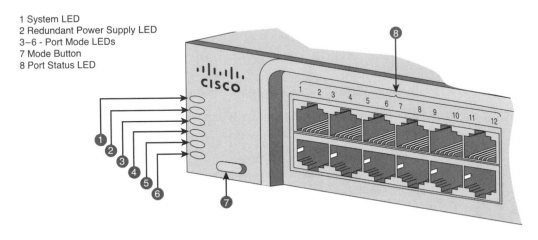

1 System LED
2 Redundant Power Supply LED
3–6 - Port Mode LEDs
7 Mode Button
8 Port Status LED

Figure 5-2 *2960 LEDs*

Connecting to the Console Port

To perform initial switch configuration, connect to the switch through the console port. The following equipment is needed to access a Cisco device through the console port:

- RJ-45–to–DB-9 console cable (also known as a rollover cable and provided with your switch)

- PC or equivalent with serial port and communications software, such as HyperTerminal, configured with these settings:

  - Speed: 9600 bits/second

  - Data bits: 8

  - Parity: None

  - Stop bit: 1

  - Flow control: None

Modern computers and notebooks rarely include built-in serial ports. Often a USB-to-RS232-compatible serial port adapter is used instead.

On newer Cisco network devices, a USB serial console connection is also supported. A suitable USB cable (USB type A–to–5-pin mini-type B) and operating system device driver are needed to establish connectivity.

> **Note**   Only one console port can be active at a time. When a cable is plugged into the USB console port, the RJ-45 port becomes inactive. When the USB cable is removed from the USB port, the RJ-45 port becomes active.

After a console connection is established, you gain access to user EXEC mode by default. To start the configuration, you must enter privileged EXEC mode by using the **enable** command.

Basic Switch Configuration

Cisco IOS Software CLI modes are hierarchically structured. After you are in privileged EXEC mode, you can access other configuration modes. Each mode is used to accomplish particular tasks and has a specific set of commands that are available in that mode. For example, to configure a switch interface, you must be in interface configuration mode. All configurations that are entered in interface configuration mode apply only to that interface.

To start, you will explore how to navigate two frequently used configuration modes: *global configuration mode* and *interface configuration mode*.

The example starts with the switch in privileged EXEC mode. To configure global switch parameters, such as the switch host name or the switch IP address that are used for switch management, use global configuration mode. To access global configuration mode, enter the configure terminal command in privileged EXEC mode:

```
Switch# configure terminal
```

After the command is executed, the prompt changes to show that the router is in global configuration mode:

```
Switch(config)#
```

Configuring interface-specific parameters is a common task. To access interface configuration mode for the Fast Ethernet 0/1 interface from global configuration mode, enter the **interface FastEthernet 0/1** command:

```
Switch(config)# interface FastEthernet 0/1
```

Or you can use a shorter version of the same command:

```
Switch(config)# interface fa 0/1
```

The prompt changes:

```
Switch(config-if)#
```

To exit interface configuration mode, use the **exit** command. Sometimes you need to execute commands on multiple interfaces at the same time. Use the **interface range** command in global configuration mode for this task:

```
Switch(config)# interface range FastEthernet 0/1 - 24
Switch(config-if-range)#
```

This example shows how to configure interfaces Fast Ethernet 0/1 through 0/24 all at the same time.

Naming the switch enables you to better manage the network by being able to uniquely identify each switch within the network. The name of the switch is considered to be the host name and is the name that is displayed at the system prompt. The switch name is assigned in global configuration mode. In the example that follows, the switch name is set to "TampaSwitch" with the use of **hostname** command. If the host name is not explicitly configured, a switch has the factory-assigned default host name of "Switch."

```
Switch(config)# hostname TampaSwitch
TampaSwitch(config)#
```

To manage a switch remotely, you need to assign an IP address to the switch. In the example that follows, you want to manage TampaSwitch from a PC, a computer that is used for managing the network, so you need to assign an IP address to TampaSwitch. This IP address is assigned to a virtual interface called a virtual local-area network (VLAN). The default configuration on the switch is to have switch management controlled through VLAN 1. Therefore, the IP address in the example is assigned to VLAN 1.

To configure an IP address and subnet mask for the switch, you must be in VLAN 1 interface configuration mode and then use the **ip address** configuration command.

You must use the **no shutdown** interface configuration command to ensure that physical interfaces are operational. The logical VLAN interface has an auto-sense behavior and can enable itself automatically, but administrators often still use the **no shutdown** command here out of good habit.

The operational VLAN interface with the assigned IP address can be used, for example, in remote management Telnet connections or if you use Simple Network Management Protocol (SNMP) to manage the switch:

```
SwitchX(config)# interface vlan 1
SwitchX(config-if)# ip address 172.20.137.5 255.255.255.0
SwitchX(config-if)# no shutdown
```

To configure the switch so that it can be accessed remotely, a default gateway is needed. This permits the switch to send packets back to the remote workstation that is managing the device. To configure a default gateway for the switch, use the **ip default-gateway** command. Enter the IP address of the next-hop router interface (172.20.137.1) that is directly connected to the switch where a default gateway is being configured.

After the default gateway is configured, the switch sends packets for all unknown IP destinations to the configured gateway, which enables switch connectivity with distant networks:

```
SwitchX(config)# ip default-gateway 172.20.137.1
```

After you enter the initial commands to configure the switch, you must save the running configuration to NVRAM with the **copy running-config startup-config** command. If the configuration is not saved to NVRAM and the switch is reloaded, the configuration is lost and the router reverts to the last configuration saved in NVRAM.

```
SwitchX# copy running-config startup-config
```

> **Note**   It is much easier to use the shortcut command **copy run star** to save the configuration. In production environments, you can even use the shortcut **wr**, which stands for **write memory**. Unfortunately, this time-saver is not guaranteed to work in the exam environments, so be sure you know **copy run star**.

Verifying the Switch Initial Startup Status

After you log in to a Catalyst switch, you can verify the switch software and hardware status using verification commands executed from privileged EXEC mode.

Use the **show version** EXEC command to display the configuration of the system hardware and the software version information. Examine this example and the explanation of key fields:

```
TampaSwitch# show version
Cisco IOS Software, C2960 Software (C2960-LANBASEK9-M), Version 15.0(1)SE3, RELEASE
  SOFTWARE (fc1)
<output omitted>
TampaSwitch uptime is 15 hours, 30 minutes
System returned to ROM by power-on
System restarted at 15:06:49 UTC Tue Aug 21 2012
System image file is "flash:/c2960-lanbasek9-mz.150-1.SE3/c2960-lanbasek9-mz. 150-1.
  SE3.bin"
<output omitted>
cisco WS-C2960-24TT-L (PowerPC405) processor (revision D0) with
65536K bytes of memory.
Processor board ID FOC1141Z8YW
<output omitted>
```

This output is from a Cisco Catalyst WS-C2960-24 switch with 24 Fast Ethernet ports. Notice the important information you can learn from this command. Some key elements are described here:

- **Cisco IOS Software version:** Cisco IOS Software, C2960 Software (C2960-LANBASEK9-M), Version 15.0(1)SE3

- **Switch uptime:** TampaSwitch uptime is 15 hours, 30 minutes

- **System image file:** flash:/c2960-lanbasek9-mz.150-1.SE3/c2960-lanbasek9-mz. 150-1. SE3.bin

- **Switch platform:** cisco WS-C2960-24TT-L

- **Memory:** 65,536K bytes of memory

- **Processor board ID:** FOC1141Z8YW

The **show interfaces** command displays status and statistical information for the network interfaces of the switch. The resulting output varies, depending on the type of interface and type of network for which an interface has been configured. Usually this command is entered with the options *type* and *slot/number*. The *type* option allows values such as FastEthernet and GigabitEthernet, and the *slot/number* option indicates slot 0 and the port number on the selected interface (for example, fa0/1).

As you might guess, the **show interfaces** command is used frequently when you are configuring and monitoring network devices.

```
TampaSwitch# show interfaces
FastEthernet 0/1 FastEthernet0/1 is up, line protocol is up (connected)
Hardware is Fast Ethernet, address is 001e.147c.bd01 (bia 001e.147c.bd01)
MTU 1500 bytes, BW 100000 Kbit/sec, DLY 100 usec,
reliability 255/255, txload 1/255, rxload 1/255
Encapsulation ARPA, loopback not set
Keepalive set (10 sec)
Full-duplex, 100Mbps, media type is 10/100BaseTX
<output omitted>
5 minute input rate 31000 bits/sec, 33 packets/sec
<output omitted>
```

Some key elements of this important output include

- **Layer 1 and Layer 2 status of the interface:** FastEthernet 0/1 FastEthernet0/1 is up, line protocol is up (connected)

- **Duplex and speed:** Full-duplex, 100 Mbps

- **Router interface statistics:** 5 minute input rate 31000 bits/sec

The **show running-config** command displays the current running (active) configuration file of the switch. This command requires privileged EXEC mode access. The IP address, subnet mask, and default gateway settings are displayed here:

```
TampaSwitch# show running-config
Building configuration... <output omitted>!
hostname TampaSwitch
!
<output omitted>
!
```

```
interface Vlan1
ip address 172.20.137.5 255.255.255.0
!
ip default-gateway 172.20.137.1
!
<output omitted>
```

Switching Operation

As you know from this chapter thus far, the switch builds and maintains a table, called a MAC address table, that matches a destination MAC address with the port used to connect to that destination system. For each incoming frame, the destination MAC address in the frame header is compared to the list of addresses in the MAC table. Switches then use MAC addresses as they decide whether to filter, forward, or flood frames.

Now it is time to break down the process the switch uses to build this MAC address table in even more detail. The following steps describe the switching process:

1. The switch receives a frame from PC A on port 1.

2. The switch enters the source MAC address and the switch port that received the frame into the MAC table. Notice that this is done transparently; the sending device is not aware that this is happening. This is why this technology is sometimes referred to as *transparent bridging*.

3. The switch checks the table for the destination MAC address. Because the destination address is not known, the switch floods the frame to all the ports except the port on which it received the frame.

4. The destination device with the matching MAC address replies to the PC A frame with a unicast frame addressed to PC A.

5. The switch enters the source MAC address of PC B and the port number of the switch port that received the frame into the MAC table. The destination address of the frame and its associated port is found in the MAC table.

6. The switch can now forward frames between the source and destination devices without flooding because it has entries in the MAC table that identify the associated ports.

Figures 5-3 and 5-4 demonstrate these important steps.

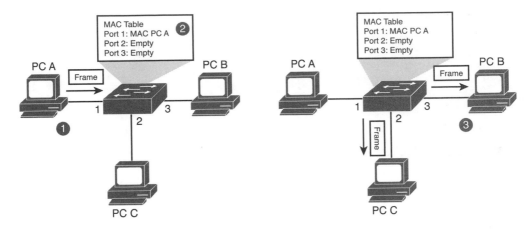

Figure 5-3 *First Three Steps of the Switching Process*

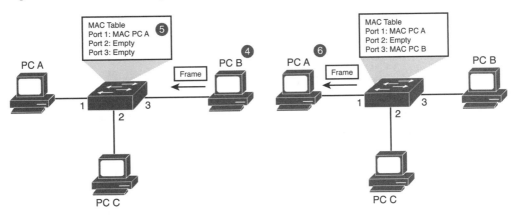

Figure 5-4 *Last Three Steps of the Switching Process*

Duplex Communication

Full-duplex communication increases effective bandwidth by allowing both ends of the connection to transmit simultaneously. However, this method of optimizing network performance requires microsegmentation before full-duplex communication can occur.

Half-duplex communication relies on a unidirectional data flow, where sending and receiving data are not performed at the same time. This behavior is similar to walkie-talkies or two-way radios in that only one person can talk at a time. If someone talks while another person is speaking, a collision occurs. As a result, half-duplex communication implements Ethernet carrier sense multiple access collision detect (CSMA/CD) to help reduce the potential for collisions and to detect them when they do happen.

Half-duplex communication has performance issues that stem from the constant waiting, because data can flow in only one direction at a time. Half-duplex connections are typically seen in older hardware, such as hubs. Nodes that are attached to hubs that share their connection to a switch port must operate in half-duplex mode because the end computers must be able to detect collisions. Nodes can operate in a half-duplex mode if the network interface card (NIC) cannot be configured for full-duplex operations. In this case, the port on the switch operates in half-duplex mode as well. Because of these limitations, full-duplex communication has replaced half-duplex in more current hardware.

In full-duplex communication, the data flow is bidirectional, so data can be sent and received at the same time. The bidirectional support enhances performance by reducing the wait time between transmissions. Most Ethernet, Fast Ethernet, and Gigabit Ethernet NICs sold today offer full-duplex capability. Frames that are sent by the two connected end nodes cannot collide because the end nodes use two separate circuits in the network cable. Each full-duplex connection uses only one port. Full-duplex connections require a switch that supports full duplex or a direct connection between two nodes that each support full duplex. Nodes that are directly attached to a dedicated switch port with NICs that support full duplex should be connected to switch ports that are configured to operate in full-duplex mode.

The duplex parameters on the Cisco Catalyst 2960 Series are as follows:

- The **auto** option sets autonegotiation of duplex mode. With autonegotiation enabled, the two ports communicate to decide the best mode of operation.

- The **full** option sets full-duplex mode.

- The **half** option sets half-duplex mode.

For Fast Ethernet and 10/100/1000 ports, the default option is **auto.** For 100BASE-FX ports, the default is **full.** The 10/100/1000 ports operate in either half- or full-duplex mode when they are set to 10 or 100 Mbps, but when they are set to 1000 Mbps, they operate only in full-duplex mode.

100BASE-FX ports operate only at 100 Mbps in full-duplex mode.

Manually set the duplex mode and speed of switch ports to avoid multivendor issues with autonegotiation. Here is an example of manually setting the duplex and speed of a switch interface:

```
TampaSwitch(config)# interface FastEthernet0/5
TampaSwitch(config-if)# duplex full
TampaSwitch(config-if)# speed 100
```

Verify the duplex settings by using the **show interfaces** command on the Cisco Catalyst 2960 Series. The **show interfaces** privileged EXEC command displays statistics and status for all interfaces or specified interfaces. This figure shows the duplex and speed settings of a Fast Ethernet interface.

Autonegotiation can at times produce unpredictable results. By default, when autonegotiation fails, the Catalyst switch sets the corresponding switch port to half-duplex mode. This type of failure happens when an attached device does not support autonegotiation. If the device is manually configured to operate in half-duplex mode, it matches the default mode of the switch. However, autonegotiation errors can happen if the device is manually configured to operate in full-duplex mode. This configuration, half-duplex on one end and full-duplex on the other end, causes late collision errors at the half-duplex end. To avoid this situation, manually set the duplex parameters of the switch to match the attached device.

If the switch port is in full-duplex mode and the attached device is in half-duplex mode, check for frame check sequence (FCS) errors on the full-duplex switch port.

Troubleshooting Common Switch Media Issues

Most issues that affect a switched network are encountered during the original implementation. Theoretically, after it is installed, a network continues to operate without problems. However, that is only true in theory. Cabling gets damaged, configurations change, and new devices are connected to the switch that require switch configuration changes. Ongoing maintenance is a fact of life. This section describes the most common media and port issues and indicates how to troubleshoot them.

Media Issues

Media issues are common. It is a fact of life that wiring gets damaged. The following are some examples of everyday situations that can cause media issues:

- In an environment using Category 3 wiring, the maintenance crew installs a new air conditioning system that introduces new electromagnetic interference (EMI) sources into the environment.

- In an environment using Category 5 wiring, cabling is run too close to an elevator motor.

- Poor cable management puts a strain on some RJ-45 connectors, causing one or more wires to break.

- New applications change traffic patterns.

- When new equipment is connected to a switch, the connection operates in a half-duplex mode or a duplex mismatch occurs, which could lead to an excessive number of collisions.

There are several ways in which light can be lost from the fiber. Some of these are manufacturing problems (for example, microbends, macrobends, and splicing fibers that do not have their cores centered), while others are physics problems (back reflections) because light reflects whenever it encounters a change in the index of refraction.

Macrobends are typically applied to the fiber during fiber installation.

There is another explanation for why light leaks out at a macrobend. Part of the traveling wave, called the *evanescent wave*, travels inside the cladding. Around the bend, part of the evanescent wave must travel faster than the speed of light in the material. This is not possible, so that part radiates out of the fiber.

Bend losses can be minimized by designing a larger index difference between the core and the cladding. Another approach is to operate at the shortest possible wavelength and perform good installations.

Splices are a way to connect two fibers by fusing their ends. The best way to align the fiber core is by using the outside diameter of the fiber as a guide. If the core is at the center of the fiber, a good splice can be achieved. If the core is off center, it is impossible to create a good splice. You would have to cut the fiber farther upstream and test again.

Another possibility is that the fibers to be spliced could have dirt on their ends. Dirt can cause many problems, particularly if the dirt intercepts some of or all the light from the core. Recall that the core for single-mode fiber (SMF) is only 9 µm.

Figure 5-5 shows an excellent troubleshooting flowchart that you can use to aid in troubleshooting switch media issues.

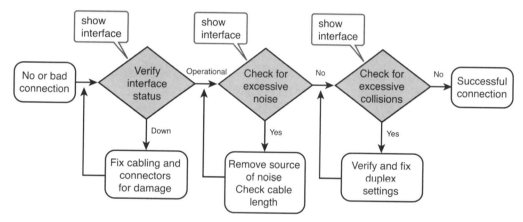

Figure 5-5 *Troubleshooting Switch Media Issues*

To troubleshoot switch media issues when you have no connection or a bad connection between a switch and another device, follow this general process:

1. Use the **show interface** command to check the interface status. If the interface is not operational, check the cable and connectors for damage.

2. Use the **show interface** command to check for excessive noise. If there is excessive noise, first find and remove the source of the noise, if possible. Verify that the cable does not exceed the maximum cable length and check the type of cable that is used. For copper cable, it is recommended that you use at least Category 5.

3. Use the **show interface** command to check for excessive collisions. If there are collisions or late collisions, verify the duplex settings on both ends of the connection.

Note A counter shows excessive values when it is constantly increasing while performing sequential verification of counter values.

One of the most important elements of the **show interface** command output is the display of the line and data link protocol status. This figure indicates the key summary line to check and the status meanings for an interface.

The first parameter refers to the hardware layer and essentially reflects whether the interface is receiving the carrier detect signal from the other end. The second parameter refers to the data link layer and reflects whether the data link layer protocol keepalives are being received.

Based on the output of the **show interface** command, possible problems can be fixed as follows:

- If the interface is up and the line protocol is down, a problem exists. There could be an encapsulation type mismatch, the interface on the other end could be error-disabled, or there could be a hardware problem.

- If the line protocol and the interface are both down, a cable is not attached or some other interface problem exists. For example, in a back-to-back connection, the other end of the connection can be administratively down.

- If the interface is administratively down, it has been manually disabled (the **shutdown** command has been issued) in the active configuration.

Figure 5-6 summarizes this important information.

Verify interface status.

```
Switch#show interface FastEthernet0/1
FastEthernet0/1 is up, line protocol is up
Hardware is Fast Ethernet, address is 0022.91c4.0e01 (bia 0022.91c4.0e01)
MTU 1500 bytes, BW 100000 Kbit, DLY 100 usec,
<output omitted>
```

Interface Status	Line Protocol Status	Link State
Up	Up	Operational
Up	Down	Connection problem
Down	Down (notconnect)	Cable unplugged; other end of the link disconnected or interface in shutdown mode.
Down	Down	Interface problem
Administratively down	Down	Disabled

Figure 5-6 *Verifying Interface Status*

Based on the output of the **show interface** command, you can find, diagnose, and correct the problem.

If you see many cyclic redundancy check (CRC) errors, there is too much noise on the link, and you should inspect the cable for damage and length. You should also search for and eliminate noise sources, if possible.

Collisions will occur in networks where half-duplex is being used. Collisions in half-duplex operations are completely normal, and you should not worry about them, as long as you are satisfied with half-duplex operations. However, you should never see collisions in a properly designed and configured network that uses full-duplex. It is highly recommended that you use full-duplex unless you have older or legacy equipment that does not support half-duplex.

Late collision refers to a collision that occurs after the preamble is transmitted. Late collisions occur when you have serious problems in a switched network, such as duplex misconfiguration. For example, you could have one end of a connection configured for full-duplex and the other for half-duplex. You would see late collisions on an interface that is configured for half-duplex. In that case, you must configure the same duplex setting on both ends.

Figure 5-7 shows an example of **show interface** command output. The example shows counters and statistics for the FastEthernet0/1 interface.

Display interface status and statistics.

```
Switch#show interface FastEthernet0/1
FastEthernet0/1 is up, line protocol is up
Hardware is Fast Ethernet, address is 0022.91c4.0e01 (bia 0022.91c4.0e01)
MTU 1500 bytes, BW 100000 Kbit, DLY 100 usec,
<output omitted>
    2295197 packets input, 305539992 bytes, 0 no buffer
    Received 1925500 broadcasts, 0 runts, 0 giants, 0 throttles
    3 input errors, 3 CRC, 0 frame, 0 overrun, 0 ignored
    0 watchdog, 68 multicast, 0 pause input
    0 input packets with dribble condition detected
    3594664 packets output, 436549843 bytes, 0 underruns
    1935 output errors, 1790 collisions, 10 interface resets
    0 unknown protocol drops
    0 babbles, 135 late collision, 0 deferred
<output omitted>
```

Figure 5-7 *Displaying the Interface Status and Statistics*

Table 5-1 describes some of the parameters in the **show interface** command output.

Table 5-1   show interface *Command Parameters*

Parameter	Description
Runts	Packets that are discarded because they are smaller than the minimum packet size for the medium. For example, any Ethernet packet that is less than 64 bytes is considered a runt.
Giants	Packets that are discarded because they exceed the maximum packet size for the medium. For example, any Ethernet packet that is greater than 1518 bytes is considered a giant.
Input Errors	Total number of errors. It includes runts, giants, no buffer, CRC, frame, overrun, and ignored counts.

Parameter	Description
CRC	CRC errors are generated when the calculated checksum is not the same as the checksum received.
Output Errors	Sum of all errors that prevented the final transmission of datagrams out of the interface that is being examined.
Collisions	Number of messages retransmitted because of an Ethernet collision. This often happens on half-duplex links when two devices transmit frames at the same time.
Late Collisions	Jammed signal could not reach to ends. Caused by a duplex mismatch or by exceeded Ethernet cable length limits.

Port Issues

A common issue with speed and duplex occurs when the duplex settings are mismatched between two switches, between a switch and a router, or between a switch and a workstation or server. This mismatch can occur when you manually hard-code the speed and duplex or from autonegotiation issues between the two devices.

Duplex mismatch is a situation in which the switch operates at full-duplex and the connected device operates at half-duplex or vice versa. The result of a duplex mismatch is extremely slow performance, intermittent connectivity, and loss of connection. Other possible causes of data-link errors at full-duplex are bad cables, a faulty switch port, or NIC software or hardware issues.

If the mismatch occurs between two Cisco devices with Cisco Discovery Protocol enabled, you will see Cisco Discovery Protocol error messages on the console or in the logging buffer of both devices. Cisco Discovery Protocol is useful in detecting errors as well as in gathering port and system statistics on nearby Cisco devices. Whenever there is a duplex mismatch (in this example, on the FastEthernet0/1 interface), these error messages are displayed on the switch consoles of Catalyst switches that run Cisco IOS Software:

```
%CDP-4-DUPLEX_MISMATCH: duplex mismatch discovered on FastEthernet0/1 (not half
    duplex)
```

Additionally, for switches with Cisco IOS Software, these messages appear for link up or down situations (in this example, on the FastEthernet0/1 interface):

```
%LINK-3-UPDOWN: Interface FastEthernet0/1, changed state to up
%LINK-3-UPDOWN: Interface FastEthernet0/1, changed state to down
```

These are examples of speed-related issues:

- One end is set to one speed and the other is set to another speed, resulting in a mismatch.

- One end is set to a higher speed and autonegotiation is enabled on the other end:

- If autonegotiation fails, the switch senses what the other end is using and reverts to optimal speed.

■ Autonegotiation is set on both ends:

- Autonegotiation fails on both ends, and they revert to their lowest speed.

- Both ends are set at lowest speed, and there is no mismatch.

Figure 5-8 shows an excellent process for troubleshooting port issues.

Troubleshooting duplex-related issues:

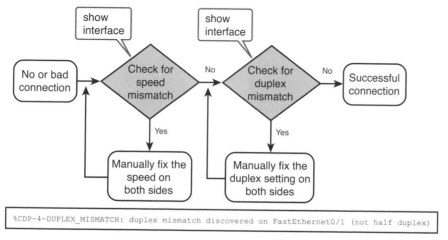

```
%CDP-4-DUPLEX_MISMATCH: duplex mismatch discovered on FastEthernet0/1 (not half duplex)
```

• Duplex mismatch detected by Cisco Discovery Protocol

Figure 5-8 *Troubleshooting Port Issues*

To troubleshoot switch port issues when you have no connection or a bad connection between a switch and another device, use this general process:

1. Use the **show interface** command to check whether there is a speed mismatch between the switch and a device on the other side (switch, router, server, and so on). If there is a speed mismatch, set the speed on both sides to the same value.

2. Use the **show interface** command to check whether there is a duplex mismatch between the switch and a device on the other side. It is recommended that you use full-duplex if both sides support it.

Chapter Summary

In this chapter, you learned that switches are the replacement technology for Layer 1 hubs. Workgroup switches operate at Layer 2 of the OSI model and can intelligently forward frames out specific ports based on MAC address learning that the switches accomplish. When connected in a full-duplex manner, the switches create a collision domain per each port. This eliminates collisions in the modern LAN and makes communications remarkably more efficient.

The installation of a switch involves providing power to the device, observing the LEDs, and observing the output at the CLI through the console port. Basic switch configurations include providing a host name to the device, configuring interfaces, and providing the switch with a default gateway and IP address so that the device can be managed remotely.

Troubleshooting switches can often be broken into two main categories: troubleshooting media issues and troubleshooting port issues. Common problems include damaged wires when it comes to media, and duplex and/or speed mismatches on ports.

Additional Resources

- Cisco Switches Homepage, Cisco Systems: www.cisco.com/go/switches

- Basic Switch Configuration Video, AJS Networking: http://ajsnetworking.com/switches

Review Questions

Use the questions here to review what you learned in this chapter. The correct answers and solutions are found in Appendix A, "Answers to Chapter Review Questions."

1. Which of the following statements about a switch are accurate? Choose two.
   a. They operate at Layer 2 of the OSI model.
   b. They must be assigned an IP address to forward frames between major network segments.
   c. They will flood or filter frames based on MAC address learning.
   d. They build a table mapping IP addresses to specific ports for forwarding.

2. What command would you use to provide a meaningful name to your switch?
   a. name
   b. hostname
   c. host
   d. prompt

3. What would be a valid first step for the physical startup of a Catalyst switch?

    a. Observe the boot sequence carefully at the CLI.

    b. Move the power switch to the ON position.

    c. Connect the AC power cable.

    d. Verify that all cable connections are secure, the PC is connected to the console port, and the console application is selected.

4. Which configuration mode would you use to configure a particular name on a switch?

    a. User EXEC mode

    b. Global Configuration mode

    c. Line Console Configuration mode

    d. Interface Configuration mode

5. Which CLI prompt and command indicate the correct way to set the port duplex operation to full?

    a. SwitchX(config-if)# **duplex default**

    b. SwitchX(config)# **duplex default**

    c. SwitchX(config)# **duplex full**

    d. SwitchX(config-if)# **duplex full**

6. Which is the Cisco IOS command that is the most useful for troubleshooting media issues?

    a. **show traffic**

    b. **show counters**

    c. **show interface**

    d. **show errors**

7. Issuing a **show interface FastEthernet 0/1** command resulted in output that stated "FastEthernet0/1 is up, line protocol is down." What does this message mean?

    a. There could be an encapsulation type mismatch on the link.

    b. The Layer 1 properties of the interface are in error.

    c. The interface has been administratively disabled.

    d. The interface is fully functional, but there is no Layer 3 address assigned to the interface.

8. How does a switch respond when it receives a frame and there is no matching MAC address in the MAC address table?

    a. It drops the frame.

    b. It forwards the frame according to the default forwarding entry.

    c. It floods the frame out all interfaces except the port on which the frame arrived.

    d. It forwards the frame to the default gateway.

9. Your switch has one router attached and eight PCs. How many broadcast domains are there if the switch is in its default configuration?

   a. 1

   b. 2

   c. 8

   d. 9

10. Your switch has one router attached and eight PCs. How many collision domains are there if the switch is in its default configuration?

   a. 1

   b. 2

   c. 8

   d. 9

Production Network Simulation Question 5-1

You supervisor has asked you to produce a configuration for a key Layer 2 switch. He wants you to type the configuration in Notepad and save it as a TXT file so that he can paste it into the device at a later time. Be sure to use the ! symbol between major sections. This character is ignored by the switch and helps the readability of configurations. Your configuration must do the following in this order:

■ Enter privileged EXEC mode

■ Enter global configuration mode

■ Set the name of the device to Lindfield2

■ Set the default gateway to 10.10.10.1

■ Configure the VLAN 1 interface with the address 10.10.10.100/24

■ Ensure that this logical interface is enabled

■ Configure the interfaces Fa0/1 through Fa0/24 to be disabled

■ Save the configuration

Chapter 6

VLANs and Trunks

This chapter includes the following sections:

- Chapter Objectives

- Implementing VLANs and Trunks

- Routing Between VLANs

- Chapter Summary

- Additional Resources

- Review Questions

- Production Network Simulation Question 6-1

Virtual local-area networks (VLAN) contribute to network performance by separating large broadcast domains into smaller segments. A VLAN allows a network administrator to create logical groups of network devices. These devices act as if they were in their own independent network, even though they share a common infrastructure with other VLANs. A VLAN is a logical broadcast domain that can span multiple physical LAN segments. Within the switched internetwork, VLANs provide segmentation and organizational flexibility. You can design a VLAN structure that lets you group stations that are segmented logically by functions, project teams, and applications, without regard to the physical location of the users. VLANs allow you to implement access and security policies to particular groups of users.

A VLAN can exist on a single switch or span multiple switches. VLANs can include stations in a single building or in multiple-building infrastructures. VLANs can also connect to other VLANs across WANs. A process of forwarding network traffic from one VLAN to another VLAN using a router is called *inter-VLAN routing*. VLANs are associated with unique IP subnets on the network. This subnet configuration facilitates the routing process in a multi-VLAN environment. When you use a router to facilitate inter-VLAN routing, the router interfaces can be connected to separate VLANs. Devices on those VLANs send traffic through the router to reach other VLANs.

Chapter Objectives

Upon completing this chapter, you will be able to describe the need for and configuration of VLANs and the trunk links that carry this traffic. These abilities include meeting the following objectives:

- Describe the issues in poorly designed LANs

- Describe the purpose and functions of VLANs

- Define the purpose and functions of trunking

- Implement and verify VLANs

- Assign ports to a VLAN

- Configure and verify 802.1Q trunking

- Describe VLAN design and creation guidelines

- Describe how redundancy in a network can cause broadcast loops and provide a solution to this problem

Implementing VLANs and Trunks

A VLAN is a logical broadcast domain that can span multiple physical LAN segments. It is used to group end stations that have a common set of requirements, independent of their physical locations. A VLAN has the same attributes as a physical LAN, except that it lets you group end stations even when they are not physically located on the same LAN segment. A VLAN also lets you group ports on a switch so that you can limit unicast, multicast, and broadcast traffic flooding. Flooded traffic that originates from a particular VLAN floods to only the ports belonging to that VLAN.

Issues in a Poorly Designed Network

Understanding how VLANs operate and what the associated protocols are is important for configuring, verifying, and troubleshooting VLANs on Cisco access switches. This section describes VLAN operations and their associated protocols.

A poorly designed network has increased support costs, reduced service availability, security risks, and limited support for new applications and solutions. Less-than-optimal performance affects end users and access to central resources directly. Some of the issues that stem from a poorly designed network include the following:

- **Failure domains:** One of the most important reasons to implement an effective network design is to minimize the extent of problems when they occur. When Layer 2 and Layer 3 boundaries are not clearly defined, failure in one network area can have a far-reaching effect.

- **Broadcast domains:** Broadcasts exist in every network. Many applications and network operations require broadcasts to function properly; therefore, it is not possible to eliminate them completely. In the same way that avoiding failure domains involves clearly defining boundaries, broadcast domains should have clear boundaries and include an optimal number of devices to minimize the negative impact of broadcasts.

- **Large amount of unknown MAC unicast traffic:** Cisco Catalyst switches limit unicast frame forwarding to ports that are associated with the specific unicast address. However, when frames arrive at a destination MAC address that is not recorded in the MAC table, they are flooded out of the switch ports in the same VLAN except for the port that received the frame. This behavior is called *unknown MAC unicast flooding*. Because this type of flooding causes excessive traffic on all the switch ports, network interface cards (NIC) must contend with a larger number of frames on the wire. When data is propagated on a wire for which it was not intended, security can be compromised.

- **Multicast traffic on ports where it is not intended:** IP multicast is a technique that allows IP traffic to be propagated from one source to a multicast group that is identified by a single IP and MAC destination-group address pair. Similar to unicast flooding and broadcasting, multicast frames are flooded out all the switch ports. A proper design allows the containment of multicast frames while allowing them to be functional.

- **Difficulty in management and support:** A poorly designed network can be disorganized and poorly documented and lack easily identified traffic flows, which can make support, maintenance, and problem resolution time-consuming and arduous tasks.

- **Possible security vulnerabilities:** A switched network that has been designed with little attention to security requirements at the access layer can compromise the integrity of the entire network.

A poorly designed network always has a negative impact and becomes a support and cost burden for any organization. Figure 6-1 shows a network with a single broadcast domain. VLANs can help alleviate some of the problems associated with this design.

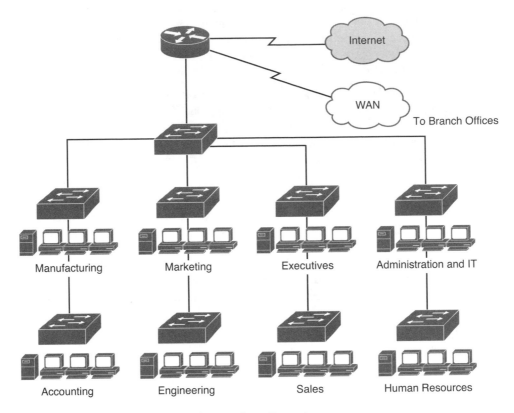

Figure 6-1   *Network with Single Broadcast Domain*

VLAN Overview

A *VLAN* is a logical broadcast domain that can span multiple physical LAN segments. In the switched internetwork, VLANs provide segmentation and organizational flexibility. You can design a VLAN structure that lets you group stations that are segmented logically by functions, project teams, and applications without regard to the physical location of the users. You can assign each switch port to only one VLAN, thereby adding a layer of security. Ports in a VLAN share broadcasts; ports in different VLANs do not. Containing broadcasts in a VLAN improves the overall performance of the network.

In the switched internetwork, VLANs provide segmentation and organizational flexibility. Using VLAN technology, you can group switch ports and their connected users into logically defined communities, such as coworkers in the same department, a cross-functional product team, or diverse user groups sharing the same network application.

A VLAN can exist on a single switch or span multiple switches. VLANs can include stations in a single building or multiple-building infrastructures. VLANs can also connect across WANs. The process of forwarding network traffic from one VLAN to another VLAN using a router is called inter-VLAN routing. VLANs are associated with unique IP subnets on the network. This subnet configuration facilitates the routing process in a multi-VLAN environment. When you are using a router to facilitate inter-VLAN routing, the router interfaces can be connected to separate VLANs. Devices on those VLANs send traffic through the router to reach other VLANs.

Each VLAN in a switched network corresponds to an IP network. Therefore, VLAN design must take into consideration the implementation of a hierarchical network-addressing scheme. Figure 6-2 shows an example of VLANs in an organization and illustrates IP address allocation between various groups in the enterprise. You will notice that each building has unique subnets. Each of these subnets would be assigned to a single VLAN. Each building has been assigned a range with four IP subnets even though only two departments are shown. The additional subnets could be used from growth.

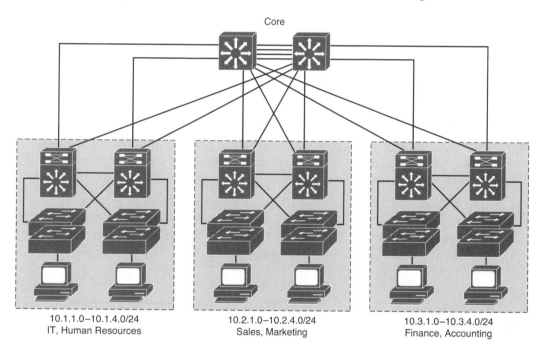

Figure 6-2 *IP Addressing per VLAN*

Understanding Trunking with 802.1Q

A *trunk* is a point-to-point link between one or more Ethernet switch interfaces and another networking device such as a router or a switch. Ethernet trunks carry the traffic of multiple VLANs over a single link and allow you to extend the VLANs across an entire network. Cisco supports IEEE 802.1Q for Fast Ethernet and Gigabit Ethernet interfaces. In addition, some Cisco switches support Cisco Inter-Switch Link (ISL) trunks, a prestandard trunking technology. ISL is being phased out now by Cisco in favor of 802.1Q technology. Figure 6-3 shows an example of trunks interconnecting Cisco Catalyst switches.

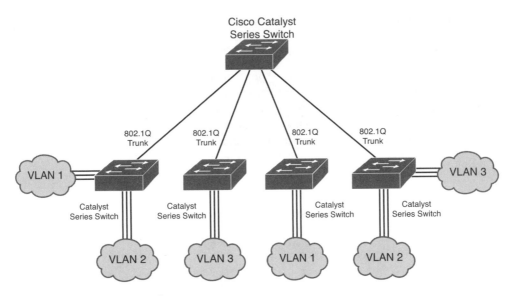

Figure 6-3 *802.1Q Trunks*

Ethernet trunk interfaces support different trunking modes. You can configure an interface as trunking or nontrunking, or you can have it negotiate trunking with the neighboring interface.

Every 802.1Q port is assigned to a trunk, and all ports on a trunk are in a native VLAN. A native VLAN is used in IEEE 802.1Q to send untagged frames to any non-802.1Q devices that might exist on the segment. Every 802.1Q port is assigned an identifier value that is based on the native VLAN ID (VID) of the port. (The default is VLAN 1.) All untagged frames are assigned to the VLAN specified in this VID parameter.

802.1Q Frame

IEEE 802.1Q uses an internal tagging mechanism that inserts a 4-byte tag field into the original Ethernet frame between the Source Address and Type or Length fields. Because 802.1Q alters the frame, the trunking device recomputes the frame check sequence (FCS) on the modified frame.

It is the responsibility of the Ethernet switch to look at the 4-byte tag field and determine where to deliver the frame. An Ether Type of 0x8100 indicates to devices that the frame has an 802.1Q tag. A tiny part of the 4-byte tag field—3 bits to be exact—is used to specify the priority of the frame. The details of this are specified in the IEEE 802.1p standard. The 802.1Q header contains the 802.1p field, so you must have 802.1Q to have 802.1p. Following the priority bit is a single flag to indicate whether the addressing is Token Ring. This is because 802.1Q tagging could also be implemented in a Token Ring environment; the flag will be 0 for an Ethernet frame. The remainder of the tag is used for the VID. Figure 6-4 shows the 802.1Q frame format.

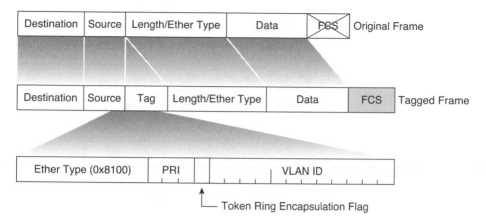

Figure 6-4   *802.1Q Frame Format*

802.1Q Native VLAN

An 802.1Q trunk and its associated trunk ports have a native VLAN value. 802.1Q does not tag frames for the native VLAN. Therefore, ordinary stations can read the native untagged frames but cannot read any other frame because the frames are tagged. Figure 6-5 shows a frame from the native VLAN being distributed across the network trunks untagged.

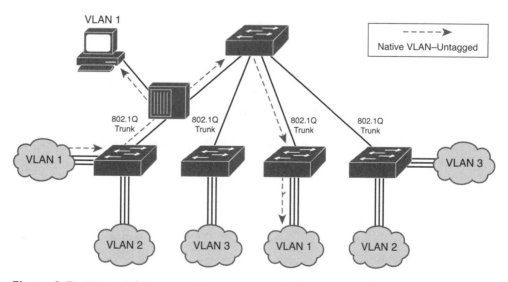

Figure 6-5   *Untagged Frame*

Note   The default native VLAN in Cisco switches is VLAN 1.

Understanding VLAN Trunking Protocol

VLAN Trunking Protocol (VTP) is a Layer 2 messaging protocol that maintains VLAN configuration consistency by managing the additions, deletions, and name changes of VLANs across networks. VTP minimizes misconfigurations and configuration inconsistencies that can cause problems, such as duplicate VLAN names or incorrect VLAN-type specifications. Figure 6-6 shows how you can use VTP to manage VLANs between switches.

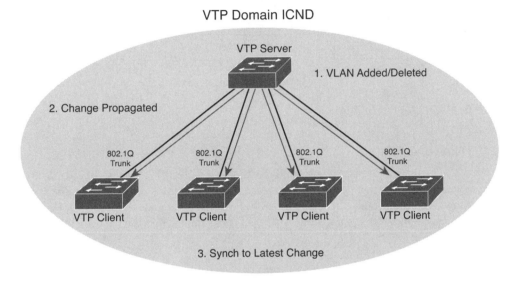

Figure 6-6 *VTP*

A VTP domain is one switch or several interconnected switches sharing the same VTP environment. You can configure a switch to be in only one VTP domain.

By default, a Cisco Catalyst switch is in the no-management-domain state until it receives an advertisement for a domain over a trunk link or until you configure a management domain. Configurations made to a VTP server are propagated across trunk links to all the connected switches in the network.

VTP Modes

VTP operates in one of three modes: server, transparent, or client. You can complete different tasks depending on the VTP operation mode. The characteristics of the three VTP modes are as follows:

- **Server:** The default VTP mode is server mode, but VLANs are not propagated over the network until a management domain name is specified or learned. When you change (create, modify, or delete) the VLAN configuration on a VTP server, the change is propagated to all switches in the VTP domain. VTP messages are transmitted out of all the trunk connections. A VTP server synchronizes its VLAN database file with other VTP servers and clients.

- **Transparent:** When you change the VLAN configuration in VTP transparent mode, the change affects only the local switch and does not propagate to other switches in the VTP domain. VTP transparent mode does forward VTP advertisements that it receives within the domain. A VTP transparent device does not synchronize its database with any other device.

- **Client:** You cannot change the VLAN configuration when in VTP client mode; however, a VTP client can send any VLANs currently listed in its database to other VTP switches. VTP advertisements are forwarded in VTP client mode. A VTP client synchronizes its database with other VTP servers and clients.

VTP clients that run Cisco Catalyst operating systems do not save the VLANs to NVRAM. When the switch is reloaded, the VLANs are not retained, and the revision number is zero. However, Cisco IOS VTP clients save VLANs to the vlan.dat file in flash memory, retaining the VLAN table and revision number.

> **Caution**   The **erase startup-config** command does not affect the vlan.dat file on Cisco IOS switches. VTP clients with a higher configuration revision number can overwrite VLANs on a VTP server in the same VTP domain. Delete the vlan.dat file and reload the switch to clear the VTP and VLAN information. See the documentation for your specific switch model to determine how to delete the vlan.dat file.

VTP Operation

VTP advertisements are flooded throughout the management domain. VTP advertisements are sent every five minutes or whenever VLAN configurations change. Advertisements are transmitted over the default VLAN (VLAN 1) using a multicast frame. A configuration revision number is included in each VTP advertisement. A higher configuration revision number indicates that the VLAN information being advertised is more current than the stored information. Figure 6-7 illustrates this operation.

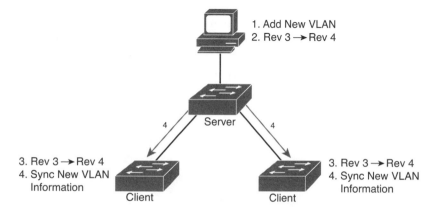

Figure 6-7   *VTP Operation*

One of the most critical components of VTP is the configuration revision number. Each time a VTP server modifies its VLAN information, the VTP server increments the configuration revision number by 1. The server then sends a VTP advertisement with the new configuration revision number. If the configuration revision number being advertised is higher than the number stored on the other switches in the VTP domain, the switches overwrite their VLAN configurations with the new information being advertised.

The configuration revision number in VTP transparent mode is always 0.

Note In the overwrite process, if the VTP server deleted all the VLANs and had the higher revision number, the other devices in the VTP domain would also delete their VLANs.

A device that receives VTP advertisements must check various parameters before incorporating the received VLAN information. First, the management domain name and password in the advertisement must match those configured in the local switch. Next, if the configuration revision number indicates that the message was created after the configuration currently in use, the switch incorporates the advertised VLAN information.

To reset the configuration revision number on some Cisco Catalyst switches, you can change the VTP domain to another name and then change it back. You can also change the VTP mode to transparent and then change it back to client or server.

VTP Pruning

VTP pruning uses VLAN advertisements to determine when a trunk connection is flooding traffic needlessly.

By default, a trunk connection carries traffic for all VLANs in the VTP management domain. In many enterprise networks, not every switch will have ports assigned to every VLAN.

Figure 6-8 shows a switched network with VTP pruning enabled. Only switches 2, 4, and 5 support ports configured in VLAN 3. Switch 5 does not forward the broadcast traffic from host X to switches 1 and 3 because traffic for VLAN 3 has been pruned on the links between switch 5 and switch 1 and switch 3, as indicated in the figure.

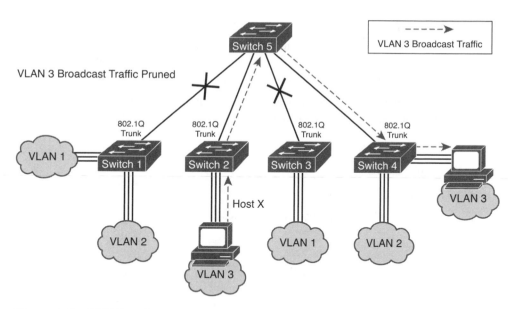

Figure 6-8 *VTP Pruning*

VTP pruning increases available bandwidth by restricting flooded traffic to those trunk links that the traffic must use to access the appropriate network devices.

You can enable pruning only on Cisco Catalyst switches that are configured for VTP servers, and not on clients.

Configuring VLANs and Trunks

By default, all the ports on a Catalyst switch are in VLAN 1. If you want to use VLANs and trunks, you need to configure them on the switches throughout the network. The steps you use to configure and verify VLANs on a switched network include the following:

- Determine whether to use VTP. If VTP will be used, enable VTP in server, client, or transparent mode.

- Enable trunking on the inter-switch connections.

- Create the VLANs on a VTP server and have those VLANs propagate to other switches.

- Assign switch ports to a VLAN using static or dynamic assignment.

- Save the VLAN configuration.

VTP Configuration

When creating VLANs, you must decide whether to use VTP in your network. With VTP, you can make configuration changes on one or more switches, and those changes are automatically communicated to all other switches in the same VTP domain.

Default VTP configuration values depend on the switch model and the software version. The default values for Cisco Catalyst switches are as follows:

- **VTP domain name:** Null

- **VTP mode:** Server

- **VTP password:** None

- **VTP pruning:** Enabled/Disabled (OS version specific)

- **VTP version:** Version 1

The VTP domain name can be specified or learned. By default, the domain name is not set. You can set a password for the VTP management domain. However, if you do not assign the same password for each switch in the domain, VTP does not function properly.

VTP pruning eligibility is one VLAN parameter that the VTP protocol advertises. Enabling or disabling VTP pruning on a VTP server propagates the change throughout the management domain.

Use the **vtp** global configuration command to modify the VTP configuration, domain name, interface, and mode:

```
SwitchX# configure terminal
SwitchX(config)# vtp mode [ server | client | transparent ]
SwitchX(config)# vtp domain domain-name
SwitchX(config)# vtp password password
SwitchX(config)# vtp pruning
SwitchX(config)# end
```

Use the **no** form of this command to remove the filename or to return to the default settings. When the VTP mode is transparent, you can save the VTP configuration in the switch configuration file by entering the **copy running-config startup-config** privileged EXEC command.

Note The domain name and password are case sensitive. You cannot remove a domain name after it is assigned; you can only reassign it.

Example: VTP Configuration

Example 6-1 demonstrates the commands that you would enter to configure VTP and display VTP status. The characteristics of the switch in this example are as follows:

- The switch is transparent in the VTP domain.

- The VTP domain name is ICND (Interconnecting Cisco Network Devices).

- Pruning is disabled.

- The configuration revision is 0.

> **Note** In the output from the **show vtp status** command, "VTP Version" identifies what version of VTP the switch is capable of running, and "VTP V2 Mode" indicates whether VTP Version 2 is being used. If "VTP V2 Mode" shows disabled, VTP Version 1 is being used.

Example 6-1 *Configuring VTP and Displaying VTP Status*

```
SwitchX(config)# vtp domain ICND
Changing VTP domain name to ICND
SwitchX(config)# vtp mode transparent
Setting device to VTP TRANSPARENT mode.
SwitchX(config)# end

SwitchX# show vtp status
VTP Version                   : 2
Configuration Revision        : 0
Maximum VLANs supported locally : 64
Number of existing VLANs      : 17
VTP Operating Mode            : Transparent
VTP Domain Name               : ICND
VTP Pruning Mode              : Disabled
VTP V2 Mode                   : Disabled
VTP Traps Generation          : Disabled
MD5 digest                    : 0x7D 0x6E 0x5E 0x3D 0xAF 0xA0 0x2F 0xAA
Configuration last modified by 10.1.1.4 at 3-3-93 20:08:05
SwitchX#
```

802.1Q Trunking Configuration

The 802.1Q protocol carries traffic for multiple VLANs over a single link on a multivendor network.

802.1Q trunks impose several limitations on the trunking strategy for a network. You should consider the following:

- Ensure that the native VLAN for an 802.1Q trunk is the same on both ends of the trunk link.

- Native VLAN frames are untagged.

Table 6-1 shows how 802.1Q trunking interacts with other switch features.

Table 6-1   *Switch Feature Trunk Interaction*

Switch Feature	Trunk Port Interaction
Secure ports	A trunk port cannot be a secure port.
Port grouping	You can group 802.1Q trunks into EtherChannel port groups, but all trunks in the group must have the same configuration.
	When you create a group, all ports follow the parameters that are set for the first port you add to the group. If you change the configuration of one of these parameters, the switch propagates the setting that you enter to all ports in the group. The settings include the following: ■ Allowed VLAN list ■ STP1 path cost for each VLAN ■ STP port priority for each VLAN ■ STP PortFast setting ■ Trunk status; if one port in a port group ceases to be a trunk, all ports cease to be trunks

1 STP = Spanning Tree Protocol

Use the **switchport mode** interface configuration command to set a Fast Ethernet or Gigabit Ethernet port to trunk mode. Many Cisco Catalyst switches support the Dynamic Trunking Protocol (DTP), which manages automatic trunk negotiation.

Four options for the **switchport mode** command are listed in Table 6-2.

Table 6-2   switchport mode *Parameters*

Parameter	Description
trunk	Configures the port into permanent 802.1Q trunk mode and negotiates with the connected device to convert the link to trunk mode.
access	Disables port trunk mode and negotiates with the connected device to convert the link to nontrunk.
dynamic desirable	Triggers the port to negotiate the link from nontrunk to trunk mode. The port negotiates to a trunk port if the connected device is in trunk state, desirable state, or auto state. Otherwise, the port becomes a nontrunk port.
dynamic auto	Enables a port to become a trunk only if the connected device has the state set to trunk or desirable. Otherwise, the port becomes a nontrunk port.

The **switchport nonegotiate** interface command specifies that DTP negotiation packets are not sent on the Layer 2 interface. The switch does not engage in DTP negotiation on this interface. This command is valid only when the interface switchport mode is access or trunk (configured by using the **switchport mode access** or the **switchport mode trunk** interface configuration command). This command returns an error if you attempt to execute it in dynamic (auto or desirable) mode. Use the **no** form of this command to return to the default setting. When you configure a port with the **switchport nonegotiate** command, the port trunks only if the other end of the link is specifically set to trunk. The **switchport nonegotiate** command does not form a trunk link with ports in either dynamic desirable or dynamic auto mode.

Table 6-3 shows the steps to configure a port as an 802.1Q trunk port, beginning in privileged EXEC mode.

Table 6-3 *Configuring a Port as an 802.1Q Trunk Port*

Step	Action	Notes
1	Enter the interface configuration mode and the port to be configured for trunking: SwitchX(config)# **interface** *int_type int_number*	After you enter the **interface** command, the command-line prompt changes from (config) #to (config-if) #.
2	Configure the port as a VLAN trunk: SwitchX(config-if)# **switchport mode trunk**	Enable trunking on the selected interface.

Some Cisco Catalyst switches support only 802.1Q encapsulation, which is configured automatically when trunking is enabled on the interface by using the **switchport mode trunk** command.

To verify a trunk configuration on many Cisco Catalyst switches, use the **show interfaces** *interface* **switchport** or the **show interfaces** *interface* **trunk** command to display the trunk parameters and VLAN information of the port, as demonstrated in Example 6-2.

Example 6-2 *Verifying Trunk Configuration, Parameters, and Port VLAN Information*

```
SwitchX# show interfaces fa0/11 switchport
Name: Fa0/11
Switchport: Enabled
Administrative Mode: trunk
Operational Mode: down
Administrative Trunking Encapsulation: dot1q
Negotiation of Trunking: On
Access Mode VLAN: 1 (default)
Trunking Native Mode VLAN: 1 (default)
```

```
SwitchX# show interfaces fa0/11 trunk

Port          Mode          Encapsulation  Status       Native vlan
Fa0/11        desirable     802.1q         trunking     1


Port          Vlans allowed on trunk
Fa0/11        1-4094


Port          Vlans allowed and active in management domain
Fa0/11        1-13
```

VLAN Creation

Before you create VLANs, you must decide whether to use VTP to maintain global VLAN configuration information for your network.

The maximum number of VLANs is switch dependent. Many access layer Cisco Catalyst switches can support up to 1001 user-defined VLANs, and this can be extended to 4094 if the switch is configured in VTP transparent mode.

Cisco Catalyst switches have a factory default configuration in which various default VLANs are preconfigured (1002–1005) to support various media and protocol types. The default Ethernet VLAN is VLAN 1. Cisco Discovery Protocol and VTP advertisements are sent on VLAN 1.

For you to be able to communicate remotely with the Cisco Catalyst switch for management purposes, the switch must have an IP address. This IP address should be in the management VLAN, which by default is VLAN 1. If VTP is configured, before you can create a VLAN, the switch must be in VTP server mode or VTP transparent mode.

Table 6-4 lists the commands to use when adding a VLAN.

Table 6-4   *Commands to Add VLANs*

Command/Variable	Description
vlan *vlan-id*	ID of the VLAN to be added and configured. For *vlan-id*, the range is 1 to 4094 when the VTP is set to transparent and 1 to 1005 when the VTP is in server mode. Do not enter leading 0s. You can enter a single VID, a series of VIDs separated by commas, or a range of VIDs separated by hyphens.
name *vlan-name*	(Optional) Specify the VLAN name, an ASCII string from 1 to 32 characters that must be unique within the administrative domain.

By default, a switch is in VTP server mode so that you can add, change, or delete VLANs. If the switch is set to VTP client mode, you cannot add, change, or delete VLANs.

Use the **vlan** global configuration command to create a VLAN and enter VLAN configuration mode:

```
SwitchX# configure terminal
SwitchX(config)# vlan 2
SwitchX(config-vlan)# name switchlab99
```

Use the **no** form of this command to delete the VLAN.

To add a VLAN to the VLAN database, assign a number and name to the VLAN. VLAN 1 is the factory default VLAN. Normal-range VLANs are identified with a number between 1 and 1001. VLAN numbers 1002 through 1005 are reserved for Token Ring and Fiber Distributed Data Interface (FDDI) VLANs. If the switch is in VTP server or VTP transparent mode, you can add, modify, or remove configurations for VLAN 2 to 1001 in the VLAN database. (VIDs 1 and 1002 to 1005 are automatically created and cannot be removed.)

Note   When the switch is in VTP transparent mode and the enhanced software image is installed, you can also create extended-range VLANs (VLANs with IDs from 1006 to 4094), but these VLANs are not saved in the VLAN database.

Configurations for VIDs 1 to 1005 are written to the vlan.dat file (VLAN database). You can display the VLANs by entering the **show vlan** privileged EXEC command. The vlan. dat file is stored in flash memory.

To add an Ethernet VLAN, you must specify at least a VLAN number. If no name is entered for the VLAN, the default is to append the VLAN number to the word **vlan**. For example, VLAN0004 would be the default name for VLAN 4 if no name were specified.

After you configure the VLAN, you should validate the parameters for that VLAN.

Use the **show vlan id** *vlan_number* or the **show vlan name** *vlan-name* command to display information about a particular VLAN, as demonstrated in Example 6-3.

Example 6-3   *Displaying VLAN Information*

```
SwitchX# show vlan id 2

VLAN Name                             Status    Ports
---- -------------------------------- --------- -------------------------------
2    switchlab99                      active    Fa0/2, Fa0/12


VLAN Type  SAID       MTU   Parent RingNo BridgeNo Stp  BrdgMode Trans1 Trans2
---- ----- ---------- ----- ------ ------ -------- ---- -------- ------ ------
2    enet  100002     1500  -      -      -        -    -        0      0

.  .  .
SwitchX#
```

Use the **show vlan brief** command to display one line for each VLAN that displays the VLAN name, the status, and the switch ports.

Use the **show vlan** command to display information on all configured VLANs. The **show vlan** command displays the switch ports assigned to each VLAN. Other VLAN parameters that are displayed include the type (the default is Ethernet); the security association ID (SAID), used for the FDDI trunk; the maximum transmission unit (MTU) (the default is 1500 for Ethernet VLANs); the STP; and other parameters used for Token Ring or FDDI VLANs.

VLAN Port Assignment

After creating a VLAN, you can manually assign a port or a number of ports to that VLAN. A port can belong to only one VLAN at a time. When you assign a switch port to a VLAN using this method, it is known as a *static-access port*.

On most Cisco Catalyst switches, you configure the VLAN port assignment from interface configuration mode using the **switchport access** command, as demonstrated in Example 6-4. Use the **vlan** *vlan_number* option to set static-access membership.

Note   By default, all ports are members of VLAN 1.

Example 6-4   *Configuring VLAN Port Assignment*

```
SwitchX# configure terminal
SwitchX(config)# interface range fastethernet 0/2 - 4
SwitchX(config-if)# switchport access vlan 2

SwitchX# show vlan

VLAN Name                             Status    Ports
---- -------------------------------- --------- ----------------------
1    default                          active    Fa0/1
2    switchlab99                      active    Fa0/2, Fa0/3, Fa0/4
```

Use the **show vlan brief** privileged EXEC command to display the VLAN assignment and membership type for all switch ports, as demonstrated in Example 6-5.

Example 6-5   *Displaying VLAN Port Assignment and Membership Type*

```
SwitchX# show vlan brief
VLAN Name                             Status    Ports
---- -------------------------------- --------- -------------------------------
1    default                          active    Fa0/1
2    switchlab99                      active    Fa0/2, Fa0/3, Fa0/4
3    vlan3                            active
```

```
4    vlan4                        active
1002 fddi-default                 act/unsup
1003 token-ring-default           act/unsup


VLAN Name                         Status    Ports
---- ---------------------------- --------- ------------------------------
1004 fddinet-default              act/unsup
1005 trnet-default
```

Alternatively, use the **show interfaces** *interface* **switchport** privileged EXEC command to display the VLAN information for a particular interface, as demonstrated in Example 6-6.

Example 6-6 *Displaying VLAN Information for a Specific Interface*

```
SwitchX# show interfaces fa0/2 switchport
Name: Fa0/2
Switchport: Enabled
Administrative Mode: dynamic auto
Operational Mode: static access
Administrative Trunking Encapsulation: dot1q
Operational Trunking Encapsulation: native
Negotiation of Trunking: On
Access Mode VLAN: 2 (switchlab99)
Trunking Native Mode VLAN: 1 (default)
--- output omitted ----
```

Adds, Moves, and Changes for VLANs

As network topologies, business requirements, and individual assignments change, VLAN requirements also change.

To add, change, or delete VLANs, the switch must be in VTP server or transparent mode. When you make VLAN changes from a switch that is in VTP server mode, the change is automatically propagated to other switches in the VTP domain. VLAN changes made from a switch in VTP transparent mode affect only the local switch; changes are not propagated to the domain.

Adding VLANs and Port Membership

After you create a new VLAN, be sure to make the necessary changes to the VLAN port assignments.

Separate VLANs typically imply separate IP networks. Be sure to plan the new IP addressing scheme and its deployment to stations before moving users to the new VLAN. Separate VLANs also require inter-VLAN routing to permit users in the new VLAN to communicate with other VLANs. Inter-VLAN routing includes setting up the appropriate IP parameters and services, including the default gateway and DHCP.

Changing VLANs and Port Membership

To modify VLAN attributes, such as the VLAN name, use the **vlan** *vlan-id* global configuration command.

> **Note**   You cannot change the VLAN number. To use a different VLAN number, create a new VLAN using a new number and then reassign all ports to this VLAN.

To move a port into a different VLAN, use the same commands that you used to make the original assignments.

You do not need to first remove a port from a VLAN to make this change. After you reassign a port to a new VLAN, that port is automatically removed from its previous VLAN.

Deleting VLANs and Port Membership

When you delete a VLAN from a switch that is in VTP server mode, the VLAN is removed from all switches in the VTP domain. When you delete a VLAN from a switch that is in VTP transparent mode, the VLAN is deleted only on that specific switch. Use the global configuration command **no vlan** *vlan-id* to remove a VLAN.

> **Note**   Before deleting a VLAN, be sure to reassign all member ports to a different VLAN. Any ports that are not moved to an active VLAN are unable to communicate with other stations after you delete the VLAN.

To reassign a port to the default VLAN (VLAN 1), use the **no switchport access vlan** command in interface configuration mode.

VLAN Design Considerations

Keep these important VLAN design considerations from Cisco in mind:

- The maximum number of VLANs is switch dependent.
- VLAN 1 is the factory default Ethernet VLAN.
- The Cisco switch IP address should be in the management VLAN.
- Keep management traffic in a separate VLAN.
- Change the native VLAN to something other than VLAN 1.
- Make sure that the native VLAN for an 802.1Q trunk is the same on both ends of the trunk link.

Typically, access layer Cisco switches support up to 64, 256, or 1024 VLANs. The maximum number of VLANs is switch dependent.

Cisco switches have a factory default configuration in which various default VLANs are preconfigured to support various media and protocol types. The default Ethernet VLAN is VLAN 1. Cisco Discovery Protocol advertisements are sent on VLAN 1. A good security practice is to separate management and user data traffic, because you do not want users to be able to establish Telnet sessions to the switch.

If you want to communicate with the Cisco switch remotely for management purposes, the switch must have an IP address. This IP address should be in the management VLAN, which by default is VLAN 1.

A good security practice is to change the native VLAN to something other than VLAN 1 (for example, VLAN 98) and tag native VLAN traffic.

Ensure that the native VLAN for an 802.1Q trunk is the same on both ends of the trunk link. If the ends are different, spanning tree loops might result. If 802.1Q trunk configuration is not the same on both ends, Cisco IOS Software will report error messages. Also ensure that native VLAN frames are untagged.

DTP offers four switch port modes: switch, trunk, dynamic auto, and dynamic desirable. A general guideline is to disable autonegotiation. That is, do not use the dynamic auto and dynamic desirable switch port modes.

Physical Redundancy in a LAN

Most complex networks include redundant devices to avoid single points of failure. Although a redundant topology eliminates some problems, it can introduce other problems. STP is a Layer 2 link management protocol that provides path redundancy while preventing undesirable loops in a switched network. It is a standard protocol as defined by IEEE 802.1D.

A redundant topology can be accomplished using multiple links, multiple devices, or both. The key is to provide multiple pathways and eliminate a single point of failure. Figure 6-9 shows a simple redundant topology between segment 1 and segment 2.

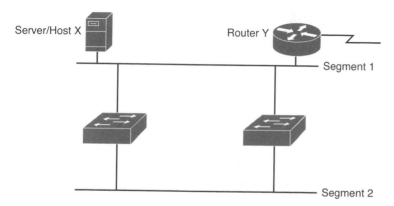

Figure 6-9 *Redundant Topology*

Although redundant designs can eliminate the possibility of a single point of failure causing a loss of function for the entire switched or bridged network, you must consider problems that redundant designs can cause. Some of the problems that can occur with redundant links and devices in switched or bridged networks are as follows:

- **Broadcast storms:** Without some loop-avoidance process in operation, each switch or bridge floods broadcasts endlessly. This situation is commonly called a *broadcast storm.*

- **Multiple frame transmission:** Multiple copies of unicast frames might be delivered to destination stations. Many protocols expect to receive only a single copy of each transmission. Multiple copies of the same frame can cause unrecoverable errors.

- **MAC database instability:** Instability in the content of the MAC address table results from copies of the same frame being received on different ports of the switch. Data forwarding can be impaired when the switch consumes the resources that are coping with instability in the MAC address table.

Layer 2 LAN protocols, such as Ethernet, lack a mechanism to recognize and eliminate endlessly looping frames. Some Layer 3 protocols like IP implement a Time-To-Live (TTL) mechanism that limits the number of times a Layer 3 networking device can retransmit a packet. Lacking such a mechanism, Layer 2 devices continue to retransmit looping traffic indefinitely.

A loop-avoidance mechanism is required to solve each of these problems.

STP provides loop resolution by managing the physical paths to given network segments. STP allows physical path redundancy while preventing the undesirable effects of active loops in the network. STP is an IEEE committee standard defined as 802.1D. Figure 6-10 illustrates how a blocked port would prevent traffic flow between the segments.

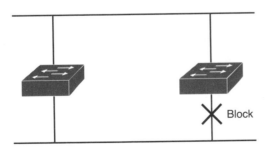

Figure 6-10 *Blocking on a Port*

STP behaves as follows:

- STP forces certain ports into a standby state so that they do not listen to, forward, or flood data frames. The overall effect is that there is only one path to each network segment that is active at any one time.

- If any of the segments in the network have a connectivity problem, STP reestablishes connectivity by automatically activating a previously inactive path, if one exists.

Figure 6-11 shows the final state of a Layer 2 network after spanning tree has performed the operations to eliminate loops.

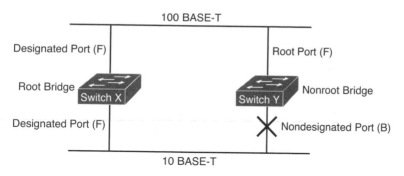

Figure 6-11 *Loop Avoidance*

Routing Between VLANs

Routing is the process of determining where to send data packets destined for addresses outside the local network. Routers gather and maintain routing information to enable the transmission and receipt of data packets. For traffic to cross from one VLAN to another, a Layer 3 process is necessary.

This section describes the operation of inter-VLAN routing using a router on a stick.

Understanding Inter-VLAN Routing

Inter-VLAN communication occurs between broadcast domains through a Layer 3 device. In a VLAN environment, frames are switched only between ports within the same broadcast domain. VLANs perform network partitioning and traffic separation at Layer 2. Inter-VLAN communication cannot occur without a Layer 3 device, such as a router.

Traditional inter-VLAN routing requires multiple physical interfaces on both the router and the switch. VLANs are associated with unique IP subnets on the network. This subnet configuration facilitates the routing process in a multi-VLAN environment. When using a router to facilitate inter-VLAN routing, the router interfaces can be connected to separate VLANs. Devices on those VLANs send traffic through the router to reach other VLANs. Figure 6-12 shows this method of inter-VLAN routing.

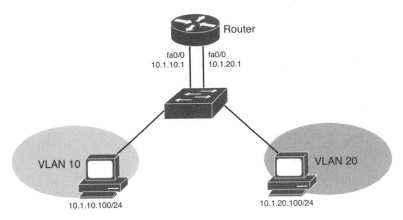

Figure 6-12 *Router with a Separate Interface for Each VLAN*

When you use a separate interface for each VLAN on a router, you can quickly run out of interfaces. This solution is not very scalable.

Another option for inter-VLAN routing is to connect the switch to a router using an 802.1Q trunk.

Example: Router on a Stick

Figure 6-13 illustrates a router attached to a core switch. The configuration between a router and a core switch is sometimes referred to as a *router on a stick*.

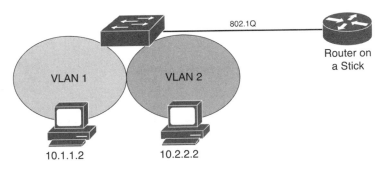

Figure 6-13 *Router on a Stick*

The router can receive packets on one VLAN and forward them to another VLAN. To perform inter-VLAN routing functions, the router must know how to reach all VLANs being interconnected. Each VLAN must have a separate connection on the router, and you must enable 802.1Q trunking on those connections. The router already knows about directly connected networks. The router must learn routes to networks to which it is not directly connected.

To support 802.1Q trunking, you must subdivide the physical Fast Ethernet interface of the router into multiple, logical, addressable interfaces, one per VLAN. The resulting logical interfaces are called *subinterfaces*. This is illustrated in Figure 6-14.

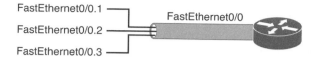

Figure 6-14 *Subinterfaces*

Without this subdivision, you would have to dedicate a separate physical interface to each VLAN.

Example: Subinterfaces

In the figure, the FastEthernet 0/0 interface is divided into multiple subinterfaces: FastEthernet 0/0.1, FastEthernet 0/0.2, and FastEthernet 0/0.3.

Configuring Inter-VLAN Routing Using Router on a Stick

To be able to route between VLANs on a switch, you will need to be able to configure inter-VLAN routing.

In Figure 6-15, the FastEthernet 0/0 interface is divided into multiple subinterfaces: FastEthernet 0/0.1 and FastEthernet 0/0.2. Each subinterface represents the router in each of the VLANs for which it routes.

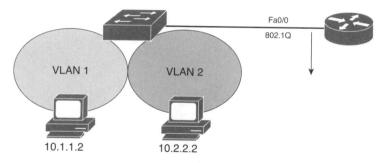

Figure 6-15 *Inter-VLAN Routing Configuration*

Use the **encapsulation dot1q** *vlan identifier* command (where *vlan identifier* is the VLAN number) on each subinterface to enable 802.1Q encapsulation trunking. The sub-interface number does not have to be the same as the dot1Q VLAN number. However, management is easier when the two numbers are the same.

The native VLAN frames in 802.1Q do not carry a tag. Therefore, the native VLAN sub-interface is configured with the **encapsulation dot1Q** *vlan identifier* **native** command. Ensure that the VLAN assigned to the native VLAN subinterface matches the native VLAN on the switch it connects to. Each subinterface will have a unique IP address for the VLAN it is associated with. This address will be used as the gateway address for workstations in that VLAN.

Using Multilayer (Layer 3) Switches

Some switches can perform Layer 3 functions, replacing the need for dedicated routers to perform basic routing on a network. Layer 3 switches are capable of performing inter-VLAN routing. Traditionally, a switch makes forwarding decisions by looking at the Layer 2 header, while a router makes forwarding decisions by looking at the Layer 3 header. A Layer 3 switch combines the functionality of a switch and a router into one device. It switches traffic when the source and destination are in the same VLAN and routes traffic when the source and destination are in different VLANs (that is, on different IP subnets). To enable a Layer 3 switch to perform routing functions, VLAN interfaces on the switch need to be properly configured. You must use the IP addresses that match the subnet that the VLAN is associated with on the network. The Layer 3 switch must also have IP routing enabled.

Layer 3 switching is more scalable than router on a stick, because the latter can only have so much traffic through the trunk link. In general, a Layer 3 switch is primarily a Layer 2 device that has been upgraded to have some routing capabilities. A router is a Layer 3 device that can perform some switching functions.

However, the line between switches and routers becomes hazier every day. Some Layer 2 switches, like the switches in the Cisco Catalyst 2960 Series, support limited Layer 3 functionality. The 2960 switch supports static routing on Switched Virtual Interface (SVI). Static routes can be configured, but routing protocols are not supported.

Figure 6-16 shows an example of inter-VLAN routing using a multilayer switch.

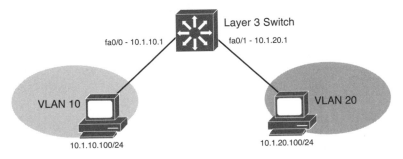

Figure 6-16   *Inter-VLAN Routing Configuration Using a Layer 3 Switch*

Chapter Summary

In this chapter, you learned why VLANs are such a common element in network designs. You learned to describe their purpose and function, and you also learned why trunk links are critical for carrying the traffic of these VLANs from network device to network device.

This chapter also ensured that you can configure and verify VLANs and trunks and provided important guidelines for both of their implementations.

The chapter concluded with an examination of the need for Spanning Tree Protocol and inter-VLAN routing solutions.

Additional Resource

■ VLANs, Trunks, and Switches, Oh My Video, AJS Networking: http://ajsnetworking. com/vlans

Review Questions

Use the questions here to review what you learned in this chapter. The correct answers and solutions are found in Appendix A, "Answers to Chapter Review Questions."

1. Which feature is required for multiple VLANs to span multiple switches?

  a. A trunk to connect the switches

  b. A router to connect the switches

  c. A bridge to connect the switches

  d. A VLAN configured between the switches

2. Which of the following are reasons for using 802.1Q? (Choose two.)

  a. To allow switches to share a trunk link with nontrunking clients

  b. To allow clients to see the 802.1Q header

  c. To provide inter-VLAN communications over a bridge

  d. To load-balance traffic between parallel links using STP

  e. To provide trunking between Cisco switches and other vendor switches

3. Which information does the **show vlan** command display?

  a. VTP domain parameters

  b. VMPS server configuration parameters

  c. Ports that are configured as trunks

  d. Names of the VLANs and the ports that are assigned to the VLANs

4. Which of the following frame types are flooded to all ports except the source port on a switch? (Choose three.)

  a. Unicast frames

  b. Multicast frames

  c. Broadcast frames

  d. Frames with a destination address mapped to a given port

  e. Frames with a destination address not yet learned by the switch

  f. Frames with an unknown source address

5. How does STP provide a loop-free network?

  a. By placing all ports in the blocking state

  b. By placing all bridges in the blocking state

  c. By placing some ports in the blocking state

  d. By placing some bridges in the blocking state

6. Which command correctly assigns a subinterface to VLAN 50 using 802.1Q trunking?

   a. Router(config) # encapsulation 50 dot1Q

   b. Router(config) # encapsulation 802.1Q 50

   c. Router(config-if) # encapsulation dot1Q 50

   d. Router(config-if) # encapsulation 50 802.1Q

7. What happens to a switch port when you delete the VLAN to which it belongs?

   a. The port becomes a member of the default VLAN 1.

   b. The port becomes a member of the default VLAN 1 and becomes inactive.

   c. The port remains in the deleted VLAN and becomes inactive.

   d. A VLAN cannot be deleted when ports are assigned to it.

8. What statement is true about the native VLAN in 802.1Q?

   a. The native VLAN must be 1.

   b. The native VLAN is the single VLAN that is not tagged.

   c. The native VLAN does not need to match on each end of the link.

   d. The native VLAN traffic does not span switches on trunk links.

9. Which of the following statements are true about VLANs? (Choose two.)

   a. The native VLAN is always tagged as VLAN 1.

   b. VLANs are IP subnets.

   c. A VLAN defines a collision domain.

   d. A route processor is needed to communicate between VLANs.

10. You notice in the output of the **show vlan brief** command on a factory default Cisco switch that some of the ports are missing from the default VLAN 1. Why is this?

   a. The ports are assigned to an inactive VLAN.

   b. The ports are disabled.

   c. The ports are nonfunctional.

   d. The ports are trunk ports.

Production Network Simulation Question 6-1

You are responsible for building an 802.1Q trunk between two switches in your organization's network. The interface on each switch you are to trunk is Fast Ethernet 0/10. You need to create two VLANs—10 and 20—and then configure the trunk. Also, ensure that interface Fast Ethernet 0/5 is placed in VLAN 10. Provide the correct configuration in Notepad.

Chapter 7

The TCP/IP Internet Layer

This chapter includes the following sections:

- Chapter Objectives

- Understanding TCP/IP's Internet Layer

- IP Network Addressing

- Addressing Services

- Chapter Summary

- Additional Resources

- Review Questions

- Production Network Simulation Questions 7-1, 7-2, 7-3

All you need to do is look at how the TCP/IP protocol suite was named and you will know that this is a very important chapter of this book. The entire suite was named after just two of the protocols used within it: Transmission Control Protocol (TCP) and Internet Protocol (IP). In this chapter, we will provide much more detail on the Internet layer of the TCP/IP model. Note that for our purposes, this is the same as discussing the network layer of the OSI model.

As you will learn, of critical importance at this layer is addressing, specifically, Internet (or IP) addressing. This is an area of much complexity, and is often an area of confusion and frustration for students. Here, we will make it simple for you—covering this topic in small, easy-to-master sections.

Chapter Objectives

Upon completing this chapter, you will be able to describe the importance of the Internet layer of the TCP/IP model and describe IP addressing and popular IP addressing services. These abilities include meeting the following objectives:

- Describe the importance of the Internet layer
- Describe the network addressing in IP
- Define IP address classes
- Identify network and broadcast addresses
- Describe private IP addresses and identify these addresses
- Identify and describe common IP addressing services

Understanding TCP/IP's Internet Layer

Among the protocols included in the TCP/IP protocol stack are a network layer protocol and a transport layer protocol. The internetworking layer handles the routing of packets of data by using IP addresses to identify each device on the network. Each computer, router, printer, or any other device attached to a network has its own unique IP address that routes packets of data.

Each IP address has a specific structure, and various classes of IP addresses exist. In addition, subnetworks and subnet masks play a role in IP addressing schemes, and different routing functions and protocols are involved in transmitting data from one network node to another using IP addresses.

The various aspects of IP addressing include calculations for constructing an IP address, classes of IP addresses designated for specific routing purposes, and public versus private IP addresses. Also, two different types of IP addresses exist: IP version 4 (IPv4) and IP version 6 (IPv6). The 32-bit IPv4 address type is currently the most common, but the 128-bit IPv6 address is also in use and will probably become the more common address type over time. This section describes 32-bit IPv4 addressing, except where IPv6 is explicitly identified.

How do end systems initially obtain their IP address information? Although manual assignment of IP address information is possible, it does not scale and is a barrier to deployment and maintenance of networks. Therefore, protocols for the automatic assignment of IP address information have evolved and now provide this essential function without end-user intervention. This section describes how IP address protocols function.

IP Network Addressing

Just as you use addresses to identify the specific locations of homes and businesses so that mail can reach them efficiently, you use IP addresses to identify the location of specific devices on a network so that data can be sent correctly to those locations. IP addressing has various aspects, including the calculations for constructing an IP address, the classes of IP addresses designated for specific routing purposes, and public versus private IP addresses.

Learning how IP addresses are structured and how they function in the operation of a network provides an understanding of how data is transmitted through Layer 3 internetworking devices using TCP/IP. To facilitate the routing of packets over a network, the TCP/IP protocol suite uses a 32-bit logical address known as an IP address. This address must be unique for each device in the internetwork.

The header of the Internet layer of TCP/IP is known as the IP header. Figure 7-1 shows the layout of the IP header.

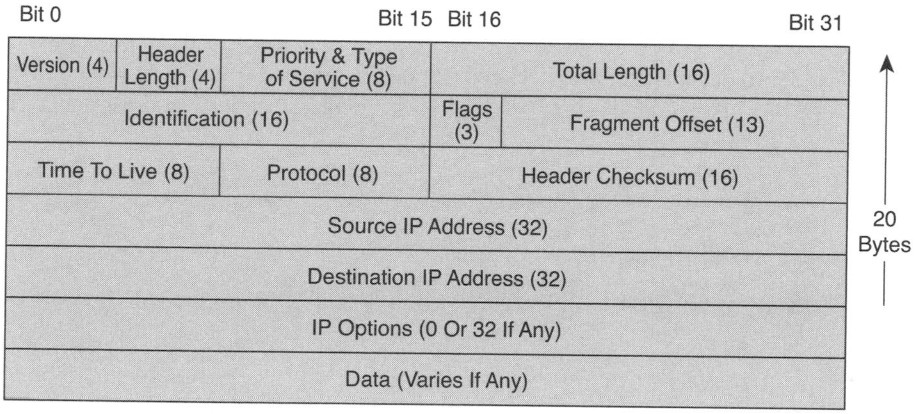

Figure 7-1 *IP Header*

Note that each IP datagram carries this header, which includes a source IP address and destination IP address that identify the source and destination network and host.

An IP address is a hierarchical address, and it consists of two parts:

- The high-order, or leftmost, bits specify the network address component (network ID) of the address.

- The low-order, or rightmost, bits specify the host address component (host ID) of the address.

Every physical or virtual LAN on the corporate internetwork is seen as a single network that must be reached before an individual host within that company can be contacted. Each LAN has a unique network address. The hosts that populate that network share those same bits, but each host is identified by the uniqueness of the remaining bits. Like a group of houses along the same road, the street address is the same, but the house number is unique.

Figure 7-2 illustrates a sample IP addressing scheme in an internetwork.

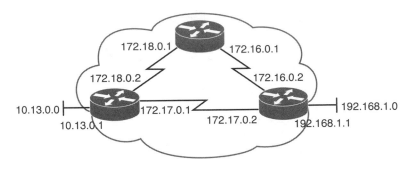

Figure 7-2   *IP Addressing*

The IP address is 32 bits in length and is binary in nature, but it is expressed in a format that can be easily understood by the human brain. Basically, the 32 bits are broken into four sections of 8 bits each, known as *octets* or bytes. Each of these octets is then converted into decimal numbers between 0 and 255, and each octet is separated from the following one by dots. Figure 7-3 illustrates the format of an IP address using 172.16.122.204 as an example.

	32 Bits			
Dotted Decimal	Network		Host	
Maximum	255	255	255	255
Binary	1 1111111 8	9 11111111 16	17 11111111 24	25 11111111 32
	128 64 32 16 8 4 2 1	128 64 32 16 8 4 2 1	128 64 32 16 8 4 2 1	128 64 32 16 8 4 2 1
Example Decimal	172	16	122	204
Example Binary	10101100	00010000	01111010	11001100

Figure 7-3   *IP Address Format*

The IP address format is known as dotted-decimal notation. Figure 7-3 shows how the dotted-decimal address is derived from the 32-bit binary value:

- Sample address: 172.16.122.204.

- Each bit in the octet has a binary weight (such as 128, 64, 32, 16, 8, 4, 2, and 1), and when all the bits are on, the sum is 255.

- The minimum decimal value for an octet is 0; it contains all 0s.

- The maximum decimal value for an octet is 255; it contains all 1s.

While many computers might share the same network address, combining the network address with a host address uniquely identifies any device connected to the network.

IP Address Classes

When IP was first developed, no classes of addresses existed, because it was assumed that 254 networks would be more than enough for an internetwork of academic, military, and research computers.

As the number of networks grew, the IP addresses were broken into categories called *classes* to accommodate different sizes of networks and to aid in identifying them. These classes are illustrated in Figure 7-4.

Assigning IP addresses to classes is known as *classful addressing*. The allocation of addresses is managed by a central authority, the American Registry for Internet Numbers (ARIN), which you can go to at www.arin.net for more information about network numbers.

	8 Bits	8 Bits	8 Bits	8 Bits
Class A:	Network	Host	Host	Host
Class B:	Network	Network	Host	Host
Class C:	Network	Network	Network	Host
Class D:	Multicast			
Class E:	Research			

Figure 7-4   *Address Classes*

Five IP address classes are used, as follows:

- **Class A:** The Class A address category was designed to support extremely large networks. A Class A address uses only the first octet to indicate the network address. The remaining three octets are used for host addresses.

  The first bit of a Class A address is always 0; therefore, the lowest number that can be represented is 00000000 (decimal 0), and the highest number that can be represented is 01111111 (decimal 127). However, these two network numbers, 0 and 127, are reserved and cannot be used as a network address. Any address that starts with a value between 1 and 126 in the first octet, then, is a Class A address.

Note   The 127.0.0.0 network is reserved for loopback testing (routers or local machines can use this address to send packets to themselves). Therefore, it cannot be assigned to a network.

- **Class B:** The Class B address category was designed to support the needs of moderate- to large-sized networks. A Class B address uses two of the four octets to indicate the network address. The other two octets specify host addresses.

The first 2 bits of the first octet of a Class B address are always binary 10. The remaining 6 bits might be populated with either 1s or 0s. Therefore, the lowest number that can be represented with a Class B address is 10000000 (decimal 128), and the highest number that can be represented is 10111111 (decimal 191). Any address that starts with a value in the range of 128 to 191 in the first octet is a Class B address.

- **Class C:** The Class C address category is the most commonly used of the original address classes. This address category was intended to support a lot of small networks.

  A Class C address begins with binary 110. Therefore, the lowest number that can be represented is 11000000 (decimal 192), and the highest number that can be represented is 11011111 (decimal 223). If an address contains a number in the range of 192 to 223 in the first octet, it is a Class C address.

- **Class D:** The Class D address category was created to enable multicasting in an IP address. A multicast address is a unique network address that directs packets with that destination address to predefined groups of IP addresses. Therefore, a single station can simultaneously transmit a single stream of datagrams to multiple recipients.

  The Class D address category, much like the other address categories, is mathematically constrained. The first 4 bits of a Class D address must be 1110. Therefore, the first octet range for Class D addresses is 11100000 to 11101111, or 224 to 239. An IP address that starts with a value in the range of 224 to 239 in the first octet is a Class D address.

  As illustrated in Figure 7-5, Class D addresses (multicast addresses) include the following range of network numbers: 224.0.0.0 to 239.255.255.255.

- **Class E:** Although a Class E address category has been defined, the Internet Engineering Task Force (IETF) reserves the addresses in this class for its own research. Therefore, no Class E addresses have been released for use in the Internet. The first 4 bits of a Class E address are always set to 1111. Therefore, the first octet range for Class E addresses is 11110000 to 11111111, or 240 to 255.

Figure 7-5 *Multicast Addresses*

Within each class, the IP address is divided into a network address (or network identifier, network ID) and the host address (or host identifier, host ID). The number of networks and hosts varies by class. A bit or bit sequence at the start of each address, known as the high-order bits, determines the class of the address, as shown in Figure 7-6.

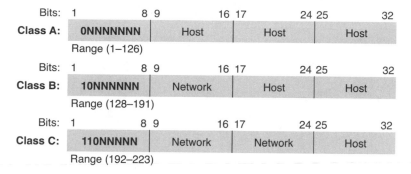

Figure 7-6 *Address Classification*

Figure 7-6 shows how the bits in the first octet identify the address class. The router uses the first bits to identify how many bits it must match to interpret the network portion of the address (based on the standard address class). Table 7-1 lists the characteristics of Class A, B, and C addresses that address network devices.

Table 7-1 *IP Address Classes*

Class A Address	Class B Address	Class C Address
The first bit is 0.	The first 2 bits are 10.	The first 3 bits are 110.
Range of network numbers: 1.0.0.0 to 126.0.0.0.	Range of network numbers: 128.0.0.0 to 191.255.0.0.	Range of network numbers: 192.0.0.0 to 223.255.255.0.
Number of possible networks: 127 (1 through 126 are usable; 127 is reserved).	Number of possible networks: 16,384.	Number of possible networks: 2,097,152.
Number of possible values in the host portion: 16,777,216.*	Number of possible values in the host portion: 65,536.*	Number of possible values in the host portion: 256.*

The number of usable hosts is 2 less than the total number possible because the host portion must be nonzero and cannot be all 1s.

Network and Broadcast Addresses

Certain IP addresses are reserved and cannot be assigned to individual devices on a network. These reserved addresses include a network address, which identifies the network itself, and a broadcast address, which is used for broadcasting packets to all the devices on a network.

An IP address that has binary 0s in all host bit positions is reserved for the network address. Therefore, as a Class A network example, 10.0.0.0 is the IP address of the network containing the host 10.1.2.3. A router uses the network IP address when it searches its IP route table for the destination network location. As a Class B network example, the IP address 172.16.0.0 is a network address, as shown in the Figure 7-7.

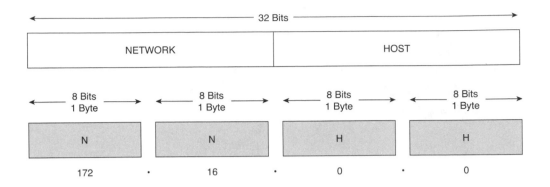

Network Address (Host Bits = All 0s)

Figure 7-7   *Network Address*

The decimal numbers that fill the first two octets in a Class B network address are assigned. The last two octets contain 0s because those 16 bits are for host numbers and are used for devices that are attached to the network. The IP address in the example (172.16.0.0) is reserved for the network address; it is never used as an address for any device that is attached to it. An example of an IP address for a device on the 172.16.0.0 network would be 172.16.16.1. In this example, 172.16 is the network-address portion and 16.1 is the host-address portion.

If you wanted to send data to all the devices on a network, you would need to use a network broadcast address. Broadcast IP addresses end with binary 1s in the entire host part of the address (the host field), as shown in Figure 7-8.

For the network in the example (172.16.0.0), in which the last 16 bits make up the host field (or host part of the address), the broadcast that is sent out to all devices on that network includes a destination address of 172.16.255.255.

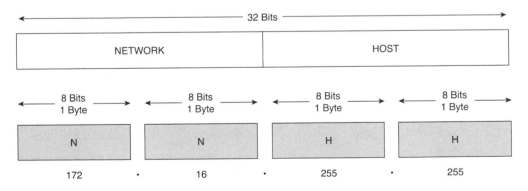

Network Address (Host Bits = All 0s)

Figure 7-8   *Network Broadcast Address*

The network broadcast is also known as a directed broadcast and is capable of being routed, because the longest match in the routing table would match the network bits. Because the host bits would not be known, the router would forward this out all the interfaces that were members of the major 172.16.0.0 network. Directed broadcast can be used to perform a denial of service (DoS) attack against routed networks. This behavior is not the default for Cisco routers, however.

If an IP device wants to communicate with all devices on all networks, it sets the destination address to all 1s (255.255.255.255) and transmits the packet. This address can be used, for example, by hosts that do not know their network number and are asking some server for it, as with Reverse Address Resolution Protocol (RARP) or DHCP. This form of broadcast is never capable of being routed, because RFC 1812 prohibits the forwarding of an all-networks broadcast. For this reason, an all-networks broadcast is called a *local broadcast* because it stays local to the LAN segment or VLAN.

The network portion of an IP address is also referred to as the network ID. It is important because hosts on a network can only directly communicate with devices in the same network. If they need to communicate with devices with interfaces assigned to some other network ID, a Layer 3 internetworking device that can route data between the networks is needed. This is true even when the devices share the same physical media segment or VLAN.

A network ID enables a router to put a packet onto the appropriate network segment. The host ID helps the router deliver the Layer 2 frame, encapsulating the packet to a specific host on the network. As a result, the IP address is mapped to the correct MAC address, which is needed by the Layer 2 process on the router to address the frame.

Specific guidelines exist for assigning IP addresses in a network. First, each device or interface must have a nonzero host number. Figure 7-9 shows devices and routers with IP addresses assigned.

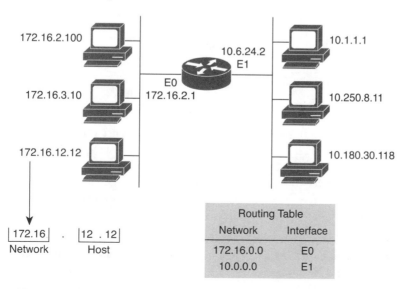

Figure 7-9 *Host Addresses*

Each wire is identified with the network address. This value is not assigned, but it is assumed. A value of 0 means "this network" or "the wire itself" (for example, 172.16.0.0). This is the information used by the router to identify each network. The routing table contains entries for network or wire addresses; it usually does not contain any information about hosts.

As soon as the network portion is determined by the classification, you can determine the total number of hosts on the network by summing all available 1 and 0 combinations of the remaining address bits and subtracting 2. You must subtract 2 because an address consisting of all 0 bits specifies the network, and an address of all 1 bits is used for network broadcasts.

The same result can be derived by using the following formula:

2N – 2 (where N is the number of bits in the host portion)

Figure 7-10 illustrates a Class B network, 172.16.0.0. In a Class B network, 16 bits are used for the host portion. Applying the formula 2N – 2 (in this case, $2^{16} - 2 = 65,534$) results in 65,534 usable host addresses.

All classful addresses have only a network portion and host portion. So, the router(s) within the internetwork know it only as a single network, and no detailed knowledge of the internal hosts is required. All datagrams addressed to network 172.16.0.0 are treated the same, regardless of the third and fourth octets of the address.

Network		Host		
172	16	0	0	
		16 15 14 13 12 11 10 9	8 7 6 5 4 3 2 1	N
10101100	00010000	00000000	00000000	1
		00000000	00000001	2
		00000000	00000011	3
		⋮	⋮	⋮
		11111111	11111101	65534
		11111111	11111110	65535
		11111111	11111111	65536
				– 2
		$2^N - 2 = 2^{16} - 2 = 65534$		65534

Figure 7-10   *Determining the Available Host Addresses*

Each class of a network allows a fixed number of hosts. In a Class A network, the first octet is assigned for the network, leaving the last three octets to be assigned to hosts. The first host address in each network (all 0s) is reserved for the actual network address, and the final host address in each network (all 1s) is reserved for broadcasts. The maximum number of hosts in a Class A network is $2^{24} - 2$ (subtracting the network and broadcast reserved addresses), or 16,777,214.

In a Class B network, the first two octets are assigned for the network, leaving the final two octets to be assigned to hosts. The maximum number of hosts in a Class B network is $2^{16} - 2$, or 65,534.

In a Class C network, the first three octets are assigned for the network. This leaves the final octet to be assigned to hosts, so the maximum number of hosts is 28 – 2, or 254.

Just as local broadcasts and directed broadcasts are special network addresses, you also find a special host address known as the loopback address that is used to test the TCP/IP stack on a host. This address is 127.0.0.1.

Another common special host address that many people run into is the autoconfiguration IP address assigned when neither a statically nor a dynamically configured IP address is found on startup. Hosts supporting IPv4 link-local addresses (RFC 3927) generate an address in the 169.254.X.X/16 prefix range. The address can be used only for local network connectivity and operates with many caveats, one of which is that it is not routed. These addresses are usually encountered when a host fails to obtain an address through startup using DHCP.

Public and Private IP Addresses

Some networks connect to each other through the Internet, whereas others are private. Public and private IP addresses are required, therefore, for both of these network types.

Internet stability depends directly on the uniqueness of publicly used network addresses. Therefore, some mechanism is needed to ensure that addresses are, in fact, unique. This responsibility originally rested within an organization known as the InterNIC (Internet Network Information Center). This organization was succeeded by the Internet Assigned Numbers Authority (IANA). IANA carefully manages the remaining supply of IP addresses to ensure that duplication of publicly used addresses does not occur. Such duplication would cause instability in the Internet and compromise its capability to deliver datagrams to networks using the duplicated addresses.

To obtain an IP address or block of addresses, you must contact an Internet service provider (ISP). The ISP allocates addresses from the range assigned by its upstream registry or its appropriate regional registry, which is managed by IANA, as follows:

- Asia Pacific Network Information Center (APNIC)
- American Registry for Internet Numbers (ARIN)
- Réseaux IP Europens Network Coordination Centre (RIPE NCC)

With the rapid growth of the Internet, public IP addresses began to run out, so new addressing schemes such as classless interdomain routing (CIDR) and IPv6 were developed to help solve the problem. CIDR and IPv6 are discussed in the next section.

Although Internet hosts require a globally unique IP address, private hosts that are not connected to the Internet can use any valid address, as long as it is unique within the private network. Because many private networks exist alongside public networks, grabbing "just any address" is strongly discouraged. Therefore, the IETF defined three blocks of IP addresses (1 Class A network, 16 Class B networks, and 256 Class C networks) in RFC

1918 for private, internal use. Addresses in this range are not routed on the Internet backbone, as shown in Table 7-2. Internet routers are configured to discard private addresses as defined by RFC 1918.

Table 7-2   *Private IP Addresses*

Class	RFC 1918 Internal Address Range
A	10.0.0.0 to 10.255.255.255
B	172.16.0.0 to 172.31.255.255
C	192.168.0.0 to 192.168.255.255

If you are addressing a nonpublic intranet, these private addresses can be used instead of globally unique addresses. If you want to connect a network using private addresses to the Internet, however, it is necessary to translate the private addresses to public addresses. This translation process is referred to as *Network Address Translation (NAT)*. A router is often the network device that performs NAT.

Address Exhaustion

The growth of the Internet has resulted in enormous demands for IP addresses. This section describes the capabilities of IPv4 in relation to that demand.

When TCP/IP was first introduced in the 1980s, it relied on a two-level addressing scheme, which at the time offered adequate scalability. The architects of TCP/IP could not have predicted that their protocol would eventually sustain a global network of information, commerce, and entertainment. Twenty years ago, IPv4 offered an addressing strategy that, although scalable for a time, eventually resulted in an inefficient allocation of addresses.

The Class A and B addresses make up 75 percent of the IPv4 address space, but a relative handful of organizations (fewer than 17,000) can be assigned a Class A or B network number. Class C network addresses are far more numerous than Class A and B addresses, although they account for only 12.5 percent of the possible 4 billion IP addresses, as shown in Figure 7-11.

Unfortunately, Class C addresses are limited to 254 hosts, which does not meet the needs of larger organizations that cannot acquire a Class A or B address.

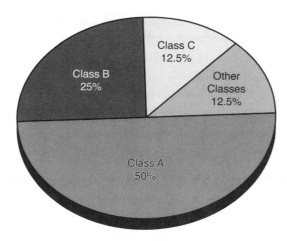

Figure 7-11 *IP Address Allocation*

As early as 1992, the IETF identified two specific concerns:

- The Class B address category was on the verge of depletion, and the remaining, unassigned IPv4 network addresses were nearly depleted at the time.

- As more Class C networks came online to accommodate the rapid and substantial increase in the size of the Internet, the resulting flood of new network information threatened the capability of Internet routers to cope effectively.

Over the past 20 years, numerous extensions to IPv4 have been developed to improve the efficiency with which the 32-bit address space can be used.

In addition, an even more extendable and scalable version of IP, IPv6, has been defined and developed. An IPv6 address is a 128-bit binary value, which can be displayed as 32 hexadecimal digits. It provides 3.4×10^{38} IP addresses. This version of IP should provide sufficient addresses for future Internet growth needs. Table 7-3 compares IPv4 and IPv6 addresses.

Table 7-3 *IPv6 Addresses*

Version	IPv4	IPv6
Number of octets	4 octets	16 octets
Binary representation of address	11000000.10101000.11001001.01110001	11010001.11011100.11001001.01110001.110100 01.11011100.110011001.01110001.11010001.110 11100.11001001.01110001.11010001.11011100.1 1001001.01110001
Notation of address	192.168.201.113	A524:72D3:2C80:DD02:0029:EC7A:002B:EA73
Total number of addresses available	4,294,467,295 IP addresses	3.4×10^{38} IP addresses

After years of planning and development, IPv6 is slowly being implemented in select networks. Eventually, IPv6 might replace IPv4 as the dominant internetwork protocol.

Another solution to the shortage of public IP addresses is a different kind of routing. CIDR is a new addressing scheme for the Internet that allows more efficient allocation of IP addresses than the old Class A, B, and C address scheme allows.

First introduced in 1993 and later deployed in 1994, CIDR dramatically improved the scalability and efficiency of IPv4 in the following ways:

- It replaced classful addressing with a more flexible and less wasteful scheme.

- It provided enhanced route aggregation, also known as *supernetting*. As the Internet grows, routers on the Internet require huge memory tables to store all the routing information. Supernetting helps reduce the size of router memory tables by combining and summarizing multiple routing information entries into one single entry. This reduces the size of router memory tables and also allows faster table lookup.

A CIDR network address looks like this:

192.168.54.0/23

The 192.168.54.0 is the network address itself and the /23 means that the first 23 bits are the network part of the address, leaving the last 9 bits for specific host addresses. The effect of CIDR is to aggregate, or combine, multiple classful networks into a single larger network. This aggregation reduces the number of entries required in the IP routing tables and allows the provisioning a larger number of hosts within the network. Both are done without using a network ID from the next larger classful address group.

With the CIDR approach, if you need more than 254 host addresses, you can be assigned a /23 address instead of wasting an entire Class B address that supports 65,534 hosts.

Figure 7-12 shows an example of using CIDR. Company XYZ asks for an address block from its ISP, not a central authority. The ISP evaluates company XYZ's needs and allocates address space from its own large *CIDR block* of addresses. CIDR blocks can be, and are, assigned by the regional authorities to governments, service providers, enterprises, and organizations.

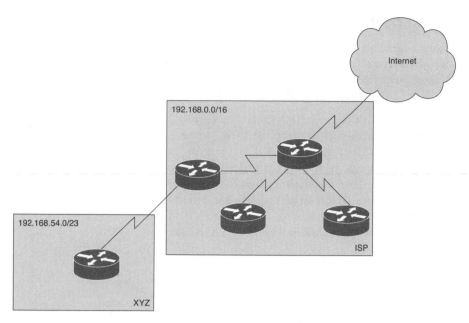

Figure 7-12   *CIDR Addressing*

Note   Figure 7-12 shows an example using private IP addresses as defined in RFC 1918. These addresses would never be used by an ISP for CIDR, but they are shown here merely as an illustration. Public addresses are not used in this example for security reasons.

In this example, the ISP owns the 192.168.0.0/16 address block. The ISP announces only this single 192.168.0.0/16 address to the Internet (even though this address block actually consists of many Class C networks). The ISP assigns the smaller 192.168.54.0/23 address block within the larger 192.168.0.0/16 address block to the XYZ company. This assignment allows the XYZ company to have a network that can have up to 510 hosts (29 − 2 = 510), or that network can be subdivided into multiple smaller subnets by the XYZ company.

Providers assume the burden of managing address space in a classless system. With this system, Internet routers keep only one summary route, or supernet route, to the provider's network, and only the individual provider keeps routes that are more specific to its own customer networks. This method drastically reduces the size of internetwork routing tables.

Addressing Services

Because of the complexity of modern IP networks, many services are necessary to provide seamless and easy-to-use internetworking. This section introduces some of these important services. They are covered in more detail later in this book.

Dynamic Host Configuration Protocol

Host addresses are assigned to devices either manually or automatically. Automated meth-
ods make administration of devices easier, so they are the ones most often employed.
Several automated methods that use protocols for assigning IP addresses exist, and
Dynamic Host Configuration Protocol (DHCP) is the most popular of those methods.

DHCP is a protocol used to assign IP addresses automatically and to set TCP/IP stack
configuration parameters, such as the subnet mask, default router, and Domain Name
System (DNS) servers for a host. DHCP is also used to provide other configuration information as necessary, including the length of time the address has been allocated to the
host. DHCP consists of two components: a protocol for delivering host-specific configuration parameters from a DHCP server to a host and a mechanism for allocating network
addresses to hosts. DCHP addresses are usually obtained on startup, and Figure 7-13
shows the communication that takes place to obtain the address.

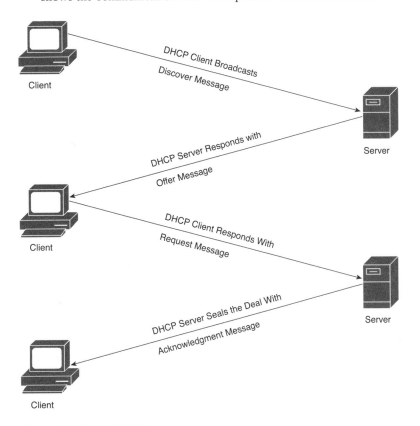

Figure 7-13   *DHCP Request*

Using DHCP, a host can obtain an IP address quickly and dynamically. All that is required
is a defined range of IP addresses on a DHCP server. As hosts come online, they contact
the DHCP server and request address information. The DHCP server selects an address

and allocates it to that host. The address is only "leased" to the host, so the host periodically contacts the DHCP server to extend the lease. This lease mechanism ensures that hosts that have been moved or are switched off for extended periods of time do not hold on to addresses that they are not using. The addresses are returned to the address pool by the DHCP server to be reallocated as necessary.

DHCP is a protocol specified by RFC 2131, superseding RFC 1541. DHCP is based on the Bootstrap Protocol (BOOTP), which it has effectively superseded.

IP addresses can also be assigned statically by configuring the host manually.

Domain Name System

Another important parameter used in TCP/IP is DNS. DNS is a mechanism for converting symbolic names into IP addresses. The DNS application frees users of IP networks from the burden of having to remember IP addresses. Without this freedom, the Internet would *not* be as popular or as usable as it is today.

The DNS address is a server that provides the DNS services. The address is typically assigned during the DCHP address assignment or can be assigned manually.

Using Common Host Tools to Determine the IP Address of a Host

Most operating systems provide a series of tools that can be used to verify host addresses and DNS addresses.

For a Microsoft Windows device, the Network Connections tab under System setup enables you to set and view the IP address configured on the PC. As shown in Figure 7-14, this PC is configured to obtain the address from a DHCP server.

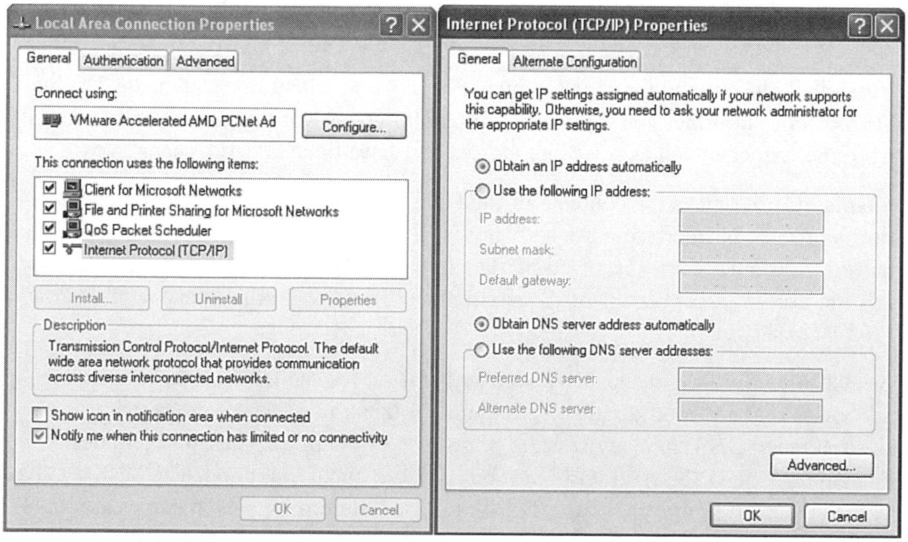

Figure 7-14   *TCP/IP Properties*

To determine the actual address of the device, the **ipconfig** command can be used from the command line to display all current TCP/IP network configuration values and refresh DHCP and DNS settings. Used without parameters, **ipconfig** displays the IP address, subnet mask, and default gateway for all adapters.

You can run **ipconfig** with various flags to determine exactly what output should be displayed. The syntax flags are as follows:

```
ipconfig [/all] [/renew [Adapter]] [/release [Adapter]] [/flushdns]
[/displaydns]    [/registerdns] [/showclassid Adapter] [/setclassid Adapter
[ClassID]]
```

The parameters are as follows:

- **/all:** Displays the full TCP/IP configuration for all adapters. Without this parameter, **ipconfig** displays only the IP address, subnet mask, and default gateway values for each adapter. Adapters can represent physical interfaces, such as installed network adapters, or logical interfaces, such as dialup connections.

- **/renew [*Adapter*]:** Renews DHCP configuration for all adapters (if an adapter is not specified) or for a specific adapter if the *Adapter* parameter is included. This parameter is available only on computers with adapters that are configured to obtain an IP address automatically. To specify an adapter name, type the adapter name that appears when you use **ipconfig** without parameters.

- **/release [*Adapter*]:** Sends a DHCPRELEASE message to the DHCP server to release the current DHCP configuration and discard the IP address configuration for either all adapters (if an adapter is not specified) or for a specific adapter if the *Adapter* parameter is included. This parameter disables TCP/IP for adapters configured to obtain an IP address automatically. To specify an adapter name, type the adapter name that appears when you use **ipconfig** without parameters.

- **/flushdns:** Flushes and resets the contents of the DNS client resolver cache. During DNS troubleshooting, you can use this procedure to discard negative cache entries from the cache, as well as any other entries that have been added dynamically.

- **/displaydns:** Displays the contents of the DNS client resolver cache, which includes both entries preloaded from the local host's file and any recently obtained resource records for name queries resolved by the computer. The DNS client service uses this information to resolve frequently queried names quickly, before querying its configured DNS servers.

- **/registerdns:** Initiates manual dynamic registration for the DNS names and IP addresses that are configured at a computer. You can use this parameter to troubleshoot a failed DNS name registration or resolve a dynamic update problem between a client and the DNS server without rebooting the client computer. The DNS settings in the advanced properties of the TCP/IP protocol determine which names are registered in DNS.

- **/showclassid** *Adapter:* Displays the DHCP class ID for a specified adapter. To see the DHCP class ID for all adapters, use the asterisk (*) wildcard character in place of *Adapter*. This parameter is available only on computers with adapters that are configured to obtain an IP address automatically.

- **/setclassid** *Adapter* [*ClassID*]: Configures the DHCP class ID for a specified adapter. To set the DHCP class ID for all adapters, use the asterisk (*) wildcard character in place of *Adapter*. This parameter is available only on computers with adapters that are configured to obtain an IP address automatically. If a DHCP class ID is not specified, the current class ID is removed.

- **/?**: Displays help at the command prompt.

Example 7-1 shows a sample of **ipconfig** usage.

Example 7-1   *Using* ipconfig *in Windows 8*

```
Microsoft Windows [Version 6.2.9200]
(c) 2012 Microsoft Corporation. All rights reserved.


C:\Users\anthonysequeira> ipconfig


Windows IP Configuration



Ethernet adapter Ethernet:

   Connection-specific DNS Suffix  . : localdomain
   IPv6 Address. . . . . . . . . . . : fdb2:2c26:f4e4:0:ad9d:b9cf:5a36:2712
   Temporary IPv6 Address. . . . . . : fdb2:2c26:f4e4:0:d021:1229:7056:bca0
   Link-local IPv6 Address . . . . . : fe80::ad9d:b9cf:5a36:2712%12
   IPv4 Address. . . . . . . . . . . : 10.211.55.6
   Subnet Mask . . . . . . . . . . . : 255.255.255.0
   Default Gateway . . . . . . . . . : 10.211.55.1


Tunnel adapter isatap.localdomain:

   Media State . . . . . . . . . . . : Media disconnected
   Connection-specific DNS Suffix  . : localdomain


Tunnel adapter Teredo Tunneling Pseudo-Interface:

   Connection-specific DNS Suffix  . :
   IPv6 Address. . . . . . . . . . . : 2001:0:9d38:953c:2479:3cd8:f52c:c8f9
   Link-local IPv6 Address . . . . . : fe80::2479:3cd8:f52c:c8f9%14
   Default Gateway . . . . . . . . . :


C:\Users\anthonysequeira>
```

Chapter Summary

This chapter examined the Internet layer of the TCP/IP protocol suite in much greater detail than we did in previous chapters. This is critically important because IP addresses and the services that accompany them are absolutely imperative in the operation of internetworks. You should consider making flash cards to assist you in memorizing many of the facts shared in this chapter. This includes the details in the many important tables presented.

Additional Resources

- The Internet Layer Video, http://ajsnetworking.com/internet
- RFC 1918 – IETF.ORG, http://tools.ietf.org/html/rfc1918

Review Questions

Use the questions here to review what you learned in this chapter. The correct answers and solutions are found in Appendix A, "Answers to Chapter Review Questions."

1. How many bits are in an IPv4 address?

   a. 16

   b. 32

   c. 48

   d. 64

   e. 128

2. In a Class B address, which of the octets are the host address portion and are assigned locally?

   a. The first octet is assigned locally.

   b. The first and second octets are assigned locally.

   c. The second and third octets are assigned locally.

   d. The third and fourth octets are assigned locally.

3. The address 172.16.128.17 is of which class?

   a. Class A

   b. Class B

   c. Class C

   d. Class D

4. Which of the following statements is true of a directed broadcast address?

    a. A broadcast address is an address that has all 0s in the host field.

    b. Any IP address in a network can be used as a broadcast address.

    c. A directed broadcast address is an address that has all 1s in the host field.

    d. None of these answers are correct.

5. Which of the following addresses are private IP addresses? (Choose two.)

    a. 10.215.34.124

    b. 172.16.71.43

    c. 176.17.10.10

    d. 225.200.15.10

6. Which of the following statements about IP are accurate? (Choose three.)

    a. IP is a connectionless protocol.

    b. IP uses relational addressing.

    c. IP delivers data reliably.

    d. IP operates at Layer 2 of the TCP/IP stack and OSI model.

    e. IP does not provide any recovery functions.

    f. IP delivers data on a best-effort basis.

7. Which of the following addresses is not a private address?

    a. 196.100.1.100

    b. 10.100.1.100

    c. 172.16.1.100

    d. 192.168.1.100

8. In a Class C address, which of the octets are the host address portion and are assigned locally?

    a. The first three octets

    b. The last octet

    c. The first octet

    d. The last three octets

9. A Class A address begins with what decimal number in the first octet?

    a. 128–191

    b. 192–224

    c. 1–192

    d. 1–126

10. What message is used to respond to a DHCP OFFER message?

   a. REPLY

   b. DISCOVER

   c. REQUEST

   d. ACKNOWLEDGMENT

Production Network Simulation Questions

Production Network Simulation Question 7-1

Your colleague has suggested that he use 27 bits for the identification of the network portion of an IP address. He wants to confirm with you regarding the number of hosts that this networking scheme can accommodate. Provide him with the correct number.

Production Network Simulation Question 7-2

You want confirmation that you have memorized the correct RFC 1918 private address space. List the complete private address ranges.

Production Network Simulation Question 7-3

Your supervisor needs a method to clear DHCP leased addresses from local hosts, and then renew addresses from the DHCP server. Provide your supervisor with a method for doing this from the command-line interface of a Windows 7 machine.

Chapter 8

IP Addressing and Subnets

This chapter includes the following sections:

- Chapter Objectives

- Understanding Binary Numbering

- Constructing a Network Addressing Scheme

- Implementing Variable-Length Subnet Masks

- Chapter Summary

- Additional Resources

- Review Questions

- Production Network Simulation Question 8-1

Subnetworks, or subnets, are very common in all but the smallest network environments. These subnetworks segment larger networks into smaller divisions that have their own network address space. To create subnet addresses, some of the bits that are used for the host portion of an IP address are "borrowed" to create the subnet address. I prefer to use the expression "stolen;" I mean after all, do we really plan on giving those bits back? No matter how you describe using bits of the host portion to create additional subnetworks in your infrastructure, this chapter reveals the exact process of creating and assigning subnets in your organization. This chapter also examines variable-length subnet masking (VLSM) and route summarization for more efficient use of network addressing.

Chapter Objectives

Upon completing this chapter, you will be able to describe the need for subnetting, and you will be able to perform the exact steps to make this addressing approach function perfectly. These abilities include meeting these objectives:

- Describe the purposes and functions of subnets and their addressing schemes

- Explain the role of a subnet mask

- Describe the octet values of a subnet mask

- Describe how end systems use subnet masks and default gateways

- Determine the number of subnets and hosts

- Identify a procedure to determine subnet addresses

- Show how to determine a subnet address

- Determine an addressing scheme

- Describe the role of VLSM

- Use VLSM to subnet a network

- Use route summarization in the network

Understanding Binary Numbering

All computers function using a system of switches that can be in one of two positions, on or off. This is called a binary system, with "off" being represented by the digit 0 and "on" being represented by the digit 1. A binary number will include only the digits 0 and 1.

Network device addresses also use this binary system to define their location on the network. The IP address is based on a dotted-decimal notation of a binary number. You must have a basic understanding of the mathematical properties of a binary system to understand networking. The following sections describe the mathematics involved in the binary numbering system and explain how to convert a decimal (base 10) number to a binary (base 2) number and vice versa.

Decimal and Binary Systems

The decimal (base 10) system is the numbering system used in everyday mathematics, and the binary (base 2) system is the foundation of computer operations.

In the decimal system, the digits are 0, 1, 2, 3, 4, 5, 6, 7, 8, and 9. When quantities higher than 9 are required, the decimal system begins with 10 and continues all the way to 99. Then the decimal system begins again with 100, and so on, with each column to the left raising the exponent by 1.

The binary system uses only the digits 0 and 1. Therefore, the first digit is 0, followed by 1. If a quantity higher than 1 is required, the binary system goes to 10, followed by 11. The binary system continues with 100, 101, 110, 111, 1000, and so on. Table 8-1 shows the binary equivalents of the decimal numbers 0 through 19.

Table 8-1 *Decimal Versus Binary Numbers*

Decimal Number	Binary Number
0	0
1	1
2	10
3	11
4	100
5	101
6	110
7	111
8	1000
9	1001
10	1010
11	1011
12	1100
13	1101
14	1110
15	1111
16	10000
17	10001
18	10010
19	10011

Least Significant Bit and Most Significant Bit

Most people are accustomed to the decimal numbering system. While the base number is important in any numbering system, it is the position of a digit that confers value. The number 10 is represented by a 1 in the tens position and a 0 in the ones position. The number 100 is represented by a 1 in the hundreds position, a 0 in the tens position, and a 0 in the ones position.

In a binary number, the digit on the rightmost side is the least significant bit (LSB), and the digit on the leftmost side is the most significant bit (MSB). The significance of any digits in between these sides is based on their proximity to either the LSB or the MSB. Figure 8-1 shows the relationships of bit significance to the values for base 10 and base 2 numbering systems.

Base-10 Decimal Conversion - 63204829

	MSB							LSB
Base^{Exponent}	10^7	10^6	10^5	10^4	10^3	10^2	10^1	10^0
Column Value	6	3	2	0	4	8	2	9
Decimal Weight	10000000	1000000	100000	10000	1000	100	10	1
Column Weight	60000000	3000000	200000	0	4000	800	20	9

60000000 + 3000000 + 200000 + 0 + 4000 + 800 + 20 + 9 = 63204829

Base-2 Binary Conversion - 1110100 (233)

	MSB							LSB
Base^{Exponent}	2^7	2^6	2^5	2^4	2^3	2^2	2^1	2^0
Column Value	1	1	1	0	1	0	0	1
Decimal Weight	128	64	32	16	8	4	2	1
Column Weight	128	64	32	0	8	0	0	1

128 + 64 + 32 + 0 + 8 + 0 + 0 + 1 = 233

Figure 8-1   *Bit Significance*

Base 2 Conversion System

Understanding the base 2 system is important because an IP version 4 (IPv4) address consists of 32 binary bits. Each digit is 1 bit. The 32 bits are divided into four sets of 8 bits, called *octets*. A dot (period) is placed between each set to separate them. (A byte is another name for 8 bits; however, for the purposes of this section, 8 bits will be referred to as an octet.)

The various classes of addresses are based on the octet boundaries, so it is helpful to get used to such groupings. It is also an ease-of-use issue, because 8-bit binary numbers are easier to convert than 32-bit binary numbers. When converting a binary IP address, you only convert one octet at a time. The highest possible binary octet is 11111111, which converts to the decimal number 255. The lowest possible binary octet is 00000000, which is the decimal number 0. That means that with 8 bits, you can have 256 different number combinations, 0 to 255 inclusive.

Powers of 2

To understand how binary numbers are used in IP addressing, you must understand the mathematical process of converting a decimal number to a binary number and vice versa.

Calculator batteries run down and charts can be misplaced, but if you know the mathematical principles, a piece of paper and pencil are all that you need to convert binary numbers to decimal numbers and to convert decimal numbers to binary numbers. There are charts available to help with decimal-to-binary conversion, showing, for example, 20 = decimal 1, 21 = decimal 2, 22 = decimal 4, and so on. Table 8-2 illustrates which decimal numbers are produced for powers of 2.

Table 8-2   *Powers of 2*

Power of 2	Calculation	Value
20	Mathematical identity	1
21	2	2
22	2*2	4
23	2*2*2	8
24	2*2*2*2	16
25	2*2*2*2*2	32
26	2*2*2*2*2*2	64
27	2*2*2*2*2*2*2	128

Decimal-to-Binary Conversion

Decimal numbers can be converted to binary numbers through a specific process, as shown in Figure 8-2.

Base^{Exponent}	2^7	2^6	2^5	2^4	2^3	2^2	2^1	2^0
Place Value	128	64	32	16	8	4	2	1
Example: Convert Decimal 35 to Binary	0	0	1	0	0	0	1	1

35	=			2^5		+		$2^1 + 2^0$
35	=			(32 * 1)		+		(2 * 1) + (1 * 1)
35	=	0 +	0 +	1 +	0 +	0 +	0 +	1 + 1
35	=	00100011						

Figure 8-2   *Decimal-to-Binary Conversion*

This example shows a simple binary conversion of the decimal number 35. The base exponent line shows base 2 numbers and their exponents (2 * 2 = 4 * 2 = 8, and so on). The decimal value of the base exponent number is listed in the second row, and the binary number is displayed in the third row. The table describes the steps to determine the binary number. Notice that the first 2 bits of the binary number are 0s; these are known as leading 0s. In reality, the decimal number 35 would only be a 6-bit binary number. Because IP addresses are laid out as four sets of octets, the binary number is made into an octet by placing 0s to the left of the 6-bit number.

The steps used in converting the number 35 to a binary number are as follows:

1. Looking at Figure 8-2, what is the greatest power of 2 that is less than or equal to 35? 128 does not go into 35, so place a 0 in that column.

2. 64 does not go into 35, so place a 0 in that column.

3. 25 (32) is smaller than 35. 32 goes into 35 one time. Place a 1 in that column.

4. Calculate how much is left over by subtracting 32 from 35. The result is 3.

5. Check to see whether 16 (the next lower power of 2) fits into 3. Because it does not, a 0 is placed in that column.

6. The value of the next number is 8, which is larger than 3, so a 0 is placed in that column, too.

7. The next value is 4, which is still larger than 3, so it too receives a 0.

8. The next value is 2, which is smaller than 3. Because 2 fits into 3 one time, place a 1 in that column.

9. Subtract 2 from 3, and the result is 1.

10. The decimal value of the last bit is 1, which fits in the remaining number. Therefore, place a 1 in the last column. The binary equivalent of the decimal number 35 is 00100011.

Binary-to-Decimal Conversion

As with decimal-to-binary conversion, there is usually more than one way to convert binary numbers to decimal numbers. You can convert binary numbers to decimal numbers using the positional values based on the powers of 2 and identifying the columns with nonzero values, which contribute to the final numerical value. Figure 8-3 illustrates this process.

Base^{Exponent}	2^7	2^6	2^5	2^4	2^3	2^2	2^1	2^0
Place Value	128	64	32	16	8	4	2	1
Example: Binary Number	1	0	1	1	1	0	0	1
Decimal Number Total: 185	128	0	32	16	8	0	0	1

1 0 1 1 1 0 0 1 = (128 * 1) + (64 * 0) + (32 * 1) + (16 * 1) + (8 * 1) + (4 * 0) + (2 * 0) + (1 * 1)
1 0 1 1 1 0 0 1 = 128 + 0 + 32 +16 + 8 + 0 + 0 + 1
1 0 1 1 1 0 0 1 = <u>185</u>

Figure 8-3 *Binary-to-Decimal Conversion*

The steps used for converting the binary number 10111001 to a decimal number are as follows:

1. Find the place value that corresponds to any 1 bit in the binary number, according to its position. For example, as shown in Figure 8-3, the binary bit in the 27 column is 1, so the decimal total is 128.

2. There is a 0 in the 26 (64) column. The decimal equation is 128 + 0 = 128.

3. There is now a 1 in the 25 (32) column. The decimal equation becomes 128 + 32 = 160.

4. There is a 1 in the 24 (16) column. Adding the value to the decimal total gives 160 + 16 = 176.

5. The next column, 23, has a 1, so add the value 8 to the decimal total, giving 176 + 8 = 184.

6. There are 0s in the 22 and 21 columns. Add 0s to the decimal total: 184 + 0 + 0 = 184.

7. Finally, there is a 1 in the 20 (1) column. Now, add 1 to 184. The result is 185. The decimal equivalent of the binary number 10111001 is 185.

Constructing a Network Addressing Scheme

Subnetworks, also known as subnets, are very common in all but the smallest of network environments, segmenting the network into smaller divisions that have their own addresses. To create subnet addresses, some of the bits used for the host portion of an IP address are "borrowed" to create the subnet address. The following sections describe how subnets function and how they are computed.

Subnetworks

Network administrators often need to divide networks, especially large networks, into subnetworks, or subnets, to provide addressing flexibility. This topic describes the purposes and functions of subnets and their addressing schemes.

A company that occupies a three-story building might have a network divided by floors, with each floor divided into offices. Think of the building as the network, the floors as the three subnets, and the offices as the individual host addresses.

A subnet segments the hosts within the network. With no subnets, the network has a flat topology. A flat topology has a short routing table and relies on Layer 2 MAC addresses to deliver packets. MAC addresses have no hierarchical structure. As the network grows, the use of the network bandwidth becomes less and less efficient.

The disadvantages of a flat network are as follows:

- All devices share the same bandwidth.

- All devices share the same Layer 2 broadcast domain.

- It is difficult to apply security policies because there are no boundaries between devices.

On an Ethernet network connected by hubs, every host on the same physical network sees all the packets on the network. On a switch-connected network, the host sees all broadcasts. In heavy traffic situations, on a shared segment connected by hubs, there can be many collisions caused by two or more devices transmitting simultaneously. The devices detect the collision, stop transmitting, and then begin transmitting at a random interval later. To users, this process is perceived as the network slowing down. Routers can be used in these situations to separate networks by breaking the network into multiple subnets. Figure 8-4 shows an example of a small network broken into three separate subnets.

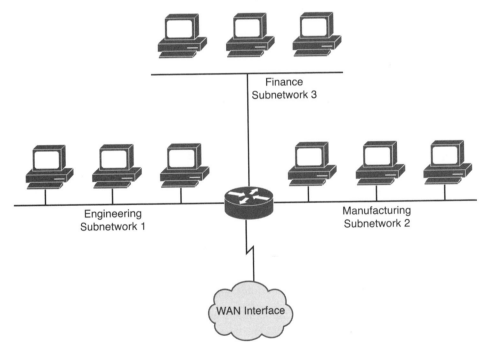

Figure 8-4 *Network Subnets*

The advantages of subnetting a network are as follows:

- Smaller networks are easier to manage and map to geographical or functional requirements.

- Overall network traffic is reduced, which can improve performance.

- You can more easily apply network security measures at the interconnections between subnets than throughout the entire network.

In multiple-network environments, each subnetwork can be connected to the Internet through a single router, as shown in Figure 8-5. In this example, the network is subdivided into multiple subnetworks. The actual details of the internal network environment and how the network is divided into multiple subnetworks are inconsequential to other IP networks.

IP addresses provide an identifier for both the network and the host of an IP subnet. As Figure 8-5 illustrates, the router must have some way of determining how much of the address is the network portion.

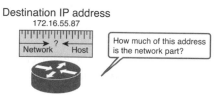

Figure 8-5   *Determining Network Addresses*

Each device on an IP network is configured with both an IP address and a subnet mask. The subnet mask identifies the network-significant portion of an IP address. The network-significant portion of an IP address is, simply, the part that identifies what network the host device is on (that is, the network address). This is important for the routing operation to be efficient.

Two-Level and Three-Level Addresses

When the IPv4 method of identifying addresses and address classes was developed, a two-level address (network and host) seemed sufficient. Each address class (A, B, and C) had a default mask associated with it, and because the mask was predefined, it was not necessary to explicitly configure the mask.

As the number of network-connected devices grew, it became clear that this was an inefficient use of network addresses. To overcome this problem, a third level of addressing, consisting of subnets, was developed.

A subnet address includes the original classful network portion plus a subnet field. This is also known as the extended network prefix. The subnet field and the host field are created from the original classful host portion. To create a subnet address, you can borrow bits from the original host field and designate them as the subnet field.

However, subnets cannot work without a way to identify the part of the address that is network significant and the part that is host significant. For this reason, explicit subnet masks need to be configured.

Subnet Creation

The subnet address is created by taking address bits from the host portion of Class A, Class B, and Class C addresses. Usually, a network administrator assigns the subnet address locally. Like IP addresses, each subnet address must be unique.

When creating subnets, many potential individual host addresses (endpoints) are lost. For this reason, you must pay close attention to the percentage of addresses that are lost when you create subnets. The algorithm used to compute the number of subnets uses powers of 2.

When taking (borrowing) bits from the host field, it is important to note that the number of additional subnets that is being created will double each time one more bit is borrowed. Borrowing 1 bit creates two possible subnets (21 = 2). Borrowing 2 bits creates four possible subnets (22 = 4). Borrowing 3 bits creates eight possible subnets (23 = 8), and so on.

Each time another bit is borrowed from the host field, the number of possible subnets created *increases* by a power of 2 and the number of individual possible host addresses on each subnet *decreases* by a power of 2. Some examples are as follows:

- Using 1 bit for the subnet field results in 2 possible subnets (21 = 2).

- Using 2 bits for the subnet field results in 4 possible subnets (22 = 4).

- Using 3 bits for the subnet field results in 8 possible subnets (23 = 8).

- Using 4 bits for the subnet field results in 16 possible subnets (24 = 16).

- Using 5 bits for the subnet field results in 32 possible subnets (25 = 32).

- Using 6 bits for the subnet field results in 64 possible subnets (26 = 64).

In general, the following formula can be used to calculate the number of usable subnets, given the number of subnet bits used:

Number of subnets = 2s (where *s* is the number of subnet bits borrowed)

Computing Usable Subnetworks and Hosts

One of the decisions you must make when creating subnets is to determine the optimal number of subnets and hosts. To accomplish this, you need to understand the classes of IP networks and know how to use the bits within these classes to create networks and allocate address space for hosts. This is done by borrowing bits from the host field in a network address space.

Computing Hosts for a Class C Subnetwork

Each time 1 bit is borrowed from a host field, there is one less bit remaining in the host field that can be used for host numbers, and the number of host addresses that can be assigned decreases by a power of 2.

As an example, consider a Class C network address in which all 8 bits in the last octet are used for the host ID. Therefore, there are 256 possible numbers. The actual number of possible addresses available to assign to hosts is 254 (256 − 2 reserved addresses).

Now, imagine that this Class C network is divided into subnets. If 2 bits are borrowed from the default 8-bit host field, the size of the host field decreases to 6 bits. All possible combinations of 0s and 1s that could occur in the remaining 6 bits produce a total number of possible hosts that could be assigned in each subnet. This number, which formerly was 256, is now 64. (You "borrowed" 2 bits to make subnets from 8 host bits total in a Class C network, so with 6 bits remaining for hosts, 26 = 64.) The number of usable host numbers decreases to 62 (64 − 2).

In the same Class C network, if 3 bits are borrowed, the size of the host field decreases to 5 bits, and the total number of assignable hosts for each subnet decreases to 32 (25). The number of usable host numbers decreases to 30 (32 − 2). The number of possible host addresses that can be assigned to a subnet is related to the number of subnets that have been created. In a Class C network, for example, with 3 bits borrowed to make subnets, the usable subnets created are 8, each having 30 (25 = 32 − 2 = 30) usable host addresses. Figure 8-6 shows the number of subnets and hosts that can be computed in a Class C address space by borrowing host bits.

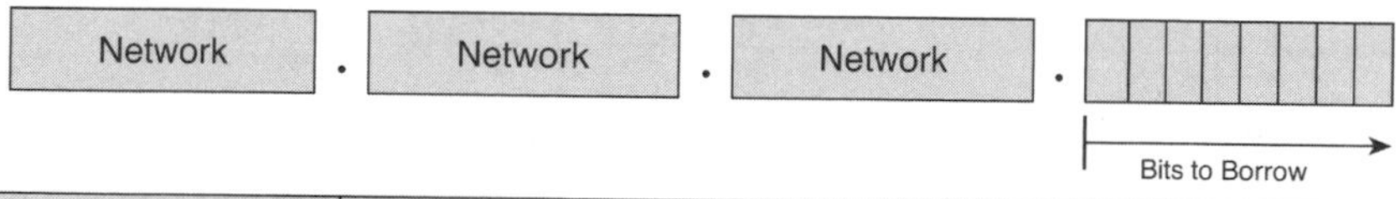

Number of Bits Borrowed (s)	Number of Subnets Possible (2^s)	Number of Bits Remaining in Host ID $(8-s=h)$	Number of Hosts Possible Per Subnet (2^h-2)
1	2	7	126
2	4	6	62
3	8	5	30
4	16	4	14
5	32	3	6
6	64	2	2
7	128	1	2

Figure 8-6   *Borrowing Bits in a Class C Network Address Space*

Computing Hosts for a Class B Subnetwork

Now consider a Class B network address, in which 16 bits are used for the network ID and 16 bits are used for the host ID. Therefore, there are 65,536 (216) possible addresses available to assign to hosts (65,534 usable addresses, after subtracting the two addresses, the broadcast and the subnet addresses, that cannot be used).

Now, imagine that this Class B network is divided into subnets. If 2 bits are borrowed from the default 16-bit host field, the size of the host field decreases to 14 bits. All possible combinations of 0s and 1s that could occur in the remaining 14 bits produce a total number of possible hosts that could be assigned in each subnet. Thus, the number of hosts assigned to each subnet is now 16,382.

In the same Class B network, if 3 bits are borrowed, making the mask 3 bits longer, the size of the host field decreases from 16 bits to 13 bits, because you borrowed 3 bits to make subnets, and now the total number of host addresses for each subnet decreases to 8192 (213). The number of usable host numbers decreases to 8190 (8192 – 2). In this Class B network, for example, the usable subnets created are 6 (23 = 8 – 2), each having 8190 (8192 – 2) usable host addresses. Figure 8-7 shows the number of subnets and hosts that can be computed in a Class B address space by borrowing host bits.

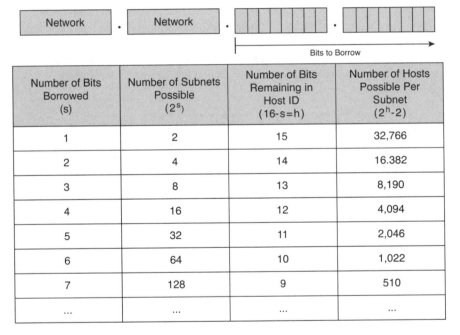

Number of Bits Borrowed (s)	Number of Subnets Possible (2^s)	Number of Bits Remaining in Host ID (16-s=h)	Number of Hosts Possible Per Subnet (2^h-2)
1	2	15	32,766
2	4	14	16.382
3	8	13	8,190
4	16	12	4,094
5	32	11	2,046
6	64	10	1,022
7	128	9	510
...	...	...	...

Figure 8-7 *Borrowing Bits in a Class B Network Address Space*

Computing Hosts for a Class A Subnetwork

Finally, consider a Class A network address, in which by default 8 bits are used for the network ID and 24 bits are used for the host ID. Therefore, there are 16,777,216 (224) possible addresses available to assign to hosts (16,777,214 usable addresses, after subtracting the two addresses, the broadcast and the subnet addresses, that cannot be used).

Now, imagine that this Class A network is divided into subnets. If 6 bits are borrowed from the default 24-bit host field, the size of the host field decreases to 18 bits. All possible combinations of 0s and 1s that could occur in the remaining 18 bits produce a total number of possible hosts that could be assigned in each subnet. This number is now 262,142, while it was formerly 16,777,216. The number of usable hosts decreases to 262,140 (262,142 − 2). Figure 8-8 shows the number of subnets and hosts that can be computed in a Class A address space by borrowing host bits.

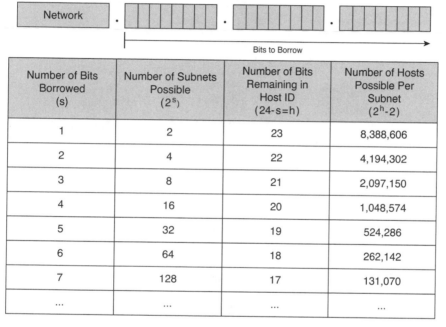

Number of Bits Borrowed (s)	Number of Subnets Possible (2^s)	Number of Bits Remaining in Host ID (24−s=h)	Number of Hosts Possible Per Subnet (2^h-2)
1	2	23	8,388,606
2	4	22	4,194,302
3	8	21	2,097,150
4	16	20	1,048,574
5	32	19	524,286
6	64	18	262,142
7	128	17	131,070
...	...	...	...

Figure 8-8   *Borrowing Bits in a Class A Network Address Space*

How End Systems Use Subnet Masks

The end system uses the subnet mask to compare the network portion of the local network address with the destination network address of the packet to be sent. Before an end system can send a packet to its destination, it must first determine whether the destination address is on the local network. This is done by comparing the bits in the destination address with the network bits of the sending station. Figure 8-9 shows how host A and host B are local because their subnetwork addresses are both 10.1.1.0.

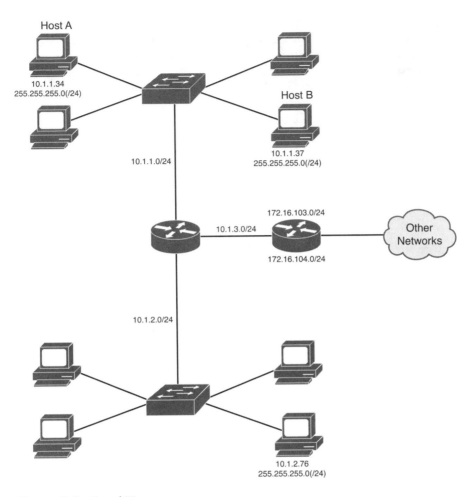

Figure 8-9   *Local Hosts*

Because these hosts are on the same subnet, the source end system will use the Address Resolution Protocol (ARP) process to bind the destination IP address to the destination MAC address. If it was not on the same subnet, the packet (frame) must be forwarded to the MAC address of the default gateway, the router on the subnet, for transmission to the destination network.

How Routers Use Subnet Masks

The subnet mask identifies the network-significant part of an IP address. Routers, like all IP hosts, need this information to determine how to get a packet to the desired destination. When a device determines that a packet does not belong on the local subnet (which would be called off-net), it will send the packet to the router (its default gateway) on its subnet. The router must then determine where to send the packet.

All routers have routing tables. Depending on the location of the router in the network hierarchy, the table can be small and simple or large and complex. Figure 8-10 shows a packet traveling from host A to host B on different networks. As the packet travels between the adjoining networks, the routers must reference their routing tables to determine where to send the packet next.

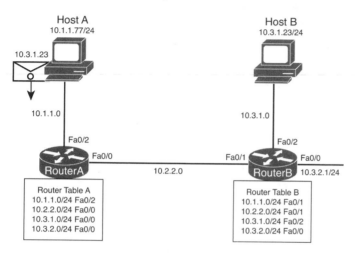

Figure 8-10   *Routing Tables*

The router populates the routing table with the network-significant part of all known networks, to compare the destination network addresses of packets that need to be forwarded. If the network is not directly attached to the router, the router stores the address of the next-hop router to which the packet should be forwarded. For routers to function without the need to store *all* destination networks in their tables, they use a default route to which packets not matching any entry in the route table are forwarded. The following list describes this behavior:

1. Host A determines that the destination network is off-net and requires the use of its default gateway router (Router A). So host A must ARP for, and deliver the frame to, Router A.

Note   Router A has a route to the destination network 10.3.1.0 and forwards the packet to Router B through the indicated interface.

2. Because the 10.3.1.0/24 network is directly connected to Router B interface Fa0/2, Router B will use ARP to determine the MAC address of host B.

When configuring routers, each interface is connected to a different network or subnet segment. An available host address from each different network or subnet must be assigned to the interface of the router that connects to that network or subnet. In Figure 8-11, RouterA has two Ethernet interfaces, one connected to the host network and one to the network connecting RouterA to RouterB.

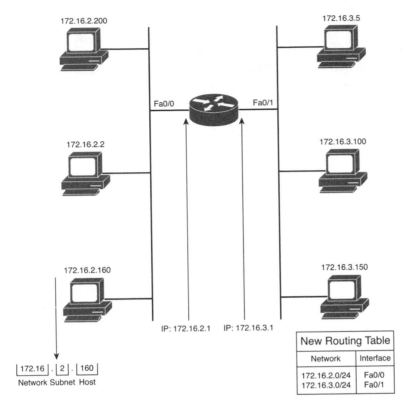

Figure 8-11   *IP Addressing on a Router Interface*

Notice Figure 8-11, the interface that is connected to the 172.16.2.0 subnetwork is assigned the IP address of 172.16.2.1, and the other interface that is connected to the 172.16.3.0 subnetwork is assigned the IP address of 172.16.3.1. All the attached hosts need to have their addresses within the range of the subnet. Any host configured with an address outside of this would *not* be reachable.

Mechanics of Subnet Mask Operation

Although subnet masks use the same format as IP addresses, they are not IP addresses themselves. Each subnet mask is 32 bits long, divided into four octets, and is usually represented in the dotted-decimal notation like IP addresses. In their binary representation, subnet masks have all 1s in the network and subnetwork portions (on the left) and all 0s in the host portion (on the right).

There are only eight valid subnet mask values per octet. The subnet field always immediately follows the network number. That is, the borrowed bits must be the first *n* bits,
starting with the most significant bit (MSB) of the default host field, where *n* is the
desired size of the new subnet field. The subnet mask is the tool used by the router to
determine which bits are routing (network and subnet) bits and which bits are host bits.

If all 8 bits in any octet are binary 1s, the octet has a decimal equivalent of 255. This is
why there is a 255 in a decimal representation of a default subnet. In Class A, the default
subnet mask is 255.0.0.0 in decimal, 11111111.00000000.00000000.00000000 in binary,
and /8 in shorthand; all three mean the same thing. If the three highest-order bits (bits to
the left) from the next highest-order host octet are borrowed (add three more 1s to the
default mask), they add up to 224 (128 + 64 + 32). This translates to 255.224.0.0, or 1111
1111.11100000.00000000.00000000. Figure 8-12 shows the common values used in subnet masking.

128	64	32	16	8	4	2	1		
1	0	0	0	0	0	0	0	=	128
1	1	0	0	0	0	0	0	=	192
1	1	1	0	0	0	0	0	=	224
1	1	1	1	0	0	0	0	=	240
1	1	1	1	1	0	0	0	=	248
1	1	1	1	1	1	0	0	=	252
1	1	1	1	1	1	1	0	=	254
1	1	1	1	1	1	1	1	=	255

Figure 8-12   *Subnet Mask Octet Values*

With IP addressing, the subnet mask identifies the network addressing information that
is necessary to send packets toward their final destinations. The subnet mask identifies
which bits within the IP address are the network and subnet bits.

Figure 8-13 shows the default subnet masks for Class A, Class B, and Class C addresses.
The subnet mask itself is indicated with 1s in the binary notation for the mask, with all
other bits indicated as 0s.

```
Example Class A Address (Decimal):    10.0.0.0
Example Class A Address (Binary):     00001010.00000000.00000000.00000000
Default Class A Mask (Binary):        11111111.00000000.00000000.00000000
Default Class A Mask (Decimal):       255.0.0.0
Default Classful Prefix Length:       /8
```

```
Example Class B Address (Decimal):    172.16.0.0
Example Class B Address (Binary):     10101100.00010000.00000000.00000000
Default Class B Mask (Binary):        11111111.11111111.00000000.00000000
Default Class B Mask (Decimal):       255.255.0.0
Default Classful Prefix Length:       /16
```

```
Example Class C Address (Decimal):    192.168.42.0
Example Class C Address (Binary):     11000000.10101000.00101010.00000000
Default Class C Mask (Binary):        11111111.11111111.11111111.00000000
Default Class C Mask (Decimal):       255.255.255.0
Default Classful Prefix Length:       /24
```

Figure 8-13 *Class A, B, and C Default Subnet Masks*

Applying Subnet Mask Operation

Most network administrators work with existing networks, complete with subnets and subnet masks in place. Network administrators need to be able to determine, from an existing IP address, which part of the address is the network and which part is the subnet. Applying the subnet mask operation provides this information.

The procedure described in the following steps explains how to select the number of subnets you need for a particular network and then apply a mask to implement subnets:

1. Determine the IP address for your network as assigned by the registry authority. Assume that you are assigned a Class B address of 172.16.0.0.

2. Based on your organization and administrative requirements and structure, determine the number of subnets required for the network. Be sure to plan for future growth. Assume that you are managing a worldwide network in 25 countries. Each country has an average of four locations. Therefore, you will need 100 subnets.

3. Based on the address class and the number of subnets you selected, determine the number of bits you need to borrow from the host ID. To create 100 subnets, you need to borrow 7 bits ($2^7 = 128$).

4. Determine the binary and decimal values of the subnet mask you select. For a Class B address with 16 bits in the network ID, when you borrow 7 bits, the mask is /23. Binary value of the mask: 11111111.11111111.11111110.00000000. Decimal value of the mask: 255.255.254.0.

5. Apply the subnet mask for the network IP address to determine the subnet and host addresses. You will also determine the network and broadcast addresses for each subnet.

6. Assign subnet addresses to specific subnets on your network.

Determining the Network Addressing Scheme

When working in a classful networking environment that uses fixed-length subnet masks, you can determine the entire network addressing based on a single IP address and its corresponding subnet mask. Figure 8-14 shows an example of the first three steps, given the following network address and mask:

- Network address: 192.168.221.37

- Subnet mask: 255.255.255.248

IP Address: 192.168.221.37   Subnet Mask /29

Step	Description	Example
1.	Write the octet that is being split in binary.	4th Octet: 00100101
2.	Write the mask or classful prefix length in binary.	Assigned Mask: 255.255.255.248 (/29) 4th Octet: 11111000
3.	Draw a line to delineate the significant bits in the assigned IP address. Cross out the mask so you can view the significant bits in the IP address.	Split Octet (Binary): 00100|101 Split Mask (Binary): 11111|000

Figure 8-14 *Determining the Addressing Scheme, Steps 1–3*

After using the subnet mask to determine the significant bits used in the host address portion, you will use Steps 4 through 8 to determine the subnetwork network address, broadcast address, first host address, last host address, and next subnet address. This is illustrated in Figure 8-15.

Step	Description	Example
4.	Copy the significant bits four times.	00100 000 (Network Address) 00100 001 (First Address in Subnet) 00100 110 (Last Address in Subnet) 00100 111 (Broadcast Address)?
5.	In the first line, define the network address by placing all zeros in the significant bit.	**Completed Subnet Addresses** Network Address: 192.168.221.32 Subnet Mask: 255.255.255.248
6.	In the last line, define the broadcast address by placing all ones in the significant bits.	First Subnet: 192.168.221.32 First Host Address: 192.168.221.33
7.	In the middle lines, define the first and last host number.	Last Host Address: 192.168.221.38 Broadcast Address: 192.168.221.39 Next Subnet: 192.168.221.40
8.	Increment the subnet bits by one.	00101000 (Next Subnet)

Figure 8-15 *Determining the Addressing Scheme, Steps 4–8*

After converting the addresses from binary to decimal, the addresses for the subnets are as follows:

- Subnet address: 192.168.221.32

- First host address: 192.168.221.33

- Last host address: 192.168.221.38

- Broadcast address: 192.168.221.39

- Next subnet address: 192.168.221.40

Notice that the range of the address block, including the subnet address and directed broadcast address in this example, is from 192.168.221.32 through 192.168.221.39, which includes eight addresses. The address block is the same size as the number of host bits (2h = 23 = 8).

Class C Example

In Figure 8-16, we will determine the addressing for a Class C network with a nondefault mask. Given the address of 192.168.5.139 and knowing that the subnet mask is 255.255.255.224, the subnet number is 11111111.11111111.11111111.11100000, or /27.

IP Address 192.168.5.139   Subnet Mask 255.255.255.224

IP Address	192	168	5	139	
IP Address	11000000	10101000	00000101	100 01011	
Subnet Mask	11111111	11111111	11111111	111 00000	/27
Subnetwork	11000000	10101000	00000101	10000000	
Subnetwork	192	168	5	128	
First Host	192	168	5	10000001=129	
Last Host	192	168	5	10011110=158	
Directed Broadcast	192	168	5	10011111=159	
Next Subnet	192	168	5	10100000=160	

Figure 8-16 *Class C Addresses with Nondefault Mask*

The following outlines the steps and shows the details of each operation in the eight-step process:

1. Write the octet that is being split in binary (10001011).

2. Write the mask bits of the same octet (11100000).

3. Draw a vertical line to delineate the network-significant bits in the assigned IP address. Put a line under the mask so that you can view the significant bits in the IP address (10000000).

4. Copy the significant bits four times.

5. In the first line, define the network address by placing 0s in the remaining host bits (10000000).

6. In the last line, define the directed broadcast address by placing all 1s in the host bits (10011111).

7. In the middle lines, define the first and last host ID for this subnet: 10000001 and 10011110.

8. Increment the subnet bits by 1 to determine the next subnet address. Repeat Steps 4 through 8 for all subnets (10100000).

Table 8-3 shows the range of subnets and broadcast addresses that would be available with the given subnet mask. Note that the subnet in Figure 8-16 is subnet 4 in the following table.

Table 8-3   *Subnet Addresses Table*

Subnet No.	Subnet ID	Host Range	Broadcast Address
1	192.168.5.0	192.168.5.1 to 192.168.5.30	192.168.5.31
2	192.168.5.32	192.168.5.33 to 192.168.5.62	192.168.5.63
3	192.168.5.64	192.168.5.65 to 192.168.5.94	192.168.5.95
4	192.168.5.96	192.168.5.97 to 192.168.5.126	192.168.5.127
5	192.168.5.128	192.168.5.128 to 192.168.5.158	192.168.5.159
6	192.168.5.160	192.168.5.161 to 192.168.5.190	192.168.5.191
7	192.168.5.192	192.168.5.193 to 192.168.5.222	192.168.5.223
8	192.168.5.224	192.168.5.225 to 192.168.5.254	192.168.5.255

Class B Example

In Figure 8-17, we will determine the addressing for a Class B network with a nondefault mask. Given the address of 172.16.139.46 and knowing that the subnet mask is 255.255.240.0, or /20, you can determine the subnet and host addresses for this network.

Base-10 Decimal Conversion - 63204829

	MSB							LSB
Base^{Exponent}	10^7	10^6	10^5	10^4	10^3	10^2	10^1	10^0
Column Value	6	3	2	0	4	8	2	9
Decimal Weight	10000000	1000000	100000	10000	1000	100	10	1
Column Weight	60000000	3000000	200000	0	4000	800	20	9

60000000 + 3000000 + 200000 + 0 + 4000 + 800 + 20 + 9 = 63204829

Base-2 Binary Conversion - 1110100 (233)

	MSB							LSB
Base^{Exponent}	2^7	2^6	2^5	2^4	2^3	2^2	2^1	2^0
Column Value	1	1	1	0	1	0	0	1
Decimal Weight	128	64	32	16	8	4	2	1
Column Weight	128	64	32	0	8	0	0	1

128 + 64 + 32 + 0 + 8 + 0 + 0 + 1 = 233

Figure 8-17 *Class B Address with Nondefault Subnet Mask*

The following outlines the steps and shows the details of each operation in the eight-step process:

1. Write the octet that is being split in binary (10001011).

2. Write the mask bits of the same octet (11110000).

3. Draw a vertical line to delineate the network-significant bits in the assigned IP address. Put a line under the mask so that you can view the significant bits in the IP address (10000000).

4. Copy the significant bits four times.

5. In the first line, define the network address by placing 0s in the remaining host bits (10000000.00000000).

6. In the last line, define the directed broadcast address by placing all 1s in the host bits (10001111.11111111).

7. In the middle lines, define the first and last host ID for this subnet—10000000.00000001 and 10001111.11111110.

8. Increment the subnet bits by 1 to determine the next subnet address. Repeat Steps 4 through 8 for all subnets (10100000.00000000).

Table 8-4 shows the range of subnets and broadcast addresses that would be available with the given subnet mask.

Table 8-4 *Subnet Addresses Table*

Subnet No.	Subnet ID	Host Range	Broadcast Address
All 0s	172.16.0.0	172.16.0.1 to 172.16.15.254	172.16.15.255
1	172.16.16.0	172.16.16.1 to 172.16.31.254	172.16.31.255
2	172.16.32.0	172.16.32.1 to 172.16.47.254	172.16.47.255
13	172.16.208.0	172.16.208.1 to 172.16.223.254	172.16.223.255
14	172.16.224.0	172.16.224.1 to 172.16.239.254	172.16.239.255
All 1s	172.16.240.0	172.16.240.1 to 172.16.255.254	172.16.255.255

Class A Example

In Figure 8-18, we will determine the addressing for a Class A network with a nondefault mask. Given the address of 10.172.16.211 and knowing that the subnet mask is /18, you can determine the subnet and host addresses for this network.

IP Address 172.16.139.46   Subnet Mask /20

IP Address	172	16	139	46	
IP Address	10101100	00010000	1000|1011	00101110	
Subnet Mask	11111111	11111111	1111|0000	00000000	/20
Subnetwork	10101100	00010000	10000000	00000000	
Subnetwork	172	16	128	0	
First Host	172	16	10000000	00000001=128.1	
Last Host	172	16	10001111	11111110=143.254	
Directed Broadcast	172	16	10001111	11111111=143.255	
Next Subnet	172	16	10010000	00000000=144.0	

Figure 8-18 *Class A Address with Nondefault Subnet Mask*

The following outlines the steps and shows the details of each operation in the eight-step process:

1. Write the octet that is being split in binary (00010000).

2. Write the mask bits of the same octet (11000000).

3. Draw a vertical line to delineate the network-significant bits in the assigned IP address. Put a line under the mask so that you can view the significant bits in the IP address (00000000).

4. Copy the significant bits four times.

5. In the first line, define the network address by placing 0s in the remaining host bits (00000000.00000000).

6. In the last line, define the directed broadcast address by placing all 1s in the host bits (00111111.11111111).

7. In the middle lines, define the first and last host ID for this subnet—00000000.00000001 and 00111111.11111110.

8. Increment the subnet bits by 1 to determine the next subnet address. Repeat Steps 4 through 8 for all subnets (01000000.00000000).

Table 8-5 shows the range of subnets and broadcast addresses that would be available with the given subnet mask.

Table 8-5   *Subnet Addresses Table*

Subnet No.	Subnet ID	Host Range	Broadcast Address
All 0s	10.0.0.0	10.0.0.1 to 10.0.63.254	10.0.63.255
1	10.0.64.0	10.0.64.1 to 10.0.127.254	10.0.127.255
2	10.0.128.0	10.0.128.1 to 10.0.191.254	10.0.191.255
1021	10.255.64.0	10.255.64.1 to 10.255.127.254	10.255.127.255
1022	10.255.128.0	10.255.128.1 to 10.255.191.254	10.255.191.255
All 1s	10.255.192.0	10.255.192.1 to 10.255.255.254	10.255.255.255

Note   There are many shortcuts to subnetting that can be implemented for faster calculations in the exam. To see a popular shortcut method, be sure to watch the videos in the Additional Resources section.

Implementing Variable-Length Subnet Masks

Variable-length subnet masks (VLSM) were developed to enable multiple levels of subnetworked IP addresses within a single network. This strategy can be used only when it is supported by the routing protocol in use, such as Routing Information Protocol version 2 (RIPv2), Open Shortest Path First (OSPF), and Enhanced Interior Gateway Routing Protocol (EIGRP). VLSM is a key technology on large, routed networks. Understanding its capabilities is important when planning large networks.

Introducing VLSMs

When an IP network is assigned more than one subnet mask for a given major network, it is considered a network with VLSMs, overcoming the limitation of a fixed number of fixed-size subnetworks imposed by a single subnet mask. Figure 8-19 shows the

172.16.0.0 network with four separate subnet masks.

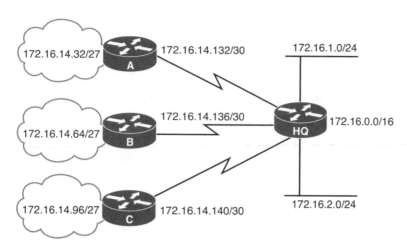

Figure 8-19   *VLSM Network*

VLSMs provide the capability to include more than one subnet mask within a network and the capability to subnet an already subnetted network address. In addition, VLSM offers the following benefits:

- **Even more efficient use of IP addresses:** Without the use of VLSMs, companies must implement a single subnet mask within an entire Class A, B, or C network number.

  For example, consider the 172.16.0.0/16 network address divided into subnets using /24 masking, and one of the subnetworks in this range, 172.16.14.0/24, further divided into smaller subnets with the /27 masking, as shown in Figure 8-19. These smaller subnets range from 172.16.14.0/27 to 172.16.14.224/27. In the figure, one of these smaller subnets, 172.16.14.128/27, is further divided with the /30 prefix, creating subnets with only two hosts to be used on the WAN links. The /30 subnets range from 172.16.14.128/30 to 172.16.14.156/30. In Figure 8-19, the WAN links used the 172.16.14.132/30, 172.16.14.136/30, and 172.16.14.140/30 subnets out of the range.

- **Greater capability to use route summarization:** VLSM allows more hierarchical levels within an addressing plan, allowing better route summarization within routing tables. For example, in Figure 8-19, subnet 172.16.14.0/24 summarizes all the addresses that are further subnets of 172.16.14.0, including those from subnet 172.16.14.0/27 and from 172.16.14.128/30.

As already discussed, with VLSMs, you can subnet an already subnetted address. Consider, for example, that you have a subnet address 172.16.32.0/20, and you need to assign addresses to a network that has ten hosts. With this subnet address, however, you have more than 4000 ($2^{12} - 2 = 4094$) host addresses, most of which will be wasted. With VLSMs, you can further subnet the address 172.16.32.0/20 to give you more network addresses and fewer hosts per network. If, for example, you subnet 172.16.32.0/20 to 172.16.32.0/26, you gain 64 (2^6) subnets, each of which could support 62 ($2^6 - 2$) hosts.

Figure 8-20 shows how subnet 172.16.32.0/20 can be divided into smaller subnets.

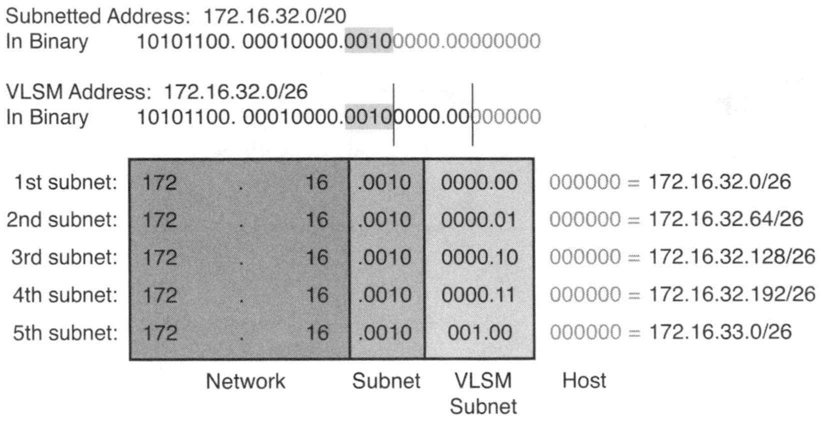

Subnetted Address: 172.16.32.0/20
In Binary   10101100. 00010000.0010 0000.00000000

VLSM Address: 172.16.32.0/26
In Binary   10101100. 00010000.0010 0000.00 000000

1st subnet:	172	. 16	.0010	0000.00	000000 = 172.16.32.0/26
2nd subnet:	172	. 16	.0010	0000.01	000000 = 172.16.32.64/26
3rd subnet:	172	. 16	.0010	0000.10	000000 = 172.16.32.128/26
4th subnet:	172	. 16	.0010	0000.11	000000 = 172.16.32.192/26
5th subnet:	172	. 16	.0010	001.00	000000 = 172.16.33.0/26

Network   Subnet   VLSM   Host
                                Subnet

Figure 8-20 *Calculating VLSM Networks*

The following procedure shows how to further subnet 172.16.32.0/20 to 172.16.32.0/26:

1. Write 172.16.32.0 in binary form.

2. Draw a vertical line between the twentieth and twenty-first bits, as shown in Figure 8-20. (/20 was the original subnet boundary.)

3. Draw a vertical line between the twenty-sixth and twenty-seventh bits, as shown in the figure. (The original /20 subnet boundary is extended 6 bits to the right, becoming /26.)

4. Calculate the 64 subnet addresses using the bits between the two vertical lines, from lowest to highest in value. Figure 8-20 shows the first five subnets available.

VLSMs are commonly used to maximize the number of possible addresses available for a network. For example, because point-to-point serial lines require only two host addresses, using a /30 subnet will not waste scarce IP addresses.

In Figure 8-21, the subnet addresses used on the Ethernets are those generated from subdividing the 172.16.32.0/20 subnet into multiple /26 subnets. The figure illustrates where the subnet addresses can be applied, depending on the number of host requirements. For example, the wide-area network (WAN) links use subnet addresses with a prefix of /30. This prefix allows only two hosts: just enough hosts for a point-to-point connection between a pair of routers.

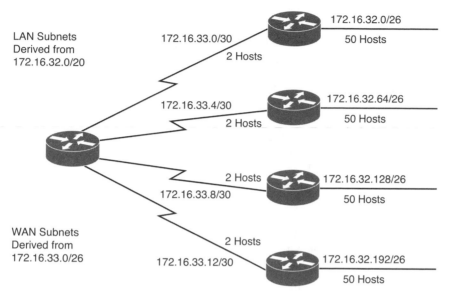

Entire Region Subnet
172.16.32.0/20

LAN Subnets
Derived from
172.16.32.0/20

WAN Subnets
Derived from
172.16.33.0/26

Figure 8-21 *VLSM Example*

To calculate the subnet addresses used on the WAN links, further subnet one of the unused /26 subnets. In this example, 172.16.33.0/26 is further subnetted with a prefix of /30. This provides four more subnet bits, and therefore 16 (2⁴) subnets for the WANs.

Note Remember that only subnets that are unused can be further subnetted. In other words, if you use any addresses from a subnet, that subnet cannot be further subnetted. In the example, four subnet numbers are used on the LANs. Another unused subnet, 172.16.33.0/26, is further subnetted for use on the WANs.

Route Summarization with VLSM

In large internetworks, hundreds or even thousands of network addresses can exist. In these environments, it is often not desirable for routers to maintain many routes in their routing table. Route summarization, also called *route aggregation* or *supernetting*, can reduce the number of routes that a router must maintain by representing a series of network numbers in a single summary address. This section describes and provides examples of route summarization, including implementation considerations.

Figure 8-22 shows that Router A can either send three routing update entries or summarize the addresses into a single network number.

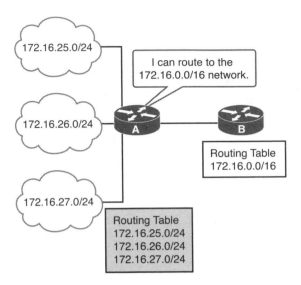

Figure 8-22   *VLSM Route Summarization*

The figure illustrates a summary route based on a full octet: 172.16.25.0/24, 172.16.26.0/24, and 172.16.27.0/24 could be summarized into 172.16.0.0/16.

Note   Router A can route to network 172.16.0.0/16, including all subnets of that network. However, if there were other subnets of 172.16.0.0 elsewhere in the network (for example, if 172.16.0.0 were discontiguous), summarizing in this way might not be valid. Discontiguous networks and summarization are discussed later in this chapter.

Another advantage to using route summarization in a large, complex network is that it can isolate topology changes from other routers. That is, if a specific link in the 172.16.27.0/24 domain were "flapping," or going up and down rapidly, the summary route would not change. Therefore, no router external to the domain would need to keep modifying its routing table because of this flapping activity. By summarizing addresses, you also reduce the amount of memory consumed by the routing protocol for table entries.

Route summarization is most effective within a subnetted environment when the network addresses are in contiguous blocks in powers of 2. For example, 4, 16, or 512 addresses can be represented by a single routing entry because summary masks are binary masks—just like subnet masks—so summarization must take place on binary boundaries (powers of 2).

Routing protocols summarize or aggregate routes based on shared network numbers within the network. Classless routing protocols, such as RIPv2, OSPF, Intermediate System–to–Intermediate System (IS-IS), and EIGRP, support route summarization based on subnet addresses, including VLSM addressing. Classful routing protocols, such as RIPv1 and Interior Gateway Routing Protocol (IGRP), automatically summarize routes on the classful network boundary and do not support summarization on any other boundaries.

RFC 1518, "An Architecture for IP Address Allocation with CIDR," describes summarization in full detail.

Suppose that a router receives updates for the following routes:

- 172.16.168.0/24

- 172.16.169.0/24

- 172.16.170.0/24

- 172.16.171.0/24

- 172.16.172.0/24

- 172.16.173.0/24

- 172.16.174.0/24

- 172.16.175.0/24

To determine the summary route, the router determines the number of highest-order bits that match in all the addresses. By converting the IP addresses to the binary format, as shown in Figure 8-23, you can determine the number of common bits shared among the IP addresses.

172.16.168.0/24 =	10101100	00010000	10101	000	00000000
172.16.169.0/24 =	172 .	16 .	10101	001	. 0
172.16.170.0/24 =	172 .	16 .	10101	010	. 0
172.16.171.0/24 =	172 .	16 .	10101	011	. 0
172.16.172.0/24 =	172 .	16 .	10101	100	. 0
172.16.173.0/24 =	172 .	16 .	10101	101	. 0
172.16.174.0/24 =	172 .	16 .	10101	110	. 0
172.16.175.0/24 =	172 .	16 .	10101	111	. 0

Number of Common Bits = 21   Noncommon
Summary: 172.16.168.0/21   Bits = 11

Figure 8-23 *Summarizing Within an Octet*

In Figure 8-23, the first 21 bits are in common among the IP addresses. Therefore, the best summary route is 172.16.168.0/21. You can summarize addresses when the number of addresses is a power of 2. If the number of addresses is not a power of 2, you can divide the addresses into groups and summarize the groups separately.

To allow the router to aggregate the highest number of IP addresses into a single route summary, your IP addressing plan should be hierarchical in nature. This approach is particularly important when using VLSMs.

A VLSM design allows maximum use of IP addresses, as well as more efficient routing update communication when using hierarchical IP addressing. In Figure 8-24, for example, route summarization occurs at two levels:

- Router C summarizes two routing updates from networks 172.16.32.64/26 and 172.16.32.128/26 into a single update, 172.16.32.0/24.

- Router A receives three different routing updates but summarizes them into a single routing update before propagating it to the corporate network.

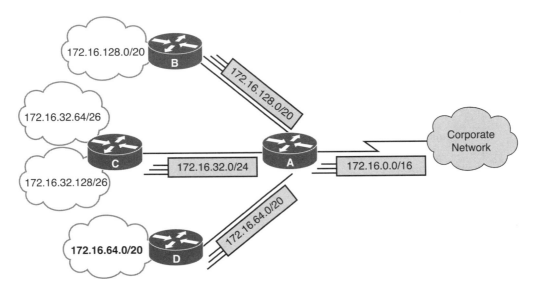

Figure 8-24   *Summarizing Addresses in a VLSM-Designed Network*

Route summarization reduces memory use on routers and routing protocol network traffic. Requirements for summarization to work correctly are as follows:

- Multiple IP addresses must share the same highest-order bits.

- Routing protocols must base their routing decisions on a 32-bit IP address and a prefix length that can be up to 32 bits.

- Routing protocols must carry the prefix length (subnet mask) with the 32-bit IP address.

Cisco routers manage route summarization in two ways:

- **Sending route summaries:** Routing protocols, such as RIP and EIGRP, perform automatic route summarization across network boundaries. Specifically, this automatic summarization occurs for those routes whose classful network address differs from the major network address of the interface to which the advertisement is being sent. For OSPF and IS-IS, you must configure manual summarization. For EIGRP and RIPv2, you can disable automatic route summarization and configure manual summarization. Whether routing summarization is automatic or not depends on the routing protocol.

It is recommended that you review the documentation for your specific routing protocols. Route summarization is not always a solution. You would not use route summarization if you needed to advertise all networks across a boundary, such as when you have discontiguous networks.

- **Selecting routes from route summaries:** If more than one entry in the routing table matches a particular destination, the longest prefix match in the routing table is used. Several routes might match one destination, but the longest matching prefix is used.

For example, if a routing table has different paths to 192.16.0.0/16 and to 192.16.5.0/24, packets addressed to 192.16.5.99 would be routed through the 192.16.5.0/24 path because that address has the longest match with the destination address.

Classful routing protocols summarize automatically at network boundaries. This behavior, which cannot be changed with RIPv1 and IGRP, has important results, as follows:

- Subnets are not advertised to a different major network.

- Discontiguous subnets are not visible to each other.

In Figure 8-25, RIPv1 does not advertise the 172.16.5.0 255.255.255.0 and 172.16.6.0 255.255.255.0 subnets because RIPv1 cannot advertise subnets; both Router A and Router B advertise 172.16.0.0. This leads to confusion when routing across network 192.168.14.0. In this example, Router C receives routes about 172.16.0.0 from two different directions, so it cannot make a correct routing decision.

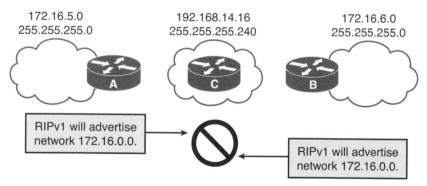

Figure 8-25 *Classful Summarization in Discontiguous Networks*

You can resolve this situation by using RIP-2, OSPF, IS-IS, or EIGRP and not using summarization because the subnet routes would be advertised with their actual subnet masks.

Note   Cisco IOS Software also provides an IP unnumbered feature that permits discontiguous subnets to be separated by an unnumbered link.

Chapter Summary

This chapter examined IP addresses and subnetting in great detail. It also examined the concept of variable-length subnet masking and route summarization for addressing modern networks in the most efficient manner possible.

Additional Resources

- CCENT Subnetting Part 1 of 2 Video, AJS Networking: http://ajsnetworking.com/subnet1

- CCENT Subnetting Part 2 of 2 Video, AJS Networking: http://ajsnetworking.com/subnet2

- IP Subnet Calculator: www.subnet-calculator.com

Review Questions

Use the questions here to review what you learned in this chapter. The correct answers and solutions are found in Appendix A, "Answers to Chapter Review Questions."

1. The decimal number 10 converts to the binary number _____.

    a. 10

    b. 1010

    c. 110

    d. 1000

2. 2 to the fifth power is _____.

    a. 2 * 5

    b. 128

    c. 2 multiplied by itself 5 times

    d. None of these answers are correct.

3. The decimal number 205 converted into a binary number is _____.

    a. 11011101

    b. 11001101

    c. 110001019

    d. 11000101

4. What is the decimal equivalent of the binary number 11000111?

   a. 218

   b. 199

   c. 179

   d. 208

5. What is the practical minimum number of bits that can be borrowed to form a subnet?

   a. 1

   b. 2

   c. 3

   d. 4

6. Using 6 subnet bits, how many usable subnets are created?

   a. 58

   b. 62

   c. 64

   d. 128

7. How many host addresses can be used in a Class C network?

   a. 253

   b. 254

   c. 255

   d. 256

   e. Discards the packet

8. Which part of the IP address 172.17.128.47 does the subnet mask 255.255.0.0 tell the router to look for regarding the network portion?

   a. 172.17.128.47

   b. 172.17.128

   c. 172.17

   d. 10.172.47

9. What is the last usable host address on the third subnet for the following address and mask combination: 192.168.1.0 255.255.255.248?

   a. 192.168.1.24

   b. 192.168.1.23

   c. 192.168.1.25

   d. 192.168.1.22

   e. 192.168.1.16

   f. 192.168.1.14

10. Which of the following is an accurate description of variable-length subnet masking?

   a. Taking an unused subnet and further subnetting it

   b. Taking the last used subnet and further subnetting it

   c. Subnetting using only major classful network addresses

   d. None of these answers are correct.

Production Network Simulation Question 8-1

You had a peer configure the IP addressing for your subnet, and several systems are unable to communicate. You check his documentation for your PC and he indicates the following:

IP Address: 192.168.1.73

Subnet Address: 255.255.255.240

You need to reconfigure the addressing for your subnet. Calculate the subnet address, the first usable host address on the subnet, the last usable host address on the subnet, and finally, the broadcast address for the subnet. Because you do not have an Internet connection and you are not at your PC, make this calculation using only pencil and paper.

Chapter 9

The TCP/IP Transport Layer

This chapter includes the following sections:

- Chapter Objectives
- Understanding TCP/IP's Transport Layer
- Chapter Summary
- Additional Resources
- Review Questions
- Production Network Simulation Questions 9-1 and 9-2

Data networks and the Internet provide seamless and reliable communication between people (locally and around the globe). Applications such as email, web browsers, and instant messaging allow people to use computers and networks to send messages and find information. Data from applications is packaged, transported, and delivered to the appropriate server or application on the destination device. The processes that are described in the TCP/IP transport layer accept data from the application layer and prepare it for addressing at the Internet layer. The transport layer is responsible for the overall end-to-end transfer of application data. The transport layer also encompasses functions to enable multiple applications to communicate over the network at the same time on a single device. This layer uses error-processing mechanisms (if required) to ensure that all the data is received reliably and in order by the correct application.

Chapter Objectives

Upon completing this chapter, you will be able to describe the transport layer of the OSI and TCP/IP models. These abilities include meeting these objectives:

- Explain the purpose and major functions of the TCP/IP transport layer
- Contrast connection-oriented transport with connectionless transport

- Explain the basic difference between TCP and UDP

- List the characteristics of UDP

- List the characteristics of TCP

- List the common applications that are provided by TCP/IP

Understanding TCP/IP's Transport Layer

When computers communicate with one another, certain rules, or protocols, are required to allow them to transmit and receive data in an orderly fashion. Throughout the world, the most widely adopted protocol suite is TCP/IP. Understanding how TCP/IP functions is important for a larger understanding of how data is transmitted in network environments.

The way in which IP delivers a packet of data across a network is a fundamental concept in the TCP/IP architecture used in large networks. Understanding how data is transmitted through IP is central to understanding how the TCP/IP suite of protocols functions overall. This, in turn, adds to an understanding of how data that is communicated across networks can be prioritized, restricted, secured, optimized, and maintained. This section describes the sequence of steps in IP packet delivery and the concepts and structures involved, such as packets, datagrams, and protocol fields, to provide a view of how data is transmitted over large networks.

For the Internet and internal networks to function correctly, data must be delivered reliably. You can ensure reliable delivery of data through development of the application and by using the services provided by the network protocol. In the Open Systems Interconnection (OSI) reference model, the transport layer manages the process of reliable data delivery. The transport layer hides details of any network-dependent information from the higher layers by providing transparent data transfer. The User Datagram Protocol (UDP) and TCP operate between the transport layer and the application layer. Learning how UDP and TCP function between the network layer and the application layer provides a more complete understanding of how data is transmitted in a TCP/IP networking environment. This section describes the function of the transport layer and how UDP and TCP operate.

The Transport Layer

Residing between the application and network layers, the transport layer, Layer 4, is in the core of the TCP/IP layered network architecture. The transport layer has the critical role of providing communication services directly to the application processes running on different hosts. Learning how the transport layer functions provides an understanding of how data is transmitted in a TCP/IP networking environment.

The transport layer protocol places a header on data that is received from the application layer. The purpose of this protocol is to identify the application from which the data was received and create segments to be passed down to the Internet layer. Some transport layer protocols also perform two additional functions: flow control (provided by sliding windows) and reliability (provided by sequence numbers and acknowledgments). Flow control is a mechanism that enables the communicating hosts to negotiate how much data is transmitted each time. Reliability provides a mechanism for guaranteeing the delivery of each packet.

Two protocols provided at the transport layer that we must be aware of are as follows:

- **TCP:** A connection-oriented, reliable protocol. In a connection-oriented environment, a connection is established between both ends before transfer of information can begin. TCP is responsible for breaking messages into segments, reassembling them at the destination station, resending anything that is not received, and reassembling messages from the segments. TCP supplies a virtual circuit between end-user applications.

- **UDP:** A connectionless and unacknowledged protocol. Although UDP is responsible for transmitting messages, no checking for segment delivery is provided at this layer. UDP depends on upper-layer protocols for reliability.

When devices communicate with one another, they exchange a series of messages. To understand and act on these messages, devices must agree on the format and the order of the messages exchanged, as well as the actions taken on the transmission or receipt of a message.

An example of a how a protocol can be used to provide this functionality is a conversation exchange between a student and a teacher in a classroom:

1. The teacher is lecturing on a particular subject. The teacher stops to ask, "Are there any questions?" This question is a broadcast message to all students.

2. You raise your hand. This action is an implicit message back to the teacher.

3. The teacher responds with "Yes, what is your question?" Here, the teacher has acknowledged your message and signals you to send your next message.

4. You ask your question. You transmit your message to the teacher.

5. The teacher hears your question and answers it. The teacher receives your message and transmits a reply back to you.

6. You nod to the teacher that you understand the answer. You acknowledge receipt of the message from the teacher.

7. The teacher asks if everything is all clear.

The transmission and receipt of messages and a set of conventional actions taken when sending and receiving these messages are at the heart of this question-and-answer protocol.

TCP provides transparent transfer of data between end systems using the services of the network layer below to move packets between the two communicating systems. TCP is a transport layer protocol. IP is a network layer protocol.

Similar to the OSI reference model, TCP/IP separates a full network protocol suite into a number of tasks. Each layer corresponds to a different facet of communication. Conceptually, you can envision TCP/IP as a protocol stack.

The services provided by TCP run in the host computers at either end of a connection, not in the network. Therefore, TCP is a protocol for managing end-to-end connections. Because end-to-end connections can exist across a series of point-to-point connections, these end-to-end connections are called *virtual circuits*. The characteristics of TCP are as follows:

- **Connection-oriented:** Two computers set up a connection to exchange data. The end systems synchronize with one another to manage packet flows and adapt to congestion in the network.

- **Full-duplex operation:** A TCP connection is a pair of virtual circuits, one in each direction. Only the two synchronized end systems can use the connection.

- **Error checking:** A checksum technique verifies that packets are not corrupted.

- **Sequencing:** Packets are numbered so that the destination can reorder packets and determine whether a packet is missing.

- **Acknowledgments:** Upon receipt of one or more packets, the receiver returns an acknowledgment to the sender indicating that it received the packets. If packets are not acknowledged, the sender can retransmit the packets or terminate the connection if the sender thinks the receiver is no longer on the connection.

- **Flow control:** If the sender is overflowing the buffer of the receiver by transmitting too quickly, the receiver drops packets. Failed acknowledgments alert the sender to slow down or stop sending. The receiver can also reduce the flow to slow the sender down.

- **Packet recovery services:** The receiver can request retransmission of a packet. If packet receipt is not acknowledged, the sender resends the packets.

TCP is a reliable transport layer protocol. Reliable data delivery services are critical for applications such as file transfers, database services, transaction processing, and other mission-critical applications in which delivery of every packet must be guaranteed.

An analogy to TCP protocol services would be sending certified mail through the postal service. For example, someone who lives in Lexington, Kentucky, wants to send this book to a friend in New York City, New York, but for some reason, the postal service handles only letters. The sender could rip the pages out and put each one in a separate envelope. To ensure that the receiver reassembles the book correctly, the sender numbers each envelope. Then, the sender addresses the envelopes and sends the first envelope by certified mail. The postal service delivers the first envelope by any truck and any route. Upon delivery of that envelope, the carrier must get a signature from the receiver and return that certificate of delivery to the sender.

The sender mails several envelopes on the same day. The postal service again delivers each envelope by any truck using any route. The sender returns to the post office each day, sending several envelopes each requiring a return receipt. The receiver signs a separate receipt for each envelope in the batch as they are received. If one envelope is lost in transit, the sender would not receive a certificate of delivery for that numbered envelope. The sender might have already sent the pages that follow the missing one, but would still be able to resend the missing page. After receiving all the envelopes, the receiver puts the pages in the right order and pastes them back together to make the book. TCP provides these levels of services.

UDP is another transport layer protocol that was added to the TCP/IP protocol suite. This transport layer protocol uses a smaller header and does not provide the reliability available with TCP.

The early IP suite consisted only of TCP and IP, although IP was not differentiated as a separate service. However, some end-user applications needed timeliness rather than accuracy. In other words, speed was more important than packet recovery. In real-time voice or video transfers, a few lost packets are tolerable. Recovering packets creates excessive overhead that reduces performance.

To accommodate this type of traffic, TCP architects redesigned the protocol suite to include UDP. The basic addressing and packet-forwarding service in the network layer was IP. TCP and UDP are in the transport layer on top of IP, and both use IP services.

UDP offers only minimal, nonguaranteed transport services and gives applications direct access to the IP layer. UDP is used by applications that do not require the level of service of TCP or that want to use communications services such as multicast or broadcast delivery, not available from TCP.

An analogy of the UDP protocol services would be using the postal service to send fliers notifying all your neighbors of your garage sale. In this example, you make a flier advertising the day, time, and location of your garage sale. You address each flier with the specific name and address of each neighbor within a two-mile radius of your house. The postal service delivers each flier by any truck and any route. However, it is not important if a flier is lost in transit or if a neighbor acknowledges receipt of the flier.

TCP/IP Applications

In addition to including the IP, TCP, and UDP protocols, the TCP/IP protocol suite also includes applications that support other services such as file transfer, email, and remote login. Some of the applications that TCP/IP supports include the following:

- **FTP:** FTP is a reliable, connection-oriented service that uses TCP to transfer files between systems that support FTP. FTP supports bidirectional binary and ASCII file transfers.

- **TFTP:** TFTP is an application that uses UDP. Routers use TFTP to transfer configuration files and Cisco IOS images and to transfer files between systems that support TFTP.

- **Terminal Emulation (Telnet):** Telnet provides the capability to remotely access another computer. Telnet enables a user to log on to a remote host and execute commands. Telnet relies upon TCP.

- **Email (SMTP):** Simple Mail Transfer Protocol allows users to send and receive messages to email applications throughout the internetwork. As you might guess, SMTP uses the reliable TCP protocol.

Transport Layer Functionality

The transport layer hides details of any network-dependent information from the higher layers by providing transparent data transfer. Learning how the TCP/IP transport layer and the TCP and UDP protocols function provides a more complete understanding of how data is transmitted with these protocols in a TCP/IP networking environment.

Transport services enable users to segment and reassemble several upper-layer applications onto the same transport layer data stream. This transport layer data stream provides end-to-end transport services. The transport layer data stream constitutes a logical connection between the endpoints of the internetwork, the originating or sending host and the destination or receiving host.

A user of a reliable transport layer service must establish a connection-oriented session with its peer system. For reliable data transfer to begin, both the sending and the receiving applications inform their respective operating systems that a connection is to be initiated, as shown in Figure 9-1.

One machine initiates a connection that must be accepted by the other. Protocol software modules in the two operating systems communicate by sending messages across the network to verify that the transfer is authorized and that both sides are ready.

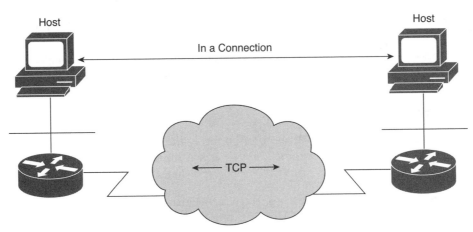

Figure 9-1 *Connection-Oriented Protocol*

After successful synchronization has occurred, the two end systems have established a connection, and data transfer can begin. During transfer, the two machines continue to verify that the connection is still valid.

Encapsulation is the process by which data is prepared for transmission in a TCP/IP network environment. This section describes the encapsulation of data in the TCP/IP stack.

The data container looks different at each layer, and at each layer the container goes by a different name, as shown in Figure 9-2.

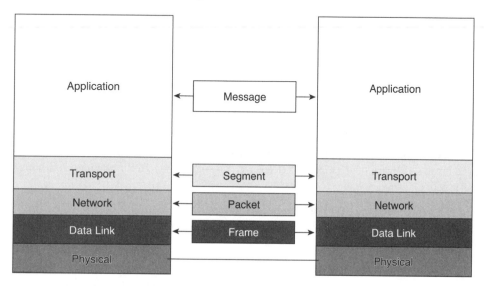

Figure 9-2 *Protocol Data Unit (PDU) Names*

The names for the data containers created at each layer are as follows:

- **Message:** The data container created at the application layer is called a *message*.

- **Segment or datagram:** The data container created at the transport layer, which encapsulates the application layer message, is called a *segment* if it comes from the transport layer's TCP protocol. If the data container comes from the transport layer's UDP protocol, it is called a *datagram*. Both TCP and UDP rely upon addressing called port numbers to carry out their functions.

- **Packet:** The data container at the network layer, which encapsulates the transport layer segment, is called a *packet*. Remember, the packet contains IP addressing to allow routing to function.

- **Frame:** The data container at the data link layer, which encapsulates the packet, is called a *frame*. This frame is then turned into a bit stream at the physical layer. Remember, the frame contains layer 2 addressing. In Ethernet networks, this layer 2 addressing is MAC addresses.

A segment or packet is the unit of end-to-end transmission containing a transport header and the data and header from the applications and protocols above in the OSI model. In general, in discussion about transmitting information from one node to another, the term *packet* is used loosely to refer to as a piece of data. However, this book refers to data formed in the transport layer as a segment, data at the network layer as a datagram or packet, and data at the link layer as a frame.

To provide communications between the segments, each protocol uses a particular header, as discussed in the next section.

TCP/UDP Header Format

TCP is known as a connection-oriented protocol because the end stations are aware of each other and are constantly communicating about the connection. A classic nontechnical example of connection-oriented communication is a telephone conversation between two people. First, a protocol lets the participants know that they have connected and can begin communicating. This protocol is analogous to an initial conversation of "Hello."

UDP is known as a connectionless protocol. An example of a connectionless conversation is the normal delivery of the U.S. postal service. You place the letter in the mail and hope that it gets delivered.

Figure 9-3 illustrates the TCP segment header format, the field definitions of which are described in Table 9-1. These fields provide the communication between end stations to control the conversation.

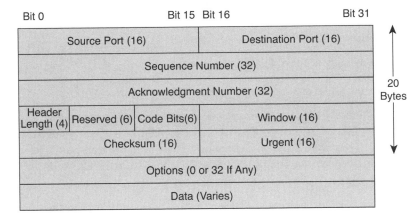

Figure 9-3   *TCP Header Fields*

Table 9-1 *TCP Header Field Descriptions*

TCP Header Field Description		Number of Bits
Source Port	Number of the calling port	16
Destination Port	Number of the called port	16
Sequence Number	Number used to ensure correct sequencing of the arriving data	32
Acknowledgment Number	Next expected TCP octet	32
Header Length	Number of 32-bit words in the header	4
Reserved	Set to zero	6
Code Bits	Control functions such as setup and termination of a session	6
Window	Number of octets that the device is willing to accept	16
Checksum	Calculated checksum of the header and data fields	16
Urgent	Indicates the end of the urgent data	16
Options	One currently defined: maximum TCP segment size	0 or 32, if any
Data	Upper-layer protocol data	Varies

The TCP header is 20 bytes. Transporting multiple packets with small data fields results in less efficient use of available bandwidth than transporting the same amount of data with fewer, larger packets. This situation is like placing several small objects into several boxes, which could hold more than one object, and shipping each box individually instead of filling one box completely with all the objects and sending only that box to deliver all the objects.

Figure 9-4 shows the UDP header fields.

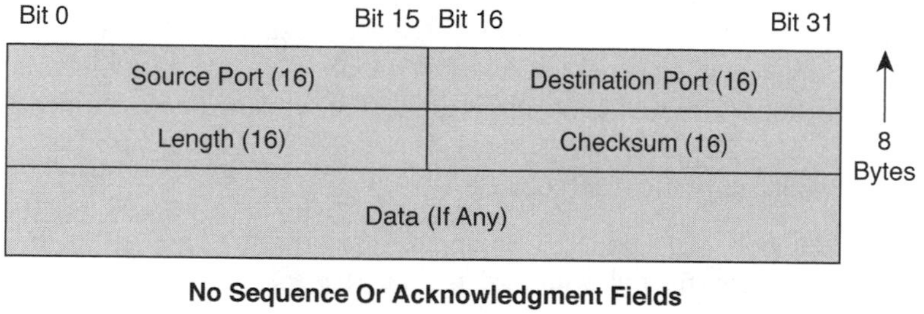

No Sequence Or Acknowledgment Fields

Figure 9-4 *UDP Header Fields*

The field definitions of the UDP header are described in Table 9-2. The UDP header length is always 64 bits.

Table 9-2   *UDP Header Field Descriptions*

UDP Header Field	Description	Number of Bits
Source Port	Number of the calling port	16
Destination Port	Number of the called port	16
Length	Length of the UDP header and UDP data	16
Checksum	Calculated checksum of the header and data fields	16
Data	Upper-layer protocol data	Varies

Protocols that use UDP include TFTP, SNMP, Network File System (NFS), and Domain Name System (DNS).

How TCP and UDP Use Port Numbers

Both TCP and UDP use port numbers to pass information to the upper layers. Port numbers keep track of different conversations crossing the network at the same time. Figure 9-5 defines some of the port numbers as used by TCP and UDP.

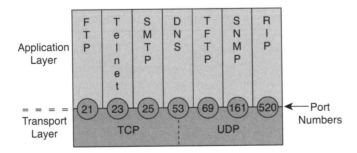

Figure 9-5   *Port Number Example*

Application software developers agree to use well-known port numbers that are controlled by the Internet Assigned Numbers Authority (IANA). For example, any conversation bound for the FTP application uses the standard port number 21. Conversations that do not involve an application with a well-known port number are assigned port numbers randomly chosen from within a specific range instead. These port numbers are used as source and destination addresses in the TCP segment.

Some ports are reserved in both TCP and UDP, but applications might not be written to support them. Port numbers have the following assigned ranges:

- Numbers below 1024 are considered well-known or assigned ports.

- Numbers 1024 and above are dynamically assigned ports.

- Registered ports are those registered for vendor-specific applications. Most are above 1024.

Note   Some applications, such as DNS, use both transport layer protocols. DNS uses UDP for name resolution and TCP for server zone transfers. Perhaps the most famous well-known port assignment is www at TCP port 80.

Figure 9-6 shows how well-known port numbers are used by hosts to connect to the application on the end station. It also illustrates the selection of a source port so that the end station knows how to communicate with the client application.

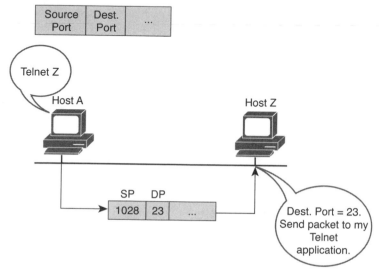

Figure 9-6   *Using Port Numbers*

RFC 1700, "Assigned Numbers," defines all the well-known port numbers for TCP/IP. For a listing of current port numbers, refer to the IANA website at www.iana.org.

End systems use port numbers to select the proper application. Originating source port numbers are dynamically assigned by the source host, some number greater than 1023.

Establishing a TCP Connection: The Three-Way Handshake

TCP is connection oriented, so it requires connection establishment before data transfer begins. For a connection to be established or initialized, the two hosts must synchronize on each other's initial sequence numbers (ISN). Synchronization is done in an exchange of connection-establishing segments carrying a control bit called SYN (for synchronize) and the initial sequence numbers. As shorthand, segments carrying the SYN bit are also called *SYNs*. Hence, the solution requires a suitable mechanism for picking an initial sequence number and a slightly involved handshake to exchange the ISN.

The synchronization requires each side to send its own initial sequence number and to receive a confirmation of its successful transmission within the acknowledgment (ACK) from the other side. Here is the sequence of events:

1. **Host A to Host B SYN:** My sequence number is 100, ACK number is 0, and ACK bit is not set. SYN bit is set.

2. **Host B to Host A SYN, ACK:** I expect to see 101 next, my sequence number is 300, and ACK bit is set. Host B to Host A SYN bit is set.

3. **Host A to Host B ACK:** I expect to see 301 next, my sequence number is 101, and ACK bit is set. SYN bit is not set.

Note   The initial sequence numbers are actually large random numbers chosen by each host.

This exchange is called the *three-way handshake*, which is illustrated in Figure 9-7.

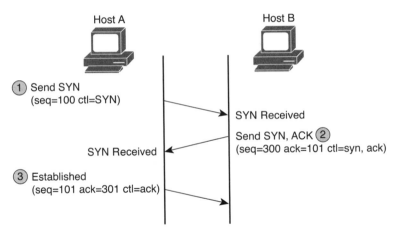

Figure 9-7   *Three-Way Handshake of TCP*

Figure 9-8 shows a data capture of the three-way handshake. Notice the sequence numbers in the three frames.

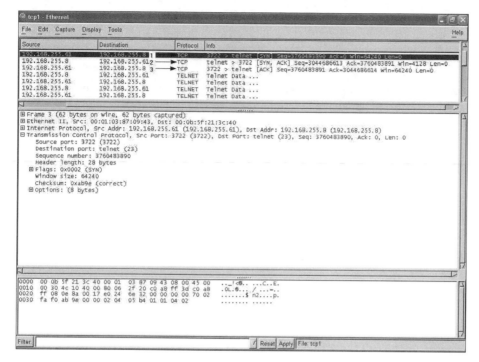

Figure 9-8   *Three-Way Handshake Captured*

A three-way handshake is necessary because sequence numbers are not tied to a global clock in the network, and IP stacks might have different mechanisms for picking the ISN. Because the receiver of the first SYN has no way of knowing whether the segment was an old delayed one, unless it remembers the last sequence number used on the connection (which is not always possible), it must ask the sender to verify this SYN. Figure 9-9 illustrates the acknowledgment process.

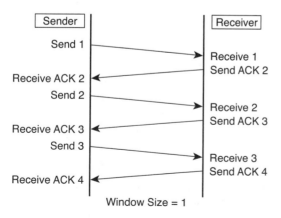

Figure 9-9   *TCP Acknowledgment Process*

The window size determines how much data, in bytes, the receiving station accepts at one time before an acknowledgment is returned. With a window size of 1 byte (as shown in Figure 9-9), each segment must be acknowledged before another segment is transmitted. This results in inefficient use of bandwidth by the hosts.

TCP provides sequencing of segments with a forward reference acknowledgment. Each datagram is numbered before transmission. At the receiving station, TCP reassembles the segments into a complete message. If a sequence number is missing in the series, that segment is retransmitted. If segments are not acknowledged within a given time period, that results in retransmission. Figure 9-10 illustrates the role that acknowledgment numbers play when datagrams are transmitted.

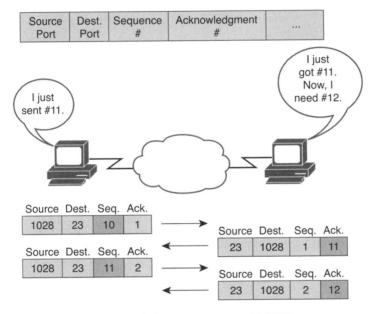

Figure 9-10 *Acknowledgments in Use with TCP*

Session Multiplexing

Session multiplexing is an activity by which a single computer, with a single IP address, is able to have multiple sessions occur simultaneously. A session is created when a source machine needs to send data to a destination machine. Most often, this involves a reply, but a reply is not mandatory. The session is created and controlled within the IP network application, which contains the functionality of OSI Layers 5 through 7.

A best-effort session is very simple. The session parameters are sent to UDP. A best-effort session sends data to the indicated IP address using the port numbers provided. Each transmission is a separate event, and no memory or association between transmissions is retained.

When using the reliable TCP service, a connection must first be established between the sender and the receiver before any data can be transmitted. TCP opens a connection and negotiates connection parameters with the destination. During data flow, TCP maintains reliable delivery of the data and, when complete, closes the connection.

For example, you enter a Uniform Resource Locator (URL) for Yahoo! into the address line in the Internet Explorer window, and the Yahoo! site corresponding to the URL appears. With the Yahoo! site open, you can open the browser again in another window and type in another URL (for example, Google). You can open another browser window and type the URL for Cisco.com, and it will open. Three sites are open using only one IP connection, because the session layer is sorting the separate requests based on the port number.

Segmentation

TCP takes data chunks from the application layers and prepares them for shipment onto the network. Each chunk is broken up into smaller segments that fit the maximum transmission unit (MTU) of the underlying network layers. UDP, being simpler, does no checking or negotiating and expects the application process to give it data that works.

Flow Control for TCP/UDP

To govern the flow of data between devices, TCP uses a flow control mechanism. The receiving TCP reports a "window" to the sending TCP. This window specifies the number of bytes, starting with the acknowledgment number, that the receiving TCP is currently prepared to receive.

TCP window sizes are variable during the lifetime of a connection. Each acknowledgment contains a window advertisement that indicates how many bytes the receiver can accept. TCP also maintains a congestion control window that is normally the same size as the receiver's window but is cut in half when a segment is lost (for example, when you have congestion). This approach permits the window to be expanded or contracted as necessary to manage buffer space and processing. A larger window size allows more data to be processed.

Note TCP window size is documented in RFC 793, "Transmission Control Protocol," and RFC 813, "Window and Acknowledgment Strategy in TCP," which you can find at www.ietf.org/rfc.html.

In Figure 9-11, the sender sends three 1-byte packets before expecting an ACK. The receiver can handle a window size of only 2 bytes (because of available memory). So, it drops packet 3, specifies 3 as the next byte to be received, and specifies a window size of 2. The sender resends packet 3 and also resends the next 1-byte packet, but still specifies its window size of 3. (For example, it can still accept three 1-byte packets.) The receiver acknowledges bytes 3 and 4 by requesting byte 5 and continuing to specify a window size of 2 bytes.

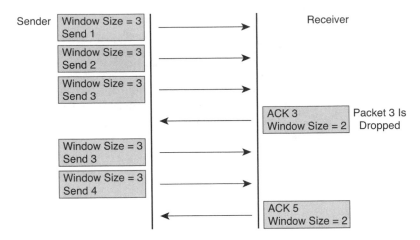

Figure 9-11 *TCP Windowing*

Many of the functions described in these sections, such as windowing and sequencing, have no meaning in UDP. Recall that UDP has no fields for sequence numbers or window sizes. Application layer protocols can provide reliability. UDP is designed for applications that provide their own error recovery process. It trades reliability for operational efficiency.

TCP, UDP, and IP and their headers are key in the communications between networks. Layer 3 devices use an internetwork protocol like TCP/IP to provide communications between remote systems.

Acknowledgment

TCP performs sequencing of segments with a forward reference acknowledgment. A forward reference acknowledgment comes from the receiving device and tells the sending device which segment the receiving device is expecting to receive next.

For the purpose of this section, the complex operation of TCP is simplified in a number of ways. Simple incremental numbers are used as the sequence numbers and acknowledgments, although in reality the sequence numbers track the number of bytes received. In a TCP simple acknowledgment, the sending computer transmits a segment, starts a timer, and waits for acknowledgment before transmitting the next segment. If the timer expires before receipt of the segment is acknowledged, the sending computer retransmits the segment and starts the timer again.

Imagine that each segment is numbered before transmission (remember that it is really the number of bytes that are tracked). At the receiving station, TCP reassembles the segments into a complete message. If a sequence number is missing in the series, that segment and all subsequent segments can be retransmitted. The steps involved with the acknowledgment process are as follows:

1. The sender and receiver agree that each segment must be acknowledged before another can be sent. This occurs during the connection setup procedure by setting the window size to 1.

2. The sender transmits segment 1 to the receiver. The sender starts a timer and waits for acknowledgment from the receiver.

3. The receiver receives segment 1 and returns ACK = 2. The receiver acknowledges the successful receipt of the previous segment by stating the expected next segment number.

4. The sender receives ACK = 2 and transmits segment 2 to the receiver. The sender starts a timer and waits for acknowledgment from the receiver.

5. The receiver receives segment 2 and returns ACK = 3. The receiver acknowledges the successful receipt of the previous segment.

6. The sender receives ACK = 3 and transmits segment 4 to the receiver. This process continues until all data is sent.

Windowing

The TCP window controls the transmission rate at a level where receiver congestion and data loss do not occur.

Fixed Windowing

In the most basic form of reliable, connection-oriented data transfers, ignoring network congestion issues, the recipient acknowledges the receipt of each data segment to ensure the integrity of the transmission. However, if the sender must wait for an acknowledgment after sending each segment, throughput is low, depending on the round-trip time (RTT) between sending the data and receiving the acknowledgment.

Most connection-oriented, reliable protocols allow more than one segment to be outstanding at a time. This approach can work because time is available after the sender completes a segment transmission and before the sender processes any acknowledgment of receipt. During this interval, the sender can transmit more data, provided that the window at the receiver is large enough to handle more than one segment at a time. The window is the number of data segments the sender is allowed to send without getting acknowledgment from the receiver, as shown in Figure 9-12.

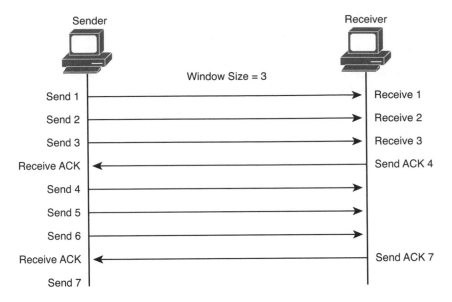

Figure 9-12   *Fixed Windowing*

Windowing enables a specified number of unacknowledged segments to be sent to the receiver, thereby reducing latency. Latency in this instance refers to the amount of time it takes for data to be sent and the acknowledgment to be returned.

Example: Throwing a Ball

Think of two people standing 50 feet apart. One person throws a football to the other, and that portion of the trip takes 3 seconds. The second person receives the football and throws a ball back (acknowledgment), and that portion of the trip takes 3 seconds. The round trip takes a total of 6 seconds. To do this process three times would take a total of 18 seconds. Now imagine that the first person has three balls and throws them one after the other. This part of the trip still takes 3 seconds. The second person throws back one ball to acknowledge the receipt of the third ball, and that portion of the trip again takes 3 seconds. The round trip takes a total of 6 seconds. (Of course, this ignores processing time and so on.)

The following steps describe the windowing process in a TCP connection:

1. The sender and receiver set an initial window size: three segments before an acknowledgment must be sent. This occurs during the connection setup procedure.

2. The sender transmits segments 1, 2, and 3 to the receiver. The sender transmits the segments, starts a timer, and waits for acknowledgment from the receiver.

3. The receiver receives segments 1, 2, and 3 and returns ACK = 4. The receiver acknowledges the successful receipt of the previous segments.

4. The sender receives ACK = 4 and transmits segments 4, 5, and 6 to the receiver. The sender transmits the segments, starts a timer, and waits for acknowledgment from the receiver.

5. The receiver receives segments 4, 5, and 6 and returns ACK = 7. The receiver acknowledges the successful receipt of the previous segments.

The numbers used in this example are simplified for ease of understanding. These numbers actually represent octets (bytes) and would be increasing in much larger numbers representing the contents of TCP segments, not the segments themselves.

TCP Sliding Windowing

TCP uses a sliding window technique to specify the number of segments, starting with the acknowledgment number that the receiver can accept.

In fixed windowing, the window size is established and does not change. In sliding windowing, the window size is negotiated at the beginning of the connection and can change dynamically during the TCP session. A sliding window results in more efficient use of bandwidth because a larger window size allows more data to be transmitted pending acknowledgment. Also, if a receiver reduces the advertised window size to 0, this effectively stops any further transmissions until a new window greater than 0 is sent.

If communications begin and the window size is 3, the sender can transmit three segments to the receiver. At that point, the sender must wait for acknowledgment from the receiver. After the receiver acknowledges receipt of the three segments, the sender can transmit three more. However, if resources at the receiver become scarce, the receiver can reduce the window size so that it does not become overwhelmed and have to drop data segments.

Each acknowledgment transmitted by the receiver contains a window advertisement that indicates the number of bytes the receiver can accept (the window size). This allows the window to be expanded or contracted as necessary to manage buffer space and processing.

TCP maintains a separate congestion window size (CWS) parameter, which is normally the same size as the window size of the receiver, but the CWS is cut in half when segments are lost. Segment loss is perceived as network congestion. TCP invokes sophisticated back-off and restart algorithms so that it does not contribute to network congestion. The following steps are taken during a sliding window operation:

1. The sender and the receiver exchange their initial window size values. In this example, the window size is three segments before an acknowledgment must be sent. This occurs during the connection setup procedure.

2. The sender transmits segments 1, 2, and 3 to the receiver. The sender waits for an acknowledgment from the receiver after sending segment 3.

3. The receiver receives segments 1 and 2, but now can handle a window size of only 2 (ACK = 3 WS = 2). The receiver's processing might slow down for many reasons, such as when the CPU is searching a database or downloading a large graphic file.

4. The sender transmits segments 3 and 4. The sender waits for an acknowledgment from the receiver after sending segment 4, when it still has two outstanding segments.

5. The receiver acknowledges receipt of segments 3 and 4, but still maintains a window size of 2 (ACK = 5, WS = 2). The receiver acknowledges the successful receipt of segments 3 and 4 by requesting transmission of segment 5.

Maximize Throughput

The congestion windowing algorithm manages the rate of sent data. This minimizes both data drop and the time spent recovering dropped data; therefore, efficiency is improved.

Global Synchronization

While the congestion windowing algorithm improves efficiency in general, it can also have an extremely negative effect on efficiency by causing global synchronization of the TCP process. Global synchronization is when all the same senders use the same algorithm and their behavior synchronizes. The senders all perceive the same congestion and all back off at the same time. Then, because the senders are all using the same algorithm, they all come back at the same time, which creates waves of congestion.

Chapter Summary

UDP is a protocol that operates at the transport layer and provides applications with access to the network layer without the overhead and reliability mechanisms of TCP. UDP is a connectionless, best-effort delivery protocol.

TCP is a protocol that operates at the transport layer and provides applications with access to the network layer. TCP is connection oriented, provides error checking, delivers data reliably, operates in full-duplex mode, and provides some data recovery functions. TCP/IP supports a number of applications, including FTP, TFTP, and Telnet.

IP uses a protocol number in the datagram header to identify which protocol to use for a particular datagram. Port numbers map Layer 4 to an application. If you use TCP as the transport layer protocol, before applications can transfer data, both sending and receiving applications inform their respective operating systems that a connection will be initiated. After synchronization has occurred, the two end systems have established a connection and data transfer can begin.

Flow control avoids the problem of a transmitting host overflowing the buffers in the receiving host and slowing network performance. TCP also provides sequencing of segments with a forward reference acknowledgement. When a single segment is sent, receipt is acknowledged, and the next segment is then sent. TCP window size decreases the transmission rate to a level at which congestion and data loss do not occur. The TCP window size allows a specified number of unacknowledged segments to be sent. A fixed window is a window with an unchanging size that can accommodate a specific flow of segments. A TCP sliding window is a window that can change size dynamically to accommodate the flow of segments.

Additional Resource

- TCP versus UDP Video, AJS Networking: http://ajsnetworking.com/tcpudp

Review Questions

Use the questions here to review what you learned in this chapter. The correct answers and solutions are found in Appendix A, "Answers to Chapter Review Questions."

1. Which of the following statements about TCP are accurate? (Choose three.)

   a. TCP operates at Layer 3 of the TCP/IP stack.

   b. TCP is a connection-oriented protocol.

   c. TCP provides no error checking.

   d. TCP packets are numbered and sequenced so that the destination can reorder packets and determine whether a packet is missing.

   e. TCP provides no recovery service.

   f. Upon receipt of one or more TCP packets, the receiver returns an acknowledgment to the sender, indicating that it received the packets.

2. When a single computer with one IP address has several websites open at once, this is called _____.

   a. windowing

   b. session multiplexing

   c. segmenting

   d. connection-oriented protocol

3. TCP is best for which of the following applications? (Choose two.)

   a. Email

   b. Voice streaming

   c. Downloading

   d. Video streaming

4. Which of the following characteristics apply to UDP? (Choose three.)

   a. Packets are treated independently.

   b. Packet delivery is guaranteed.

   c. Packet delivery is not guaranteed.

   d. Lost or corrupted packets are not resent.

5. Which of the following characteristics apply to TCP? (Choose two.)

   a. Packet delivery is not guaranteed.

   b. Lost or corrupted packets are not resent.

   c. Lost or corrupted packets are resent.

   d. A TCP segment contains a sequence number and an acknowledgment number.

6. Proprietary applications use which kind of port?

   a. Dynamically assigned ports

   b. Well-known ports

   c. Registered ports

   d. Assigned ports

7. Ports that are used only for the duration of a specific session are called _____.

   a. Dynamically assigned ports

   b. Well-known ports

   c. Registered ports

   d. Assigned ports

8. The source port in both a UDP header and a TCP header is a _____.

   a. 16-bit number of the called port

   b. 16-bit length of the header

   c. 16-bit sum of the header and data fields

   d. 16-bit number of the calling port

9. Which field in a TCP header ensures that data arrives in the correct order?

   a. Acknowledgment number

   b. Sequence number

   c. Reserved

   d. Options

10. In a TCP connection setup, the initiating device sends which message?

   a. ACK

   b. Receive SYN

   c. Send SYN

   d. Discover

Production Network Simulation Questions

Production Network Simulation Question 9-1

A peer at work is studying for the Network+ exam and has asked you to describe the difference between TCP and UDP in plain English so that he can understand it. Provide this assistance.

Production Network Simulation Question 9-2

Your work peer has graciously thanked you for your assistance with TCP and UDP. Now this peer has come to you for confirmation of which protocol is used for the network services in the list below and what port number is assigned to each. Provide this assistance.

- FTP
- TFTP
- Telnet
- SMTP
- SNMP
- RIP
- DNS
- WWW

Chapter 10

The Functions of Routing

This chapter includes the following sections:

- Chapter Objectives

- Exploring the Functions of Routing

- Chapter Summary

- Additional References

- Review Questions

- Production Network Simulation Question 10-1

Routing is the process that forwards data packets between networks or subnetworks, using a TCP/IP Internet layer device. As you probably know by now from previous chapters, this device is a router. The routing process uses network routing tables, protocols, and algorithms to determine the most efficient path for forwarding an IP packet. The routing protocols use a routing algorithm to ensure these efficient paths. Remember that routing protocols function for a routed protocol. There is only one routed protocol we need to worry about here and that is TCP/IP, either version 4, version 6, or both.

Routers gather routing information and update other routers about changes in the network. Routers greatly expand the scalability of networks by terminating Layer 2 collisions and broadcast domains. Understanding how routers function will help you to understand the broader topic of how networks are connected and how data is transmitted over networks. This chapter describes the operation of routing.

Chapter Objectives

Upon completing this chapter, you will be able to describe the functions of routing. These abilities include meeting these objectives:

- Describe the role of a router in the IP packet delivery process

- Describe the physical characteristics of a router

- Describe the functions of a router

- Describe the method that is used to determine the optimal path for forwarding IP packets

- Describe the functions of the routing table in the routing process

- List the types of routes

- Describe the function of dynamic routing protocols

Exploring the Functions of Routing

Routing is the process that forwards data packets between networks or subnetworks using a Layer 3 device: a router or gateway. The routing process uses network routing tables, protocols, and algorithms to determine the most efficient path for forwarding a given packet. Routers greatly expand the scalability of networks by terminating Layer 2 collisions and broadcast domains. Understanding how routers function will help you understand the broader topic of how networks are connected and how data is transmitted over networks. The following sections describe the operation of routers.

Routers

A *router* or *gateway* is a network device that determines the optimal path for transmitting data from one network to another. A router is a specialized computing device running programs and algorithms that aid in the optimal delivery of network traffic. Certain characteristics are common to all routers. Figure 10-1 shows a picture of various Cisco 2800 Series routers.

Figure 10-1   *Cisco 2800 Series Routers*

Routers are essential components of large networks that use TCP/IP, because routers provide the ability to accommodate growth across wide geographical areas. The following characteristics are common to all routers:

- Routers have these components, which are also found in computers and switches:

    - CPU

    - Motherboard

    - RAM

    - ROM

- Routers have network adapters to which IP addresses are assigned.

- Routers can have these types of ports:

    - **Console port:** The router uses a console port for the attachment of a terminal used for management, configuration, and control. A console port might not be found on all routers.

    - **Network port:** The router has a number of network ports, including different LAN or WAN media ports.

Routers have the following two key functions:

- **Path determination:** Routers must maintain their routing tables and ensure that other routers know about changes in the network. Routers do this by using a routing protocol to communicate the network information to other routers from a routing table on the router. It is possible to statically populate the routing tables, but statically populating does not scale and leads to problems when the network topology changes, either by design or as a result of outages.

■ **Packet forwarding:** Routers use the routing table to determine where to forward packets. Routers forward packets through a network interface toward the destination network identified by the destination IP address in the packet.

Path Determination

During the path determination part of transmitting data over a network, routers evaluate the available paths to remote destinations. This section describes how routers determine the most efficient path for forwarding packets.

There can be many paths to get from one network to another. These paths, also known as *routes*, can have many different characteristics, such as speed, latency, and media type. The purpose of a router is to communicate with other routers to learn and select the best path, as shown in Figure 10-2.

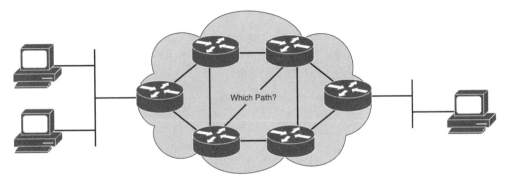

Figure 10-2 *Routers Perform Path Selection*

These routes are held in routing tables within the software of the router and are then used to determine where to send a packet based on the destination addressing. The following three types of entries in routing tables can be used to select the best path to a remote destination:

■ **Static routing:** This type of routing requires that you manually enter route information into a routing table.

■ **Dynamic routing:** This type of routing builds a routing table dynamically, using routing information that is obtained from routing protocols.

■ **Default routing:** This type of routing replaces the need to hold an explicit route to every network. The default route entry can be either statically configured or learned from a dynamic routing protocol.

The routing table can hold one or more entries per network. Different routing protocols use different metrics to measure the distance and desirability of a path to a destination network. Because it is not possible to directly select from information provided by different routing protocols, the Cisco routing process assigns a weight, known as the *administrative distance*, to each source of information. The best, most trusted source has the lowest administrative distance score and is the routing protocol that is "believed." For example, if your Cisco router learns of a remote prefix from Enhanced Interior Gateway Routing Protocol (EIGRP) (internal) and Open Shortest Path First (OSPF), it chooses the EIGRP information as more believable and trustworthy than the OSPF information by default. Why does it do this? Because Cisco wrote the EIGRP protocol.

Routing Tables

As part of the path determination process, the routing process builds a routing table that identifies known networks and knows how to reach them. Figure 10-3 shows how a routing table maintains network locations.

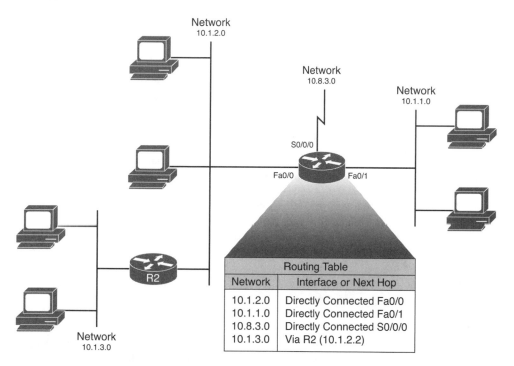

Figure 10-3 *Routing Tables*

Routing metrics vary depending on the routing protocol used. Figure 10-3 shows how routers keep a table of information used to decide how to forward packets.

Routing Table Information

The routing table consists of an ordered list of "known" network addresses—that is, those addresses that have been learned dynamically by the routing process or the statically configured, directly connected networks. Routing tables also include information on destinations and next-hop associations. These associations tell a router that a particular destination is either directly connected to the router or that it can be reached through another router, called the *next-hop router*, on the way to the final destination. When a router receives an incoming packet, it uses the destination address and searches the routing table to find the best path. If no entry can be found, the router will discard the packet after sending an Internet Control Message Protocol (ICMP) message to the source address of the packet.

In Figure 10-3, the routing table of the router in the middle shows that when it receives a packet with a destination address on the 10.1.3.0 network, it must forward the packet to R2.

Routing Update Messages

Routers communicate with each other and maintain their routing tables by transmitting routing update messages. Depending on the particular routing protocol, routing update messages can be sent periodically or only when there is a change in the network topology. The information contained in the routing update messages includes the destination networks that the router can reach and the routing metric and the next-hop address to reach each destination. By analyzing routing updates from neighboring routers, a router can build and maintain its routing table.

Static, Dynamic, Directly Connected, and Default Routes

Routers can learn about other networks through static, dynamic, directly connected, and default routes. The routing tables can be populated by the following methods:

- **Directly connected networks:** This entry comes from having router interfaces or subinterfaces (loopback) directly attached to network segments and is the most certain method of populating a routing table. If the interface fails or is administratively shut down, the entry for that network will be removed from the routing table. The administrative distance is 0 and, therefore, will preempt all other entries for that destination network, because the entry with the lowest administrative distance is the best, most trusted source.

- **Static routes:** Static routes are manually entered directly into the configuration of a router by a system administrator. The default administrative distance for a static route is 1; therefore, the static routes will be included in the routing table unless there is a direct connection to that network. Static routes can be an effective method for small, simple networks.

- **Dynamic routes:** Dynamic routes are learned by the router, and the information is responsive to changes in the network so that it is constantly being updated. There is, however, always a lag between the time that a network changes and when all the routers become aware of the change. The time delay for a router to match a network change is called *convergence time*. The shorter the convergence time, the better, and different routing protocols perform differently in this regard. Larger networks require the dynamic routing method because there are usually many addresses and constant changes, which, if not acted upon immediately, would result in loss of connectivity.

■ **Default route:** A default route is used when no explicit path to a destination is found in the routing table. The default route can be manually inserted or populated from a dynamic routing protocol. The default route is typically used in stub networks. A stub network is one in which there is only one single path into and out of the stub network section. It makes perfect sense, therefore, to route everything over this one "bridge" into and out of the network section.

Dynamic Routing Protocols

Some routing protocols use their own rules and metrics to build and update routing tables automatically. These protocols are known as dynamic routing protocols because they can adjust dynamically to changes in the network topology.

Routing Metrics

When a routing protocol updates a routing table, the primary objective of the protocol is to determine the best information to include in the table. The routing algorithm generates a number, called the *metric value*, for each path through the network. Sophisticated routing protocols can base route selection on multiple metrics, combining them in a single metric. Typically, the smaller the metric number, the better the path. Figure 10-4 shows some network criteria that can be used to establish metrics.

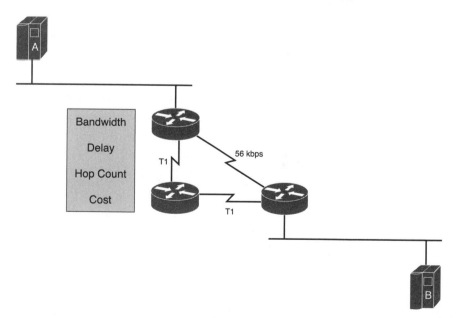

Figure 10-4 *Establishing Routing Metrics*

Metrics can be based on either a single characteristic or several characteristics of a path. The metrics that are most commonly used by routing protocols are as follows:

- **Bandwidth:** The data capacity of a link (the connection between two network devices).

- **Delay:** The length of time required to move a packet along each link from source to destination—depends on the bandwidth of intermediate links, port queues at each router, network congestion, and physical distance.

- **Hop count:** The number of routers that a packet must travel through before reaching its destination. (In Figure 10-4, the hop count from host A to host B would be 1 or 2 depending on the path.)

- **Cost:** An arbitrary value assigned by a network administrator or operating system, usually based on bandwidth, administrator preference, or other measurement.

Routing Methods

In addition to the metrics used to select paths, there are also a variety of routing protocol methods. Most routing protocols are designed around one of the following two routing methods: distance vector or link-state.

Distance vector routing: In this method, a router does not have to know the entire path to every network segment; the router only has to know the direction, or vector, in which to send the packet. The distance vector routing approach determines the direction (vector) and distance (hop count) to any network in the internetwork. Distance vector algorithms periodically (such as every 30 seconds by default for Routing Information Protocol [RIP]) send all or portions of their routing table to their adjacent neighbors. Routers running a distance vector routing protocol will send periodic updates, even if there are no changes in the network. By receiving the routing table of a neighbor, a router can verify all the known routes and make changes to its local routing table based on updated information received from the neighboring router. This process is also known as "routing by rumor," because the understanding that a router has of the network topology is based on the perspective of the routing table of a neighbor router. Figure 10-5 shows how distance vector protocols determine routes.

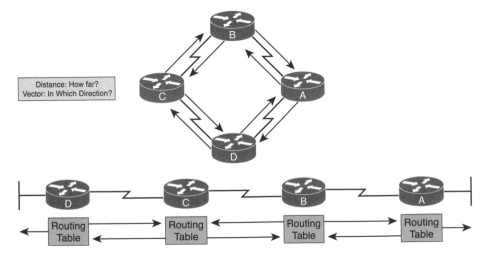

Figure 10-5 *Distance Vector Protocols*

An example of a distance vector protocol is RIP, which is a commonly used routing protocol that uses hop count as its routing metric.

Link-state routing: In this method, each router tries to build its own internal map of the network topology. Each router sends messages into the network when it first becomes active, listing the routers to which it is directly connected and providing information about whether the link to each router is active. The other routers use this information to build a map of the network topology and then use the map to choose the best path to the destination. Link-state routing protocols respond quickly to network changes, sending triggered updates when a network change has occurred and sending periodic updates (link-state refreshes) at long time intervals, such as every 30 minutes.

When a link changes state, the device that detected the change creates an update message regarding that link (route), and that update message is propagated to all routers (running the same routing protocol). Each router takes a copy of the update message, updates its routing tables, and forwards the update message to all neighboring routers. This flooding of the update message is required to ensure that all routers update their databases before creating an updated routing table that reflects the new topology. Figure 10-6 shows how link-state protocols determine routes.

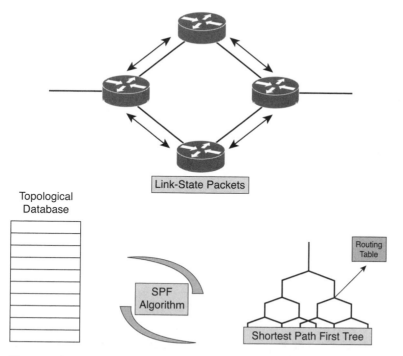

Figure 10-6 *Link-State Protocols*

Examples of link-state routing protocols are OSPF and Intermediate System–to–Intermediate System (IS-IS).

Note   Cisco developed EIGRP, which combines the best features of distance vector and link-state routing protocols. Many consider this protocol as a new category of routing protocols called hybrid protocols. There is much debate on whether EIGRP is more distance vector than it is link-state or vice versa. For our purposes, just know that EIGRP does indeed provide features of both forms.

Chapter Summary

Routers have certain components that are also found in computers and switches. These components include the CPU, motherboard, RAM, and ROM. Routers have two primary functions in the IP packet delivery process: maintaining routing tables and determining the best path to use to forward packets. Routers determine the optimal path for forwarding IP packets between networks. Routers can use different types of routes to reach the destination networks, including static, dynamic, directly connected, and default routes.

Routing tables provide an ordered list of best paths to known networks and include information such as destination, next-hop associations, and routing metrics.

Routing algorithms process the received updates and populate the routing table with the best route. Commonly used routing metrics include bandwidth, delay, hop count, and cost.

Distance vector routing protocols build and update routing tables automatically by sending all or some portion of their routing table to neighbors. The distance vector routing approach determines the direction (vector) and distance to any network in the internetwork.

Link-state routing protocols build and update routing tables automatically, running the shortest path first (SPF) algorithms against the link-state database to determine the best paths, and flood routing information about their own links to all the routers in the network.

Cisco developed EIGRP, which combines the best features of distance vector and link-state routing protocols.

Additional Reference

- Routing Video, AJS Networking: http://ajsnetworking.com/routing

Review Questions

Use the questions here to review what you learned in this chapter. The correct answers and solutions are found in Appendix A, "Answers to Chapter Review Questions."

1. Which of the following components is used by a router and a PC to store information during a session and is erased when the device is rebooted?

   a. RAM

   b. CPU

   c. Motherboard

   d. Keyboard

2. Which of the following statements best describe the functions of a router in a network? (Choose two.)

   a. Routers maintain their routing tables and ensure that other routers know of changes in the network.

   b. Routers use the routing table to determine where to forward packets.

   c. Routers strengthen the signal over large distances in a network.

   d. Routers create larger collision domains.

   e. Routers use ICMP to communicate network information from their own routing table with other routers.

3. Which of the following statements about the path determination process are accurate? (Choose three.)

   a. Routers evaluate the available paths to a destination.

   b. The routing process uses metrics and administrative distances when evaluating network paths.

   c. Dynamic routing occurs when the network administrator configures information on each router.

   d. Dynamic routing occurs when information is learned using routing information that is obtained from routing protocols.

   e. A default route holds an explicit route to every network.

4. Arrange the following steps of the routing process in the correct order.

   Step 1

   Step 2

   Step 3

   Step 4

   Step 5

   a. The router deencapsulates the frame and uses the protocol information of the frame to determine that the network layer packet will pass to the IP process.

   b. If the destination network is on a directly attached network, the router will use the ARP process to obtain the MAC address of the host and forward it to the network segment. If the network is reachable through another router, the router will use the MAC address of the next-hop router and forward the packet out the interface indicated in the routing table.

   c. The router checks the destination address in the IP header. Either the packet is destined for the router itself or it needs to be forwarded. If the packet needs to be forwarded, the router searches its routing table to determine where to send the packet.

   d. The outgoing interface process encapsulates the packet appropriately to the media and sends the packet onto the network segment.

   e. The router receives a packet on one of its interfaces.

5. Which of the following is the criterion used by a router to select the best path and varies from routing protocol to routing protocol?

   a. IP address

   b. The metric

   c. Routing table

   d. Routing protocol

6. Which of the following statements describe the function of routing tables? (Choose three.)

   a. Routing tables provide an ordered list of known network addresses.

   b. Routing tables are maintained through the transmission of MAC addresses.

   c. Routing tables contain metrics that are used to determine the desirability of the route.

   d. Routing table associations tell a router that a particular destination is either directly connected to the router or that it can be reached through another router (the next-hop router) on the way to the final destination.

   e. When a router receives an incoming packet, it uses the source address and searches the routing table to find the best path for the data from that source.

   f. Although routing protocols vary, routing metrics do not.

7. Match each of the following method of populating a routing table to its definition.

   1. This entry comes from having interfaces attached to network segments. This entry is obviously the most certain; if the interface fails or is administratively shut down, the entry for that network will be removed from the routing table.

   2. This is an optional entry that is used when no explicit path to a destination is found in the routing table. This entry can be manually inserted or be populated from a dynamic routing protocol.

   3. These routes are entered manually by a system administrator directly into the configuration of a router.

   4. These routes are learned by the router, and the information is responsive to changes in the network so that the router is constantly being updated.

   a. Static routing

   b. Dynamic routing

   c. Default route

   d. Directly connected network

8. Which of the following metrics are most commonly used by routing protocols to determine a network path? (Choose three.)

a. Hop count

b. Bandwidth

c. Delay

d. Packet length

e. Distance

f. Quantity

9. Which of the following statements accurately describe a distance vector protocol? (Choose two.)

a. An example of this protocol includes RIP.

b. Using these protocols, a router needs to know the entire path to every network segment.

c. This process is also known as "routing by rumor."

d. Routers running a distance vector routing protocol send periodic updates only when there are changes in the network.

10. Which of the following statements accurately describe a link-state routing protocol? (Choose three.)

a. The link-state database is used to calculate the paths with the highest bandwidths on the network.

b. Link-state routing protocols respond quickly to network changes.

c. In link-state routing protocols, each router periodically sends messages to the network, listing the routers to which it is directly connected and also information about whether the link to each router is active.

d. Link-state routing protocols send periodic updates (link-state refreshes) at long time intervals, approximately once every 30 minutes.

e. In link-state routing protocols, every router tries to build its own internal map of the network topology.

f. Link-state routing protocols send periodic updates even if no network changes have occurred.

Production Network Simulation Question 10-1

You need to present to the junior administrators in your consulting agency. They are struggling with the difference between metrics and administrative distances in routing architectures. Present this information to them in plain language.

Chapter 11

The Packet Delivery Process

This chapter includes the following sections:

- Chapter Objectives

- Exploring the Packet Delivery Process

- Chapter Summary

- Additional Resources

- Review Questions

- Production Network Simulation Question 11-1

Understanding the packet delivery process is a fundamental part of understanding networking devices. You must understand host-to-host communications to administer a network. This chapter describes host-to-host communications through a router by providing a graphic representation. The beginning of the chapter illustrates the role of Layer 2 and Layer 3 addresses in packet delivery. The role of ARP follows. The chapter ends with a step-by-step analysis of the packet delivery process that shows all the mechanisms in a network scenario.

Chapter Objectives

Upon completing this chapter, you will be able to describe the packet delivery process in IP-based networks. These abilities include meeting these objectives:

- Describe Layer 2 addressing

- Describe Layer 3 addressing

- Explain the role of ARP

- Describe the host-to-host packet delivery process

Exploring the Packet Delivery Process

In this book up to now, you learned much about the elements that govern host-to-host communications. You also need to understand how these elements interact. This section covers host-to-host communications by providing a graphic representation. Although much of this chapter might be review for you, remember to focus on the way in which these elements interact.

Layer 1 Devices and Their Functions

Layer 1 defines the electrical, mechanical, procedural, and functional specifications for activating, maintaining, and deactivating the physical link between end systems. Some common examples are Ethernet segments and serial links like Frame Relay and T1. Repeaters (Hubs) that provide signal amplification are also considered Layer 1 devices. Figure 11-1 shows some common Layer 1 devices.

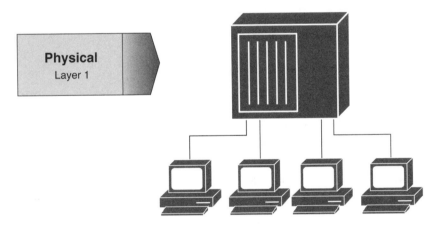

Figure 11-1   *Layer 1 Devices*

The physical interface on the network interface card (NIC) can also be considered part of Layer 1.

Layer 2 Devices and Their Functions

Layer 2 defines how data is formatted for transmission and how access to the physical media is controlled. A common example of a Layer 2 device is a network interface card. Even though these devices possess an IP address, these devices also provide an interface between the Layer 2 device and the physical media. Layer 2 devices also include switches and the devices that predate them, bridges. Figure 11-2 shows an example of Layer 2 devices.

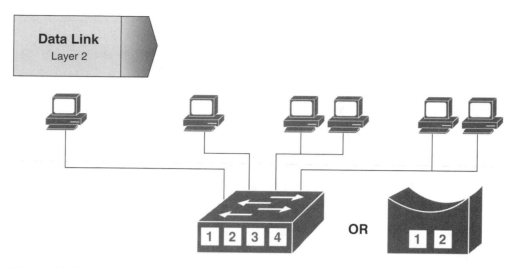

Figure 11-2   *Layer 2 Devices*

Layer 2 Addressing

Host communications require a Layer 2 address. Figure 11-3 shows an example of a MAC address for a Layer 2 Ethernet frame.

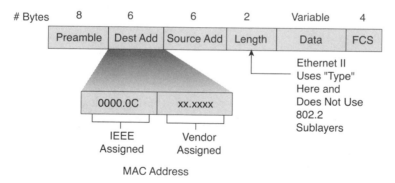

Figure 11-3   *Layer 2 MAC Address*

When host-to-host communications were first developed, several network layer protocols were called network operating systems (NOS). Early NOSs were NetWare, IP, ISO, and Banyan-Vines. It became apparent that a need for a Layer 2 address that was independent of the NOS existed, so the MAC address was created.

MAC addresses are assigned to end devices such as hosts, as well as the Layer 2 and Layer 3 devices that forward their traffic, including switches and routers. Although MAC addresses are the Layer 2 addresses found in Ethernet LANs, it is important to realize that other types of Layer 2 addresses are used in WAN environments. For example, a type of Layer 2 address that has been used for decades in WAN technologies is the Data Link Connection Identifier (DLCI) in Frame Relay environments.

Layer 3 Devices and Their Functions

The network layer provides connectivity and path selection between two host systems that might be located on geographically separated networks. In the case of a host, this is the path between the data link layer and the upper layers of the NOS. In the case of a router, it is the actual path across the network. Figure 11-4 shows Layer 3 devices.

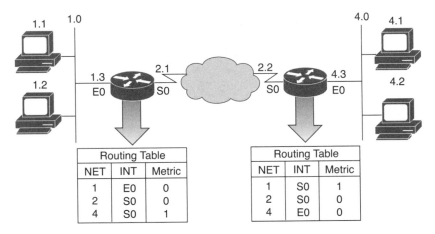

Figure 11-4 *Layer 3 Devices*

Layer 3 Addressing

Each NOS has its own Layer 3 address format. For example, the Open Systems Interconnection (OSI) reference model uses an identifying label for a service access point (SAP) called a network service access point (NSAP), while TCP/IP uses an IP address. Both concepts are roughly comparable and are used to specify devices attached to a network. This text focuses on TCP/IP. Figure 11-5 shows an example of Layer 3 addressing.

Network Layer End-Station Packet

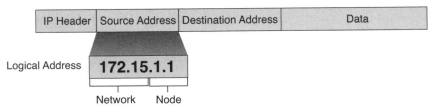

Figure 11-5 *Layer 3 Addressing*

Remember that the IP address shown in Figure 11-5 is hierarchical. This means it is divided into parts. The subnet mask (not shown) designates that the first 16 bits (in our example) represent the network portion of the host, and the last 16 bits designate a host on that network.

Mapping Layer 2 Addressing to Layer 3 Addressing

For IP communication on Ethernet-connected networks to take place, the logical (IP) address needs to be bound to the physical (MAC) address of its destination. This process is carried out by the Address Resolution Protocol (ARP). Figure 11-6 shows an example of mapping a Layer 2 address to a Layer 3 address.

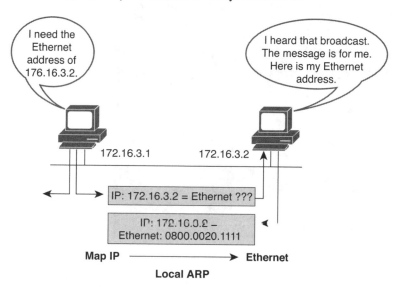

Figure 11-6 *ARP*

To send data to a destination, a host on an Ethernet network must know the physical (MAC) address of the destination. If the destination is on a remote network, the host needs to know the physical MAC address of its default gateway (router). ARP provides the essential service of mapping IP addresses to physical addresses on a network.

The term *address resolution* refers to the process of binding a network layer IP address of a remote device to its locally reachable, data link layer MAC address. The address is "resolved" when ARP broadcasts the known information (the target destination IP address and its own IP address). The broadcast is received by all devices on the Ethernet segment. When the target recognizes itself by reading the contents of the ARP request packet, it responds with the required MAC address in its ARP reply. The address resolution procedure is completed when the originator receives the reply packet (containing the required MAC address) from the target and updates the table containing all the current bindings. (This table is usually called the ARP cache or ARP table.) The ARP table maintains a correlation between each IP address and its corresponding MAC address.

The bindings in the table are kept current by a process of aging out unused entries after a period of inactivity. The default time for this aging is usually 300 seconds (5 minutes), ensuring that the table does not contain information for systems that might be switched off or that have been moved. The ARP table is covered in much more detail for you next.

ARP Table

The ARP table, or ARP cache, keeps a record of recent bindings of IP addresses to MAC addresses. Figure 11-7 shows an example of an ARP table.

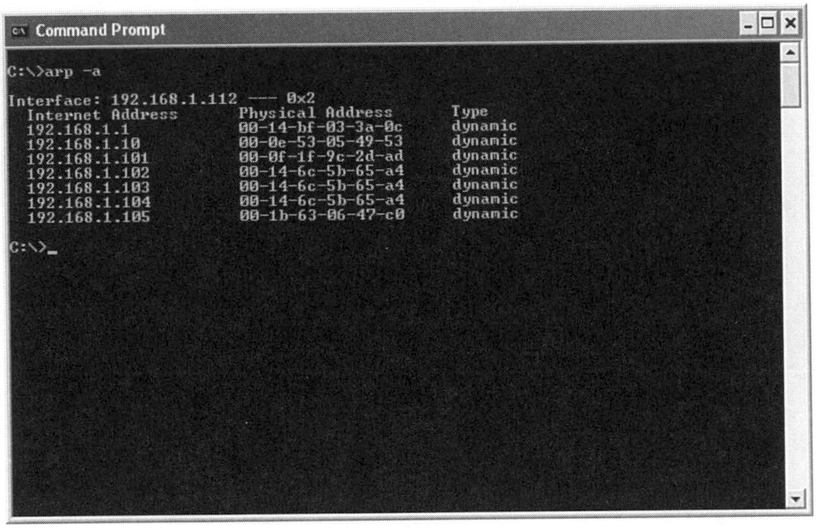

Figure 11-7   *ARP Table*

Each IP device on a network segment maintains an ARP table in its memory. This table maps the IP addresses of other devices on the network with their physical (MAC) addresses. When a host wants to transmit data to another host on the same network, it searches the ARP table to see whether an entry exists. If an entry does exist, the host uses it, but if not, ARP is used to get an entry.

The ARP table is created and maintained dynamically, adding and changing address relationships as they are used on the local host. The entries in an ARP table usually expire after a period of time; however, when the local host wants to transmit data again, the entry in the ARP table is regenerated through the ARP process.

Host-to-Host Packet Delivery

In Figure 11-8, an application on the host with a Layer 3 address of 192.168.3.1 wants to send some data to the host with a Layer 3 address of 192.168.3.2. The application wants to use a reliable connection. The application requests this service from the transport layer.

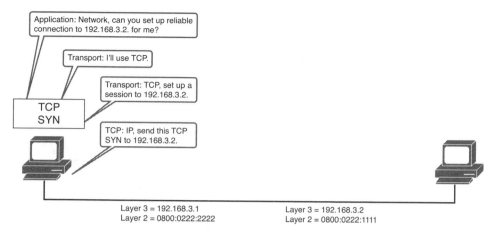

Figure 11-8   *Host-to-Host Packet Delivery*

The transport layer selects TCP to set up the session. TCP initiates the session by passing a TCP header with the SYN bit set and the destination Layer 3 address (192.168.3.2) to the IP layer.

The IP layer encapsulates the TCP's SYN in a Layer 3 packet by prepending the local Layer 3 address and the Layer 3 address that IP received from TCP. IP then passes the packet to Layer 2. Figure 11-9 shows this operation.

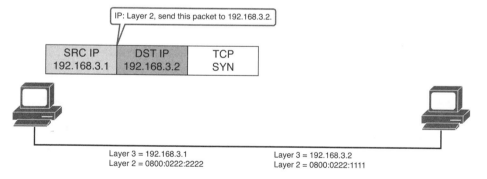

Figure 11-9   *Sending the Packet to Layer 2*

Layer 2 needs to encapsulate the Layer 3 packet into a Layer 2 frame. To do this, Layer 2 needs to map the Layer 3 destination address of the packet to its MAC address. It does this by requesting a mapping from the ARP program.

ARP checks its table. In this example, it is assumed that this host has not communicated with the other host, so you see no entry in the ARP table. This results in Layer 2 holding the packet until ARP can provide a mapping. Figure 11-10 shows this operation.

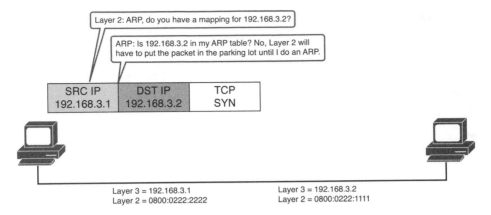

Figure 11-10 *Checking the ARP Table*

The ARP program builds an ARP request and passes it to Layer 2, telling Layer 2 to send the request to a broadcast (all Fs) address. Layer 2 encapsulates the ARP request in a Layer 2 frame using the broadcast address provided by ARP as the destination MAC address and the local MAC address as the source. Figures 11-11 and 11-12 show this operation.

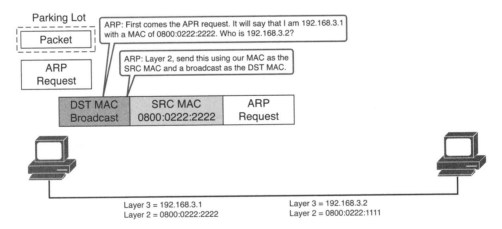

Figure 11-11 *Preparing the ARP Request*

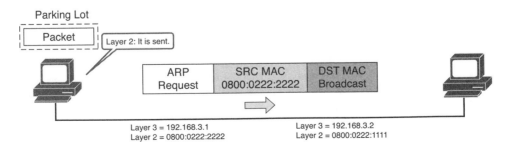

Figure 11-12 *ARP Request Sent*

When host 192.168.3.2 receives the frame, it notes the broadcast address and strips the Layer 2 encapsulation. Figure 11-13 shows this operation.

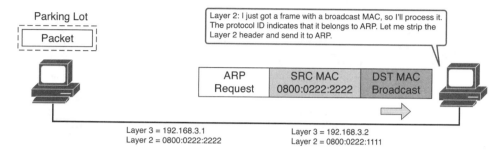

Figure 11-13   *Sending the Frame to ARP*

The remaining ARP request is passed to ARP. Figure 11-14 shows this operation.

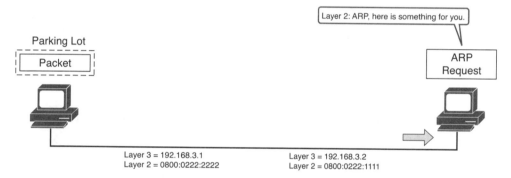

Figure 11-14   *ARP Receives the Information*

Using the information in the ARP request, ARP updates its table. Figure 11-15 shows this operation.

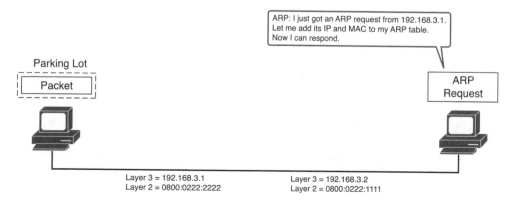

Figure 11-15   *ARP Updates Its Table*

ARP builds a response and passes it to Layer 2, telling Layer 2 to send the response to MAC address 0800:0222:2222 (host 192.168.3.1). Figure 11-16 shows this operation.

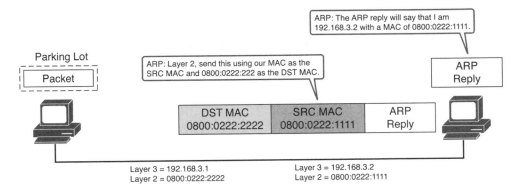

Figure 11-16 *ARP Prepares a Response*

Layer 2 encapsulates the ARP in a Layer 2 frame using the destination MAC address provided by ARP and the local source MAC address. Figure 11-17 shows this operation.

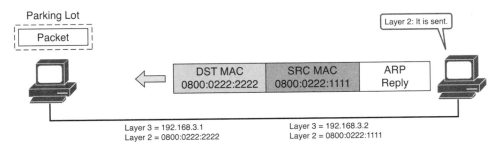

Figure 11-17 *ARP Reply Is Sent*

When host 192.168.3.1 receives the frame, it notes that the destination MAC address is the same as its own address. It strips the Layer 2 encapsulation. Figure 11-18 shows this operation.

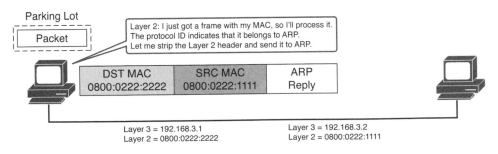

Figure 11-18 *ARP Reply Is Received*

The remaining ARP reply is passed to ARP. Figure 11-19 shows this operation.

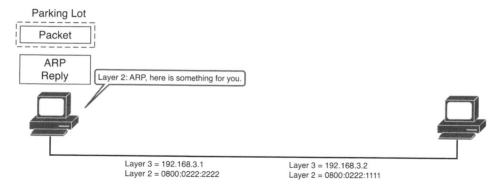

Figure 11-19 *ARP Reply Is Passed to ARP*

ARP updates its table and passes the mapping to Layer 2. Figure 11-20 shows this operation.

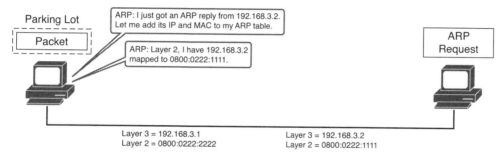

Figure 11-20 *ARP Updates the Table*

Layer 2 can now send the pending Layer 2 packet. Figure 11-21 shows this operation.

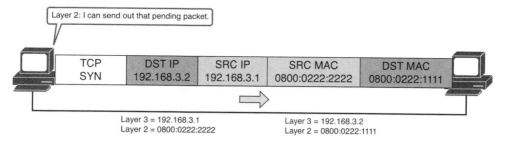

Figure 11-21 *Sending the Pending Packet*

At host 192.168.3.2, the frame is passed up the stack, where encapsulation is removed. The remaining protocol data unit (PDU) is passed to TCP. Figure 11-22 shows this operation.

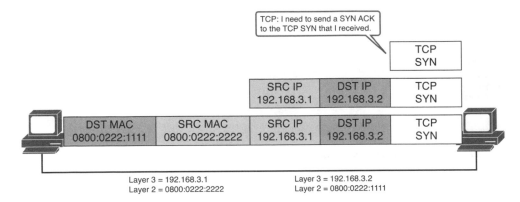

Figure 11-22   *Receiving the TCP SYN*

In response to the SYN, TCP passes a SYN ACK down the stack to be encapsulated. Figure 11-23 shows this operation.

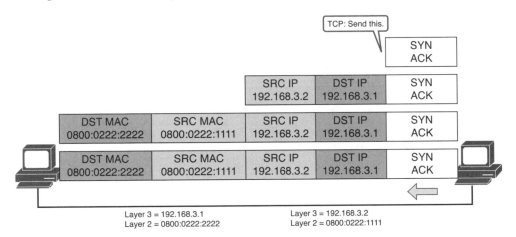

Figure 11-23   *SYN ACK Is Sent*

The sender receives the ACK from the receiver that it must respond to. This is shown in Figure 11-24.

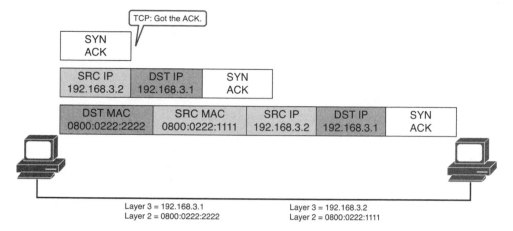

Figure 11-24 *Sender Receives the ACK*

The sender sends the ACK to the receiver that it must respond to. With the three-way handshake completed, TCP can inform the application that the session has been established. This is shown in Figure 11-25.

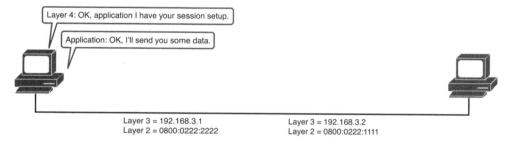

Figure 11-25 *Informing the Application Layer*

Now the application can send the data over the session, relying on TCP for error detection. Figures 11-26 through 11-28 show this operation.

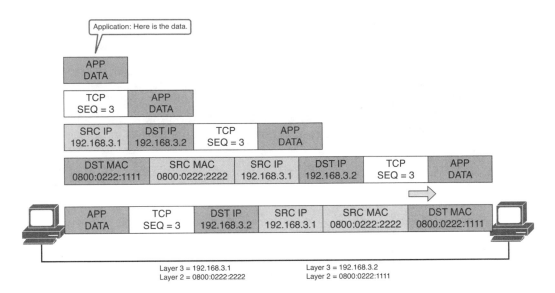

Figure 11-26 *Data Is Sent*

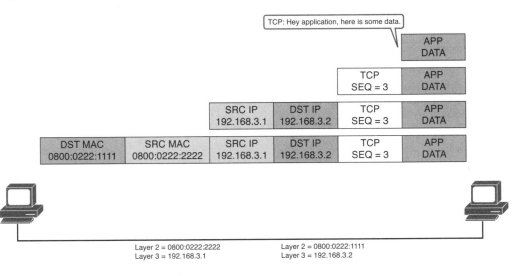

Figure 11-27 *Data Is Received*

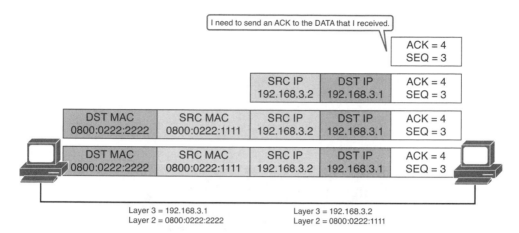

Figure 11-28   *Data Is Acknowledged*

The data exchange continues until the application stops sending data.

Function of the Default Gateway

In the host-to-host packet delivery example, the host was able to use ARP to map a destination's MAC address to the destination's IP address. However, this option is available only if the two hosts are on the same network. If the IP is not local, the gateway (router) will see this (remember, the ARP request is broadcast so that all hosts on the LAN will see the request). The router will look in its routing table, and if it has a route to the destination network, it will reply with its own MAC address. The sending host must send the data to the default gateway, which forwards the data to the destination. Figure 11-29 shows role of the default gateway in data transfers.

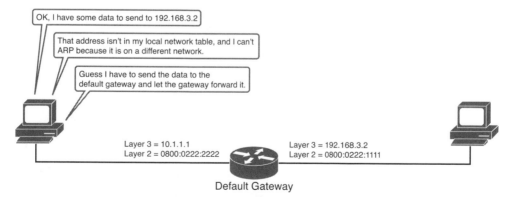

Figure 11-29   *Default Gateway*

Using Common Host Tools to Determine the Path Between Two Hosts Across a Network

Ping is a computer network tool used to test whether a particular host is reachable across an IP network. Ping works by sending Internet Control Message Protocol (ICMP) "echo request" packets to the target host and listening for ICMP "echo response" replies. Using interval timing and response rates, ping estimates the round-trip time (RTT) (generally in milliseconds) and packet-loss rate between hosts. Figure 11-30 shows the ping output from a Windows command line.

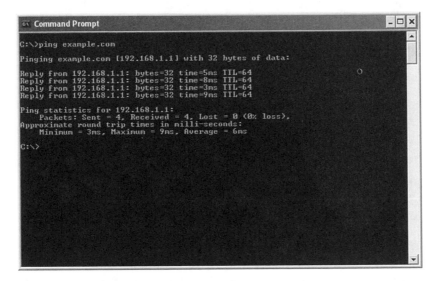

Figure 11-30   *Displaying the ARP Table*

The syntax for a Windows ping is as follows:

```
ping [-t] [-a] [-n Count] [-l Size] [-f] [-i TTL] [-v TOS] [-r Count] [-s
Count]
[{-j HostList | -k HostList}] [-w Timeout] [TargetName]
```

The syntax flags are as follows:

- **-t:** Specifies that ping continues sending echo request messages to the destination until interrupted. To interrupt and display statistics, press **Ctrl-BREAK**. To interrupt and quit ping, press **Ctrl-C**.

- **-a:** Specifies that reverse name resolution is performed on the destination IP address. If this is successful, ping displays the corresponding host name.

- **-n** *Count:* Specifies the number of echo request messages sent. The default is 4.

- **-l** *Size:* Specifies the length, in bytes, of the Data field in the echo request messages sent. The default is 32. The maximum size is 65,527.

- **-f:** Specifies that echo request messages are sent with the Don't Fragment flag in the IP header set to 1. The echo request message cannot be fragmented by routers in the path to the destination. This parameter is useful for troubleshooting path maximum transmission unit (PMTU) problems.

- **-i** *TTL:* Specifies the value of the Time-to-Live (TTL) field in the IP header for echo request messages sent. The default is the default TTL value for the host. For Windows XP hosts, this is typically 128. The maximum TTL is 255.

- **-v** *TOS:* Specifies the value of the type of service (TOS) field in the IP header for echo request messages sent. The default is 0. TOS is specified as a decimal value from 0 to 255.

- **-r** *Count:* Specifies that the Record Route option in the IP header is used to record the path taken by the echo request message and corresponding echo reply message.

  Each hop in the path uses an entry in the Record Route option. If possible, specify a *Count* that is equal to or greater than the number of hops between the source and destination. The *Count* must be a minimum of 1 and a maximum of 9.

- **-s** *Count:* Specifies that the Internet Timestamp option in the IP header is used to record the time of arrival for the echo request message and corresponding echo reply message for each hop. The *Count* must be a minimum of 1 and a maximum of 4.

- **-j** *HostList:* Specifies that the echo request messages use the Loose Source Route option in the IP header with the set of intermediate destinations specified in *HostList*. With loose source routing, successive intermediate destinations can be separated by one or multiple routers. The maximum number of addresses or names in the host list is nine. The *HostList* is a series of IP addresses (in dotted-decimal notation) separated by spaces.

- **-k** *HostList:* Specifies that the echo request messages use the Strict Source Route option in the IP header with the set of intermediate destinations specified in *HostList*. With strict source routing, the next intermediate destination must be directly reachable (it must be a neighbor on an interface of the router). The maximum number of addresses or names in the host list is nine. The *HostList* is a series of IP addresses (in dotted decimal notation) separated by spaces.

- **-w** *Timeout:* Specifies the amount of time, in milliseconds, to wait for the echo reply message that corresponds to a given echo request message to be received. If the echo reply message is not received within the timeout, the "Request timed out" error message is displayed. The default timeout is 4000 (4 seconds).

- *TargetName:* Specifies the destination, which is identified by either IP address or host name.

- **/?:** Displays help at the command prompt.

The Windows **arp** command, shown in Figure 11-31, displays and modifies entries in the ARP cache, which contains one or more tables that store IP addresses and their resolved Ethernet physical addresses. A separate table exists for each Ethernet or Token Ring network adapter installed on your computer. Used without parameters, **arp** displays help.

```
Command Prompt                                                    _ □ ×

C:\>arp -a

Interface: 192.168.1.112 --- 0x2
  Internet Address      Physical Address      Type
  192.168.1.1           00-14-bf-03-3a-0c     dynamic
  192.168.1.10          00-0e-53-05-49-53     dynamic
  192.168.1.101         00-0f-1f-9c-2d-ad     dynamic
  192.168.1.102         00-14-6c-5b-65-a4     dynamic
  192.168.1.103         00-14-6c-5b-65-a4     dynamic
  192.168.1.104         00-14-6c-5b-65-a4     dynamic
  192.168.1.105         00-1b-63-06-47-c0     dynamic

C:\>_
```

Figure 11-31   *arp command*

The syntax for the command is as follows:

```
arp [-a [InetAddr] [-N IfaceAddr]] [-g [InetAddr] [-N IfaceAddr]] [-d InetAddr
[IfaceAddr]] [-s InetAddr EtherAddr [IfaceAddr]]
```

The following are the parameters associated with the windows **arp** command:

- **-a** [*InetAddr*] [**-N** *IfaceAddr*]: Displays current ARP cache tables for all interfaces. To display the ARP cache entry for a specific IP address, use **arp -a** with the *InetAddr* parameter, where *InetAddr* is an IP address. To display the ARP cache table for a specific interface, use the **-N** *IfaceAddr* parameter, where *IfaceAddr* is the IP address assigned to the interface. The **-N** parameter is case sensitive.

- **-g** [*InetAddr*] [**-N** *IfaceAddr*]: Identical to **-a**.

- **-d** *InetAddr* [*IfaceAddr*]: Deletes an entry with a specific IP address, where *InetAddr* is the IP address. To delete an entry in a table for a specific interface, use the *IfaceAddr* parameter, where *IfaceAddr* is the IP address assigned to the interface. To delete all entries, use the asterisk (*) wildcard character in place of *InetAddr*.

- **-s** *InetAddr EtherAddr* [*IfaceAddr*]: Adds a static entry to the ARP cache that resolves the IP address *InetAddr* to the physical address *EtherAddr*. To add a static ARP cache entry to the table for a specific interface, use the *IfaceAddr* parameter, where *IfaceAddr* is an IP address assigned to the interface.

- **/?**: Displays help at the command prompt.

The TRACERT (traceroute) diagnostic utility determines the route to a destination by sending ICMP echo packets to the destination. In these packets, TRACERT uses varying IP TTL values. Because each router along the path is required to decrement the packet's TTL by at least 1 before forwarding the packet, the TTL is effectively a hop counter. When the TTL on a packet reaches zero (0), the router sends an ICMP "Time Exceeded" message back to the source computer.

TRACERT sends the first echo packet with a TTL of 1 and increments the TTL by 1 on each subsequent transmission until the destination responds or until the maximum TTL is reached. The ICMP "Time Exceeded" messages that intermediate routers send back show the route. Note, however, that some routers silently drop packets with expired TTL values, and these packets are invisible to TRACERT.

TRACERT prints out an ordered list of the intermediate routers that return ICMP "Time Exceeded" messages. Using the **-d** option with the **tracert** command instructs TRACERT not to perform a DNS lookup on each IP address so that TRACERT reports the IP address of the near-side interface of the routers.

The syntax for a Windows traceroute is as follows:

```
tracert -d -h maximum_hops -j HostList -w Timeout target_host
```

The following are the parameters associated with the Windows traceroute command:

- **-d:** Specifies to not resolve addresses to host names

- **-h** *maximum_hops:* Specifies the maximum number of hops to search for the target

- **-j** *HostList:* Specifies loose source route along the host list

- **-w** *Timeout:* Waits the number of milliseconds specified by timeout for each reply

- *target_host:* Specifies the name or IP address of the target host

Figure 11-32 demonstrates the use of TRACERT on a Windows 7 machine.

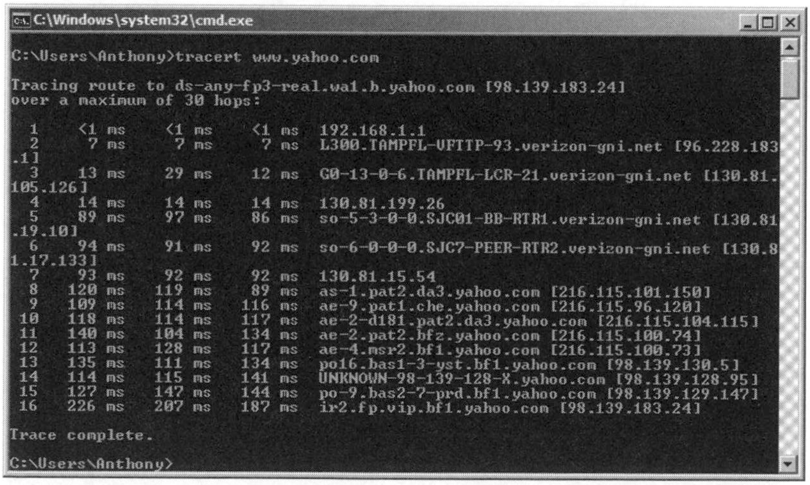

Figure 11-32 *TRACERT*

Summary

Layer 1 devices provide the connection to the physical media and its encoding. Layer 2 devices provide an interface between the Layer 2 device and the physical media. Layer 2 addresses are MAC addresses.

The network layer provides connectivity and path selection between two host systems. Layer 3 addresses provide identification of a network and a host, such as an IP address.

Before a host can send data to another host, it must know the MAC address of the other device or the default gateway. ARP is a protocol that maps IP addresses to MAC addresses. Most operating systems offer tools to view the device ARP table as well as tools like ping and traceroute to test IP connectivity.

Additional Resource

- The Packet Delivery Process Video, AJS Networking: http://ajsnetworking.com/packetdelivery

Review Questions

Use the questions here to review what you learned in this chapter. The correct answers and solutions are found in Appendix A, "Answers to Chapter Review Questions."

1. Which of the following is an example of a Layer 1 network device?

    a. Bridge

    b. Switch

    c. Router

    d. Hub

2. Which of the following are examples of a Layer 2 network device? (Choose two.)

    a. Repeater

    b. Switch

    c. Router

    d. NIC in host

3. What is an example of a Layer 2 network address?

    a. IP address

    b. MAC address

    c. IPv6 address

    d. TCP port address

4. What protocol is responsible for mapping Layer 2 addresses to Layer 3 addresses?

   a. DNS

   b. DHCP

   c. NAT

   d. ARP

5. When an ARP request is sent, what is the destination MAC address field populated with?

   a. The destination MAC of the default gateway

   b. The destination MAC of the host

   c. The multicast ARP group address

   d. The broadcast MAC address

6. When an ARP reply is sent, what is the destination MAC address field populated with?

   a. The MAC address of the host that sent the ARP request

   b. The broadcast MAC address

   c. The multicast ARP group address

   d. None of these answers are correct.

7. What is an example of a network address that is used at Layer 3?

   a. MAC address

   b. IP address

   c. TCP port address

   d. Winsocket address

8. What protocol is used by ping?

   a. DHCP

   b. DNS

   c. RIP

   d. ICMP

9. What command on a PC allows you to view the ARP cache?

   a. arp -a

   b. arp -l

   c. arp -v

   d. arp -s

10. What diagnostic tool allows you to see the network path that a packet has taken through an internetwork?

   a. traceroute

   b. ping

   c. arp

   d. debug ip packet

Production Network Simulation Question 11–1

Your supervisor has asked you for your recommendation on tools that can be used from a Windows 7 machine for troubleshooting the network. Specifically, your boss wants to know an appropriate tool for each of the situations listed below. Provide her with this information and be specific with the commands required.

1. Examine the Layer 2–to–Layer 3 name resolution cache information.

2. Display the current configuration at the command of the TCP/IP information including DNS information.

3. Confirm the reachability of the default gateway at the IP address 10.10.10.1.

4. See the various routers that a packet will pass through in route to a destination of www.cisco.com.

Chapter 12

Configuring a Cisco Router

This chapter includes the following sections:

- Chapter Objectives

- Starting a Cisco Router

- Configuring a Cisco Router

- Chapter Summary

- Additional Resources

- Review Questions

- Production Network Simulation Question 12-1

After hardware installation, when a Cisco router is turned on, it goes through its startup procedure. After the operating system is loaded, you can start configuring the router. This chapter describes basic configuration, how to configure interfaces, and how to use Cisco Discovery Protocol to discover connected neighboring devices.

Chapter Objectives

Upon completing this chapter, you will be able to describe how a router is started and the basic configurations you perform on these devices. These abilities include meeting these objectives:

- Describe router startup

- Perform initial router setup

- Configure router interfaces

- Configure a router interface IP address

- Verify the router interface configuration
- Describe the need for a network discovery protocol
- Describe Cisco Discovery Protocol
- Use the CLI to discover neighbors on a network using Cisco Discovery Protocol

Starting a Cisco Router

When you remove your shiny new Cisco router from its packaging, plug it in, and turn it on, the router goes through its startup, sees that there is no previously saved configuration, and prompts you to enter a startup configuration guide or wizard. Recognizing correct router startup is the first step in installing a Cisco router. The router must start successfully and have a valid configuration to operate on the network. This chapter describes how the router starts up and explains how to verify its initial operation.

Initial Startup of a Cisco Router

The startup of a Cisco router requires verifying the physical installation, powering up the router, and viewing the Cisco IOS Software output on the console. To start router operations, the router completes the following tasks:

- Runs the power-on self test (POST) to test the hardware
- Finds and loads the Cisco IOS Software that the router uses for its operating system
- Finds and applies the configuration statements about router-specific attributes, protocol functions, and interface addresses

When a Cisco router powers up, it performs a POST. During the POST, the router executes diagnostics to verify the basic operation of the CPU, memory, and interface circuitry.

After verifying the hardware functions, the router proceeds with software initialization, during which it finds and loads the Cisco IOS image, and then it finds and loads the configuration file, if one exists.

The following list describes the steps required for the initial startup of a Cisco router:

1. Before starting the router, verify the following:

   - All network cable connections are secure.
   - Your terminal is connected to the console port.
   - Your console terminal application, such as HyperTerminal, is selected.

2. Move the power switch to "On" or plug in the device if there is no On/Off switch.

3. Observe the boot sequence and the Cisco IOS Software output on the console.

Initial Setup of a Cisco Router

Upon boot, the Cisco router looks for a device configuration file. If it does not find one, the router executes a question-driven initial configuration routine, called "setup." Setup is a prompt-driven program that allows a minimal device configuration. After a router completes the POST and loads a Cisco IOS image, it looks for a device configuration file in its NVRAM. The NVRAM of the router is a type of memory that retains its contents even when power is turned off. If the router has a startup configuration file in NVRAM, the user-mode prompt appears after entering the console password, if one has been set.

Obviously when starting a new Cisco router, there is no configuration file. If no valid configuration file exists in NVRAM, the operating system executes a question-driven initial configuration routine, referred to as the system configuration dialog, or setup mode.

Setup mode is not intended for entering complex protocol features in the router. Use setup mode to bring up a minimal configuration. Rather than using the setup mode, you can use other various configuration modes to configure the router.

The primary purpose of the setup mode is to rapidly bring up a minimal-feature configuration for any router that cannot find its configuration from some other source. Setup mode can be entered when the router boots up without a configuration, or it can be entered at any time after the router is booted and operational, by entering the **setup** privileged EXEC mode command. Example 12-1 shows how to enter setup from the privileged EXEC mode prompt.

Example 12-1   *Entering Setup*

```
Router# setup


        --- System Configuration Dialog ---

Continue with configuration dialog? [yes/no]: yes

At any point you may enter a question mark '?' for help.
Use ctrl-c to abort configuration dialog at any prompt.
Default settings are in square brackets '[]'.


Basic management setup configures only enough connectivity
for management of the system, extended setup will ask you
to configure each interface on the system

Would you like to enter basic management setup? [yes/no]: no
```

For many of the prompts in the dialog of the **setup** command facility, default answers appear in square brackets ([ ]) following the question. Pressing **Enter** allows the use of the defaults.

When prompted with "Would you like to enter basic management setup?" the system configuration dialog can be discontinued by entering **no** at the prompt. To begin the initial configuration process, enter **yes**. Normally, you enter **no** at the "basic management setup" prompt so that extended setup can be entered to configure more specific system parameters.

Pressing **Ctrl-C** will terminate the process and start over at any time. When using the command form of setup (Router# **setup**), **Ctrl-C** returns to the privileged EXEC prompt (Router#).

If you enter **yes** at the "Would you like to enter basic management setup?" prompt, you are prompted with "First, would you like to see the current interface summary?" Enter **yes** to view the router interfaces. Example 12-2 shows the output indicating the current status of each router interface. This information includes the interface IP address and current configuration.

Example 12-2   *Current Status of Interfaces*

```
Any interface listed with OK? value "NO" does not have a valid configuration


Interface                IP-Address       OK? Method Status           Protocol
FastEthernet0/0          unassigned       NO  unset  up                  up
FastEthernet0/1          unassigned       NO  unset  up                  up
Serial0/0/0              unassigned       NO  unset  up                  up
Serial0/0/1              unassigned       NO  unset  down
```

Continuing through the setup dialog, you are prompted for global parameters. Enter the global parameters at the prompts, using the configuration values that were determined for the router.

The first global parameter sets the router host name. This host name will precede Cisco IOS prompts for all configuration modes. The default router name is shown between the square brackets as [Router].

Use the next global parameters shown to set the various passwords used on the router. Example 12-3 illustrates the default settings in brackets and shows entering global parameters.

Example 12-3   *Default Settings and Global Parameters*

```
Configuring global parameters:

  Enter host name [Router]: RouterA


The enable secret is a password used to protect access to privileged EC and
  configuration modes. This password, after entered, becomes encrypted in the
  configuration.
  Enter enable secret: Cisco1
```

```
The enable password is used when you do not specify an enable secret password,
  with some older software versions, and some boot images.
  Enter enable password: SanFran3


The virtual terminal password is used to protect access to the router over a network
  interface.
  Enter virtual terminal password: SanJose
  Configure SNMP Network Management? [no]:
```

Continuing through the setup dialog, you are prompted for additional global parameters. Enter the global parameters at the prompts, using the configuration values that were determined for your router. The example shows the prompts for routing protocols as they appear during setup.

If you enter **yes** at a prompt to indicate that you want to configure a protocol, additional subordinate prompts appear about that protocol. Example 12-4 illustrates this feature.

Example 12-4   *Additional Configuration Prompts*

```
Configure IP? [yes]:
    Configure RIP routing? [yes]: no
Configure CLNS? [no]:
  Configure bridging? [no]:
```

Continuing through the setup dialog, you are prompted for parameters for each installed interface. Use the configuration values that were determined for the interface to enter the proper parameters at the prompts. Example 12-5 illustrates the configuration of interface FastEthernet 0/0.

Example 12-5   *Configuring Interface FastEthernet 0/0*

```
Configuring interface parameters:

Do you want to configure FastEthernet0/0 interface? [yes]:
  Use the 100 Base-TX (RJ-45) connector? [yes]:
  Operate in full-duplex mode? [no]:
  Configure IP on this interface? [yes]:
    IP address for this interface: 10.2.2.11
    Subnet mask for this interface [255.0.0.0] : 255.255.255.0
    Class A network is 10.0.0.0, 24 subnet bits; mask is /24

Do you want to configure FastEthernet0/1 interface? [yes]: no

Do you want to configure Serial0/0/0 interface? [yes]: no

Do you want to configure Serial0/0/1 interface? [yes]: no
```

A newer feature in Cisco IOS is Cisco AutoSecure. Cisco AutoSecure is a Cisco IOS security CLI command feature that is used to disable services most often used to attack routers and networks. You can deploy one of these two modes, depending on your needs:

- **Interactive mode:** Prompts the user with options to enable and disable services and other security features

- **Noninteractive mode:** Automatically executes a Cisco AutoSecure command with the recommended Cisco default settings

Caution   Cisco AutoSecure attempts to ensure maximum security by disabling the services most commonly used by hackers to attack a router. However, some of these services might be needed for successful operation in your network. For this reason, you should not use the Cisco AutoSecure feature until you fully understand its operations and the requirements of your network.

Cisco AutoSecure performs the following functions:

- Disables these global services:
  - Finger
  - Packet assembler/disassembler (PAD)
  - Small servers
  - BOOTP (Bootstrap Protocol) servers
  - HTTP service
  - Identification service
  - Cisco Discovery Protocol
  - Network Time Protocol (NTP)
  - Source routing
- Enables these global services:
  - Password encryption service
  - Tuning of scheduler interval and allocation
  - TCP synwait time
  - TCP keepalive messages
  - Security policy database (SPD) configuration
  - Internet Control Message Protocol (ICMP) unreachable messages

- Disables these services per interface:

  - ICMP

  - Proxy Address Resolution Protocol (ARP)

  - Directed broadcast

  - Maintenance Operation Protocol (MOP) service

  - ICMP unreachables

  - ICMP mask reply messages

- Provides logging for security, including these functions:

  - Enables sequence numbers and timestamp

  - Provides a console log

  - Sets log buffered size

  - Provides an interactive dialog to configure the logging server IP address

- Secures access to the router, including these functions:

  - Checks for a banner and provides the ability to add text for automatic configuration

  - Login and password

  - Transport input and output

  - **exec-timeout** commands

  - Local authentication, authorization, and accounting (AAA)

  - Secure Shell (SSH) timeouts and **ssh authentication-retries** commands

  - Enables only SSH and Secure Copy Protocol (SCP) for access and file transfers to and from the router

  - Disables Simple Network Management Protocol (SNMP) if not being used

- Secures the forwarding plane, including these functions:

  - Enables Cisco Express Forwarding or distributed Cisco Express Forwarding on the router, when available

  - Antispoofing

  - Blocks all Internet Assigned Numbers Authority (IANA) reserved IP address blocks

  - Blocks private address blocks, if customer desires

  - Installs a default route to Null0, if a default route is not being used

  - Configures a TCP intercept for a connection timeout, if the TCP intercept feature is available and the user desires

■ Starts an interactive configuration for Context-Based Access Control (CBAC) on interfaces facing the Internet, when using a Cisco IOS Firewall image

■ Enables NetFlow on software forwarding platforms

When you complete the configuration process for all installed interfaces on the router, the **setup** command shows the configuration command script that was created, as shown in Example 12-6.

Example 12-6 *Configuration Command Script*

```
The following configuration command script was created:

hostname RouterX
enable secret 5 $1$aNMG$kV3mxjlWDRGXmfwjEBNAf1
enable password cisco
line vty 0 4
password sanjose
no snmp-server
!
ip routing
no clns routing
no bridge 1
!
interface FastEthernet0/0
media-type 100BaseX
half-duplex
ip address 10.2.2.11 255.255.255.0
no mop enabled
!
interface FastEthernet0/1
shutdown
no ip address
!
interface Serial0/0/0
shutdown
no ip address
!
interface Serial0/0/1
shutdown
no ip address
dialer-list 1 protocol ip permit
!
end
[0] Go to the IOS command prompt without saving this config.
[1] Return back to the setup without saving this config.
[2] Save this configuration to nvram and exit.

Enter your selection [2]: 2
```

The **setup** command offers the following three choices:

- [0]: Go to the EXEC prompt without saving the created configuration.

- [1]: Go back to the beginning of setup without saving the created configuration.

- [2]: Accept the created configuration, save it to NVRAM, and exit to the EXEC mode.

If you choose [2], the configuration is executed and saved to NVRAM, and the system is ready to use. To modify the configuration, you must reconfigure it manually.

The script file generated by the setup command is additive. You can turn features on with the **setup** command, but not off. In addition, the **setup** command does not support many of the advanced features of the router or those features that require a more complex configuration.

Logging In to the Cisco Router

When you configure a Cisco router from the CLI on a console or remote terminal, the Cisco IOS Software provides a command interpreter called the EXEC. The EXEC interprets the commands that are entered and carries out the corresponding operations. You must log in to the router before entering an EXEC command.

After you have configured a Cisco router from the setup utility, you can reconfigure it or add to the configuration from the user interface that runs on the router console or auxiliary port. You can also configure a Cisco router using a remote-access application such as SSH.

For security purposes, the EXEC has the following two levels of access to commands:

- **User mode:** Typical tasks include those that check the router status.

- **Privileged mode:** Typical tasks include those that change the router configuration.

When you first log in to the router, a user-mode prompt is displayed. EXEC commands available in user mode are a subset of the EXEC commands available in privileged mode. These commands provide a means to display information without changing router configuration settings.

To access the full set of commands, you must enable the privileged mode with the **enable** command and supply the enable password, if it is configured.

Note The enable password is displayed in clear text using the **show run** command. The secret password is encrypted, so it is not displayed in clear text. If both the enable and secret passwords are configured, the secret password will override the enable password.

The EXEC prompt then displays as a pound sign (#) while in the privileged mode. From the privileged level, you can access global configuration mode and the other specific configuration modes, such as interface, subinterface, line, router, route-map, and several others.

Use the **disable** command to return to the user EXEC mode from the privileged EXEC mode. Use the **exit** or **logout** command to end the current session. Figure 12-1 illustrates the navigation through these modes.

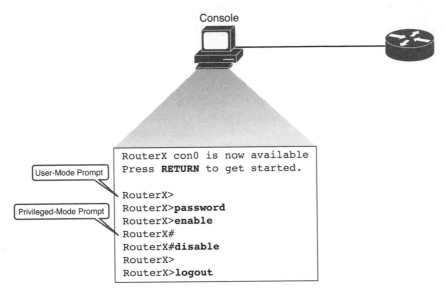

Figure 12-1   *User Mode Navigation*

You can enter a question mark (**?**) at the user-mode prompt or the privileged-mode prompt to display a list of commands available in the current mode. Example 12-7 shows getting help at the user-mode prompt.

Example 12-7   *Getting Help in User Mode*

```
RouterX> ?

Exec commands:
  access-enable    Create a temporary Access-List entry
  access-profile   Apply user-profile to interface
  clear            Reset functions
  connect          Open a terminal connection
  disable          Turn off privileged commands
  disconnect       Disconnect an existing network connection
  enable           Turn on privileged commands
  exit             Exit from the EXEC
  help             Description of the interactive help system
  lat              Open a lat connection
  lock             Lock the terminal
  login            Log in as a particular user
  logout           Exit from the EXEC
-- More --
```

Note   The available commands vary with the different Cisco IOS Software versions.

Notice the -- More -- at the bottom of the sample display. This indicates that multiple screens are available as output. Additional commands follow, and you can perform any of the following tasks:

- Press the spacebar to display the next available screen.

- Press the **Return** key (or, on some keyboards, the **Enter** key) to display the next line.

- Press any other key to return to the prompt.

Enter the **enable** user-mode command to access privileged EXEC mode. Normally, if an enable password has been configured, you must also enter the enable password before you can access privileged EXEC mode.

Enter the **?** command at the privileged-mode prompt to display a list of the available privileged EXEC commands. Example 12-8 shows getting privileged-mode help.

Example 12-8   *Getting Help in Privileged Mode*

```
RouterX# ?

Exec commands:
  access-enable     Create a temporary Access-List entry
  access-profile    Apply user-profile to interface
  access-template   Create a temporary Access-List entry
  bfe               For manual emergency modes setting
  cd                Change current directory
  clear             Reset functions
  clock             Manage the system clock
  configure         Enter configuration mode
  connect           Open a terminal connection
  copy              Copy from one file to another
  debug             Debugging functions (see also 'undebug')
  delete            Delete a file
  dir               List files on a filesystem
  disable           Turn off privileged commands
  disconnect        Disconnect an existing network connection
  enable            Turn on privileged commands
  erase             Erase a filesystem
  exit              Exit from the EXEC
  help              Description of the interactive help system
-- More --
```

Note   The available commands vary with the different Cisco IOS Software versions.

Showing the Router Initial Startup Status

After logging in to a Cisco router, the router hardware and software status can be verified by using the following router status commands: **show version**, **show running-config**, and **show startup-config**.

Use the **show version** EXEC command to display the configuration of the system hardware, the software version, the memory size, and the configuration register setting. Example 12-9 shows the output from a **show version** command.

Example 12-9   show version *Command Output*

```
Cisco IOS Software, 2800 Software (C2800NM-ADVIPSERVICESK9-M), Version 12.4(12),
  RELEASE SOFTWARE (fc1)
Technical Support: http://www.cisco.com/techsupport
Copyright (c) 1986-2006 by Cisco Systems, Inc.
Compiled Fri 17-Nov-06 12:02 by prod_rel_team


ROM: System Bootstrap, Version 12.4(13r)T, RELEASE SOFTWARE (fc1)


RouterX uptime is 2 days, 21 hours, 15 minutes
System returned to ROM by power-on
System image file is "flash:c2800nm-advipservicesk9-mz.124-12.bin"



This product contains cryptographic features and is subject to United States and
local country laws governing import, export, transfer and use. Delivery of Cisco
cryptographic products does not imply third-party authority to import, export,
distribute or use encryption. Importers, exporters, distributors and users are
responsible for compliance with U.S. and local country laws. By using this
product you agree to comply with applicable laws and regulations. If you are
unable to comply with U.S. and local laws, return this product immediately.


A summary of U.S. laws governing Cisco cryptographic products may be found at:
http://www.cisco.com/wwl/export/crypto/tool/stqrg.html


If you require further assistance please contact us by sending email to
export@cisco.com.


Cisco 2811 (revision 53.50) with 249856K/12288K bytes of memory.
Processor board ID FTX1107A6BB
2 FastEthernet interfaces
2 Serial(sync/async) interfaces
1 Virtual Private Network (VPN) Module
DRAM configuration is 64 bits wide with parity enabled.
239K bytes of non-volatile configuration memory.
```

```
62720K bytes of ATA CompactFlash (Read/Write)

Configuration register is 0x2102

RouterX#
```

In the example, the RAM is assigned with 249,856 KB available for main memory and 12,288 KB available for I/O memory (shared by all the interfaces). The I/O memory is used for holding packets while they are in the process of being routed.

Note   When you order a new Cisco router with, let's say, 256 MB of RAM and 64 MB of flash memory, do not be surprised when the **show version** command displays a bit less than this actual amount. Parts of the memory are reserved and consumed by the router right away and will not display as available.

The router has two Fast Ethernet interfaces and two serial interfaces. This is useful for confirming that the expected interfaces are recognized at startup and are functioning, from a hardware perspective.

The router has 239 KB used for startup configuration storage in the NVRAM and 62,720 KB of flash storage for the Cisco IOS Software image.

Summary of Starting a Cisco Router

The following list summarizes the key points that were discussed in the previous sections:

- The router startup sequence is similar to the startup sequence of the Catalyst switch. The router first performs the POST, and then the router finds and loads the Cisco IOS image. Finally, it finds and loads the device configuration file.

- Use the **enable** command to access the privileged EXEC mode from the user EXEC mode.

- After logging in to a Cisco router, the initial startup status of a router can be verified by using the router status commands **show version**, **show running-config**, and **show**.

Configuring a Cisco Router

When the hardware installation is complete and the Cisco router has the initial configuration, you can begin configuring the router for a specific internetwork. You must be familiar with the Cisco IOS command-line interface (CLI), its modes, and its operation before configuring more advanced features such as IP routing. The following sections describe how to implement a basic configuration for a Cisco router.

Cisco Router Configuration Modes

From privileged EXEC mode, you can enter global configuration mode, providing access to the specific router configuration modes. Figure 12-2 illustrates the different configuration modes and shows how to navigate them.

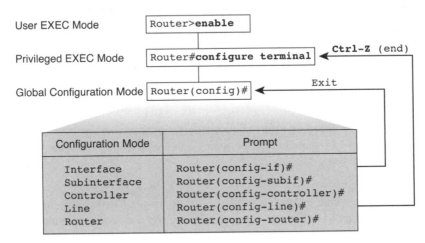

Figure 12-2 *Navigating Configuration Modes*

From the privileged EXEC mode, you can enter the global configuration mode with the **configure terminal** command. From the global configuration mode, you can access the specific configuration modes, which include the following:

- **Interface:** Supports commands that configure operations on a per-interface basis

- **Subinterface:** Supports commands that configure multiple virtual interfaces on a single physical interface

- **Controller:** Supports commands that configure controllers (for example, E1 and T1 controllers)

- **Line:** Supports commands that configure the operation of a terminal line, for example, the console or the vty ports

- **Router:** Supports commands that configure an IP routing protocol

If you enter the **exit** command, the router will back out one level, eventually logging out. In general, you can enter the **exit** command from one of the specific configuration modes to return to global configuration mode. Press **Ctrl-Z** to leave the configuration mode and return the router to the privileged EXEC mode.

In terminal configuration mode, an incremental compiler is invoked. Each configuration command entered is parsed as soon as the **Enter** key is pressed.

If there are no syntax errors, the command is executed and stored in the running configuration, and it is effective immediately.

Commands that affect the entire router are called *global* commands. The **hostname** and **enable password** commands are examples of global commands.

Commands that point to or indicate a process or interface that will be configured are called *major* commands. When entered, major commands cause the CLI to enter a specific configuration mode. Major commands have no effect unless a subcommand that supplies the configuration entry is immediately entered. For example, the major command **interface serial 0** has no effect unless it is followed by a subcommand that tells what is to be done to that interface.

The following are examples of some major commands and subcommands that go with them:

```
Router(config)# interface serial 0 (major command)
Router(config-if)# shutdown (subcommand)
Router(config-if)# line console 0 (major command)
Router(config-line)# password cisco (subcommand)
Router(config-line)# router rip (major command)
Router(config-router)# network 10.0.0.0 (subcommand)
```

Notice that entering a major command switches from one configuration mode to another. It is not necessary to return to the global configuration mode first before entering another configuration mode.

After you enter the commands to configure the router, you must save the running configuration to NVRAM with the **copy running-config startup-config** command. If the configuration is not saved to NVRAM and the router is reloaded, the configuration will be lost and the router will revert to the last configuration saved in NVRAM. Example 12-10 shows saving the configuration file to startup.

Example 12-10 *Saving Configuration File*

```
Router#
Router# copy running-config startup-config

Destination filename [startup-config]?
Building configuration...

Router#
```

Configuring a Cisco Router from the CLI

The configuration mode of the CLI is used to configure the router name, password, and other console commands.

One of the first tasks in configuring a router is to name it. Naming the router helps you to better manage the network by enabling you to uniquely identify each router within the network. The name of the router is considered to be the host name, and is the name displayed at the system prompt. If no name is configured, the default router name is Router. The router name is assigned in global configuration mode. In Example 12-11, the router name is set to RouterA.

Example 12-11 *Assigning the Router Name*

```
Router(config)# hostname RouterA

RouterA(config)#
RouterA(config)# banner motd #  You have entered a secured system. Authorized access
  only!#
```

You can configure a message-of-the-day (MOTD) banner to be displayed on all connected terminals. This banner is displayed at login and is useful for conveying messages, such as impending system shutdowns that might affect network users. When you enter the **banner motd** command, follow the command with one or more blank spaces and a delimiting character of any choice. In the example, the delimiting character is a pound sign (#). After entering the banner text, terminate the message with the same delimiting character.

You can also add a description to an interface to help remember specific information about that interface, such as the network serviced by that interface. This description is meant solely as a comment to help identify how the interface is being used. The description will appear in the output when the configuration information that exists in router memory is displayed, as well as in a **show interfaces** command display.

Other useful console-line commands include the **exec-timeout** command. In the following example, the **exec-timeout** command sets the timeout for the console EXEC session to 20 minutes and 30 seconds, which changes the session from the default timeout of 10 minutes.

The **logging synchronous** console-line command is useful when console messages are being displayed while you are attempting to input EXEC or configuration commands. Instead of the console messages being interspersed with the input, the input is redisplayed on a single line at the end of each console message that "interrupts" the input. This makes reading the input and the messages much easier. Example 12-12 shows how to configure these console settings.

Example 12-12 *Configuring Console Settings*

```
RouterA(config)# line console 0
RouterA(config-line)# exec-timeout 20 30
RouterA(config-line)# logging synchronous
```

> **Caution**   Setting the exec-timeout settings too high or disabling this setting can be a security risk.

Configuring Cisco Router Interfaces

The main function of a router is to forward packets from one network device to another. To do that, you must define the characteristics of the interfaces through which the packets are received and sent.

The router interface characteristics include, but are not limited to, the IP address of the interface, the data-link encapsulation method, media type, and bandwidth.

You can enable many features on a per-interface basis. Interface configuration-mode commands modify the operation of Ethernet, serial, and many other interface types. When you enter the **interface** command, you must define the interface type and number. The number is assigned to each interface based on the physical location of the interface hardware in the router and is used to identify each interface.

This identification is critical when there are multiple interfaces of the same type in a single router. Examples of an interface type and number are as follows:

```
Router(config)# interface serial 0
Router(config)# interface fa 0/0
```

An interface in a Cisco 2800 and 3800 Series Integrated Services Router, or other modular router, is specified by the physical slot in the router and port number on the module in that slot, as follows:

```
Router(config)# interface fa 1/0
```

To quit the interface configuration mode, enter the **exit** command at the Router (config-if)# prompt.

To add a description to an interface configuration, use the **description** command in interface configuration mode. To remove the description, use the **no description** command. The description will show up when using the **show interface** command.

You might want to disable an interface to perform hardware maintenance on a specific interface or segment of a network. You might also want to disable an interface if a problem exists on a specific segment of the network and you must isolate that segment from the rest of the network.

The **shutdown** subcommand administratively turns off an interface. To reinstate the interface, use the **no shutdown** subcommand. Example 12-13 shows the commands and output for these commands.

Example 12-13   *Disabling and Enabling Serial Interfaces*

```
RouterX# configure terminal
RouterX(config)# interface serial 0
RouterX(config-if)# shutdown

%LINK-5-CHANGED: Interface Serial0, changed state to administratively down
%LINEPROTO-5-UPDOWN: Line protocol on Interface Serial0, changed state to down
RouterX# configure terminal
RouterX(config)# interface serial 0
RouterX(config-if)# no shutdown

%LINK-3-UPDOWN:  Interface Serial0, changed state to up
%LINEPROTO-5-UPDOWN: Line Protocol on Interface Serial0, changed state to up
```

When an interface is first configured, unless in setup mode, you must administratively enable the interface before it can be used to transmit and receive packets. Use the **no shutdown** subcommand to allow the Cisco IOS Software to use the interface.

Configuring the Cisco Router IP Address

Each interface on a Cisco router must have its own IP address to uniquely identify it on the network. Figure 12-3 illustrates unique IP addresses for each network attached to the router.

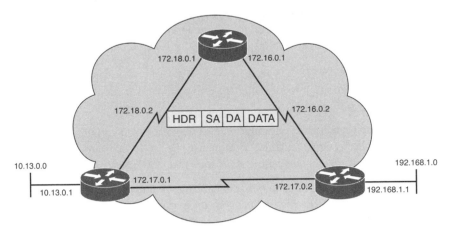

Figure 12-3   *Interface Addresses*

To configure an interface on a Cisco router, follow these steps:

1. Enter global configuration mode using the **configure terminal** command:

   ```
   Router# configure terminal
   ```

2. Identify the specific interface that requires an IP address by using the **interface** *type slot/port* command:

   ```
   Router(config)# interface fa 0/0
   ```

3. Set the IP address and subnet mask for the interface by using the **ip address** *ip-address mask* command:

```
Router(config-if)# ip address 192.168.1.1 255.255.255.0
```

4. Enable the interface to change the state from administratively down to up by using the **no shutdown** command:

```
Router(config-if)# no shutdown
```

5. Exit configuration mode for the interface by using the **exit** command:

```
Router(config-if)# exit
```

Verifying the Interface Configuration

When you have completed the router interface configuration, you can verify the configuration by using the **show interfaces** command.

The **show interfaces** command displays the status and statistics of all network interfaces on the router. Alternatively, the status for a specific interface can be displayed by using the **show interfaces type slot** command. Example 12-14 shows common output for the **show interfaces** command.

Example 12-14   show interfaces *Command Output*

```
RouterA# show interfaces

Ethernet0 is up, line protocol is up
  Hardware is Lance, address is 00e0.1e5d.ae2f (bia 00e0.1e5d.ae2f)
  Internet address is 10.1.1.11/24
  MTU 1500 bytes, BW 10000 Kbit, DLY 1000 usec, rely 255/255, load 1/255
  Encapsulation ARPA, loopback not set, keepalive set (10 sec)
  ARP type: ARPA, ARP Timeout 04:00:00
  Last input 00:00:07, output 00:00:08, output hang never
  Last clearing of "show interface" counters never
  Queueing strategy: fifo
  Output queue 0/40, 0 drops; input queue 0/75, 0 drops
  5 minute input rate 0 bits/sec, 0 packets/sec
  5 minute output rate 0 bits/sec, 0 packets/sec
     81833 packets input, 27556491 bytes, 0 no buffer
     Received 42308 broadcasts, 0 runts, 0 giants, 0 throttles
     1 input errors, 0 CRC, 0 frame, 0 overrun, 1 ignored, 0 abort
     0 input packets with dribble condition detected
     55794 packets output, 3929696 bytes, 0 underruns
     0 output errors, 0 collisions, 1 interface resets
     0 babbles, 0 late collision, 4 deferred
     0 lost carrier, 0 no carrier
     0 output buffer failures, 0 output buffers swapped out
```

Output fields for an Ethernet interface and their meanings are shown in Table 12-1.

Table 12-1   show interfaces *Output Field Descriptions*

Output	Description
Ethernet . . . is {up | down | administratively down}	Indicates whether the interface hardware is currently active or down, or whether an administrator has taken it down.
line protocol is {up | down}	Indicates whether the software processes that handle the line protocol consider the interface usable (that is, whether keepalives are successful). If the interface misses three consecutive keepalives, the line protocol is marked as down.
Hardware	Hardware type (for example, MCI Ethernet, serial communications interface [SCI], cBus Ethernet) and address.
Internet address	IP address followed by the prefix length (subnet mask).
MTU	Maximum transmission unit (MTU) of the interface.
BW	Bandwidth of the interface, in kilobits per second. The bandwidth parameter is used to compute routing protocol metrics and other calculations.
DLY	Delay of the interface, in microseconds.
rely	Reliability of the interface as a fraction of 255 (255/255 is 100 percent reliability), calculated as an exponential average over 5 minutes.
load	Load on the interface as a fraction of 255 (255/255 is completely saturated), calculated as an exponential average over 5 minutes.
Encapsulation	Encapsulation method assigned to an interface.
keepalive	Indicates whether keepalives are set.
ARP type:	Type of Address Resolution Protocol (ARP) assigned.
loopback	Indicates whether loopback is set.
Last input	Number of hours, minutes, and seconds since the last packet was successfully received by an interface. Useful for knowing when a dead interface failed.
output	Number of hours, minutes, and seconds since the last packet was successfully transmitted by an interface. Useful for knowing when a dead interface failed.
output hang	Number of hours, minutes, and seconds (or never) since the interface was last reset because of a transmission that took too long. When the number of hours in any of the previous fields exceeds 24 hours, the number of days and hours is printed. If that field overflows, asterisks are printed.

Output	Description
Last clearing	Time at which the counters that measure cumulative statistics shown in this report (such as number of bytes transmitted and received) were last reset to 0. Note that variables that might affect routing (for example, load and reliability) are not cleared when the counters are cleared. Asterisks indicate elapsed time too large to be displayed.
Output queue, input queue, drops	Number of packets in output and input queues. Each number is followed by a slash (/), the maximum size of the queue, and the number of packets dropped because of a full queue.
Five minute input rate, Five minute output rate	Average number of bits and packets transmitted per second in the last 5 minutes. If the interface is not in promiscuous mode, it senses network traffic that it sends and receives (rather than all network traffic). The 5-minute input and output rates should be used only as an approximation of traffic per second during a given 5-minute period. These rates are exponentially weighted averages with a time constant of 5 minutes. A period of four time constants must pass before the average will be within 2 percent of the instantaneous rate of a uniform stream of traffic over that period.
packets input	Total number of error-free packets received by the system.
bytes input	Total number of bytes, including data and MAC encapsulation, in the error-free packets received by the system.
no buffers	Number of received packets discarded because there was no buffer space in the main system. Compare with "ignored count." Broadcast storms on Ethernet are often responsible for no input buffer events.
Received...broadcasts	Total number of broadcast or multicast packets received by the interface. The number of broadcasts should be kept as low as practicable. An approximate threshold is less than 20 percent of the total number of input packets.
runts	Number of Ethernet frames that are discarded because they are smaller than the minimum Ethernet frame size. Any Ethernet frame that is less than 64 bytes is considered a runt. Runts are usually caused by collisions. If there is more than one runt per million bytes received, it should be investigated.
giants	Number of Ethernet frames that are discarded because they exceed the maximum Ethernet frame size. Any Ethernet frame that is larger than 1518 bytes is considered a giant.
input error	Includes runts, giants, no buffer, cyclic redundancy check (CRC), frame, overrun, and ignored counts. Other input-related errors can also cause the input error count to be increased, and some datagrams can have more than one error. Therefore, this sum might not balance with the sum of enumerated input error counts.

Output	Description
CRC	CRC generated by the originating LAN station or far-end device does not match the checksum calculated from the data received. On a LAN, this usually indicates noise or transmission problems on the LAN interface or the LAN bus itself. A high number of CRCs is usually the result of collisions or a station transmitting bad data.
frame	Number of packets received incorrectly having a CRC error and a noninteger number of octets. On a LAN, this is usually the result of collisions or a malfunctioning Ethernet device.
overrun	Number of times the receiver hardware was unable to hand-receive data to a hardware buffer because the input rate exceeded the ability of the receiver to handle the data.
ignored	Number of received packets ignored by the interface because the interface hardware ran low on internal buffers. These buffers are different from the system buffers mentioned in the buffer description. Broadcast storms and bursts of noise can cause the ignored count to be increased.
input packets with dribble condition detected	Dribble bit error indicates that a frame is slightly too long. This frame error counter is incremented just for informational purposes; the router accepts the frame.
packets output	Total number of messages transmitted by the system.
bytes	Total number of bytes, including data and MAC encapsulation, transmitted by the system.
underruns	Number of times that the transmitter has been running faster than the router can handle. This might never be reported on some interfaces.
output errors	Sum of all errors that prevented the final transmission of datagrams out of the interface being examined. Note that this might not balance with the sum of the enumerated output errors, because some datagrams might have more than one error, and others might have errors that do not fall into any of the specifically tabulated categories.
collisions	Number of messages retransmitted because of an Ethernet collision. This is usually the result of an overextended LAN (Ethernet or transceiver cable too long, more than two repeaters between stations, or too many cascaded multiport transceivers). A packet that collides is counted only once in output packets.
interface resets	Number of times that an interface has been completely reset. This can happen if packets queued for transmission were not sent within several seconds. On a serial line, this can be caused by a malfunctioning modem that is not supplying the transmit clock signal, or it can be caused by a cable problem. If the system notices that the carrier detect line of a serial interface is up but the line protocol is down, it periodically resets the interface in an effort to restart it. Interface resets can also occur when an interface is looped back or shut down.

One of the most important elements of the **show interfaces** command output is the display of the line and data-link protocol status. For other types of interfaces, the meanings of the status line can be slightly different. Figure 12-4 highlights the key output for this command.

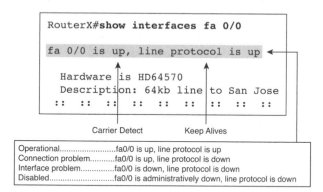

Figure 12-4 *Interface State*

The first parameter refers to the hardware layer and essentially reflects whether the interface is receiving the carrier detect signal from the other end. The second parameter refers to the data link layer and reflects whether the data link layer protocol keepalives are being received.

Based on the output of the **show interfaces** command, possible problems can be fixed as follows:

- If the interface is up and the line protocol is down, a problem exists. Some possible causes include the following:

  - No keepalives

  - Mismatch in encapsulation type

- If both the line protocol and the interface are down, a cable might never have been attached when the router was powered up, or some other interface problem must exist. For example, in a back-to-back connection, the other end of the connection might be administratively down.

- If the interface is administratively down, it has been manually disabled (the **shutdown** command has been issued) in the active configuration.

After configuring a serial interface, use the **show interface serial** command to verify the changes.

Verifying the Interface Configuration

If no documentation about the network topology is available or if the existing documentation is not up to date, you might find yourself in a position of needing to discover the neighboring devices of a router. You can sometimes do this manually, by inspecting the physical wiring if the devices are installed next to each other. When neighboring devices are in other buildings or cities, you must use a different method.

One possibility is to use a dynamic discovery protocol that gathers information about directly connected devices.

Cisco devices support Cisco Discovery Protocol (CDP), which provides information about directly connected Cisco devices and their functions and capabilities.

Cisco Discovery Protocol is a proprietary tool that enables you to access a summary of protocol and address information about Cisco devices that are directly connected. By default, each Cisco device sends periodic messages, known as Cisco Discovery Protocol advertisements, to other directly connected Cisco devices. These advertisements contain information such as the types of devices that are connected, the router interfaces to which they are connected, the interfaces that are used to make the connections, and the model numbers of the devices.

Information that is gathered from other devices can assist you in making network design decisions, troubleshooting, and making changes to equipment. Cisco Discovery Protocol can be used as a network discovery tool, helping you to build a logical topology of a network when such documentation is missing or lacking in detail.

Cisco Discovery Protocol runs over the OSI data link layer, connecting the physical media to the upper-layer protocols. Because Cisco Discovery Protocol operates at the data link layer, two or more Cisco network devices can learn about each other even if they are using different network layer protocols, if they are not configured, or if IP addressing, for example, is misconfigured on neighboring routers.

LLDP is a standardized vendor-independent discovery protocol that discovers neighboring devices from different vendors. It is standardized by IEEE as the 802.1AB standard, and it performs functions similar to the Cisco Discovery Protocol. As you might guess, this protocol is not supported on some older Cisco hardware, but on the newer hardware from Cisco, LLDP (Link Layer Discovery Protocol) is very useful for discovering non-Cisco devices in your network.

Figure 12-5 shows the output from the **show cdp neighbors** command for router Branch.

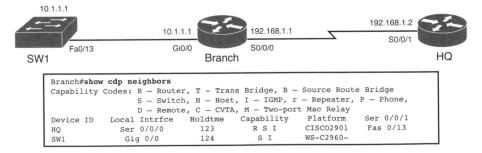

Figure 12-5 show cdp neighbors *Command Output*

For each Cisco Discovery Protocol neighbor, this information is displayed:

- Neighbor device ID

- Local interface

- Hold time value, in seconds

- Neighbor device capability code

- Neighbor hardware platform

- Neighbor remote port ID

Note   The command output in the figure clearly shows OSI Layer 2 and OSI Layer 3 neighbors, a switch and router, respectively.

The format of the **show cdp neighbors** output varies among different types of devices, but the available information is generally consistent across devices.

The **show cdp neighbors** command can also be used on a Cisco Catalyst switch to display the Cisco Discovery Protocol updates that were received on the local interfaces. Note that on a switch, the local interface is referred to as the local port.

Figure 12-6 shows the use of the **show cdp neighbors detail** command on the Branch router.

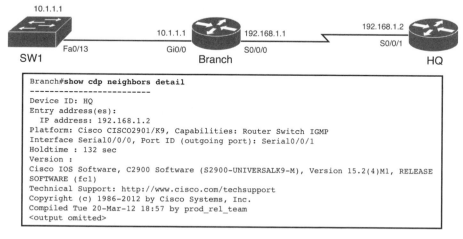

Figure 12-6   show cdp neighbors detail *Command Output*

The **show cdp neighbors detail** or **show cdp entry** * command displays detailed information about neighboring devices. Figure 12-6 shows this command. To display information about a specific neighbor, the command string must include the IP address or device ID of the neighbor. The **show cdp entry** command shows the following information:

Neighbor device ID (router HQ in the figure)

OSI Layer 3 protocol information (for example, IP address 192.168.1.2 in the figure)

Device platform (Cisco 2901 in the figure)

Device capabilities (router, switch, IGMP in the figure)

Local interface type and outgoing remote port ID (Serial 0/0/0 in the figure)

Hold time value, in seconds (132 seconds in the figure)

Cisco IOS Software type and release (C2900 Software [C2900-UNIVERSALK9-M], Version 15.2[4]M1, in the figure)

Chapter Summary

The router startup sequence begins with POST; then the Cisco IOS image is found and loaded. At the last step, the configuration file is loaded if it exists. If the router starts without a configuration, the Cisco IOS executes a question-driven configuration dialog that can be skipped. The main function of a router is to relay packets from one network device to another.

Interface characteristics, such as the IP address and description, are configured using interface configuration mode. When you have completed router interface configuration, you can verify it by using the **show ip interface brief** and **show interfaces** commands.

Cisco Discovery Protocol is an information-gathering tool used by network administrators to obtain information about directly connected devices. Cisco Discovery Protocol exchanges hardware and software device information with its directly connected Cisco Discovery Protocol neighbors. The **show cdp neighbors** command displays information about the Cisco Discovery Protocol neighbors of a router. The **show cdp neighbors detail** command displays detailed Cisco Discovery Protocol information on a Cisco device.

Additional Resource

- Configuring Cisco Routers Video, AJS Networking: http://ajsnetworking.com/configrouter

Review Questions

Use the questions here to review what you learned in this chapter. The correct answers and solutions are found in Appendix A, "Answers to Chapter Review Questions."

1. When you start a Cisco router, what should you see on the console?

    a. Cisco IOS debug messages

    b. The Diagnostic Console menu

    c. Cisco IOS Software output text

    d. A graphical picture showing the real-time status of the LED

2. What is the primary purpose of setup utility on a Cisco router?

   a. To display the current router configuration

   b. To complete hardware and interface testing

   c. To bring up a minimal feature configuration

   d. To fully configure a Cisco router for IP routing

3. Which statement best describes what the user EXEC mode commands allow you to configure on a Cisco router?

   a. Minimal configuration capabilities; the user mode commands are used to display information.

   b. The user EXEC mode allows you to perform global configuration tasks that affect the entire router.

   c. The user EXEC mode commands allow you to enter a secret password so that you can configure the router.

   d. The user EXEC mode commands allow you to configure interfaces, subinterfaces, lines, and routers.

4. Which Cisco IOS command is used to return to user EXEC mode from the privileged EXEC mode?

   a. exit

   b. quit

   c. disable

   d. userexec

5. What information does the **show running-config** command provide on a Cisco router?

   a. Current (running) configuration in RAM

   b. System hardware and names of configuration files

   c. Amount of NVRAM used to store the configuration

   d. Version of Cisco IOS Software running on the router

6. Which Cisco IOS command displays the configuration of the system hardware and the software version information?

   a. show version

   b. show interfaces

   c. show startup-config

   d. show running-config

7. Match each of the following router prompts to its configuration mode.

___ Console

___ OSPF

___ Interface

___ Controller

___ Subinterface

a. Router(config-if)#

b. Router(config-line)#

c. Router(config-subif)#

d. Router(config-router)#

e. Router(config-controller)#

8. Which Cisco IOS command creates a message to be displayed upon router login?

a. hostname *hostname*

b. banner motd *message*

c. hostname interface description

d. description interface description

9. If both the **enable secret** and the **enable password** commands are configured on your router, how do you get to the # prompt?

a. Enter the **enable secret** command.

b. Enter the **enable password** command.

c. Enter either the **enable secret** or the **enable password** command.

d. Enter both the **enable secret** and the **enable password** commands.

10. A serial interface displays "Serial1 is up, line protocol is down." Which of the following situations can cause this error? (Choose two.)

a. The clock rate has not been set.

b. The interface has been manually disabled.

c. No cable is attached to the serial interface.

d. There is a mismatch in the encapsulation type.

Production Network Simulation Question 12-1

You have been asked to provide a configuration in Notepad for a key Cisco router in your organization. Provide the configuration that meets the following requirements:

- The network name of the router will be Branch.

- The timeout on the console port should be set to 1 minute 45 seconds.

- Synchronous logging should be enabled.

- The Serial 0/0 interface should be enabled.

- The Serial 0/0 interface should possess the last usable host address on the 192.168.0.64 subnet using the subnet mask /26.

Chapter 13

Static Routing

This chapter includes the following sections:

- Chapter Objectives

- Enabling Static Routing

- Chapter Summary

- Additional Resources

- Review Questions

- Production Network Simulation Questions 13-1 and 13-2

Routing is the process by which a packet moves from one location to another. In terms of computer networks, it is the process of determining where to send data packets destined for addresses outside of the local network.

A router is a special-purpose computer that performs packet forwarding by learning about remote networks and maintaining routing information. The router is the junction or intersection that connects multiple IP networks. The primary forwarding decision of the router is based on OSI Layer 3 information, which is the destination IP address.

To effectively manage an IP network, you must understand how both static and dynamic routing operate and know the impact that they have on IP networks. This chapter introduces static IP routing.

Chapter Objectives

Upon completing this chapter, you will be able to describe the differences between static and dynamic routing protocols. You will also be able to configure and verify static routes. These abilities include meeting these objectives:

- Describe the basic characteristics of routing operations

- Explain the differences between static and dynamic routing

- Explain when to use static routing

- Configure static routes

- Configure default routes

- Verify static route configuration

Enabling Static Routing

Routing is the process of determining where to send data packets destined for addresses outside the local network. Routers gather and maintain routing information to enable the transmission and receipt of such data packets.

Conceptually, routing information takes the form of entries in a routing table, with one entry for each identified route. You can statically (manually) configure the entries in the routing table, or the router can use a routing protocol to create and maintain the routing table dynamically to accommodate network changes when they occur.

To manage an IP network effectively, you must understand the operation of both static and dynamic routing and know the impact that they have on an IP network. This section introduces IP static routing.

Routing Overview

To be able to route anything, a router, or any entity that performs routing, must do the following:

- **Identify the destination address:** Determine the destination (or address) of the packet that needs to be routed.

- **Identify the sources of routing information:** Determine from which sources (other routers) the router can learn the paths to given destinations.

- **Identify routes:** Determine the initial possible routes, or paths, to the intended destination.

- **Select routes:** Select the best path to the intended destination.

- **Maintain and verify routing information:** Determine whether the known paths to the destination are the most current.

The routing information that a router obtains from other routers is placed in its routing table. The router relies on this table to tell it which interfaces to use when forwarding addressed packets. Figure 13-1 shows that the router on the left uses interface s0/0/0 to get to the 172.16.1.0 subnet.

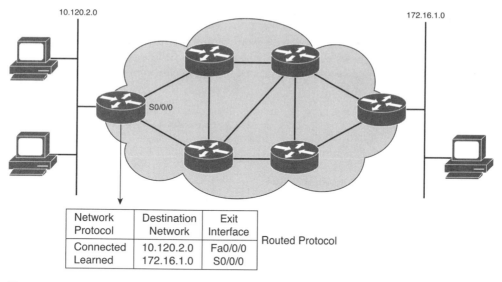

Figure 13-1 *Routes to Destination*

If the destination network is directly connected, the router already knows which interface to use when forwarding packets. If destination networks are not directly attached, the router must learn the best route to use when forwarding packets.

The destination information can be learned in two ways:

- You can enter routing information manually.
- You can collect routing information through the dynamic routing process that runs in the routers.

Static and Dynamic Route Comparison

Routers can forward packets over static routes or dynamic routes based on the router configuration. The two ways to tell the router where to forward packets to destination networks that are not directly connected are as follows:

- **Static route:** The router learns routes when an administrator manually configures the static route. The administrator must manually update this static route entry whenever an internetwork topology change requires an update. Static routes are user-defined routes that specify the path that packets take when moving between a source and a destination. These administrator-defined routes allow very precise control over the routing behavior of the IP internetwork.

- **Dynamic route:** The router dynamically learns routes after an administrator configures a routing protocol that helps determine routes. Unlike the situation with static routes, after the network administrator enables dynamic routing, the routing process automatically updates route knowledge whenever new topology information is received. The router learns and maintains routes to the remote destinations by exchanging routing updates with other routers in the internetwork.

Static Route Configuration

Static routes are commonly used when you are routing from a network to a destination. Static routes can also be useful for specifying a "gateway of last resort" to which all packets with an unknown destination address are sent. Following is the syntax for configuring a static route:

```
RouterX(config)# ip route network [mask] {address | interface}[distance]
[permanent]
```

Example: Understanding Static Routes

In Figure 13-2, Router A is configured with a static route to reach the 172.16.1.0 subnet through the serial interface of Router A given either configuration method. Router B is configured with a static or default route to reach the networks behind Router A through the serial interface of Router B.

> **Note** The static route is configured for connectivity to remote networks that are not directly connected to your router. For end-to-end connectivity, a static route must be configured in both directions.

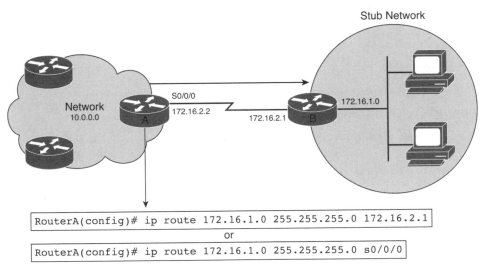

Figure 13-2 *Static Route Example*

To configure a static route, enter the **ip route** command in global configuration mode. The parameters identified in Table 13-1 further define the static route. A static route allows manual configuration of the routing table. No dynamic changes to the routing table entry occur as long as the path is active.

Table 13-1   ip route *Parameters*

ip route Command Parameters	Description
network	Destination network, subnetwork, or host.
mask	Subnet mask.
address	IP address of the next-hop router.
interface	Name of the interface to use to get to the destination network. The interface should be a point-to-point interface. The command does not work properly if the interface is multi-access (for example, a shared media Ethernet interface), unless Proxy ARP is enabled on the other router.
distance	(Optional) Defines the administrative distance.
permanent	(Optional) Specifies that the route will not be removed, even if the interface shuts down.

Example: Configuring Static Routes

In this example, the static route is configured as follows:

```
Router(config)#ip route 172.16.1.0 255.255.255.0 172.16.2.1
```

or

```
Router(config)#ip route 172.16.1.0 255.255.255.0 s0/0/0
```

Table 13-2 lists the **ip route** command parameters for this example.

Table 13-2   *Static Route Example Parameters*

ip route Command Parameters	Description
ip route	Identifies the static route.
172.16.1.0	IP address of a static route to the destination subnetwork.
255.255.255.0	Indicates the subnet mask. There are 8 bits of subnetting in effect.
172.16.2.1	IP address of the next-hop router in the path to the destination.
s0/0/0	Optional: If next-hop address is not used, the interface to send the packet out can be used instead.

The assignment of a static route to reach the stub network 172.16.1.0 is proper for Router A because only one way to reach that network exists.

290   Interconnecting Cisco Network Devices, Part 1 (ICND1) Foundation Learning Guide

Default Route Forwarding Configuration

You should use a default route in situations in which the destination is not known or when it is not feasible for the router to maintain many routes in its routing table, such as the one shown in Figure 13-3.

Use the **ip route** command to configure default route forwarding. In Figure 13-3, Router B is configured to forward all packets that do not have the destination network listed in the Router B routing table to Router A.

In the default route example, the default route is configured as follows:

```
Router(config)# ip route 0.0.0.0 0.0.0.0 172.16.2.2
```

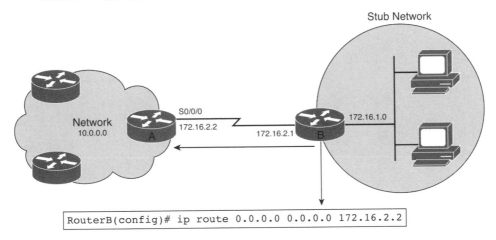

Figure 13-3   *Using Default Routes*

Table 13-3 lists the **ip route** command parameters for this example.

Table 13-3   *Default Route Example Parameters*

ip route Command Parameters	Description
ip route	Identifies the static route.
0.0.0.0	Routes to networks not in the routing table.
0.0.0.0	Special mask indicating the default route.
172.16.2.2	IP address of the next-hop router to be used as the default for packet forwarding.

Static Route Verification

To verify that you have properly configured static routing, enter the **show ip route** command and look for static routes signified by "S." You should see a verification output as indicated:

```
RouterA# show ip route
Codes: C - connected, S - static, I - IGRP, R - RIP, M - mobile, B - BGP
       D - EIGRP, EX - EIGRP external, O - OSPF, IA - OSPF inter area
       E1 - OSPF external type 1, E2 - OSPF external type 2, E - EGP
       i - IS-IS, L1 - IS-IS level-1, L2 - IS-IS level-2, * - candidate default
       U - per-user static route

Gateway of last resort is 0.0.0.0 to network 0.0.0.0

     10.0.0.0/8 is subnetted, 1 subnets
C       10.1.1.0 is directly connected, Serial0/0/0
S*   0.0.0.0/0 is directly connected, Serial0
```

Chapter Summary

Routing is the process by which items get from one location to another. In networking, a router is the device used to route traffic. Routers can forward packets over static routes or dynamic routes based on the router configuration.

Routers configured for static routing use a route that a network administrator enters into the router manually. Dynamic routes use a router that a network routing protocol adjusts automatically for topology or traffic changes.

Unidirectional static routes must be configured to and from a stub network to allow communications to occur. The **ip route** command can be used to configure default route forwarding.

The **show ip route** command verifies that static routing is properly configured. Static routes are signified in the command output by "S."

Additional Resource

■ Static Routing Video, AJS Networking: http://ajsnetworking.com/static

Review Questions

Use the questions here to review what you learned in this chapter. The correct answers and solutions are found in Appendix A, "Answers to Chapter Review Questions."

1. Which statement most accurately describes static and dynamic routes?

   a. Dynamic routes are manually configured by a network administrator, whereas static routes are automatically learned and adjusted by a routing protocol.

   b. Static routes are manually configured by a network administrator, whereas dynamic routes are automatically learned and adjusted by a routing protocol.

   c. Static routes tell the router how to forward packets to networks that are not directly connected, whereas dynamic routes tell the router how to forward packets to networks that are directly connected.

   d. Dynamic routes tell the router how to forward packets to networks that are not directly connected, whereas static routes tell the router how to forward packets to networks that are directly connected.

2. What does the **ip route 186.157.5.0 255.255.255.0 10.1.1.3** command specify?

   a. Both 186.157.5.0 and 10.1.1.3 use a mask of 255.255.255.0.

   b. The router should use network 186.157.5.0 to get to address 10.1.1.3.

   c. You want the router to trace a route to network 186.157.5.0 through 10.1.1.3.

   d. The router should use address 10.1.1.3 to get to devices on network 186.157.5.0.

3. Which command displays information about only the static route configurations on a Cisco router?

   a. show route ip

   b. show ip route

   c. show ip route static

   d. show route ip static

4. What command causes the router to send traffic for unknown destinations to a specific router?

   a. ip route 0 0 10.1.1.3

   b. ip route * * 10.1.1.3

   c. ip route 0.0.0.0 255.255.255.255 10.1.1.3

   d. ip route 0.0.0.0 0.0.0.0 10.1.1.3

Production Network Simulation Questions

Production Network Simulation Question 13-1

You need to provide a static route on a key branch router in your organization. This static route must provide reachability to the 192.168.2.0/28 network. The next-hop device is 10.10.10.1/24. Provide the static route configuration.

Production Network Simulation Question 13-2

You need to provide a default static route on another device pointing to 10.20.20.1/24. Supply this configuration.

Chapter 14

Dynamic Routing Protocols

This chapter includes the following sections:

- Chapter Objectives
- Dynamic Routing Protocol Overview
- Classful Routing Versus Classless Routing Protocols
- Distance Vector Route Selection
- Understanding Link-State Routing Protocols
- Chapter Summary
- Additional Resources
- Review Questions
- Production Network Simulation Question 14-1

Routing is the process of determining where to send data packets that are destined for addresses outside the local network. Routers gather and maintain routing information to enable the transmission and receipt of these data packets. Routing information takes the form of entries in a routing table, with one entry for each identified route. The router can use a routing protocol to create and maintain the routing table dynamically so that network changes can be accommodated whenever they occur.

To effectively manage an IP network, you must understand the operation of dynamic routing protocols and the impact that they have on an IP network. This chapter discusses the need for routing protocols and describes the differences between interior and exterior routing protocols and also between link-state and distance vector routing protocols. The operation of link-state protocols is explained.

Chapter Objectives

Upon completing this chapter, you will be able to describe the various types of dynamic routing protocols. These abilities include meeting these objectives:

■ Describe the purpose of dynamic routing protocols

■ Compare interior and exterior routing protocols

■ Compare link-state and distance vector routing protocols

■ Describe the operation and characteristics of link-state routing protocols

Dynamic Routing Protocol Overview

A routing protocol defines the rules that are used by a router when it communicates with neighboring routers. Dynamic routing relies on a routing protocol to disseminate knowledge. In contrast, static routing defines the format and use of the fields within a packet. Packets are generally conveyed from end system to end system. Figure 14-1 shows how a router uses a routing protocol to learn the locations of other networks.

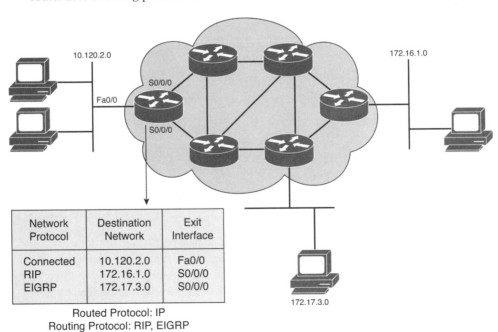

Figure 14-1 *Routing Protocols Learn About Networks*

Further examples of the information that routing protocols describe are as follows:

■ How updates are conveyed

■ What knowledge is conveyed

- When to convey knowledge

- How to locate recipients of the updates

Figure 14-2 shows the two types of routing protocols, interior gateway protocols and exterior gateway protocols.

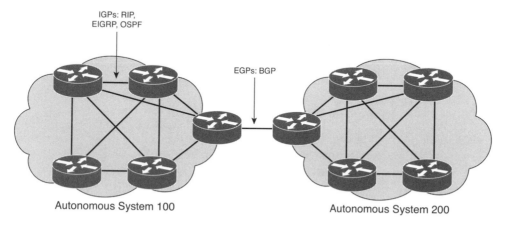

Figure 14-2 *Routing Protocol Types*

- **Interior gateway protocols (IGP):** These routing protocols are used to exchange routing information within an autonomous system. Routing Information Protocol version 1 (RIPv1), RIPv2, Enhanced Interior Gateway Routing Protocol (EIGRP), and Open Shortest Path First (OSPF) are examples of IGPs.

- **Exterior gateway protocols (EGP):** These routing protocols are used to connect autonomous systems. An autonomous system is a collection of networks under a common administration and sharing a common routing strategy. Border Gateway Protocol (BGP) is an example of an EGP.

Note The Internet Assigned Numbers Authority (IANA) assigns autonomous system numbers for many jurisdictions. The use of IANA numbering is required if your organization plans to use an EGP, such as BGP. However, it is good practice to be aware of private versus public autonomous system numbering schema.

In addition to types like internal and external, routing protocols can further be classified as to how the routing protocols operate, as shown in Figure 14-3.

In an autonomous system, most IGP routing algorithms can be classified as conforming to one of the following algorithms:

- **Distance vector:** The distance vector routing approach determines the direction (vector) and distance (hops) to any link in the internetwork.

■ **Link-state:** The link-state approach, also known as the shortest path first (SPF) algorithm, creates an abstraction of the exact topology of the entire internetwork, or at least of the partition in which the router is situated.

■ **Balanced hybrid:** The balanced hybrid approach combines aspects of link-state and distance vector algorithms.

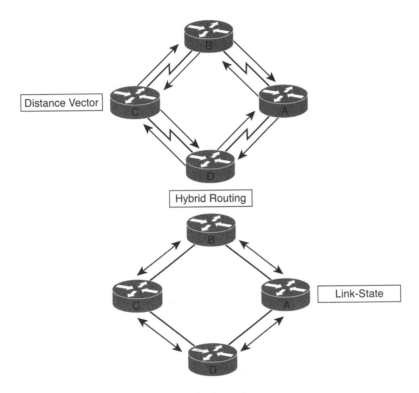

Figure 14-3 *Routing Protocol Algorithms*

No single best routing algorithm exists for all internetworks. Each routing protocol provides information differently.

Features of Dynamic Routing Protocols

Multiple routing protocols and static routes can be used at the same time. If several sources for routing information exist, an administrative distance value rates the trustworthiness of each routing information source. By specifying administrative distance values, Cisco IOS Software can discriminate between sources of routing information.

Example: Administrative Distance

An administrative distance is an integer from 0 to 255. A routing protocol with a lower administrative distance is more trustworthy than one with a higher administrative distance. As shown in Figure 14-4, if Router A receives a route to network E from EIGRP and RIP at the same time, Router A uses the administrative distance to determine that EIGRP is more trustworthy. Router A would then add the EIGRP route to the routing table.

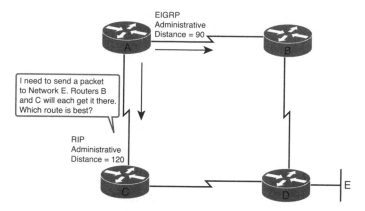

Figure 14-4 *Administrative Distance*

Table 14-1 shows the default administrative distance for selected routing information sources.

Table 14-1 *Default Administrative Distances*

Route Source	Default Distance
Connected interface	0
Static route address	1
EIGRP	90
OSPF	110
RIPv1, RIPv2	120
External EIGRP	170
Unknown or unbelievable	255 (will not be used to pass traffic)

If nondefault values are necessary, you can use Cisco IOS Software to configure administrative distance values on a per-router, per-protocol, and per-route basis.

Classful Routing Versus Classless Routing Protocols

Routing protocols are also identified by how they handle IP address space. RIP version 1 is a classful routing protocol. Classful routing is a consequence of the fact that subnet masks are *not* advertised in the routing advertisements that are generated by most distance vector routing protocols.

When a classful routing protocol is used, all subnetworks of the same major network (Class A, B, or C) must use the same subnet mask. Routers that are running a classful routing protocol perform automatic route summarization across network boundaries.

Upon receiving a routing update packet, a router that is running a classful routing protocol takes one of the following actions to determine the network portion of the route:

■ If the routing update information contains the same major network number as is configured on the receiving interface, the router applies the subnet mask that is configured on the receiving interface.

■ If the routing update information contains a major network that is different from that configured on the receiving interface, the router applies the default classful mask (by address class) as follows:

   ■ For Class A addresses, the default classful mask is 255.0.0.0.

   ■ For Class B addresses, the default classful mask is 255.255.0.0.

   ■ For Class C addresses, the default classful mask is 255.255.255.0.

RIP version 2 is a classless routing protocol. Classless routing protocols can be considered second-generation protocols because they are designed to address some of the limitations of the earlier classful routing protocols. One of the most serious limitations in a classful network environment is that the subnet mask is not exchanged during the routing update process, thus requiring the same subnet mask to be used on all subnetworks within the same major network.

Another limitation of the classful approach is the need to automatically summarize to the classful network boundary at major network boundaries.

In the classless environment, the summarization process is controlled manually and can usually be invoked at any bit position within the address. Because subnet routes are propagated throughout the routing domain, manual summarization might be required to keep the size of the routing tables manageable. Classless routing protocols include RIPv2, EIGRP, OSPF, and Intermediate System–to–Intermediate System (IS-IS).

Note   Even though RIPv2 and EIGRP are classless routing protocols, they default to a classful type of operation by automatically summarizing prefixes to classful boundaries. This is easily turned off with a **no auto-summary** router configuration command, but it is worth noting. Also interesting is the fact this command is now a default for EIGRP in 15.x IOS router code.

Distance Vector Route Selection

In addition to supporting both classful and classless routing, RIP can be characterized as a distance vector routing protocol. The periodic routing updates that most distance vector routing protocols generate are addressed only to directly connected routing devices. The addressing scheme that is most commonly used is a logical broadcast. Routers that are running a distance vector routing protocol send periodic updates even if no changes exist in the network.

In a pure distance vector environment, the periodic routing update includes a complete routing table. Upon receiving a full routing table from its neighbor, a router can verify all known routes and make changes to the local routing table based on updated information. This process is also known as "routing by rumor" because the router's understanding of the network is based on the neighboring router's perspective of the network topology. Figure 14-5 demonstrates how distance vector protocols operate.

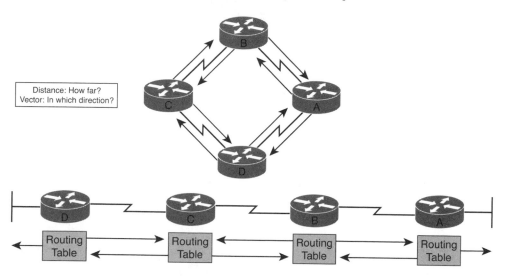

Figure 14-5 *Distance Vector Protocols*

Example: Distance Vector Routing Protocols

Router B receives periodic routing updates from Router A. Router B adds a distance vector metric (such as the hop count) to each route learned from Router A, increasing the distance vector. Router B then passes its own routing table to its neighbor, Router C. This step-by-step process occurs in all directions between directly connected neighbor routers.

Traditionally, distance vector protocols were also classful protocols. RIPv2 and EIGRP are examples of more advanced distance vector protocols that exhibit classless behavior. EIGRP also exhibits some link-state characteristics.

In Figure 14-6, the interface to each directly connected network is shown as having a distance of 0.

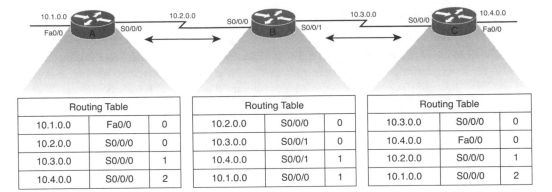

Figure 14-6 *Distance Vector Example*

As the distance vector network discovery process continues, routers discover the best path to destination networks that are not directly connected, based on accumulated metrics from each neighbor. Neighboring routers provide information for routes that are not directly connected.

Example: Sources of Information and Discovering Routes

Router A learns about networks that are not directly connected (10.3.0.0 and 10.4.0.0) based on information that it receives from Router B. Each network entry in the routing table has an accumulated metric to show how far away that network is in a given direction.

Understanding Link-State Routing Protocols

In addition to distance vector–based routing, the second basic algorithm used for routing is the link-state algorithm. Link-state protocols build routing tables based on a topology database. This database is built from link-state packets that are passed between all the routers to describe the state of a network. The shortest path first algorithm uses the database to build the routing table. Figure 14-7 shows the components of a link-state protocol.

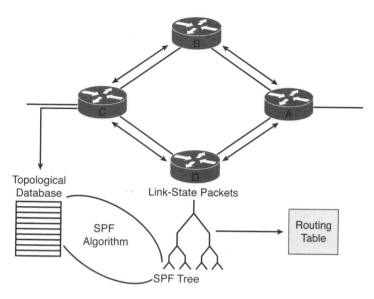

Figure 14-7 *Link-State Protocols*

Understanding the operation of link-state routing protocols is critical to being able to enable, verify, and troubleshoot their operation.

Link-state-based routing algorithms—also known as *shortest path first (SPF)* algorithms—maintain a complex database of topology information. Whereas the distance vector algorithm has nonspecific information about distant networks and no knowledge of distant routers, a link-state routing algorithm maintains full knowledge of distant routers and how they interconnect.

Link-state routing uses link-state advertisements (LSA), a topological database, the SPF algorithm, the resulting SPF tree, and finally, a routing table of paths and ports to each network.

Open Shortest Path First (OSPF) and Intermediate System–to–Intermediate System (IS-IS) are classified as link-state routing protocols. RFC 2328 describes OSPF link-state concepts and operations. Link-state routing protocols collect routing information from all other routers in the network or within a defined area of the internetwork. After all the information is collected, each router, independently of the other routers, calculates its best paths to all destinations in the network. Because each router maintains its own view of the network, it is less likely to propagate incorrect information provided by any one particular neighboring router.

Link-state routing protocols were designed to overcome the limitations of distance vector routing protocols. Link-state routing protocols respond quickly to network changes, send triggered updates only when a network change has occurred, and send periodic updates (known as *link-state refreshes*) at long intervals, such as every 30 minutes with OSPF. A hello mechanism determines the reachability of neighbors.

When a failure occurs in the network, such as when a neighbor becomes unreachable, link-state protocols flood LSAs using a special multicast address throughout an area. Each link-state router takes a copy of the LSA, updates its link-state (topological) database, and forwards the LSA to all neighboring devices. LSAs cause every router within the area to recalculate routes. Because LSAs need to be flooded throughout an area and all routers within that area need to recalculate their routing tables, you should limit the number of link-state routers that can be in an area.

A link is similar to an interface on a router. The state of the link is a description of that interface and of its relationship to its neighboring routers. A description of the interface would include, for example, the IP address of the interface, the mask, the type of network to which it is connected, the routers connected to that network, and so on. The collection of link states forms a link-state, or topological, database. The link-state database is used to calculate the best paths through the network. Link-state routers find the best paths to a destination by applying Dr. Edsger Dijkstra's SPF algorithm against the link-state database to build the SPF tree. The best paths are then selected from the SPF tree and placed in the routing table.

As networks become larger in scale, link-state routing protocols become more attractive for the following reasons:

- Link-state protocols always send updates when a topology changes.

- Periodic refresh updates are more infrequent than for distance vector protocols.

- Networks running link-state routing protocols can be segmented into area hierarchies, limiting the scope of route changes.

- Networks running link-state routing protocols support classless addressing.

- Networks running link-state routing protocols support route summarization.

Link-state protocols use a two-layer network hierarchy, as shown in Figure 14-8.

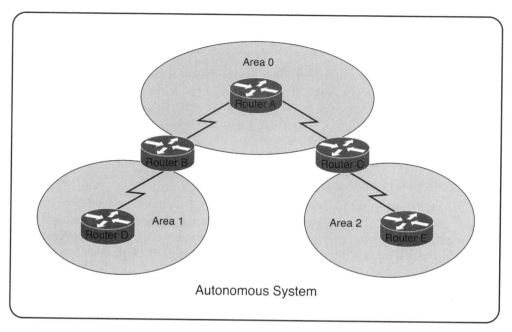

Figure 14-8 *Link-State Network Hierarchy*

The two-layer network hierarchy contains two primary elements:

- **Area:** An area is a grouping of networks. Areas are logical subdivisions of the autonomous system (AS).

- **Autonomous system:** An AS consists of a collection of networks under a common administration that share a common routing strategy. An AS, sometimes called a domain, can be logically subdivided into multiple areas.

Within each AS, a contiguous backbone area must be defined. All other nonbackbone areas are connected off the backbone area. The backbone area is the transition area because all other areas communicate through it. For OSPF, the nonbackbone areas can be additionally configured as a stub area, a totally stubby area, a not-so-stubby area (NSSA), or a totally not-so-stubby area to help reduce the link-state database and routing table size.

Routers operating within the two-layer network hierarchy have different routing entities. The terms used to refer to these entities are different for OSPF than IS-IS. Refer to the following examples from Figure 14-8:

- Router A is called the backbone router in OSPF and the L2 router in IS-IS. The backbone, or L2, router provides connectivity between different areas.

- Routers B and C are called area border routers (ABR) in OSPF and L1/L2 routers in IS-IS. ABR, or L1/L2, routers attach to multiple areas, maintain separate link-state databases for each area to which they are connected, and route traffic destined for or arriving from other areas.

- Routers D and E are called nonbackbone internal routers in OSPF or L1 routers in IS-IS. Nonbackbone internal, or L1, routers are aware of the topology within their respective areas and maintain identical link-state databases about the areas.

- The ABR, or L1/L2, router will advertise a default route to the nonbackbone internal, or L1, router. The L1 router will use the default route to forward all interarea or inter-domain traffic to the ABR, or L1/L2, router. This behavior can be different for OSPF, depending on how the OSPF nonbackbone area is configured (stub area, totally stubby area, or not-so-stubby area).

Link-State Routing Protocol Algorithms

Link-state routing algorithms, known collectively as SPF protocols, maintain a complex database of the network topology. Unlike distance vector protocols, link-state protocols develop and maintain full knowledge of the network routers and how they interconnect. This is achieved through the exchange of link-state packets (LSP) with other routers in a network.

Each router that has exchanged LSPs constructs a topological database using all received LSPs. An SPF algorithm is then used to compute reachability to networked destinations. This information is used to update the routing table. The process can discover changes in the network topology caused by component failure or network growth.

In fact, the LSP exchange is triggered by an event in the network, instead of running periodically. This can greatly speed the convergence process because it is unnecessary to wait for a series of timers to expire before the networked routers can begin to converge.

If the network shown in Figure 14-9 uses a link-state routing protocol, connectivity between New York City and San Francisco is not a concern. Depending on the actual protocol used and the metrics selected, it is highly likely that the routing protocol could discriminate between the two paths to the same destination and try to use the best one.

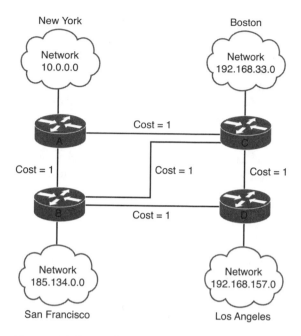

Figure 14-9 *Link-State Algorithms*

Table 14-2 summarizes the contents of the routing database of each router in the figure.

Table 14-2 *Link-State Routing Database*

Router	Destination	Next Hop	Cost
A	185.134.0.0	B	1
	192.168.33.0	C	1
	192.168.157.0	B	2
	192.168.157.0	C	2
B	10.0.0.0	A	1
	192.168.33.0	C	1
	192.168.157.0	D	1
C	10.0.0.0	A	1
	185.134.0.0	B	1
	192.168.157.0	D	1
D	10.0.0.0	B	2
	10.0.0.0	C	2
	185.134.0.0	B	1
	192.168.33.0	C	1

As shown in the table, link-state database entries for the New York (Router A) to Los Angeles (Router D) routes, a link-state protocol would remember both routes. Some link-state protocols can even provide a way to assess the performance capabilities of these two routes and bias toward the better-performing one. If the better-performing path, such as the route through Boston (Router C), experienced operational difficulties of any kind, including congestion or component failure, the link-state routing protocol would detect this change and begin forwarding packets through San Francisco (Router B).

Link-state routing might flood the network with LSPs during initial topology discovery and can be both memory- and processor-intensive. This section describes the benefits of link-state routing, the caveats to consider when using it, and the potential problems.

The following list highlights some of the many benefits that link-state routing protocols have over the traditional distance vector algorithms, such as RIPv1 or the now obsolete Interior Gateway Routing Protocol (IGRP):

■ Link-state protocols use cost metrics to choose paths through the network. For Cisco IOS devices, the cost metric reflects the capacity of the links on those paths.

■ By using triggered, flooded updates, link-state protocols can immediately report changes in the network topology to all routers in the network. This immediate reporting generally leads to fast convergence times.

■ Because each router has a complete and synchronized picture of the network, it is difficult for routing loops to occur.

■ Because LSPs are sequenced and aged, routers always base their routing decisions on the latest set of information.

■ With careful network design, the link-state database sizes can be minimized, leading to smaller SPF calculations and faster convergence.

The link-state approach to dynamic routing can be useful in networks of any size. In a well-designed network, a link-state routing protocol enables your network to gracefully adapt to unexpected topology changes. Using events, such as changes, to drive updates, rather than fixed-interval timers, enables convergence to begin that much more quickly after a topological change.

The overhead of the frequent, time-driven updates of a distance vector routing protocol is also avoided. This makes more bandwidth available for routing traffic rather than for network maintenance, provided that you design your network properly.

A side benefit of the bandwidth efficiency of link-state routing protocols is that they facilitate network scalability better than either static routes or distance vector protocols. When compared to the limitations of static routes or distance vector protocols, you can easily see that link-state routing is best in larger, more complex networks, or in networks that must be highly scalable. Initially, configuring a link-state protocol in a large network can be challenging, but it is well worth the effort in the long run.

Link-state protocols do, however, have the following limitations:

- They require a topology database, an adjacency database, and a forwarding database, in addition to the routing table. This can require a significant amount of memory in large or complex networks.

- Dijkstra's algorithm requires CPU cycles to calculate the best paths through the network. If the network is large or complex (that is, the SPF calculation is complex), or if the network is unstable (that is, the SPF calculation is running on a regular basis), link-state protocols can use significant CPU power.

- To avoid excessive memory or CPU power, a strict hierarchical network design is required, dividing the network into smaller areas to reduce the size of the topology tables and the length of the SPF calculation. However, this dividing can cause problems because areas must remain contiguous at all times. The routers in an area must always be capable of contacting and receiving LSPs from all other routers in their area. In a multiarea design, an area router must always have a path to the backbone, or it will have no connectivity to the rest of the network. In addition, the backbone area must remain connected at all times to avoid some areas from becoming isolated (partitioned).

- The configuration of link-state networks is usually simple, provided that the underlying network architecture has been soundly designed. If the network design is complex, the operation of the link-state protocol might have to be tuned to accommodate it.

- During the initial discovery process, link-state routing protocols can flood the network with LSPs and significantly decrease the capability of the network to transport data because no traffic is passed until after the initial network convergence. This performance compromise is temporary but can be noticeable. Whether this flooding process will noticeably degrade network performance depends on two things: the amount of available bandwidth and the number of routers that must exchange routing information. Flooding in large networks with relatively small links, such as low-bandwidth links, is much more noticeable than a similar exercise on a small network with large links, such as T3s and Ethernet.

- Link-state routing is both memory- and processor-intensive. Consequently, more fully configured routers are required to support link-state routing than distance vector routing. This increases the cost of the routers that are configured for link-state routing.

The following are some of the benefits of a link-state routing protocol:

- Troubleshooting is usually easier in link-state networks because every router has a complete copy of the network topology, or at least of its own area of the network. However, interpreting the information stored in the topology, neighbor databases, and routing table requires an understanding of the concepts of link-state routing.

- Link-state protocols usually scale to larger networks than distance vector protocols, particularly the traditional distance vector protocols such as RIPv1 and IGRP.

You can address and resolve the potential performance impacts of both drawbacks through foresight, planning, and engineering.

Chapter Summary

Dynamic routing requires administrators to configure either a distance vector or a link-state routing protocol. Distance vector routing protocols incorporate solutions such as split horizon, route poisoning, and hold-down timers to prevent routing loops. These protocols must engage in these protection mechanisms because of their simplistic operation. Link-state routing protocols scale to large network infrastructures better than distance vector routing protocols, but they require more planning to implement.

Additional Resources

- Dynamic Routing Protocols Video, AJS Networking: http://ajsnetworking.com/dynrouting

- Routing Basics, Cisco Systems: http://docwiki.cisco.com/wiki/Routing_Basics

Review Questions

Use the questions here to review what you learned in this chapter. The correct answers and solutions are found in Appendix A, "Answers to Chapter Review Questions."

1. Which of the following protocols is an example of an exterior gateway protocol?

   a. RIP

   b. BGP

   c. IGRP

   d. EIGRP

2. In which situation is an administrative distance required?

   a. When static routes are defined

   b. When dynamic routing is enabled

   c. When the same route is learned through multiple routing protocols

   d. When multiple paths are available to the same destination and they are all learned through the same routing protocol

3. When a router receives a packet with a destination address that is in an unknown subnetwork of a directly attached network, what is the default behavior if the **ip classless** command is not enabled?

   a. Drop the packet

   b. Forward the packet to the default route

   c. Forward the packet to the next hop for the directly attached network

   d. Broadcast the packet through all interfaces except the one on which it was received

4. How does a distance vector router learn about paths for networks that are not directly connected?

   a. From the source router

   b. From neighboring routers

   c. From the destination router

   d. A distance vector router can only learn directly connected networks

5. What does a distance vector router send to neighboring routers as part of a periodic routing-table update?

   a. The entire routing table

   b. Information about new routes

   c. Information about routes that have changed

   d. Information about routes that no longer exist

6. How can link-state protocols limit the scope of route changes?

   a. By supporting classless addressing

   b. By sending the mask along with the address

   c. By sending only updates of a topology change

   d. By segmenting the network into area hierarchies

7. What is the purpose of link-state advertisements?

   a. To construct a topological database

   b. To specify the cost to reach a destination

   c. To determine the best path to a destination

   d. To verify that a neighbor is still functioning

8. What is the administrative distance of OSPF?

   a. 110

   b. 120

   c. 20

   d. 90

9. What algorithm is used to calculate best paths used by OSPF?

   a. DUAL

   b. SPF

   c. Bellman-Ford

   d. STP

10. What is the name of the area in OSPF that connects all other areas?

   a. The start area

   b. The central area

   c. The core area

   d. The backbone area

Production Network Simulation Question 14-1

You have a production network router that is participating in your IGP of OSPF. This router has one interface in Area 0 and one interface in Area 2. What is this router called in OSPF, and how many link-state databases does it possess?

Chapter 15

OSPF

This chapter includes the following sections:

- Chapter Objectives

- Introducing OSPF

- Troubleshooting OSPF

- Chapter Summary

- Additional Resources

- Review Questions

- Production Network Simulation Question 15-1

Open Shortest Path First (OSPF) is an interior gateway protocol (IGP) that was designed by the Internet Engineering Task Force (IETF). Because OSPF is a widely deployed standard protocol, knowledge of its configuration and maintenance is essential. This chapter describes the function of OSPF and explains how to configure a single-area OSPF network on a Cisco router.

Chapter Objectives

Upon completing this chapter, you will be able to describe the OSPF protocol in a fair amount of detail. You will also be able to configure single-area OSPF. These abilities include meeting these objectives:

- Describe the features of OSPF

- Explain how OSPF routers become neighbors

- Explain how OSPF decides which is the best path through the network

- Explain the OSPF router ID
- Configure a single-area OSPF network
- Verify a single-area OSPF configuration

Introducing OSPF

Open Shortest Path First is a link-state routing protocol. You can think of a *link* as an interface on a router. The state of the link is a description of that interface and of its relationship to its neighboring routers. A description of the interface would include, for example, the IP address of the interface, the subnet mask, the type of network to which it is connected, the routers that are connected to that network, and so on. The collection of all these link states forms a link-state database.

A router sends link-state advertisement (LSA) packets to advertise its state periodically (every 30 minutes) and immediately when the router state changes. Information about attached interfaces, metrics used, and other variables is included in OSPF LSAs. As OSPF routers accumulate link-state information, they use the shortest path first (SPF) algorithm to calculate the shortest path to each node.

A topological (link-state) database is, essentially, an overall picture of networks in relation to routers. The topological database contains the collection of LSAs received from all routers in the same area. Because routers within the same area share the same information, they have identical topological databases.

OSPF can operate within a hierarchy. The largest entity within the hierarchy is the autonomous system, which is a collection of networks under a common administration that share a common routing strategy. An autonomous system can be divided into a number of areas, which are groups of contiguous networks and attached hosts. Figure 15-1 shows an example of an OSPF hierarchy.

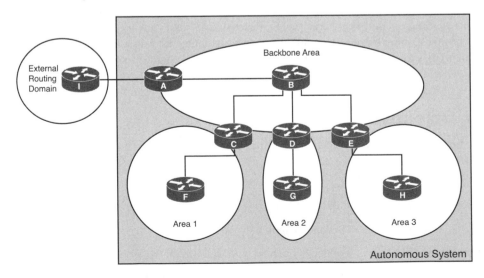

Figure 15-1 *OSPF Hierarchy*

OSPF uses a two-layer network hierarchy that has two primary elements:

- **Autonomous system:** An autonomous system consists of a collection of networks under a common administration that share a common routing strategy. An autonomous system, sometimes called a domain, can be logically subdivided into multiple areas.

- **Area:** An area is a grouping of contiguous networks. Areas are logical subdivisions of the autonomous system.

Within each autonomous system, a contiguous backbone area must be defined. All other nonbackbone areas are connected off the backbone area. The backbone area is the transition area because all other areas communicate through it. For OSPF, the nonbackbone areas can be additionally configured as stub areas, totally stubby areas, or not-so-stubby areas (NSSA) to help reduce the link-state database and routing table size.

OSPF special areas such as NSSAs, totally stubby areas, and stub areas are beyond the scope of this text. Routers that operate within the two-layer network hierarchy have different routing entities and different functions in OSPF. The following are some examples based on Figure 15-1:

- Router B is the backbone router. The backbone router provides connectivity between different areas.

- Routers C, D, and E are area border routers (ABR). ABRs attach to multiple areas, maintain separate link-state databases for each area to which they are connected, and route traffic destined for or arriving from other areas. An ABR is often the point at which route summarization is accomplished in the network.

- Routers F, G, and H are nonbackbone, internal routers. Nonbackbone, internal routers are aware of the topology within their respective areas and maintain identical link-state databases about the areas.

- Depending on the configuration of the OSPF nonbackbone area (stub area, totally stubby area, or NSSA) the ABR advertises a default route to the nonbackbone, internal router. The nonbackbone, internal router uses the default route to forward all interarea or interdomain traffic to the ABR.

- Router A is the autonomous system boundary router (ASBR) that connects to an external routing domain, or autonomous system.

- Router I is a router that belongs to another routing domain, or autonomous system.

Establishing OSPF Neighbor Adjacencies

Neighbor OSPF routers must recognize each other on the network before they can share information because OSPF routing depends on the status of the link between two routers. This process is done using the Hello protocol. The Hello protocol establishes and maintains neighbor relationships by ensuring bidirectional (two-way) communication between neighbors. Bidirectional communication occurs when a router recognizes itself listed in the hello packet received from a neighbor. Figure 15-2 illustrates the hello packet.

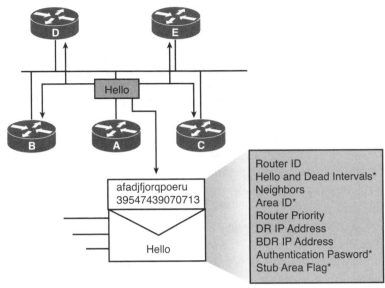

*Entry must match on neighboring routers.

Figure 15-2 *OSPF Hello*

Each interface that is participating in OSPF uses IP multicast address 224.0.0.5 to periodically send hello packets. A hello packet contains the following information:

■ **Router ID:** The router ID is a 32-bit number that uniquely identifies the router. The highest IP address on an active interface is chosen by default, unless a loopback interface or the router ID is configured. For example, IP address 172.16.12.1 would be chosen over 172.16.1.1. This identification is important in establishing and troubleshooting neighbor relationships and coordinating route exchanges.

■ **Hello and dead intervals:** The hello interval specifies the frequency in seconds at which a router sends hello packets. The default hello interval on multiaccess networks is 10 seconds. The dead interval is the time in seconds that a router waits to hear from a neighbor before declaring the neighboring router out of service. By default, the dead interval is four times the hello interval. These timers must be the same on neighboring routers; otherwise, an adjacency will not be established.

■ **Neighbors:** The Neighbors field lists the adjacent routers with established bidirectional communication. This bidirectional communication is indicated when the router recognizes itself listed in the Neighbors field of the hello packet from the neighbor.

■ **Area ID:** To communicate, two routers must share a common segment, and their interfaces must belong to the same OSPF area on that segment. The neighbors must also share the same subnet and mask. All these routers will have the same link-state information.

- **Router priority:** The router priority is an 8-bit number that indicates the priority of a router. OSPF uses the priority to select a designated router (DR) and a backup DR (BDR). A value of 0 specifies that the router should not participate in the election process. Higher values are preferred.

- **DR and BDR IP addresses:** These are the IP addresses of the DR and BDR for the specific network, if they are known.

Note   OSPF DRs and BDRs are discussed in greater detail in the Cisco Certified Networking Professional (CCNP) curriculum.

- **Authentication password:** If router authentication is enabled, two routers must exchange the same password. OSPF has three types of authentication: null (no authentication), simple (plain-text passwords), and message digest algorithm 5 (MD5). Authentication is not required, but if it is enabled, all peer routers must have the same password and authentication type.

- **Stub area flag:** A stub area is a special area. Designating a stub area is a technique that reduces routing updates by replacing them with a default route. Two routers must agree on the stub area flag in the hello packets.

Note   OSPF special areas, such as stub areas, are discussed in greater detail in the CCNP curriculum.

SPF Algorithm

The SPF algorithm places each router at the root of a tree and calculates the shortest path to each node, using Dijkstra's algorithm, based on the cumulative cost that is required to reach that destination. LSAs are flooded throughout the area using a reliable algorithm, which ensures that all routers in an area have the same topological database. Each router uses the information in its topological database to calculate a shortest-path tree, with itself as the root. The router then uses this tree to route network traffic. Figure 15-3 represents the Router A view of the network, where Router A is the root and calculates pathways assuming this view.

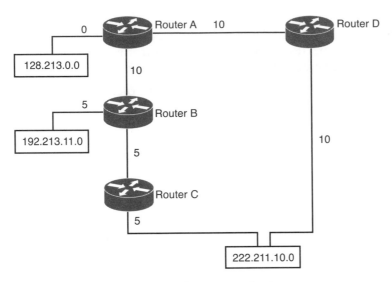

Figure 15-3   *SPF Algorithm for Route Selection*

Each router has its own view of the topology, even though all the routers build a shortest-path tree using the same link-state database.

The cost, or *metric*, of an interface is an indication of the overhead that is required to send packets across a certain interface. The interface cost is inversely proportional to the bandwidth, so a higher bandwidth indicates a lower cost. There is more overhead, higher cost, and more time delays involved in crossing a T1 serial line than in crossing a 10-Mbps Ethernet line.

The formula used to calculate OSPF cost is as follows:

Cost = Reference bandwidth / Interface bandwidth (in bps)

The default reference bandwidth is 108, which is 100,000,000 or the equivalent of the bandwidth of Fast Ethernet. Therefore, the default cost of a 10-Mbps Ethernet link will be 108 / 107 = 10, and the cost of a T1 link will be 108 / 1,544,000 = 64.

To adjust the reference bandwidth for links with bandwidths greater than Fast Ethernet, use the **ospf auto-cost reference-bandwidth** *ref-bw* command configured in the OSPF routing process configuration mode. This configuration is typically made in modern high-speed LAN environments. This is to ensure that gigabit-per-second links can be distinguished from other Fast Ethernet links.

Configuring and Verifying OSPF

The **router ospf** command uses a process identifier as an argument. The process ID is a unique, arbitrary number that you select to identify the routing process. The process ID does not need to match the OSPF process ID on other OSPF routers.

The **network** command identifies which IP interfaces on the router are part of the OSPF network. For each network, you must also identify the OSPF area to which the networks belong. The **network** command takes the three arguments listed in Table 15-1. The table defines the parameters of the **network** command.

Table 15-1   network *Command Parameters*

OSPF Config Command Parameters	Description
address	The network, subnet, or interface address.
wildcard-mask	The wildcard mask. This mask identifies the part of the IP address that is to be matched, where 0 is a match and 1 is "don't care." For example, a wildcard mask of 0.0.0.0 indicates a match of all 32 bits in the address.
area-id	The area that is to be associated with the OSPF address range. It can be specified either as a decimal value or in dotted-decimal notation, like an IP address.

Calculating wildcard masks on non-8-bit boundaries can be prone to error. You can avoid calculating wildcard masks by having a network statement that matches the IP address on each interface and uses the 0.0.0.0 mask. This configuration also ensures precision in your configuration, allowing you to specify the exact interfaces that are to participate in OSPF.

Figure 15-4 shows an example of a single-area OSPF configuration on Router B.

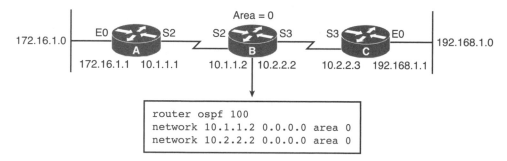

Figure 15-4   *Single-Area OSPF*

Loopback Interfaces

The OSPF router ID is used to uniquely identify each router in the OSPF network. By default, this ID is selected by the operating system from the configured IP addresses on the router. To modify the OSPF router ID to use a loopback address, first define a loopback interface with the following command:

```
RouterX(config)# interface loopback number
```

The highest IP address, used as the router ID by default, can be overridden by configuring an IP address on a loopback interface. OSPF is more reliable if a loopback interface is configured because the interface is always active and cannot be in a down state like a "real" interface can. For this reason, the loopback address should be used on all key routers. If the loopback address is going to be published with the **network area** command, using a private IP address will save on registered IP address space. Note that a loopback address requires a different subnet for each router, unless the host address is advertised.

Using an address that is not advertised saves real IP address space, but unlike an address that is advertised, the unadvertised address does not appear in the OSPF table and thus cannot be accessed across the network. Therefore, using a private IP address represents a trade-off between the ease of debugging the network and conservation of address space. Figure 15-5 highlights some of the advantages and disadvantages of using advertised and unadvertised loopback addresses.

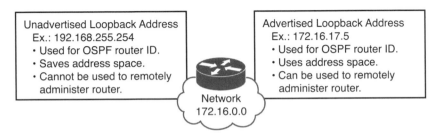

Figure 15-5   *Loopback Addresses*

Verifying the OSPF Configuration

You can use any one of a number of **show** commands to display information about an OSPF configuration. The **show ip protocols** command displays parameters about timers, filters, metrics, networks, and other information for the entire router.

The **show ip route** command displays the routes that are known to the router and how they were learned. This command is one of the best ways to determine connectivity between the local router and the rest of the internetwork. Example 15-1 shows the output from the **show ip route ospf** command for a router running OSPF.

Example 15-1   *Displaying Routes Known by Router*

```
RouterX# show ip route ospf

Codes: I - IGRP derived, R - RIP derived, O - OSPF derived,
       C - connected, S - static, E - EGP derived, B - BGP derived,
       * - candidate default route, IA - OSPF inter area route,
       i - IS-IS derived, ia - IS-IS, U - per-user static route,
       o - on-demand routing, M - mobile, P - periodic downloaded static route,
       D - EIGRP, EX - EIGRP external, E1 - OSPF external type 1 route,
```

```
        E2 - OSPF external type 2 route, N1 - OSPF NSSA external type 1 route,
        N2 - OSPF NSSA external type 2 route

Gateway of last resort is 10.119.254.240 to network 10.140.0.0

O 10.110.0.0 [110/5] via 10.119.254.6, 0:01:00, Ethernet2
O IA 10.67.10.0 [110/10] via 10.119.254.244, 0:02:22, Ethernet2
O 10.68.132.0 [110/5] via 10.119.254.6, 0:00:59, Ethernet2
O 10.130.0.0 [110/5] via 10.119.254.6, 0:00:59, Ethernet2
O E2 10.128.0.0 [170/10] via 10.119.254.244, 0:02:22, Ethernet2
```

Table 15-2 describes the significant fields shown in the **show ip route** display.

Table 15-2   *IP Routing Table Fields*

Value	Description
O	This field indicates the learning method that derived the route. It can be one of the following values:
	I: IGRP1-derived
	R: RIP2-derived
	O: OSPF-derived (the value displayed in the example)
	C: Connected
	S: Static
	E: EGP3-derived
	B: BGP4-derived
	D: EIGRP5-derived
	EX: EIGRP external
	i: IS-IS6-derived
	ia: IS-IS
	M: Mobile
	P: Periodic downloaded static route
	U: Per-user static route
	o: On-demand routing

Value	Description
E2	This field indicates the type of route. It can be one of the following values:
IA	*: Indicates the last path used when a packet was forwarded. It pertains only to the nonfast-switched packets. However, it does not indicate which path will be used next when forwarding a nonfast-switched packet, except when the paths are equal cost.
	IA: OSPF interarea route
	E1: OSPF external type 1 route
	E2: OSPF external type 2 route (the value displayed in the example)
	L1: IS-IS level 1 route
	L2: IS-IS level 2 route
	N1: OSPF NSSA external type 1 route
	N2: OSPF NSSA external type 2 route
172.150.0.0	This address indicates the address of the remote network.
[110/5]	The first number in the brackets is the administrative distance of the information source; the second number is the metric for the route.
via 10.119.254.6	This value specifies the address of the next router to the remote network.
0:01:00	This field specifies the last time the route was updated (in hours:minutes:seconds).
Ethernet2	This field specifies the interface through which the specified network can be reached.

Use the **show ip ospf** command to verify the OSPF router ID. This command also displays OSPF timer settings and other statistics, including the number of times the SPF algorithm has been executed. In addition, this command has optional parameters so that you can further specify the information that is to be displayed.

Example 15-2 shows the output from this command when it is executed on Router X.

Example 15-2   show ip ospf *Command Output*

```
RouterX# show ip ospf
 Routing Process "ospf 50" with ID 10.64.0.2
 Supports only single TOS(TOS0) routes
 Supports opaque LSA
 Supports Link-local Signaling (LLS)
 Supports area transit capability
 Initial SPF schedule delay 5000 msecs
 Minimum hold time between two consecutive SPFs 10000 msecs
 Maximum wait time between two consecutive SPFs 10000 msecs
 Incremental-SPF disabled
 Minimum LSA interval 5 secs
 Minimum LSA arrival 1000 msecs
 LSA group pacing timer 240 secs
 Interface flood pacing timer 33 msecs
 Retransmission pacing timer 66 msecs
 Number of external LSA 0. Checksum Sum 0x000000
 Number of opaque AS LSA 0. Checksum Sum 0x000000
 Number of DCbitless external and opaque AS LSA 0
 Number of DoNotAge external and opaque AS LSA
 Number of areas in this router is 1. 1 normal 0 stub 0 nssa
 Number of areas transit capable is 0
External flood list length 0
    Area BACKBONE(0)
    Area BACKBONE(0)
        Area has no authentication
        SPF algorithm last executed 00:01:25.028 ago
        SPF algorithm executed 7 times
        Area ranges are
        Number of LSA 6. Checksum Sum 0x01FE3E
        Number of opaque link LSA 0. Checksum Sum 0x000000
        Number of DCbitless LSA 0
        Number of indication LSA 0
        Number of DoNotAge LSA 0
        Flood list length 0
```

The **show ip ospf interface** command verifies that interfaces have been configured in the intended areas. If no loopback address is specified, the interface with the highest address is chosen as the router ID. This command also displays the timer intervals, including the hello interval, and shows the neighbor adjacencies. Example 15-3 demonstrates output from the **show ip ospf interface** command.

Example 15-3   show ip ospf interface *Command Output*

```
RouterX# show ip ospf interface ethernet 0

Ethernet 0 is up, line protocol is up
Internet Address 192.168.254.202, Mask 255.255.255.0, Area 0.0.0.0
AS 201, Router ID 192.168.99.1, Network Type BROADCAST, Cost: 10
Transmit Delay is 1 sec, State OTHER, Priority 1
Designated Router id 192.168.254.10, Interface address 192.168.254.10
Backup Designated router id 192.168.254.28, Interface addr 192.168.254.28
Timer intervals configured, Hello 10, Dead 60, Wait 40, Retransmit 5
Hello due in 0:00:05
Neighbor Count is 8, Adjacent neighbor count is 2
 Adjacent with neighbor 192.168.254.28 (Backup Designated Router)
  Adjacent with neighbor 192.168.254.10 (Designated Router)
```

Table 15-3 describes the output for the **show ip ospf interface** command.

Table 15-3   show ip ospf interface *Output*

Field	Description
Ethernet	Status of physical link and operational status of protocol
Internet Address	Interface IP address, subnet mask, and area address
AS	Autonomous system number (OSPF process ID), router ID, network type, link-state cost
Transmit Delay	Transmit delay, interface state, and router priority
Designated Router	Designated router ID and respective interface IP address
Backup Designated Router	Backup designated router ID and respective interface IP address
Timer Intervals Configured	Configuration of timer intervals
Hello	Number of seconds until the next hello packet is sent out of this interface
Neighbor Count	Count of network neighbors and list of adjacent neighbors

The **show ip ospf neighbor** command displays OSPF neighbor information on a per-interface basis.

Example 15-4 shows output from the **show ip ospf neighbor** command, with a single line of summary information for each neighbor in the output.

Example 15-4 show ip ospf neighbor *Command Output*

```
RouterX# show ip ospf neighbor

ID                Pri  State          Dead Time  Address         Interface
10.199.199.137    1    FULL/DR        0:00:31    192.168.80.37   FastEthernet0/0
172.16.48.1       1    FULL/DROTHER   0:00:33    172.16.48.1     FastEthernet0/1
172.16.48.200     1    FULL/DROTHER   0:00:33    172.16.48.200   FastEthernet0/1
10.199.199.137    5    FULL/DR        0:00:33    172.16.48.189   FastEthernet0/1
```

For more specific information about a given neighbor, use the same command, but specify the address of a given neighbor. Example 15-5 shows how to get specific information for the neighbor 10.199.199.137.

Example 15-5 show ip ospf neighbor *Command Output for a Specific Neighbor*

```
RouterX# show ip ospf neighbor 10.199.199.137
Neighbor 10.199.199.137, interface address 192.168.80.37
In the area 0.0.0.0 via interface Ethernet0
Neighbor priority is 1, State is FULL
Options 2
Dead timer due in 0:00:32
Link State retransmission due in 0:00:04
Neighbor 10.199.199.137, interface address 172.16.48.189
In the area 0.0.0.0 via interface Fddi0
Neighbor priority is 5, State is FULL
Options 2
Dead timer due in 0:00:32
Link State retransmission due in 0:00:03
```

Table 15-4 describes the significant fields for the **show ip ospf neighbor** command output.

Table 15-4 show ip ospf neighbor *Output*

Field	Description
Neighbor	Neighbor router ID.
Interface Address	IP address of the interface.
In the Area	Area and interface through which the OSPF neighbor is known.
Neighbor Priority	Router priority of the neighbor, neighbor state.
State	OSPF state.
State Changes	Number of state changes since the neighbor was created. This value can be reset using the **clear ip ospf counters neighbor** command.
DR	Router ID of the designated router for the interface.

Field	Description
BDR	Router ID of the backup designated router for the interface.
Options	Hello packet options field contents. (E-bit only. Possible values are 0 and 2. 2 indicates that the area is not a stub; 0 indicates that the area is a stub.)
LLS Options..., Last OOB-Resync	LLS1 and OOB2 link-state database resynchronization performed hours:minutes:seconds ago (Cisco NSF3 information). The field indicates the last successful OOB resynchronization with the Cisco NSF-capable router.
Dead Timer Due In	Expected time before Cisco IOS Software will declare the neighbor dead.
Neighbor Is Up For	Number of hours:minutes:seconds since the neighbor went into a two-way state.
Index	Neighbor location in the area-wide and autonomous system–wide retransmission queue.
Retransmission Queue Length	Number of elements in the retransmission queue.
Number of Retransmission	Number of times update packets have been resent during flooding.
First	Memory location of the flooding details.
Next	Memory location of the flooding details.
Last Retransmission Scan Length	Number of LSAs in the last retransmission packet.
Maximum	Maximum number of LSAs that can be sent in any retransmission packet.
Last Retransmission Scan Time	Time taken to build the last retransmission packet.
Maximum	Maximum time taken to build any retransmission packet.

Using OSPF debug Commands

The **debug ip ospf events** command output shown in Example 15-6 might appear if any of the following situations occur:

- The IP subnet masks for the routers on the same network do not match.
- The OSPF hello interval for the router does not match the OSPF hello interval that is configured on a neighbor.
- The OSPF dead interval for the router does not match the OSPF dead interval that is configured on a neighbor.

Example 15-6   debug ip ospf events *Command Output*

```
RouterX# debug ip ospf events

OSPF:hello with invalid timers on interface Ethernet0
hello interval received 10 configured 10
net mask received 255.255.255.0 configured 255.255.255.0
dead interval received 40 configured 30

OSPF: hello packet with mismatched E bit
```

If a router that is configured for OSPF routing is not seeing an OSPF neighbor on an attached network, perform the following tasks:

- Ensure that both routers have been configured with the same IP subnet mask and that the OSPF hello interval and dead intervals match on both routers.

- Ensure that both neighbors are part of the same area number and area type.

- Ensure that authentication type and passwords match.

In Example 15-6, which shows output from the **debug ip ospf events** command, the neighbor router and this router are not part of a stub area, denoted by the mismatched E bit. That is, one router is configured for the area to be a transit area, and the other router is configured for the area to be a stub area, as explained in RFC 2328.

To display information about each OSPF packet that is received, use the **debug ip ospf packet** privileged EXEC command. The **no** form of this command disables the debugging output.

The **debug ip ospf packet** command produces one set of information for each packet that is received. The output varies slightly depending on which authentication is used. The table shows sample output from the **debug ip ospf packet** command when message digest algorithm 5 (MD5) authentication is used. Example 15-7 shows an OSPF message received and displayed when using this **debug** command.

Example 15-7   debug ip ospf packet *Command Output*

```
RouterX# debug ip ospf packet

OSPF: rcv. v:2 t:1 l:48 rid:200.0.0.116
        aid:0.0.0.0 chk:0 aut:2 keyid:1 seq:0x0
```

Table 15-5 describes the significance of the fields in this output.

Table 15-5 debug ip ospf packet *Fields*

Field	Description
v:	OSPF version
t:	OSPF packet type; possible packet types are as follows: ■ Hello ■ Data description ■ Link-state request ■ Link-state update ■ Link-state acknowledgment
l:	OSPF packet length in bytes
rid:	OSPF router ID
aid:	OSPF area ID
chk:	OSPF checksum
aut:	OSPF authentication type; possible authentication types are as follows: 0: No authentication 1: Simple password 2: MD5
auk:	OSPF authentication key
keyid:	MD5 key ID
seq:	Sequence number

Load Balancing with OSPF

Load balancing is a standard functionality of Cisco IOS Software that is available across all router platforms. It is inherent to the forwarding process in the router, and it enables a router to use multiple paths to a destination when it forwards packets. The number of paths used is limited by the number of entries that the routing protocol puts in the routing table. Four entries is the default in Cisco IOS Software for IP routing protocols except for BGP. BGP has a default of one entry. The maximum number of paths you can configure is 16.

Figure 15-6 shows an example of configuring an OSPF router to load-balance across six equal-cost paths.

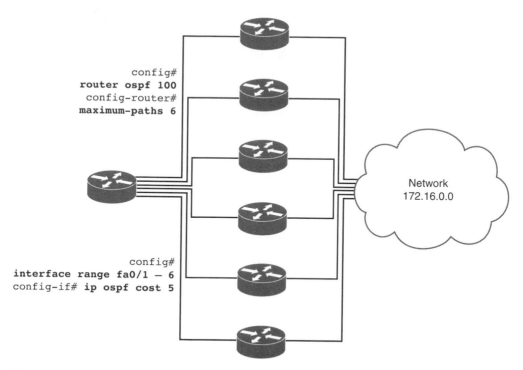

Figure 15-6   *OSPF Equal-Cost Load Balancing*

The cost (or metric) of an interface in OSPF indicates the overhead that is required to send packets across a certain interface. The cost of an interface is inversely proportional to its bandwidth. A higher bandwidth indicates a lower cost. By default, Cisco routers calculate the cost of an interface based on the bandwidth. However, you can force the cost of an interface with the **ip ospf cost** {*value*} command in interface configuration mode.

If equal-cost paths exist to the same destination, the Cisco implementation of OSPF can keep track of up to 16 next hops to the same destination in the routing table (which is called *load balancing*). By default, the Cisco router supports up to four equal-cost paths to a destination for OSPF. Use the **maximum-paths** command in the OSPF router process configuration mode to set the number of equal-cost paths in the routing table, as shown in Example 15-8.

Example 15-8   *Setting the Number of Equal-Cost Paths in the Routing Table*

```
RouterX(config)# router ospf 1
RouterX(config-router)# maximum-paths ?
<1-16>  Number of paths
RouterX(config-router)# maximum-paths 3
```

You can use the **show ip route** command to find equal-cost routes. Following is an example of the **show ip route** command output for a specific subnet that has multiple routes available in the routing table. Example 15-9 shows three equal-cost paths to the 194.168.20.0 network.

Example 15-9 *Finding Equal-Cost Routes with the show ip route Command*

```
RouterX# show ip route 194.168.20.0
 Routing entry for 194.168.20.0/24
  Known via "ospf 1", distance 110, metric 74, type intra area
  Redistributing via ospf 1
  Last update from 10.10.10.1 on Serial1, 00:00:01 ago
  Routing Descriptor Blocks:
  * 20.20.20.1, from 204.204.204.1, 00:00:01 ago, via Serial2
      Route metric is 74, traffic share count is 1
    30.30.30.1, from 204.204.204.1, 00:00:01 ago, via Serial3
      Route metric is 74, traffic share count is 1
    10.10.10.1, from 204.204.204.1, 00:00:01 ago, via Serial1
      Route metric is 74, traffic share count is 1
```

Notice the three routing descriptor blocks. Each block is one available route. Also note the asterisk (*) next to one of the block entries. The asterisk corresponds to the active route that is used for new traffic. The term *new traffic* corresponds to a single packet or an entire flow to a destination, depending on whether the router is performing per-destination or per-packet load balancing.

OSPF Authentication

OSPF neighbor authentication (also called *neighbor router authentication* or *route authentication*) can be configured so that routers can participate in routing based on predefined passwords.

When you configure neighbor authentication on a router, the router authenticates the source of each routing update packet that it receives. This authentication is accomplished by the exchange of an authenticating key (sometimes referred to as a *password*) that is known to both the sending and receiving router.

Types of Authentication

By default, OSPF uses null authentication (Type 0), which means that routing exchanges over a network are not authenticated. OSPF supports two other authentication methods:

- Plaintext (or simple) password authentication (Type 1)

- MD5 authentication (Type 2)

OSPF MD5 authentication includes an increasing sequence number in each OSPF packet to protect against replay attacks.

Configuring Plaintext Password Authentication

To configure OSPF plaintext password authentication, complete the following steps:

1. Use the interface level **ip ospf authentication-key** *password* command to assign a password to use with neighboring routers that use the OSPF simple password authentication. The *password* can be any continuous string of characters that can be entered from the keyboard, up to eight characters in length.

Note   In Cisco IOS Release 12.4, the router gives a warning message if you try to configure a password longer than eight characters; only the first eight characters are used. Some earlier Cisco IOS Software releases did not provide this warning.

2. The password that is created by this command is used as a "key" that is inserted directly into the OSPF header when Cisco IOS Software originates routing protocol packets. A separate password can be assigned to each network on a per-interface basis. All neighboring routers on the same network must have the same password to be able to exchange OSPF information.

Note   If you do not use the **service password-encryption** command when configuring OSPF authentication, the key is stored as plaintext in the router configuration. If you configure the global **service password-encryption** command, the key is stored and displayed in an encrypted form; when it is displayed, an encryption type of 7 is specified before the encrypted key.

3. Specify the authentication type using the interface level **ip ospf authentication** command. Table 15-6 explains the parameters for this command.

Table 15-6   ip ospf authentication *Command Parameters*

Parameter	Description
message-digest	(Optional) Specifies that MD5 authentication will be used.
null	(Optional) No authentication is used. This option is useful for overriding password or MD5 authentication if configured for an area.

4. For plaintext password authentication, use the **ip ospf authentication** command with no parameters. Before using this command, configure a password for the interface using the **ip ospf authentication-key** command. The **ip ospf authentication** command was introduced in Cisco IOS Release 12.0. For backward compatibility, the authentication type for an area is still supported. If the authentication type is not specified for an interface, the authentication type for the area is used. (The area default is null authentication.) To enable authentication for an OSPF area, use the **area** *area-id* **authentication** [*message-digest*] router configuration command. Table 15-7 explains the parameters for this command.

Table 15-7   area authentication *Parameters*

Parameter	Description
area-id	Identifier of the area for which authentication is to be enabled. The identifier can be specified as either a decimal value or an IP address.
message-digest	(Optional) Enables MD5 authentication on the area specified by the *area-id* argument.

Example: Plaintext Password Authentication Configuration

Figure 15-7 shows the network that is used to illustrate the configuration, verification, and troubleshooting of plaintext password authentication.

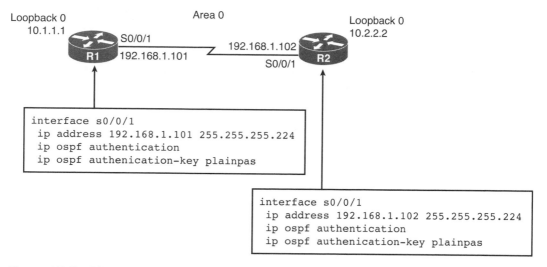

Figure 15-7 *Plaintext Password Authentication*

Plaintext password authentication is configured on interface serial 0/0/1 with the **ip ospf authentication** command. The interface is configured with an authentication key of "plainpas."

Notice that the connecting interfaces on both Router 1 and Router 2 are configured for the same type of authentication with the same authentication key.

Verifying Plaintext Password Authentication

Example 15-10 shows output from the **show ip ospf neighbor** and **show ip route** commands for a router that was configured with authentication.

Example 15-10 *Verifying Authentication with the* **show ip ospf** neighbor *and* **show ip route** *Commands*

```
RouterX# show ip ospf neighbor
Neighbor ID    Pri      State      Dead Time     Address          Interface
10.2.2.2        0       FULL/      00:00:32      192.168.1.102    Serial0/0/1


RouterX# show ip route
<output omitted>
Gateway of last resort is not set
10.0.0.0/8 is variably subnetted, 2 subnets, 2 masks
O       10.2.2.2/32 [110/782] via 192.168.1.102, 00:01:17, Serial0/0/1
C       10.1.1.0/24 is directly connected, Loopback0
     192.168.1.0/27 is subnetted, 1 subnets
C       192.168.1.96 is directly connected, Serial0/0/1
```

Notice that the neighbor state is FULL, indicating that the two routers have successfully formed an OSPF adjacency. The routing table verifies that the 10.2.2.2 address has been learned through OSPF over the serial connection.

The results of a ping to the Router Y loopback interface address are also displayed to illustrate that the link is working, as shown in Example 15-11.

Example 15-11   *Using* ping *Output to Verify Link Operation*

```
RouterX# ping 10.2.2.2
Type escape sequence to abort.
Sending 5, 100-byte ICMP Echos to 10.2.2.2, timeout is 2 seconds:
!!!!!
Success rate is 100 percent (5/5), round-trip min/avg/max = 28/29/32 ms
```

Troubleshooting OSPF

Because it is a link-state routing protocol, OSPF scales well with a growing network. But this scalability introduces complexity in design, configuration, and maintenance. This section introduces some of the common issues surrounding an OSPF network and offers a flowchart approach to troubleshooting these issues.

Components of Troubleshooting OSPF

Troubleshooting OSPF requires an understanding of the operation of the protocol as well as a specific approach methodology. Figure 15-8 shows the major components of OSPF troubleshooting and the order in which the process flows.

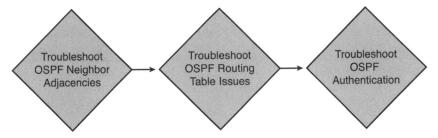

Figure 15-8   *Components of Troubleshooting OSPF*

The major components of OSPF troubleshooting include the following:

- OSPF neighbor adjacencies
- The OSPF routing table
- OSPF authentication

Troubleshooting OSPF Neighbor Adjacencies

The first component to troubleshoot and verify is the OSPF neighbor adjacency. Figure 15-9 shows the verification/troubleshooting components for neighbor adjacencies.

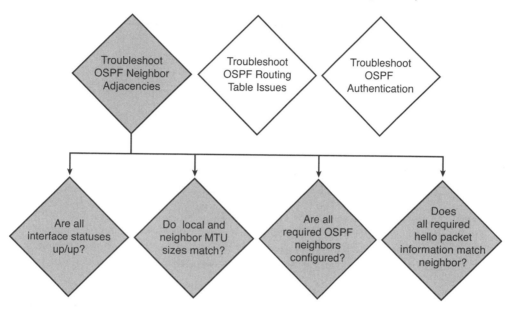

Figure 15-9 *Troubleshooting OSPF Neighbor Adjacencies*

A healthy OSPF neighbor state is "Full." If the OSPF neighbor state remains in any other state, it can indicate a problem. Example 15-12 demonstrates sample output from the **show ip ospf neighbor** command to gather this information.

Example 15-12 *Verifying OSPF Neighbor State*

```
RouterX# show ip ospf neighbor
Neighbor ID      Pri   State       Dead Time      Address         Interface
172.16.31.100    0     Full/  -    00:00:31       10.140.1.1      Serial0/0/0
192.168.1.81     0     Full/  -    00:00:31       10.23.23.2      Serial0/0/1
```

To determine whether a possible Layer 1 or Layer 2 problem exists with a connection, display the status of an interface using the **show ip ospf neighbor** command. "Administratively Down" indicates that the interface is not enabled. If the status of the interface is not up/up, there will be no OSPF neighbor adjacencies. In Example 15-13, serial 0/0/1 is up/up.

Example 15-13 *Verifying Interface Status*

```
RouterX# show ip ospf interface
Serial0/0/1 is up, line protocol is up
  Internet Address 10.23.23.1/24, Area 0
  Process ID 100, Router ID 192.168.1.65, Network Type POINT_TO_POINT, Cost: 1562
```

For OSPF to create an adjacency with a directly connected neighbor router, both routers must agree on the maximum transmission unit (MTU) size. To check the MTU size of an interface, use the **show interface** command. In Example 15-14, the MTU size is 1500 bytes.

Example 15-14   *Verifying Interface MTU Size*

```
RouterX# show ip interface fa0/0
FastEthernet0/0 is up, line protocol is up
  Internet address is 10.2.2.3/24
  Broadcast address is 255.255.255.255
  Address determined by setup command
  MTU is 1500 bytes
  Helper address is not set
  Directed broadcast forwarding is disabled
  Outgoing access list is not set
  Inbound  access list is not set
```

The **network** command that you configure under the OSPF routing process indicates which router interfaces participate in OSPF and determines in which area the interface belongs. If an interface appears under the **show ip ospf interface** command, that interface is running OSPF. In Example 15-15, interfaces serial 0/0/1 and serial 0/0/0 are running OSPF.

Example 15-15   *Verifying Whether an Interface Is Running OSPF*

```
RouterX# show ip ospf interface
Serial0/0/1 is up, line protocol is up
  Internet Address 10.23.23.1/24, Area 0
  Process ID 100, Router ID 192.168.1.65, Network Type POINT_TO_POINT, Cost: 1562
  Transmit Delay is 1 sec, State POINT_TO_POINT,
  Timer intervals configured, Hello 10, Dead 40, Wait 40, Retransmit 5
    oob-resync timeout 40
    Hello due in 00:00:04
  Neighbor Count is 1, Adjacent neighbor count is 1
    Adjacent with neighbor 192.168.1.81
  Suppress hello for 0 neighbor(s)
  Simple password authentication enabled

Serial0/0/0 is up, line protocol is up
  Internet Address 10.140.1.2/24, Area 0
  Process ID 100, Router ID 192.168.1.65, Network Type POINT_TO_POINT, Cost: 1562
  Transmit Delay is 1 sec, State POINT_TO_POINT,
```

OSPF routers exchange hello packets to create neighbor adjacencies. Four items in an OSPF hello packet must match before an OSPF adjacency can occur:

- Area ID

- Hello and dead intervals

- Authentication password

- Stub area flag

To determine whether any of these hello packet options do not match, use the **debug ip ospf adj** command. The output in Example 15-16 illustrates a successful adjacency on the serial 0/0/1 interface.

Example 15-16 *Verifying OSPF Adjacencies*

```
RouterX# debug ip ospf adj *Feb 17 18:41:51.242: OSPF: Interface Serial0/0/1 going
  Up
*Feb 17 18:41:51.742: OSPF: Build router LSA for area 0, router ID 10.1.1.1, seq
  0x80000013
*Feb 17 18:41:52.242: %LINEPROTO-5-UPDOWN: Line protocol on Interface Serial0/0/1,
  changed state to up
*Feb 17 18:42:01.250: OSPF: 2 Way Communication to 10.2.2.2 on Serial0/0/1, state
  2WAY
*Feb 17 18:42:01.250: OSPF: Send DBD to 10.2.2.2 on Serial0/0/1 seq 0x9B6 opt 0x52
  flag 0x7
  len 32
*Feb 17 18:42:01.262: OSPF: Rcv DBD from 10.2.2.2 on Serial0/0/1 seq 0x23ED opt0x52
  flag 0x7
  len 32  mtu 1500 state EXSTART
*Feb 17 18:42:01.262: OSPF: NBR Negotiation Done. We are the SLAVE
*Feb 17 18:42:01.262: OSPF: Send DBD to 10.2.2.2 on Serial0/0/1 seq 0x23ED opt 0x52
  flag 0x2
  len 72
*Feb 17 18:42:01.294: OSPF: Rcv DBD from 10.2.2.2 on Serial0/0/1 seq 0x23EE opt0x52
  flag 0x3
  len 72  mtu 1500 state EXCHANGE
*Feb 17 18:42:01.294: OSPF: Send DBD to 10.2.2.2 on Serial0/0/1 seq 0x23EE opt 0x52
  flag 0x0
  len 32
*Feb 17 18:42:01.294: OSPF: Database request to 10.2.2.2
*Feb 17 18:42:01.294: OSPF: sent LS REQ packet to 192.168.1.102, length 12
*Feb 17 18:42:01.314: OSPF: Rcv DBD from 10.2.2.2 on Serial0/0/1 seq 0x23EF opt0x52
  flag 0x1
  len 32  mtu 1500 state EXCHANGE
*Feb 17 18:42:01.314: OSPF: Exchange Done with 10.2.2.2 on Serial0/0/1
*Feb 17 18:42:01.314: OSPF: Send DBD to 10.2.2.2 on Serial0/0/1 seq 0x23EF opt 0x52
  flag 0x0
  len 32
*Feb 17 18:42:01.326: OSPF: Synchronized with 10.2.2.2 on Serial0/0/1, state FULL
*Feb 17 18:42:01.330: %OSPF-5-ADJCHG: Process 10, Nbr 10.2.2.2 on Serial0/0/1
  from LOADING to FULL, Loading Done
*Feb 17 18:42:01.830: OSPF: Build router LSA for area 0, router ID 10.1.1.1, seq
  0x80000014
```

Troubleshooting OSPF Routing Tables

After you verify that the adjacencies are correct, the next step is to troubleshoot/verify the routing tables. Figure 15-10 shows the procedures for verifying the routing tables.

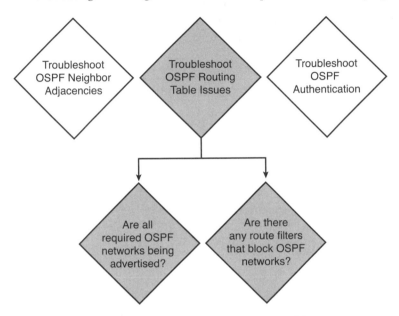

Figure 15-10   *Troubleshooting OSPF Routing Tables*

An OSPF route found in the routing table can have a variety of different codes:

- **O:** OSPF intra-area, within the same area, route from a router within the same OSPF area

- **O IA:** OSPF inter-area, from another area in the OSPF network, route from a router in a different OSPF area

- **O E1 or E2:** An external OSPF route from another autonomous system

If you have a single OSPF area, you should not see O IA routes in the routing table. Example 15-17 has both an O IA and an O E2 route.

Example 15-17   *Determining OSPF Route Types*

```
RouterX# show ip route
Codes: C - connected, S - static, R - RIP, M - mobile, B - BGP
       D - EIGRP, EX - EIGRP external, O - OSPF, IA - OSPF inter area
       N1 - OSPF NSSA external type 1, N2 - OSPF NSSA external type 2
       E1 - OSPF external type 1, E2 - OSPF external type 2
       ia - IS-IS inter area, * - candidate default,
        o - ODR, P - periodic downloaded static route
```

```
Gateway of last resort is not set
172.16.0.0/32 is subnetted, 1 subnets
O       172.16.31.100 [110/1563] via 10.140.1.1, 00:03:15, Serial0/0/0
     10.0.0.0/24 is subnetted, 5 subnets
C       10.2.2.0 is directly connected, FastEthernet0/0
O IA     10.1.1.0 [110/1563] via 10.140.1.1, 00:03:15, Serial0/0/0
O       10.140.2.0 [110/3124] via 10.140.1.1, 00:03:15, Serial0/0/0
                   [110/3124] via 10.23.23.2, 00:03:15, Serial0/0/1
     192.168.1.0/24 is variably subnetted, 2 subnets, 2 masks
C       192.168.1.64/28 is directly connected, Loopback0
E2   192.168.1.81/32 [110/1563] via 10.23.23.2, 00:03:17, Serial0/0/1
```

The **network** command that you configure under the OSPF routing process also indicates which networks OSPF advertises.

The **show ip protocols** command indicates whether any route filters have been implemented, which can affect which routes are seen in the routing table. The command, as shown in Example 15-18, also displays the networks that have been configured to be advertised to other OSPF routers.

Example 15-18 *Determining Whether Route Filters Have Been Implemented*

```
RouterX# show ip protocols
Routing Protocol is "ospf 100"
  Outgoing update filter list for all interfaces is not set
  Incoming update filter list for all interfaces is not set
  Router ID 192.168.1.65
  Number of areas in this router is 1. 1 normal 0 stub 0 nssa
  Maximum path: 4
  Routing for Networks:
    10.2.2.3 0.0.0.0 area 0
    10.23.23.1 0.0.0.0 area 0
    10.140.1.2 0.0.0.0 area 0
    192.168.1.65 0.0.0.0 area 0
 Reference bandwidth unit is 100 mbps
  Routing Information Sources:
    Gateway         Distance      Last Update
    192.168.1.81        110       00:04:52
    172.16.31.100       110       00:04:52
  Distance: (default is 110)
```

Troubleshooting Plaintext Password Authentication

If you are using OSPF password authentication, you must also be prepared to troubleshoot any authentication problems that might occur during the adjacency process.

You can use the **debug ip ospf adj** command to display OSPF adjacency-related events. This command is useful when troubleshooting authentication.

If plaintext password authentication is configured on the Router X serial 0/0/1 interface but no authentication is configured on the Router Y serial 0/0/1 interface, the routers will not be able to form an adjacency over that link. The output of the **debug ip ospf adj** command shown in Example 15-19 illustrates that the routers report a mismatch in authentication type; no OSPF packets will be sent between the neighbors.

Example 15-19   *Determining Whether an Authentication Mismatch Exists*

```
RouterX# debug ip ospf adj
*Feb 17 18:51:31.242: OSPF: Rcv pkt from 192.168.1.102, Serial0/0/1 :
  Mismatch Authentication type. Input packet specified type 0, we use type 1

RouterY# debug ip ospf adj
*Feb 17 18:50:43.046: OSPF: Rcv pkt from 192.168.1.101, Serial0/0/1 :
  Mismatch Authentication type. Input packet specified type 1, we use type 0
```

Note   The different types of authentication have these codes:

```
Null is type 0
Simple password is type 1
MD5 is type 2
```

If plaintext password authentication is configured on the Router X serial 0/0/1 interface and on the Router Y serial 0/0/1 interface, but the interfaces are configured with different passwords, the routers will not be able to form an adjacency over that link.

The output of the **debug ip ospf adj** command shown in Example 15-20 illustrates that the routers report a mismatch in authentication key; no OSPF packets will be sent between the neighbors.

Example 15-20   **debug ip ospf adj** *Command Output Confirms an Authentication Mismatch*

```
RouterX# debug ip ospf adj
*Feb 17 18:54:01.238: OSPF: Rcv pkt from 192.168.1.102, Serial0/0/1 :
  Mismatch Authentication Key - Clear Text

RouterY# debug ip ospf adj
*Feb 17 18:53:13.050: OSPF: Rcv pkt from 192.168.1.101, Serial0/0/1 :
  Mismatch Authentication Key - Clear Text
```

Chapter Summary

OSPF is a classless, link-state routing protocol that uses an area hierarchy for fast convergence. OSPF exchanges hello packets to establish neighbor adjacencies between routers. The SPF algorithm uses a cost metric to determine the best path. Lower costs indicate a better path. The **router ospf** *process-id* command is used to enable OSPF on the router. Use a loopback interface to keep the OSPF router ID consistent. The **show ip ospf neighbor** command displays OSPF neighbor information on a per-interface basis. OSPF will load-balance across up to four equal-cost metric paths by default. OSPF authentication can be two types: plaintext and MD5.

The commands **debug ip ospf events** and **debug ip ospf packets** can be used to troubleshoot OSPF problems. Troubleshooting OSPF involves looking at neighbor adjacencies, routing tables, and authentication issues. Use the **show ip interface** command to verify the MTU of an OSPF interface. Use the **show ip ospf** interface command to help troubleshoot whether OSPF is enabled on an interface. Use the **debug ip ospf adj** command to troubleshoot OSPF authentication.

Additional Resources

- OSPF Video, AJS Networking: http://ajsnetworking.com/ospf
- OSPF, Cisco Systems: http://docwiki.cisco.com/wiki/Open_Shortest_Path_First

Review Questions

Use the questions here to review what you learned in this chapter. The correct answers and solutions are found in Appendix A, "Answers to Chapter Review Questions."

1. Which of the following are characteristics of OSPF? (Choose two.)
   a. OSPF uses a two-layer hierarchy.
   b. OSPF is a proprietary routing protocol.
   c. OSPF is an open standard.
   d. OSPF is similar to the RIP routing protocol.
   e. OSPF is a distance vector routing protocol.

2. OSPF routes packets within a single _____.
   a. Area
   b. Network
   c. Segment
   d. Autonomous system

3. With OSPF, each router builds its SPF tree using the same link-state information, but each will have a separate _____ of the topology.

   a. State

   b. View

   c. Version

   d. Configuration

4. Which component of the SPF algorithm is inversely proportional to bandwidth?

   a. Link cost

   b. Root cost

   c. Link state

   d. Hop count

5. Which command correctly starts an OSPF routing process using process ID 191?

   a. Router(config)# **router ospf 191**

   b. Router(config)# **network ospf 191**

   c. Router(config-router)# **network ospf 191**

   d. Router(config-router)# **router ospf process-id 191**

6. What is the purpose of the **show ip ospf interface** command?

   a. To display OSPF-related interface information

   b. To display general information about OSPF routing processes

   c. To display OSPF neighbor information on a per-interface basis

   d. To display OSPF neighbor information on a per-interface type basis

7. Which command configures OSPF on the Fa0/0 (10.1.1.1) interface?

   a. network interface fa0/0 area 0

   b. network 10.1.1.1 area 0

   c. network 10.1.1.1 255.255.255.255 area 0

   d. network 10.1.1.1 0.0.0.0 area 0

8. Which of the following methods of OSPF authentication are available? (Choose two.)

   a. Clear text

   b. DES

   c. MD5

   d. 3DES

9. Which OSPF neighbor state indicates that two neighbors have exchanged routes and are no longer in the process of forming an adjacency?

    a. Init

    b. Two-way

    c. Loading

    d. Full

10. What command allows you to view a table of all the adjacent OSPF routers?

    a. show ip ospf process neighbor

    b. show ospf adjacencies

    c. show ospf neighbor

    d. show ip ospf neighbor

Production Network Simulation Question 15-1

You have been asked to provide a configuration for a key router in your organization. This configuration must accomplish the following:

■ Provide a name of Tampa1.

■ Configure the Gi0/0 interface with the address 10.10.10.1/24 and enable the interface.

■ Configure the Gi0/1 interface with the address 10.20.20.1/24 and enable the interface.

■ Configure the Gi0/2 interface with the address 192.168.1.1/24 and enable the interface.

■ Configure OSPF process ID 1 and assign a router ID of 1.1.1.1. Do not use a loop-back interface for this task.

■ Configure the Gi0/0 and Gi0/1 interfaces for OSPF area 0 using a single network command and an 8-bit wildcard mask.

■ Configure the Gi0/2 interface for OSPF area 1 using a wildcard mask as specific as possible.

Chapter 16

DHCP and NAT

This chapter includes the following sections:

- Chapter Objectives

- Using a Cisco Router as a DHCP Server

- Scaling the Network with NAT and PAT

- Chapter Summary

- Additional Resources

- Review Questions

- Production Network Simulation Questions 16-1 and 16-2

Dynamic Host Configuration Protocol (DHCP) is a critical service in the network for automatically providing hosts with the TCP/IP address configuration that they require to communicate. This chapter discusses this important protocol and teaches you how to configure this valuable service on a Cisco router. This chapter also discusses Network Address Translation (NAT). NAT permits private internal-use-only IP addresses to be translated into public, Internet-routable addresses for communication on public networks. This chapter will teach you how to configure this important service as well.

Chapter Objectives

Upon completing this chapter, you will be able to describe both DHCP and NAT services in the network, including the configuration of these important services. These abilities include meeting these objectives:

- Describe DHCP and its role in the network

- Configure DHCP on a Cisco router

- Configure and verify static, dynamic, and overloading NAT

- Identify key **show** and **debug** command parameters that are required for trouble-shooting NAT and PAT

Using a Cisco Router as a DHCP Server

Originally, network administrators had to manually configure the host address, default gateway, and other network parameters on each host. However, DHCP provides configuration parameters to IP hosts. DHCP consists of these two components:

- A protocol for delivering host-specific configuration parameters from a DHCP server to a host

- A mechanism for tracking address assignments in the network

Understanding DHCP

DHCP is built on a client-server model. The DHCP server hosts allocate network addresses and deliver configuration parameters to dynamically configured hosts. The term *client* refers to a host requesting initialization parameters from a DHCP server.

DHCP supports these three mechanisms for IP address allocation:

- **Automatic allocation:** DHCP assigns a permanent IP address to a client.

- **Dynamic allocation:** DHCP assigns an IP address to a client for a limited period of time (or until the client explicitly relinquishes the address).

- **Manual allocation:** A client IP address is assigned by the network administrator, and DHCP is used simply to convey the assigned address to the client.

Dynamic allocation is the only one of the three mechanisms that allows automatic reuse of an address that is no longer needed by the client to which it was assigned. Dynamic allocation is particularly useful for assigning an address to a client that will be connected to the network only temporarily, or for sharing a limited pool of IP addresses among a group of clients that do not need permanent IP addresses. Dynamic allocation can also be a good choice for assigning an IP address to a new client being permanently connected to a network in which IP addresses are sufficiently scarce that it is important to reclaim them when old clients are retired.

DHCPDISCOVER

When a DHCP client boots up for the first time, it transmits a DHCPDISCOVER message on its local physical subnet. Because the client has no way of knowing the subnet to which it belongs, the DHCPDISCOVER is an all-subnets (all-hosts) broadcast (destination IP address of 255.255.255.255). The client does not have a configured IP address; therefore, the source IP address of 0.0.0.0 is used.

DHCPOFFER

A DHCP server that receives a DHCPDISCOVER message can respond with a DHCPOFFER message, which contains initial configuration information for the client. For example, the DHCP server provides the requested IP address. The subnet mask and default gateway are specified in the options field, subnet mask, and router options, respectively. Other common options in the DHCPOFFER message include IP address lease time, renewal time, domain name server, and NetBIOS Name Service (Microsoft Windows Internet Name Service [Microsoft WINS]).

DHCPREQUEST

After the client receives a DHCPOFFER message, it responds with a DHCPREQUEST message, indicating its intent to accept the parameters in the DHCPOFFER.

DHCPACK

After the DHCP server receives the DHCPREQUEST message, it acknowledges the request with a DHCPACK message, thus completing the initialization process.

Configuring a Cisco Router as a DHCP Client

An ISP sometimes provides a static address for an interface that is connected to the Internet. In other cases, an address is provided using DHCP. If the ISP uses DHCP to provide interface addressing, no manual address can be configured. Instead, the interface is configured to operate as a DHCP client.

If a router received the optional DHCP parameter called the default gateway together with the assigned IP address, the default route will get injected into the routing table pointing to the default gateway IP address.

Configuration is simple, as shown here:

```
R1(config)# interface Gi0/0
R1(config-if)# ip address dhcp
```

Using a Cisco Router as a DHCP Server

Cisco routers running Cisco IOS Software provide full support for a router to be a DHCP server. The Cisco IOS DHCP server is a full DHCP server implementation that assigns and manages IP addresses from specified address pools within the router to DHCP clients. You can configure a DHCP server to assign additional parameters, such as the IP address of the Domain Name System (DNS) server and the default router.

The Cisco IOS DHCP server accepts address assignment requests and renewals and assigns the addresses from predefined groups of addresses contained within DHCP address pools. These address pools can also be configured to supply additional information to the requesting client, such as the IP address of the DNS server, the default router, and other configuration parameters. The Cisco IOS DHCP server can accept broadcasts from locally attached LAN segments or from DHCP requests that have been forwarded by other DHCP relay agents within the network.

The configuration of DHCP on a Cisco router or switch is simple. Examine Example 16-1.

Example 16-1 *Configuring DHCP*

```
Branch(config)# ip dhcp pool Guests
Branch(dhcp-config)# network 10.1.50.0 /24
Branch(dhcp-config)# default-router 10.1.50.1
Branch(dhcp-config)# dns-server 10.1.50.1
Branch(dhcp-config)# domain-name example.com
Branch(dhcp-config)# lease 0 12
Branch(dhcp-config)# exit
Branch(config)# ip dhcp excluded-address 10.1.50.1 10.1.50.50
```

Notice how in this example, the **ip dhcp pool** command defines the name of your DHCP pool on the Cisco device and enters configuration mode for the pool. The **network** command allows you to create the address scheme that will be leased to DHCP clients. The **default-router** command allows you to configure the default gateway address on the clients. The **dns-server** and **domain-name** commands allow you to specify the DNS server address and the domain name of the client. The **lease** command specifies that the client can maintain the information for 0 days and 12 hours. Finally, the **ip dhcp excluded-address** command is issued in global configuration mode and ensures that the addresses 10.1.50.1 to 10.1.50.50 are not leased out to clients. Notice that these addresses are reserved for servers in the LAN, as shown by the DNS server at 10.1.50.1.

You can verify configured DHCP parameters using the **show ip dhcp pool** command in privileged EXEC mode. The total number of available addresses, configured address range, and number of leased addresses is displayed. Keep in mind that the total addresses number does not take excluded IP addresses into account.

To verify the operation of a DHCP server, use the **show ip dhcp binding** command, which displays a list of all IP address–to–MAC address bindings that have been provided by the DHCP service. Additionally, the lease expiration time and type of DHCP allocation are listed.

To display address conflicts that are found by a DHCP server when addresses are offered to the client, use the **show ip dhcp conflict** command in user EXEC or privileged EXEC mode.

The server uses ping to detect conflicts. The client uses GARP (Gratuitous Address Resolution Protocol) to detect conflicts. If an address conflict is detected, the address is removed from the pool and the address is not assigned until an administrator resolves the conflict.

You can clear conflicting IP addresses by using the privileged EXEC command **clear ip dhcp conflict**.

Using a Cisco Router as a DHCP Relay Agent

When DHCP clients try to obtain an IP address, they search for a DHCP server within their segment. Managing one DHCP server in each network segment can represent considerable administrative work. If DHCP servers are spread across different physical locations and are managed by different administrators, there is also a greater chance of human error.

A centralized DHCP solution enables an administrator to manage IP address assignment in one place for an entire organization. While DHCP servers are usually positioned in the center of the network infrastructure, other network devices can be configured with the DHCP relay agent functionality to enable clients to obtain an IP address from a central DHCP server.

DHCP clients use UDP broadcasts to send their initial DHCP discover message, because they do not have information about the network to which they are attached. If the client is on a network that does not include a DHCP server, broadcasts are normally not forwarded by the attached router.

To allow DHCP clients on subnets that are not directly served by DHCP servers to communicate with DHCP servers, DHCP relay agents can be installed on these subnets. You can configure the relay agent for a specific segment with the interface configuration command **ip helper-address** *address*, where you specify the IP address of a DHCP server.

When the DHCP relay agent receives the broadcast DHCP discover message, it transmits it to one or more DHCP servers as a unicast packet, after it stores its own IP address in the gateway IP address (GIADDR) field of the DHCP packet. The DHCP server uses the GIADDR to determine the subnet on which the relay agent received the broadcast and allocates an IP address belonging to the same subnet. When the DHCP server replies to the client, it sends the reply to the GIADDR address, again using unicast. The relay agent receives the response and retransmits it on the local network.

Note   The **ip helper-address** command enables forwarding of all the well-known UDP ports that might be included in a UDP broadcast message.

Scaling the Network with NAT and PAT

Two Internet scalability challenges are the depletion of registered IP version 4 (IPv4) address space and scaling in routing. Cisco IOS Network Address Translation (NAT) and Port Address Translation (PAT) are mechanisms for conserving registered IPv4 addresses in large networks and simplifying IPv4 address management tasks. NAT and PAT translate IPv4 addresses within private internal networks to legal IPv4 addresses for transport over public external networks, such as the Internet, without requiring a registered subnet address. Incoming traffic is translated back for delivery within the inside network.

This translation of IPv4 addresses eliminates the need for host renumbering and allows the same IPv4 address range to be used in multiple intranets. This section describes the features that are offered by NAT and PAT and shows you how to configure NAT and PAT on Cisco routers.

Introducing NAT and PAT

NAT operates on a Cisco router and is designed for IPv4 address conservation. NAT enables private IPv4 internetworks that use nonregistered IPv4 addresses to connect to the Internet. Usually, NAT connects two networks and translates the private (inside local) addresses in the internal network into public addresses (inside global) before packets are forwarded to another network. As part of this functionality, you can configure NAT to advertise only one address for the entire network to the outside world. Advertising only one address effectively hides the internal network from the world, thus providing additional security. Figure 16-1 shows an example of address translation between a private and public network. "SA" in the figure refers to Source Address.

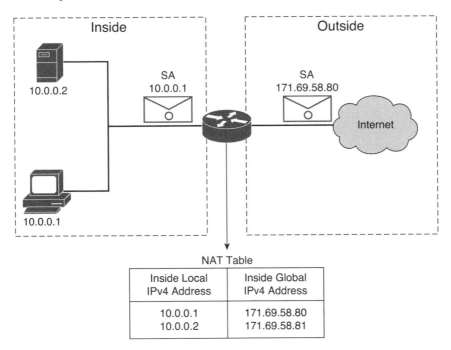

Figure 16-1 *Network Address Translation*

Any device that is between an internal network and the public network—such as a firewall, a router, or a computer—uses NAT, which is defined in RFC 1631.

In NAT terminology, the *inside network* is the set of networks that are subject to translation. The *outside network* refers to all other addresses. Usually these are valid addresses located on the Internet.

Cisco defines the following list of NAT terms:

- **Inside local address:** The IPv4 address that is assigned to a host on the inside network. The inside local address is likely not an IPv4 address assigned by the Network Information Center or service provider.

- **Inside global address:** A legitimate IPv4 address typically assigned by a service provider that represents one or more inside local IPv4 addresses to the outside world.

- **Outside local address:** The IPv4 address of an outside host as it appears to the inside network. Not necessarily legitimate, the outside local address is allocated from a routable address space on the inside.

- **Outside global address:** The IPv4 address that is assigned to a host on the outside network by the host owner. The outside global address is allocated from a globally routable address or network space.

NAT has many forms and can work in the following ways:

- **Static NAT:** Maps an unregistered IPv4 address to a registered IPv4 address (one to one). Static NAT is particularly useful when a device must be accessible from outside the network.

- **Dynamic NAT:** Maps an unregistered IPv4 address to a registered IPv4 address from a group of registered IPv4 addresses.

- **NAT overloading:** Maps multiple unregistered IPv4 addresses to a single registered IPv4 address (many to one) by using different ports. Overloading is also known as PAT and is a form of dynamic NAT.

NAT offers these benefits over using public addressing:

- Permits the use of the private address space internally.

- Conserves addresses through application port-level multiplexing. With NAT, internal hosts can share a single registered IPv4 address for all external communications. In this type of configuration, relatively few external addresses are required to support many internal hosts, thus conserving IPv4 addresses.

- Protects network security. Because private networks do not advertise their addresses or internal topology, they remain reasonably secure when they gain controlled external access in conjunction with NAT.

One of the main features of NAT is PAT, which is also referred to as "overload" in Cisco IOS configuration. PAT allows you to translate multiple internal addresses into a single external address, essentially allowing the internal addresses to share one external address. Figure 16-2 shows an example of Port Address Translation. The following list highlights the operations of PAT.

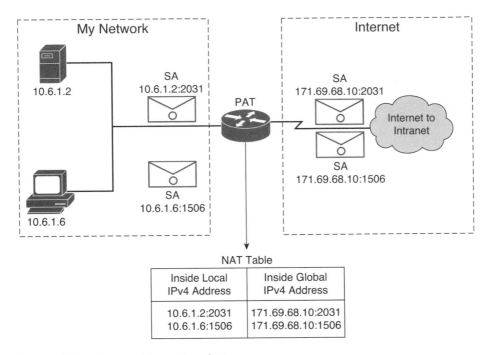

Figure 16-2   *Port Address Translation*

■ PAT uses unique source port numbers on the inside global IPv4 address to distinguish between translations. Because the port number is encoded in 16 bits, the maximum number of internal sessions that NAT can translate into one external address is, theoretically, 65,536.

■ PAT attempts to preserve the original source port. If the source port is already allocated, PAT attempts to find the first available port number. It starts from the beginning of the appropriate port group, 0 to 511, 512 to 1023, or 1024 to 65535. If PAT does not find an available port from the appropriate port group and if more than one external IPv4 address is configured, PAT moves to the next IPv4 address and tries to allocate the original source port again. PAT continues trying to allocate the original source port until it runs out of available ports and external IPv4 addresses.

Translating Inside Source Addresses

You can translate your own IPv4 addresses into globally unique IPv4 addresses when you are communicating outside your network. You can configure static or dynamic inside source translation.

Figure 16-3 illustrates a router that is translating a source address inside a network into a source address outside the network.

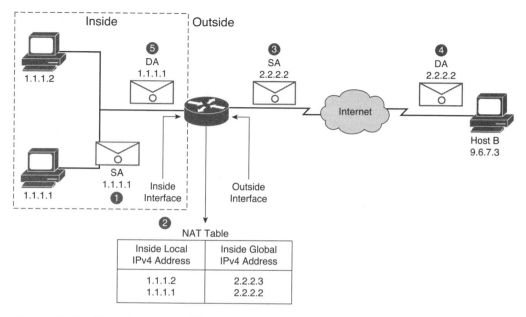

Figure 16-3   *Translating an Address*

The steps for translating an inside source address are as follows:

1. The user at host 1.1.1.1 opens a connection to host B.

2. The first packet that the router receives from host 1.1.1.1 causes the router to check its NAT table:

   ■ If a static translation entry was configured, the router goes to Step 3.

   ■ If no static translation entry exists, the router determines that the source address 1.1.1.1 (SA 1.1.1.1) must be translated dynamically. The router then selects a legal, global address from the dynamic address pool and creates a translation entry (in the example, 2.2.2.2). This type of entry is called a *simple entry*.

3. The router replaces the inside local source address of host 1.1.1.1 with the translation entry global address and forwards the packet.

4. Host B receives the packet and responds to host 1.1.1.1 by using the inside global IPv4 destination address 2.2.2.2 (DA 2.2.2.2).

5. When the router receives the packet with the inside global IPv4 address, the router performs a NAT table lookup by using the inside global address as a key. The router then translates the address back to the inside local address of host 1.1.1.1 and forwards the packet to host 1.1.1.1. Host 1.1.1.1 receives the packet and continues the conversation. The router performs Steps 2 through 5 for each packet.

The order in which the router processes traffic depends on whether the NAT translation is a global-to-local translation or a local-to-global translation. Table 16-1 illustrates the order in which a router processes traffic, depending on the direction of the translation.

Table 16-1   *Router Processing Order*

Local-to-Global	Global-to-Local
1. Check input access list if using IPsec1.	1. Check input access list if using IPsec.
2. Perform decryption—for Cisco Encryption Technology or IPsec.	2. Perform decryption—for Cisco Encryption Technology or IPsec.
3. Check inbound access list.	3. Check inbound access list.
4. Check input rate limits.	4. Check input rate limits.
5. Perform input accounting.	5. Perform input accounting.
6. Perform policy routing.	6. Perform NAT outside to inside (global to local translation).
7. Route packet.	7. Perform policy routing.
8. Redirect to web cache.	8. Route packet.
9. Perform NAT inside-to-outside (local-to-global) translation.	9. Redirect to web cache.
10. Check crypto map and mark for encryption if appropriate.	10. Check crypto map and mark for encryption if appropriate.
11. Check outbound access list.	11. Check outbound access list.
	12. Inspect CBAC2.
	13. Intercept TCP.
	14. Perform encryption.
	15. Perform queuing.

To configure static inside source address translation on a router, follow these steps:

1. Establish static translation between an inside local address and an inside global address.

   ```
   RouterX(config)# ip nat inside source static local-ip global-ip
   ```

   Enter the **no ip nat inside source static** global command to remove the static source translation.

2. Specify the inside interface.

```
RouterX(config)# interface type number
```

After you enter the **interface** command, the CLI prompt changes from (config)# to (config-if)#.

3. Mark the interface as connected to the inside.

```
RouterX(config-if)# ip nat inside
```

4. Specify the outside interface.

```
RouterX(config-if)# interface type number
```

5. Mark the interface as connected to the outside.

```
RouterX(config-if)# ip nat outside
```

Use the **show ip nat translations** command in EXEC mode to display active translation information, as demonstrated here:

```
RouterX# show ip nat translations
    Pro      Inside global    Inside local   Outside local   Outside global
    ---          192.168.1.2      10.1.1.2
```

Static NAT Address Mapping

The example shows the use of discrete address mapping with static NAT translations for the network in Figure 16-4. The router translates packets from host 10.1.1.2 to a source address of 192.168.1.2.

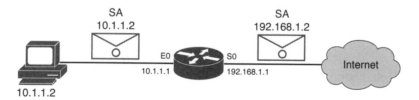

Figure 16-4 *Static NAT Address Mapping*

To configure dynamic inside source address translation, follow these steps:

1. Define a pool of global addresses to be allocated as needed.

```
RouterX(config)# ip nat pool name start-ip end-ip {netmask netmask |
  prefix-length prefix-length}
```

Enter the **no ip nat pool** global command to remove the pool of global addresses.

2. Define a standard access control list (ACL) that permits the addresses that are to be translated.

```
RouterX(config)# access-list access-list-number permit source [source-wildcard]
```

Enter the **no access-list** *access-list-number* global command to remove the ACL.

3. Establish dynamic source translation, specifying the ACL that was defined in the prior step.

```
RouterX(config)# ip nat inside source list access-list-number   pool name
```

Enter the **no ip nat inside source** global command to remove the dynamic source translation.

4. Specify the inside interface.

```
RouterX(config)# interface type number
```

After you enter the **interface** command, the CLI prompt changes from (config)# to (config-if)#.

5. Mark the interface as connected to the inside.

```
RouterX(config-if)# ip nat inside
```

6. Specify the outside interface.

```
RouterX(config-if)# interface type number
```

7. Mark the interface as connected to the outside.

```
RouterX(config-if)# ip nat outside
```

Caution   The ACL must permit only those addresses that are to be translated. Remember that there is an implicit **deny any** statement at the end of each ACL. An ACL that is too permissive can lead to unpredictable results. Using **permit any** can result in NAT consuming too many router resources, which can cause network problems.

Use the **show ip nat translations** command in EXEC mode to display active translation information.

Dynamic Address Translation

The example in Figure 16-5 shows how the device translates all source addresses that pass ACL 1, which means a source address from the 192.168.1.0/24 network, into an address from the pool named net-208. The pool contains addresses from 171.69.233.209/28 to 171.69.233.222/28.

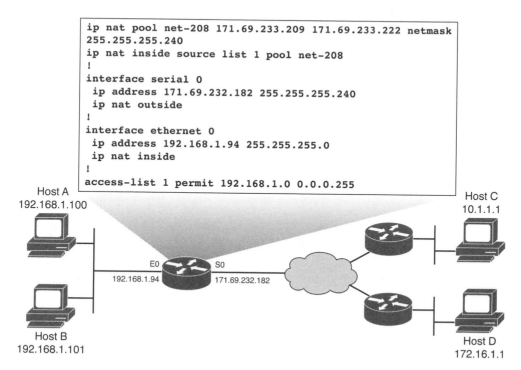

```
ip nat pool net-208 171.69.233.209 171.69.233.222 netmask
255.255.255.240
ip nat inside source list 1 pool net-208
!
interface serial 0
 ip address 171.69.232.182 255.255.255.240
 ip nat outside
!
interface ethernet 0
 ip address 192.168.1.94 255.255.255.0
 ip nat inside
!
access-list 1 permit 192.168.1.0 0.0.0.255
```

Figure 16-5 *Dynamic Address Translation*

Overloading an Inside Global Address

You can conserve addresses in the inside global address pool by allowing the router to use one inside global address for many inside local addresses. When this overloading is configured, the router maintains enough information from higher-level protocols—for example, TCP or User Datagram Protocol (UDP) port numbers—to translate the inside global address back into the correct inside local address. When multiple inside local addresses map to one inside global address, the TCP or UDP port numbers of each inside host distinguish between the local addresses.

Figure 16-6 illustrates NAT operation when one inside global address represents multiple inside local addresses. The TCP port numbers act as differentiators.

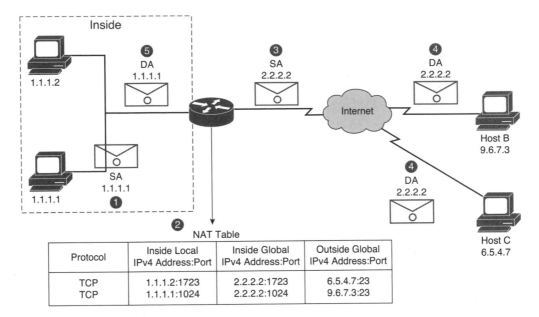

Figure 16-6 *Overloading an Inside Global Address*

Both host B and host C think they are talking to a single host at address 2.2.2.2. They are actually talking to different hosts; the port number is the differentiator. In fact, many inside hosts could share the inside global IPv4 address by using many port numbers.

The router performs the following process when it overloads inside global addresses:

1. The user at host 1.1.1.1 opens a connection to host B.

2. The first packet that the router receives from host 1.1.1.1 causes the router to check its NAT table.

   If no translation entry exists, the router determines that address 1.1.1.1 must be translated and sets up a translation of inside local address 1.1.1.1 into a legal inside global address. If overloading is enabled and another translation is active, the router reuses the inside global address from that translation and saves enough information to be able to translate back. This type of entry is called an *extended entry*.

3. The router replaces the inside local source address 1.1.1.1 with the selected inside global address and forwards the packet.

4. Host B receives the packet and responds to host 1.1.1.1 by using the inside global IPv4 address 2.2.2.2.

5. When the router receives the packet with the inside global IPv4 address, the router performs a NAT table lookup. Using the inside global address and port and outside global address and port as a key, the router translates the address back into the inside local address 1.1.1.1 and forwards the packet to host 1.1.1.1. Host 1.1.1.1 receives the packet and continues the conversation. The router performs Steps 2 through 5 for each packet.

To configure overloading of inside global addresses, follow these steps:

1. Define a standard ACL that permits the addresses that are to be translated.

   ```
   RouterX(config)# access-list access-list-number permit source    [source-wildcard]
   ```

   Enter the **no access-list** *access-list-number* global command to remove the ACL.

2. Establish dynamic source translation, specifying the ACL that was defined in the prior step.

   ```
   RouterX(config)# ip nat inside source list access-list-number    interface interface
   overload
   ```

   Enter the **no ip nat inside source** global command to remove the dynamic source translation. The keyword **overload** enables PAT.

3. Specify the inside interface.

   ```
   RouterX(config)# interface type number
   RouterX(config-if)# ip nat inside
   ```

   After you enter the **interface** command, the CLI prompt changes from (config)# to (config-if)#.

4. Specify the outside interface.

   ```
   RouterX(config-if)# interface type number
   RouterX(config-if)# ip nat outside
   ```

Use the **show ip nat translations** command in EXEC mode to display active translation information.

The NAT inside-to-outside process comprises this sequence of steps:

1. The incoming packet goes to the route table and the next hop is identified.

2. NAT statements are parsed so that the interface serial 0 IPv4 address can be used in overload mode. PAT creates a source address to use.

3. The router encapsulates the packet and sends it out on interface serial 0.

For the return traffic, the NAT outside-to-inside address translation process works in the following sequence of steps:

1. NAT statements are parsed. The router looks for an existing translation and identifies the appropriate destination address.

2. The packet goes to the route table, and the next-hop interface is determined.

3. The packet is encapsulated and sent out to the local interface.

No internal addresses are visible during this process. As a result, hosts do not have an external public address, which leads to improved security.

By default, dynamic address translations time out from the NAT and PAT translation tables after some period of nonuse. The default timeout periods differ among various protocols. You can reconfigure the default timeouts with the **ip nat translation** command. The syntax for this command is as follows:

```
ip nat translation {timeout | udp-timeout | dns-timeout | tcp-timeout |
  finrst-timeout |
  icmp-timeout | pptp-timeout | syn-timeout | port-timeout} {seconds | never}
```

Table 16-2 describes the parameters for this command.

Table 16-2   ip nat translation *Parameters*

Parameter	Description
timeout	Specifies that the timeout value applies to dynamic translations except for overload translations. The default is 86,400 seconds (24 hours).
udp-timeout	Specifies the timeout value for the UDP port. The default is 300 seconds (5 minutes).
dns-timeout	Specifies the timeout value for connections to the DNS1. The default is 60 seconds.
tcp-timeout	Specifies the timeout value for the TCP port. The default is 86,400 seconds (24 hours).
finrst-timeout	Specifies the timeout value for the Finish and Reset TCP packets, which terminate a connection. The default is 60 seconds.
	Specifies the timeout value for ICMP2 flows. The default is 60 seconds.
	Specifies the timeout value for NAT PPTP3 flows. The default is 86,400 seconds (24 hours).
	Specifies the timeout value for TCP flows immediately after a synchronous transmission message that consists of digital signals that are sent with precise clocking. The default is 60 seconds.
	Specifies that the timeout value applies to the TCP/UDP port.
	Number of seconds after which the specified port translation times out. The default is 0.
never	Specifies that the port translation never times out.

Table 16-3 lists commands you can use to clear the entries before they time out.

Table 16-3   clear ip nat translation *Commands*

Command	Description
clear ip nat translation *	Clears all dynamic address translation entries from the NAT translation table.
clear ip nat translation inside [outside]	Clears a simple dynamic translation entry that contains an inside translation or both an inside and outside translation.
clear ip nat translation outside	Clears a simple dynamic translation entry containing an outside translation.
clear ip nat translation protocol inside [outside]	Clears an extended dynamic translation entry (PAT entry).

Resolving Translation Table Issues

When you have IPv4 connectivity problems in a NAT environment, it is often difficult to determine the cause of the problem. Many times NAT is blamed, when in reality there is an underlying problem. When you are trying to determine the cause of an IPv4 connectivity problem, it helps to eliminate NAT as the potential problem. Follow these steps to verify that NAT is operating as expected:

1. Based on the configuration, clearly define what NAT is supposed to achieve. You might determine that the NAT configuration has a problem.

2. Use the **show ip nat translations** command to determine whether the correct translations exist in the translation table.

3. Verify whether the translation is occurring by using **show** and **debug** commands.

4. Review in detail what is happening to the translated packet, and verify that routers have the correct routing information for the translated address to move the packet.If the appropriate translations are not in the translation table, verify the following items:

   - There are no inbound ACLs that are denying the packet entry into the NAT router.

      - The ACL that is referenced by the NAT command is permitting all necessary networks.

      - The NAT pool has enough addresses.

   - The router interfaces are appropriately defined as NAT inside or NAT outside.

In a simple network environment, it is useful to monitor NAT statistics with the **show ip nat statistics** command. However, in a more complex NAT environment with several translations taking place, this **show** command is no longer useful. In this case, it might be necessary to run **debug** commands on the router.

The **debug ip nat** command displays information about every packet that is translated by the router, which helps you verify the operation of the NAT feature. The **debug ip nat detailed** command generates a description of each packet that is considered for translation. This command also outputs information about certain errors or exception conditions, such as the failure to allocate a global address. The **debug ip nat detailed** command will generate more overhead than the **debug ip nat** command, but it can provide the detail that you need to troubleshoot the NAT problem.

Example 16-2 demonstrates sample **debug ip nat** output.

Example 16-2   *Displaying Information About Packets Translated by the Router*

```
RouterX# debug ip nat
NAT: s=192.168.1.95->172.31.233.209, d=172.31.2.132 [6825]
NAT: s=172.31.2.132, d=172.31.233.209->192.168.1.95 [21852]
NAT: s=192.168.1.95->172.31.233.209, d=172.31.1.161 [6826]
NAT*: s=172.31.1.161, d=172.31.233.209->192.168.1.95 [23311]
NAT*: s=192.168.1.95->172.31.233.209, d=172.31.1.161 [6827]
NAT*: s=192.168.1.95->172.31.233.209, d=172.31.1.161 [6828]
NAT*: s=172.31.1.161, d=172.31.233.209->192.168.1.95 [23312]
NAT*: s=172.31.1.161, d=172.31.233.209->192.168.1.95 [23313]
```

Note   Be careful when debugging NAT in production environments because of the amount of information that can result.

In Example 16-2, the first two lines show the debugging output that a server request and reply produce where the server address is 172.31.2.132. The remaining lines show the debugging output from a Telnet connection from a host on the inside of the network to a host on the outside of the network.

The asterisk (*) next to NAT indicates that the translation is occurring in the fast-switched path. The first packet in a conversation is always process switched. The remaining packets go through the fast-switched path if a cache entry exists.

The final entry in each line, within brackets ([ ]), provides the identification number of the packet. You can use this information to correlate with other packet traces from protocol analyzers.

Another useful command when verifying the operation of NAT is the **show ip nat statistics** command. This command is shown in Example 16-3.

Example 16-3   show ip nat statistics *Command Output*

```
RouterX# show ip nat statistics
 Total active translations: 1 (1 static, 0 dynamic; 0 extended)
 Outside interfaces:
 Ethernet0, Serial2
 Inside interfaces:
 Ethernet1
 Hits: 0  Misses: 0
 Expired translations: 0
 Dynamic mappings:
 -- Inside Source
 access-list 7 pool test refcount 0
 pool test: netmask 255.255.255.0
 start 172.16.11.70 end 172.16.11.71
 type generic, total addresses 2, allocated 0 (0%), misses 0
```

Table 16-4 describes the **show ip nat statistics** fields.

Table 16-4   show ip nat statistics *Field Descriptions*

Field	Description
Total translations	Number of translations that are active in the system. This number is incremented each time a translation is created and is decremented each time a translation is cleared or times out.
Outside interfaces	List of interfaces that are marked as outside with the **ip nat outside** command.
Inside interfaces	List of interfaces that are marked as inside with the **ip nat inside** command.
Hits	Number of times the software looks up an entry in the translations table and finds an entry.
Misses	Number of times the software looks up a translations table, fails to find an entry, and must try to create one.
Expired translations	Cumulative count of translations that have expired since the router was booted.
Dynamic mappings	Indicates that the information that follows is about dynamic mappings.
Inside source	Indicates that the information that follows is about an inside source translation.
access-list	ACL number that is being used for the translation.
pool	Name of the pool (in this case, test).
refcount	Number of translations that are using this pool.
netmask	IPv4 network mask that is used in the pool.

Field	Description
start	Starting IPv4 address in the pool range.
end	Ending IPv4 address in the pool range.
type	Type of pool. Possible types are generic or rotary.
total addresses	Number of addresses in the pool that are available for translation.
allocated	Number of addresses that are being used.
misses	Number of failed allocations from the pool.

Resolving Issues by Using the Correct Translation Entry

You know from the configuration that the source address (10.10.10.4) should be statically translated to 172.16.6.14. You can use the **show ip nat translation** command to verify that the translation does exist in the translation table, as demonstrated here:

```
RouterX# show ip nat translation
Pro Inside global      Inside local     Outside local      Outside global
---    172.16.6.14       10.10.10.4        ---                ---
```

Next, ensure that the translation is occurring. You can confirm this in two ways: by running a NAT **debug** command or by monitoring NAT statistics with the **show ip nat statistics** command. Because **debug** commands should always be used as a last resort, start with the **show ip nat statistics** command.

To determine whether the translation is taking place, monitor the hits counter to see whether it increases as traffic is sent through the router. The hits counter increments every time a translation in the translation table is used to translate an address. First, clear the statistics and then display them. Next, try to execute a ping through the router and then display the statistics again, as demonstrated in Example 16-4.

Example 16-4   *Verifying That Address Translation Is Occurring*

```
RouterX# clear ip nat statistics
RouterX#
RouterX# show ip nat statistics
 Total active translations: 1 (1 static, 0 dynamic; 0 extended)
 Outside interfaces:
 Ethernet0, Serial2
 Inside interfaces:
 Ethernet1
 Hits: 0  Misses: 0
 Expired translations: 0
 Dynamic mappings:
 -- Inside Source
```

```
access-list 7 pool test refcount 0
pool test: netmask 255.255.255.0
start 172.16.11.70 end 172.16.11.71
type generic, total addresses 2, allocated 0 (0%), misses 0
```

After you ping through the router, the NAT statistics show, as demonstrated in Example 16-5.

Example 16-5 show ip nat statistics *Command to Verify Translation*

```
RouterX# show ip nat statistics
 Total active translations: 1 (1 static, 0 dynamic; 0 extended)
 Outside interfaces:
 Ethernet0, Serial2
 Inside interfaces:
 Ethernet1
 Hits: 5  Misses: 0
 Expired translations: 0
 Dynamic mappings:
 -- Inside Source
 access-list 7 pool test refcount 0
 pool test: netmask 255.255.255.0
 start 172.16.11.70 end 172.16.11.71
 type generic, total addresses 2, allocated 0 (0%), misses 0
```

You can see from the output of the **show** command that the number of hits incremented by 5 after the NAT statistics were cleared. In a successful ping, the number of hits should increase by 10. The five ICMP echoes that were sent by the source should be translated, and the five echo reply packets from the destination should be translated, for a total of 10 hits. The five missing hits are most likely because of the echo replies not being translated or not being sent from the destination router.

To determine why the echo reply is not being returned when you issue a ping, check the default gateway of the destination default gateway router for a route back to the translated address, as demonstrated in Example 16-6.

Example 16-6 *Verifying the Default Gateway*

```
RouterY# show ip route
Codes: C - connected, S - static, I - IGRP, R - RIP, M - mobile, B - BGP
       D - EIGRP, EX - EIGRP external, O - OSPF, IA - OSPF inter area
       N1 - OSPF NSSA external type 1, N2 - OSPF NSSA external type 2
       E1 - OSPF external type 1, E2 - OSPF external type 2, E - EGP
       i - IS-IS, L1 - IS-IS level-1, L2 - IS-IS level-2, ia - IS-IS inter are
       * - candidate default, U - per-user static route, o - ODR
       P - periodic downloaded static route

Gateway of last resort is not set
```

```
        172.16.0.0/24 is subnetted, 4 subnets
C          172.16.12.0 is directly connected, Serial0.8
C          172.16.9.0 is directly connected, Serial0.5
C          172.16.11.0 is directly connected, Serial0.6
C          172.16.5.0 is directly connected, Ethernet0
```

The routing table of Router B does not have a route for 172.16.6.14, which is the translated address. Therefore, the echo replies in response to the ping fail. After you add this return route, the ping works.

In Figure 16-7, the network administrator is experiencing the following symptom: Host A (192.168.1.2) cannot ping host B (192.168.2.2).

The next several examples show how to troubleshoot this issue.

To troubleshoot the problem, use the **show ip nat translations** command to see whether any translations are currently in the table:

```
RouterA# show ip nat translations
      Pro Inside global    Inside local    Outside local    Outside global
      --- ---              ---             ---              ---
```

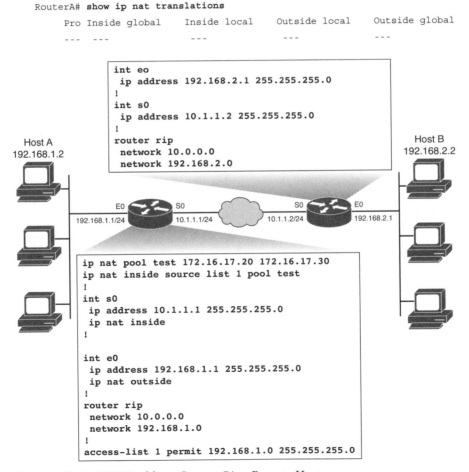

Figure 16-7 *NAT Problem: Cannot Ping Remote Host*

You find that no translations are in the table. This could indicate a problem, or it could mean that no traffic is currently being translated.

Next, you must verify whether any translations have ever taken place and identify the interfaces between which translation should be occurring. Use the **show ip nat statistics** command to determine this information, as demonstrated in Example 16-7.

Example 16-7   *Identifying Translations and Interfaces*

```
RouterA# show ip nat statistics
    Total active translations: 0 (0 static, 0 dynamic; 0 extended)
    Outside interfaces:
    Ethernet0
    Inside interfaces:
    Serial0
    Hits: 0  Misses: 0
    ...
```

From the results in Example 16-7, you determine that the NAT counters are at 0, verifying that no translation has occurred. You also find that the router interfaces are incorrectly defined as NAT inside or NAT outside.

After you correctly define the NAT inside and outside interfaces, generate another ping from host A to host B. In the example, the ping still fails. Issue the **show ip nat transla-tions** and **show ip nat statistics** commands again to troubleshoot the problem. In the example, you find that translations are still not occurring.

Next, you should use the **show access-list** command to verify whether the ACL that is referenced by the NAT command is permitting all the necessary networks:

```
RouterA# show access-list

Standard IP access list 1
    10 permit 192.168.1.1, wildcard bits 255.255.255.0
```

From this output, you determine that an incorrect wildcard bit mask has been used in the ACL that defines the addresses to be translated.

After correcting the ACL wildcard bit mask, you generate another ping from host A to host B. The ping still fails. However, when you reissue the **show ip nat translations** and **show ip nat statistics** commands, you find that translations are now occurring:

```
RouterA#
    Pro   Inside global      Inside local      Outside local    Outside global
    ---   172.16.17.20       192.168.1.2          ---              ---
```

Next, you use the **show ip route** command on Router B to verify the existence of a return route to the translated address.

From the results in Example 16-8, you discover that Router B has no route to the translated network address of 172.16.0.0.

Example 16-8   *Verifying a Return Route to the Translated Address*

```
RouterB# show ip route

Codes: C - connected, S - static, R - RIP, M - mobile, B - BGP

Gateway of last resort is not set

     10.0.0.0/24 is subnetted, 1 subnets
C       10.1.1.0/24 is directly connected, Serial0
     192.168.2.0/24 is subnetted, 1 subnets
R       192.168.2.0/24 is directly connected, Ethernet0
     192.168.1.0/24 is variably subnetted, 3 subnets, 2 masks
R       192.168.1.0/24 [120/1] via 10.1.1.1, 2d19h, Serial0
```

You return to Router A and enter the **show ip protocol** command to determine whether Router A is advertising the translated address of 172.16.0.0, as demonstrated in Example 16-9.

Example 16-9   *Verifying Advertisement of a Translated Address*

```
RouterA# show ip protocol
Routing Protocol is "rip"
  Outgoing update filter list for all interfaces is not set
  Incoming update filter list for all interfaces is not set
  Sending updates every 30 seconds, next due in 0 seconds
  Invalid after 180 seconds, hold down 180, flushed after 240
  Redistributing: rip
  Default version control: send version 1, receive any version
  Automatic network summarization is in effect
  Maximum path: 4
  Routing for Networks:
    192.168.0.0
  Routing Information Sources:
    Gateway         Distance      Last Update
  Distance: (default is 120)
```

You find that Router A is advertising 192.168.1.0, which is the network that is being translated, instead of advertising network 172.16.0.0, which is the network to which the addresses are being translated.

So, to fix the original problem where host A (192.168.1.2) could not ping host B (192.168.2.2), you changed the following configurations on Router A:

- Interface S0 is now the outside interface, rather than the inside interface.

- Interface E0 is now the inside interface, rather than the outside interface.

- The wildcard mask now matches any host on the 192.168.1.0 network. Previously, the **access-list 1** command did not match the inside local IPv4 address.

- Router A is now configured to advertise network 172.16.0.0. Previously, Router B did not know how to reach the 172.16.17.0/24 subnet. The configuration is done by creating a loopback interface and modifying the Routing Information Protocol (RIP) network statements.

Chapter Summary

Your router or switch can function as a DHCP server with a very simple configuration. Remember, DHCP is a four-step process for automatically applying an IP address configuration to your end systems.

Network Address Translation (NAT) is a critical service for IPv4 systems as a result of the shortage of IP addresses we currently endure. NAT can be configured statically or dynamically, or can even be configured to overload a singe public address. When this configuration is applied, it is referred to as PAT (Port Address Translation).

Additional Resources

- DHCP Video, AJS Networking: http://ajsnetworking.com/dhcp

- NAT Video, AJS Networking: http://ajsnetworking.com/nat

Review Questions

Use the questions here to review what you learned in this chapter. The correct answers and solutions are found in Appendix A, "Answers to Chapter Review Questions."

1. What happens when a DHCP server receives a DISCOVER message from a host?

   a. It responds with a REQUEST message.

   b. It responds with a REPLY message.

   c. It responds with an OFFER message.

   d. It responds with an ACK message.

2. What function on a Cisco router enables the device to forward a DHCP DISCOVER broadcast as a unicast packet to a DHCP server on another subnet?

   a. DHCP Forwarder

   b. DHCP Relay Agent

   c. DHCP Proxy

   d. DHCP Assistant

3. Match each NAT term with its definition.

___ Static NAT

___ Dynamic NAT

___ Inside local

___ Inside global

a. Address that is subject to translation with NAT

b. Address of an inside host as it appears to the outside network

c. Maps an unregistered IPv4 address to a registered IPv4 address on a one-to-one basis

d. Maps an unregistered IPv4 address to a registered IPv4 address from a group of registered IPv4 addresses

4. Which Cisco IOS command would you use to define a pool of global addresses that can be allocated as needed?

a. ip nat pool

b. ip nat inside pool

c. ip nat outside pool

d. ip nat inside source static

5. What does the **ip nat inside source static** command do?

a. Selects the inside static interface

b. Marks the interface as connected to the outside

c. Creates a pool of global addresses that can be allocated as needed

d. Establishes permanent translation between an inside local address and an inside global address

6. Match each of these commands, which are used to configure NAT overloading, with its function.

___ **ip nat inside**

___ **ip nat outside**

___ **access-list 1 permit 10.1.1.0 0.0.0.255**

___ **ip nat inside source list 1 pool nat-pool overload**

___ **ip nat pool nat-pool 192.1.1.17 192.1.1.20 netmask 255.255.255.240**

a. Marks an interface as connected to the inside

b. Marks an interface as connected to the outside

c. Defines a pool of inside global addresses that can be allocated as needed

d. Establishes dynamic port address translation using the defined ACL

e. Defines a standard ACL that will permit the addresses that are to be translated

7. Which command clears a specific extended dynamic translation entry from the NAT translation table?

   a. clear ip nat translation *

   b. clear ip nat translation inside

   c. clear ip nat translation outside

   d. clear ip nat translation protocol inside

8. The output of which command displays the active translations for a NAT translation table?

   a. show ip nat statistics

   b. show ip nat translations

   c. clear ip nat translation *

   d. clear ip nat translation outside

9. You are troubleshooting a NAT connectivity problem on a Cisco router. You determine that the appropriate translation is not installed in the translation table. Which of the following actions should you take? (Choose three.)

   a. Determine whether the NAT pool has enough addresses.

   b. Run **debug ip nat detailed** to determine the source of the problem.

   c. Use the **show ip route** command to verify that the selected route exists.

   d. Verify that the router interfaces are appropriately defined as NAT inside or NAT outside.

   e. Verify that the ACL that is referenced by the NAT command is permitting all necessary inside local IPv4 addresses.

10. The output of which command provides information about certain errors or exceptional conditions, such as the failure to allocate a global address?

   a. debug nat verbose

   b. debug ip nat detailed

   c. show ip nat statistics

   d. show ip nat translations

Production Network Simulation Questions

Production Network Simulation Question 16-1

Your boss has asked you to create a configuration in Notepad that will accomplish the following:

- Create a DHCP pool named MYPOOL

- Assign the address space 10.1.50.0/24

- Assign a default gateway address of 10.1.50.1

- Assign a DNS server address of 10.1.50.2

- Assign a domain name of ciscopress.com

- Feature a lease duration of 12 hours

- Ensure that you exclude addresses from 10.1.50.1 to 10.1.50.50

Production Network Simulation Question 16-2

You must also produce a configuration in Notepad that performs the following:

- Creates access control list 1 permitting the 10.10.10.0/24 network

- Configures dynamic inside NAT to use PAT ACL 1 to the IP address on gi0/0

- Configures the gi0/1 interface as the inside NAT interface

- Configures the gi0/0 interface as the outside NAT interface

Chapter 17

Securing the Network

This chapter includes the following sections:

- Chapter Objectives

- Securing the Network

- Understanding Cisco Device Security

- Chapter Summary

- Additional Resources

- Review Questions

- Production Network Simulation Question 17-1

Open any major newspaper these days, and chances are you will find at least one article discussing network security attacks. This chapter provides a broad, high-level examination of network security attacks, and it also provides specific guidance on steps to ensure that Cisco devices are protected against the most common forms of attack.

Chapter Objectives

Upon completing this chapter, you will be able to discuss the importance of network security and describe its basic principles. You will also be able to configure Cisco devices to ensure a minimum acceptable level of security. These abilities include meeting these objectives:

- Describe the importance of network security

- Discuss specific attack types and typical attackers

- Provide examples of common attack mitigation techniques

- Configure Cisco routers and switches with important security settings

Securing the Network

Security is a fundamental component of every network design. When planning, building, and operating a network, you should understand the importance of a strong security policy. How important is it to have a strong network security policy? The Computer Security Institute (CSI) produced a report from the "Computer Crime and Security Survey" that provided an updated look at the impact of computer crime in the United States. One of the major participants was the San Francisco Federal Bureau of Investigation (FBI) Computer Intrusion Squad. Based on responses from over 700 computer security practitioners in U.S. corporations, government agencies, financial institutions, medical institutions, and universities, the survey confirms that the threat from computer crime and other information security breaches continues unabated and that the financial toll is mounting.

The application of an effective security policy is the most important step that an organization must take to protect itself. An effective security policy is the foundation for all the activities undertaken to secure network resources.

Need for Network Security

In the past, hackers were highly skilled programmers who understood the intricacies of computer communications and knew how to exploit vulnerabilities. Today almost anyone can become a hacker by downloading tools from the Internet. These sophisticated attack tools and generally open networks have generated an increased need for network security and dynamic security policies.

The easiest way to protect a network from an outside attack is to close it off completely from the outside world. A closed network provides connectivity only to trusted known parties and sites; a closed network does not allow a connection to public networks. Figure 17-1 shows an example of a closed network.

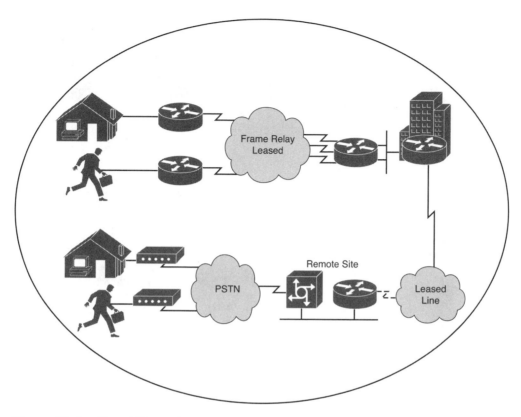

Figure 17-1   *Closed Network*

Because they have no Internet connectivity, networks designed in this way can be considered safe from Internet attacks. However, internal threats still exist. The CSI in San Francisco, California, estimates that 60 to 80 percent of network misuse comes from inside the enterprise where the misuse has taken place.

Today, corporate networks require access to the Internet and other public networks. Most of these networks have several access points to public and other private networks, as shown in Figure 17-2. Securing open networks is important.

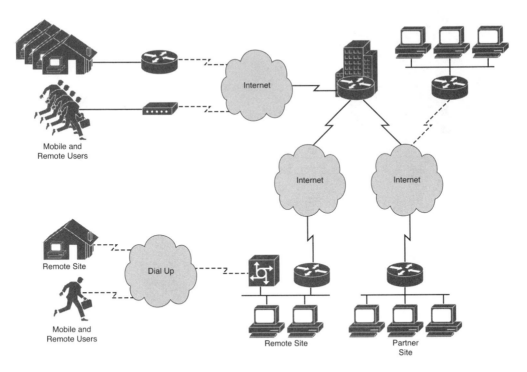

Figure 17-2   *Open Network*

As previously mentioned, one of the challenges to security is that hacking a network has become easier for those with little or no computer skills. Figure 17-3 illustrates how the increasing sophistication of hacking tools and the decreasing skill needed to use these tools have combined to pose increasing threats to open networks.

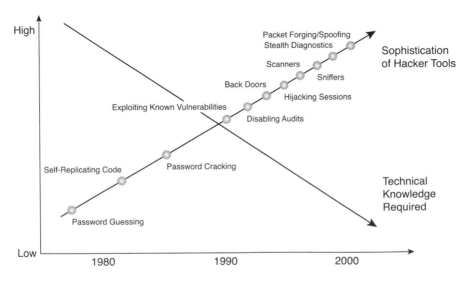

Figure 17-3   *Hacking Skills Matrix*

With the development of large open networks, security threats have increased significantly in the past 20 years. Hackers have discovered more network vulnerabilities, and because you can now download applications that require little or no hacking knowledge to implement, applications intended for troubleshooting and maintaining and optimizing networks can, in the wrong hands, be used maliciously and pose severe threats.

Balancing Network Security Requirements

The overall security challenge is to find a balance between two important needs: open networks to support evolving business requirements and freedom-of-information initiatives versus the protection of private, personal, and strategic business information. Figure 17-4 shows the relationship between expanding the business value and increasing security risks.

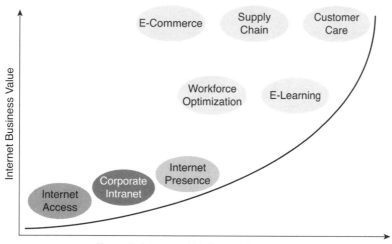

Figure 17-4   *Security Challenge*

Security has moved to the forefront of network management and implementation. The survival of many businesses depends on allowing open access to network resources and ensuring that data and resources are as secure as possible. The escalating importance of e-business and the need for private data to traverse potentially unsafe public networks both increase the need for the development and implementation of a corporate-wide network security policy. Establishing a network security policy should be the first step in changing a network to a secure infrastructure.

The Internet has created expectations for a company to build stronger relationships with customers, suppliers, partners, and employees. E-business challenges companies to become more agile and competitive. The benefit of this challenge is that new applications for e-commerce, supply chain management, customer care, workforce optimization, and e-learning have been created. These applications streamline and improve processes, lowering costs while increasing turnaround times and user satisfaction.

As enterprise network managers open their networks to more users and applications, they also expose the networks to greater risks. The result has been an increase in business security requirements. Security must be included as a fundamental component of any e-business strategy.

E-business requires mission-critical networks that can accommodate ever-increasing constituencies and ever-increasing demands on capacity and performance. These networks also need to handle voice, video, and data traffic as networks converge into multiservice environments.

Adversaries, Hacker Motivations, and Classes of Attack

To defend against attacks on information and information systems, organizations must define the threat in these three terms:

- **Adversaries:** Potential adversaries might include nation-states, terrorists, criminals, hackers, disgruntled employees, and corporate competitors.

- **Hacker motivations:** Hackers' motivations might include intelligence gathering, the theft of intellectual property, denial of service (DoS), the embarrassment of the company or clients, or the challenge of exploiting a notable target.

- **Classes of attack:** Classes of attack might include passive monitoring of communications, active network attacks, close-in attacks, exploitation by insiders, and attacks through the service provider.

Information systems and networks offer attractive targets and should be resistant to attack from the full range of threat agents, from hackers to nation-states. A system must be able to limit damage and recover rapidly when attacks occur.

Classes of Attack

There are five classes of attack:

- **Passive:** Passive attacks include traffic analysis, monitoring of unprotected communications, decrypting weakly encrypted traffic, and capturing authentication information such as passwords. Passive interception of network operations enables adversaries to see upcoming actions. Passive attacks result in the disclosure of information or data files to an attacker without the consent or knowledge of the user. Examples include the disclosure of personal information such as credit card numbers and medical files.

- **Active:** Active attacks include attempts to circumvent or break protection features, to introduce malicious code, and to steal or modify information. These attacks are mounted against a network backbone, exploit information in transit, electronically penetrate an enclave, or attack an authorized remote user during an attempt to connect to an enclave. Active attacks result in the disclosure or dissemination of data files, DoS, or modification of data.

- **Close-in:** Close-in attacks consist of regular individuals attaining close physical proximity to networks, systems, or facilities for the purpose of modifying, gathering, or denying access to information. Close physical proximity is achieved through surreptitious entry into the network, open access, or both.

- **Insider:** Insider attacks can be malicious or nonmalicious. Malicious insiders intentionally eavesdrop, steal, or damage information; use information in a fraudulent manner; or deny access to other authorized users. Nonmalicious attacks typically result from carelessness, lack of knowledge, or intentional circumvention of security for such reasons as performing a task.

- **Distributed:** Distribution attacks focus on the malicious modification of hardware or software at the factory or during distribution. These attacks introduce malicious code such as a back door to a product to gain unauthorized access to information or to a system function at a later date.

Mitigating Common Threats

Improper and incomplete network device installation is an often-overlooked security threat that, if left unaddressed, can have dire results. Software-based security measures alone cannot prevent premeditated or even accidental network damage caused by poor installation. The following sections describe how to mitigate common security threats to Cisco routers and switches.

Physical Installations

Hardware threats involve threats of physical damage to the router or switch hardware. Mission-critical Cisco network equipment should be located in wiring closets or in computer or telecommunications rooms that meet these minimum requirements:

- The room must be locked with only authorized personnel allowed access.

- The room should not be accessible through a dropped ceiling, raised floor, window, ductwork, or point of entry other than the secured access point.

- If possible, use electronic access control with all entry attempts logged by security systems and monitored by security personnel.

- If possible, security personnel should monitor activity through security cameras with automatic recording.

Environmental threats, such as temperature extremes (too hot or too cold) or humidity extremes (too wet or too dry), also require mitigation. Take these actions to limit environmental damage to Cisco network devices:

- Supply the room with dependable temperature and humidity control systems. Always verify the recommended environmental parameters of the Cisco network equipment with the supplied product documentation.

■ Remove any sources of electrostatic and magnetic interference in the room.

■ If possible, remotely monitor and alarm the environmental parameters of the room.

Electrical threats, such as voltage spikes, insufficient supply voltage (brownouts), unconditioned power (noise), and total power loss, can be limited by adhering to these guidelines:

■ Install uninterruptible power supply (UPS) systems for mission-critical Cisco network devices.

■ Install backup generator systems for mission-critical supplies.

■ Plan for and initiate regular UPS or generator testing and maintenance procedures
based on the manufacturer-suggested preventative maintenance schedule.

■ Install redundant power supplies on critical devices.

■ Monitor and alarm power-related parameters at the power supply and device levels.

Maintenance threats include poor handling of key electronic components, electrostatic discharge (ESD), lack of critical spares, poor cabling, poor labeling, and so on.
Maintenance-related threats are a broad category that includes many items. Follow the
general rules listed here to prevent maintenance-related threats:

■ Clearly label all equipment cabling and secure the cabling to equipment racks to prevent accidental damage, disconnection, or incorrect termination.

■ Use cable runs, raceways, or both to traverse rack-to-ceiling or rack-to-rack connections.

■ Always follow ESD procedures when replacing or working with internal router and
switch device components.

■ Maintain a stock of critical spares for emergency use.

■ Do not leave a console connected to and logged in to any console port. Always log
off administrative interfaces when leaving a station.

■ Do not rely upon a locked room as the only necessary protection for a device.
Always remember that no room is ever totally secure. After intruders are inside a
secure room, nothing is left to stop them from connecting a terminal to the console
port of a Cisco router or switch.

Reconnaissance Attacks

Reconnaissance is the unauthorized discovery and mapping of systems, services, or vulnerabilities. Reconnaissance is also known as information gathering and, in most cases,
precedes an actual access or denial of service (DoS) attack. First, the malicious intruder
typically conducts a ping sweep of the target network to determine which IP addresses

are alive. Then the intruder determines which services or ports are active on the live IP addresses. From this information, the intruder queries the ports to determine the type and version of the application and operating system running on the target host.

Reconnaissance is somewhat analogous to a thief investigating a neighborhood for vulnerable homes, such as an unoccupied residence or a house with an easy-to-open door or window. In many cases, intruders look for vulnerable services that they can exploit later when less likelihood that anyone is looking exists.

Access Attacks

Access attacks exploit known vulnerabilities in authentication services, FTP services, and web services to gain entry to web accounts, confidential databases, and other sensitive information.

Password Attacks

A password attack usually refers to repeated attempts to identify a user account, password, or both. These repeated attempts are called brute-force attacks. Password attacks are implemented using other methods, too, including Trojan horse programs, IP spoofing, and packet sniffers.

A security risk lies in the fact that passwords are stored as plaintext. You need to encrypt passwords to overcome risks. On most systems, passwords are processed through an encryption algorithm that generates a one-way hash on passwords. You cannot reverse a one-way hash back to its original text. Most systems do not decrypt the stored password during authentication; they store the one-way hash. During the login process, you supply an account and password, and the password encryption algorithm generates a one-way hash. The algorithm compares this hash to the hash stored on the system. If the hashes are the same, the algorithm assumes that the user supplied the proper password.

Remember that passing the password through an algorithm results in a password hash. The hash is not the encrypted password, but rather a result of the algorithm. The strength of the hash is that the hash value can be re-created only with the original user and password information and that retrieving the original information from the hash is impossible. This strength makes hashes perfect for encoding passwords for storage. In granting authorization, the hashes, rather than the plain password, are calculated and compared.

Password attack threat-mitigation methods include these guidelines:

- Do not allow users to have the same password on multiple systems. Most users have the same password for each system they access, as well as for their personal systems.

- Disable accounts after a specific number of unsuccessful logins. This practice helps to prevent continuous password attempts.

- Do not use plaintext passwords. Use either a one-time password (OTP) or an encrypted password.

■ Use strong passwords. Strong passwords are at least eight characters long and contain uppercase letters, lowercase letters, numbers, and special characters. Many systems now provide strong password support and can restrict users to strong passwords only.

Understanding Cisco Device Security

After physical access has been secured, there is a growing need to ensure that access to the router or switch ports is secure through any EXEC session connection, such as securing the console (CON) port and securing the Telnet (VTY) ports. In addition, it is important to ensure that unused device ports do not become security holes. The following sections describe how to mitigate hardware, environmental, electrical, and maintenance-related security threats to Cisco IOS devices.

Physical and Environmental Threats

Improper and incomplete network device installation is an often-overlooked security threat that, if left uncorrected, can have dire results. Just like a typical PC or server configured with default settings presents a security threat, the same is true for Cisco devices. But software-based security configuration measures alone cannot prevent premeditated or even accidental network damage because of poor installation.

Beyond insecure configuration settings, there are four classes of insecure installations or physical access threats:

■ **Hardware threats:** The threat of physical damage to the switch or switch hardware

■ **Environmental threats:** Threats such as temperature extremes (too hot or too cold) or humidity extremes (too wet or too dry)

■ **Electrical threats:** Threats such as voltage spikes, insufficient supply voltage (brownouts), unconditioned power (noise), and total power loss

■ **Maintenance threats:** Threats such as poor handling of key electronic components (electrostatic discharge), lack of critical spare parts, poor cabling, and poor labeling

Configuring Password Security

The command-line interface (CLI) is used to configure the password and other console commands. Examples 17-1, 17-2, 17-3, and 17-4 show the various passwords to be configured on a switch. These same commands are used on a Cisco router.

Example 17-1 *Switch Password Configuration: Console Password Configuration*

```
SwitchX(config)# line console 0
SwitchX(config-line)# login
SwitchX(config-line)# password cisco
```

Example 17-2 *Switch Password Configuration: Virtual Terminal (Telnet) Password Configuration*

```
SwitchX(config)# line vty 0 4
SwitchX(config-line)# login
SwitchX(config-line)# password sanjose
```

Example 17-3 *Switch Password Configuration: Enable Password Configuration*

```
SwitchX(config)# enable password cisco
```

Example 17-4 *Switch Password Configuration: Secret Password Configuration*

```
SwitchX(config)# enable secret sanfran
```

Caution   The passwords used in this text are for instructional purposes only. Passwords used in an actual implementation should meet the requirements of a "strong" and "complex" password. This would involve using a randomly generated string of uppercase and lowercase numbers, numeric symbols, and special characters. For example, a strong password would be Due63NNu3$^@nnqmzlP. Because these passwords are obviously difficult to remember, password storage applications that are heavily encrypted are recommended today.

You can secure a switch by using passwords to restrict various levels of access. Using passwords and assigning privilege levels are simple ways of providing both local and remote terminal access control in a network. Passwords can be established on individual lines, such as the console, and to the privileged EXEC (enable) mode. Passwords are case sensitive.

Each Telnet (VTY) port on the switch is known as a virtual type terminal (vty). By default, there are five VTY ports on the switch, allowing five concurrent Telnet sessions, noting that other Cisco devices might have more than five logical VTY ports. The five total VTY ports are numbered from 0 through 4 and are referred to all at once as **line vty 0 4** (notice the space between the 0 and 4). By syntax, this would include the range from 0 to 4, so it includes all five logical VTY ports, 0–4.

Use the **line console 0** command, followed by the **password** and **login** subcommands, to require login and establish a login password on the console terminal or on a VTY port. By default, login is not enabled on the console or on VTY ports.

Note that you cannot establish a Telnet connection unless you first set all the vty passwords. If there are no vty passwords set, when you try to telnet in, you get a "password required . . . but none set . . ." error message, and your attempt to telnet is rejected.

The **line vty 0 4** command, followed by the **password** and **login** subcommands, requires login and establishes a login password on incoming Telnet sessions.

Again, for Telnet VTY ports to accept a Telnet EXEC session, you *must* set the vty passwords.

The **login local** command can be used to enable password checking on a per-user basis using the username and password specified with the **username** global configuration command. The **username** command establishes username authentication with encrypted passwords.

The **enable password** global command restricts access to the privileged EXEC (enable) mode. You can assign an encrypted form of the enable password, called the enable secret password, by entering the **enable secret** command with the desired password at the global configuration mode prompt. If the enable secret password is configured, it is used (and required) instead of the enable password, not in addition to it.

You can also add a further layer of security, which is particularly useful for passwords that cross the network or are stored on a TFTP server. Cisco provides a feature that allows the use of encrypted passwords. To set password encryption, enter the **service password-encryption** command in global configuration mode.

Passwords that are displayed or set after you configure the **service password-encryption** command will be encrypted in the output. This includes the encrypting of the passwords that might otherwise be displayed in plain text on the screen in the terminal output of a **show** command, such as **show run**.

To disable a command, enter **no** before the command. For example, use the **no service password-encryption** command to disable the **service-password encryption** command:

```
SwitchX(config)# service password-encryption
SwitchX(config)# no service password-encryption
```

Configuring the Login Banner

The CLI is used to configure the "message of the day" and other console commands. This banner can be used to warn others that they have accessed a secure device and that they might be monitored.

You can define a customized banner to be displayed before the username and password login prompts by using the **banner login** command in global configuration mode. To disable the login banner, use the **no** form of this command.

When the **banner login** command is entered, follow the command with one or more blank spaces and a delimiting character of any choice. In the example, the delimiting character is a double quotation mark ("). After the banner text has been added, terminate the message with the same delimiting character.

```
SwitchX# banner login " Access for authorized users only. Please enter your
    username and password. "
```

Warning Use caution when selecting the words that are used in the login banner. Words like *welcome* can imply that access is not restricted and can allow a hacker to defend his actions.

Telnet Versus SSH Access

Telnet is the most common method of accessing a remote network device. However, Telnet is an insecure way of accessing a network device because it passes all command keystrokes, and all output back to the terminal, in unencrypted clear text. Secure Shell (SSH) Protocol is a secure replacement for Telnet that gives the same type of access. Communication between the client and server is encrypted in both Secure Shell version 1 (SSHv1) and Secure Shell version 2 (SSHv2). Implement SSHv2 when possible because it uses a more enhanced security encryption algorithm.

First, test the authentication without SSH to make sure that authentication works with the switch. Authentication can be with a local username and password or with an authentication, authorization, and accounting (AAA) server that runs Terminal Access Controller Access Control System Plus (TACACS+) or Remote Authentication Dial-In User Service (RADIUS). (Authentication through the line password is not possible with SSH.) The following example shows local authentication, which lets you use Telnet to get access to the switch with username **cisco** and password **cisco**.

```
!--- The username command create the username and password for the SSH session
username cisco password 0 cisco
ip domain-name mydomain.com
crypto key generate rsa
ip ssh version 2
line vty 0 4
  login local
  transport input ssh
```

To test authentication with SSH, you have to add to the previous configuration statements to enable SSH. Then you can test SSH from the PC and UNIX (Uniplexed Information and Computing System) stations.

If you want to prevent non-SSH connections, add the **transport input ssh** command under the lines to limit the switch to SSH connections only. Straight (non-SSH) Telnets are refused.

```
line vty 0 4
!--- Prevent non-SSH Telnets.
transport input ssh
```

Test to make sure that non-SSH users cannot telnet to the switch.

Port Security Configuration on Switches

You can use the port security feature to restrict input to an interface by limiting and identifying MAC addresses of the stations allowed to access the port. When you assign secure MAC addresses to a secure port, the port does not forward packets with source addresses outside the group of defined addresses.

Note   Before port security can be activated, the port mode must be set to access using the **switchport mode access** command.

With the Cisco Catalyst 2960 Series, use the **switchport port-security** interface command *without* keywords to enable port security on an interface. The default behavior is to permit one dynamically learned MAC address on the port. The port will be error disabled should this condition not be met. Use the **switchport port-security** interface command *with* keywords to configure a secure MAC address, a maximum number of secure MAC addresses, or the violation mode. Use the **no** form of this command to disable port security or to set the parameters to their default state. Example 17-5 shows the commands used to configure port security.

Example 17-5   *Configuring Port Security*

```
SwitchX(config)# interface fa0/5
SwitchX(config-if)# switchport mode access
SwitchX(config-if)# switchport port-security
SwitchX(config-if)# switchport port-security maximum 1
SwitchX(config-if)# switchport port-security mac-address sticky
SwitchX(config-if)# switchport port-security violation shutdown
```

A port must be in access mode (not trunk mode) to enable port security.

You can add secure (specific) MAC addresses to the MAC address table after you set the maximum number of secure MAC addresses allowed on a port in these ways:

- Manually configure all the addresses (**switchport port-security mac-address 0008. eeee.eeee**).

- Allow the port to dynamically configure all the addresses (**switchport port-security mac-address sticky**).

- Configure a number of MAC addresses and allow the rest of the addresses to be dynamically configured.

You can configure an interface to convert the dynamic MAC addresses to sticky secure MAC addresses and to add them to the running configuration by enabling *sticky learning*. To enable sticky learning, enter the **switchport port-security mac-address sticky** interface configuration command. When you enter this command, the interface converts all the dynamic secure MAC addresses, including those that were dynamically learned before sticky learning was enabled, to sticky secure MAC addresses.

The sticky secure MAC addresses do not automatically become part of the configuration file, which is the startup configuration that is used each time the switch restarts. If you save the sticky secure MAC addresses in the configuration file, when the switch restarts, the interface does not need to relearn these addresses. If you do not save the configuration, the MAC addresses are lost. If sticky learning is disabled, the sticky secure MAC addresses are converted to dynamic secure addresses and are removed from the running configuration. While it will vary from switch model to switch model, a secure port on many lower-end switches can have from 1 to 132 associated secure addresses. The total number of available secure addresses on many Cisco switches is 1024.

Security violation situations are as follows:

- The maximum number of secure MAC addresses has been added to the address table, and a station whose MAC address is not in the address table attempts to access the interface.

- An address learned or configured on one secure interface is seen on another secure interface in the same VLAN.

Note Port security is disabled by default.

On the Catalyst 2960 Series, use the **show port-security interface** privileged EXEC command, as shown in Example 17-6, to display the port security settings defined for an interface.

Example 17-6 *Displaying Port Security Settings*

```
SwitchX# show port-security interface fastethernet 0/5

Port Security              : Enabled
Port Status                : Secure-up
Violation Mode             : Shutdown
Aging Time                 : 20 mins
Aging Type                 : Absolute
SecureStatic Address Aging : Disabled
Maximum MAC Addresses      : 1
Total MAC Addresses        : 1
Configured MAC Addresses   : 0
Sticky MAC Addresses       : 0
Last Source Address        : 0000.0000.0000
Security Violation Count   : 0
```

An address violation occurs when a secured port receives a source address that has been assigned to another secured port or when a port tries to learn an address that exceeds its address table size limit, which is set with the **switchport port-security maximum** command.

Table 17-1 lists the parameters that can be used with the **show port-security** command.

Table 17-1   show port-security *Command Parameters*

Command	Description
interface *interface-id*	(Optional) Displays the port security settings for the specified interface
address	(Optional) Displays all the secure addresses on all ports
begin	(Optional) Sets the display to begin with the line that matches the specified expression
exclude	(Optional) Sets the display to exclude lines that match the specified expression
include	(Optional) Sets the display to include lines that match the specified expression
expression	Enters the expression that will be used as a reference point in the output

Use the **show port-security address** command, as shown in Example 17-7, to display the secure MAC addresses for all ports. Use the **show port-security** command without keywords to display the port security settings for the switch. Example 17-8 demonstrates this.

Example 17-7   show port-security address *Command*

```
SwitchX# show port-security address

         Secure Mac Address Table
--------------------------------------------------------------------
Vlan    Mac Address        Type               Ports   Remaining Age
                                                       (mins)

----    -----------        ----               -----   -------------
 1      0008.dddd.eeee     SecureConfigured   Fa0/5       -
--------------------------------------------------------------------
Total Addresses in System (excluding one mac per port)      : 0
```

Example 17-8   show port-security *Command*

```
SwitchX# show port-security

Secure Port  MaxSecureAddr  CurrentAddr  SecurityViolation  Security Action
             (Count)        (Count)      (Count)

----------------------------------------------------------------------------
    Fa0/5        1              1              0             Shutdown
----------------------------------------------------------------------------
Total Addresses in System (excluding one mac per port)    : 0
Max Addresses limit in System (excluding one mac per port) : 1024
```

Securing Unused Ports

In a home, an unlocked door can be a security risk. The same is true of an unused port on a router or a switch. A hacker can plug a switch into an unused port and become part of the network. Therefore, unsecured ports can create a security hole. To prevent the issue, you should secure unused ports by disabling unused interfaces (ports).

To disable an interface, use the **shutdown** command in interface configuration mode. To restart, or bring up, a disabled interface, use the **no** form of this command: **no shutdown**.

Chapter Summary

Security is an important part of any computer network. When you are building a network, a strong security policy should be part of the foundation.

Sophisticated attack tools and open networks continue to generate an increased need for network security policies and infrastructure to protect organizations from internally and externally based attacks.

The strategy of information assurance affects network architecture. Organizations must balance network security needs against e-business processes, legal issues, and government policies. Establishing a network security policy is the first step in changing a network over to a secure infrastructure. Providing physical installation security for network devices is very important.

Some excellent security best practices taught in this chapter include:

- Network devices should be protected against password attacks through controlled access methods and strong passwords.

- User and privileged passwords can be used to restrict access levels to users who have different access needs for the device.

- The login banner can be used to display a message before the user is prompted for a username.

- Port security can be used to limit a MAC address to a port. Unused ports should be shut down.

Additional Resource

- Network Security Video, AJS Networking: http://ajsnetworking.com/security

Review Questions

Use the questions here to review what you learned in this chapter. The correct answers and solutions are found in Appendix A, "Answers to Chapter Review Questions."

1. What is the main threat to a closed network?

   a. A deliberate attack from outside

   b. A deliberate or accidental attack from inside

   c. Misuse by customers

   d. Misuse by partners

2. Which of the following factors have recently influenced the increase in threats from hackers? (Choose two.)

   a. Hacker tools require more technical knowledge to use.

   b. Hacker tools have become more sophisticated.

   c. The number of reported security threats has remained constant from year to year.

   d. Hacker tools require less technical knowledge to use.

3. Which of the following attacks is classified as a reconnaissance attack?

   a. Password attacks

   b. DDoS

   c. Trojan horse

   d. Ping sweep

4. Which of the following cannot be protected with a password?

   a. Console access

   b. VTY access

   c. TTY access

   d. User-level access

   e. EXEC-level access

5. Which of the following is a customized text that is displayed before the username and password login prompts?

   a. Message of the day

   b. Entry banner

   c. Access warning

   d. User banner

   e. Warning message

6. Which of the following is the most secure method of remotely accessing a network device?

   a. HTTP

   b. Telnet

   c. SSH

   d. RMON

   e. SNMP

7. Which of the following is an IOS command that can be used to control access to a switch port based on a MAC address?

   a. shutdown

   b. switchport port-security

   c. switchport mac-secure

   d. firewall

8. Which of the following is an IOS command that can be used to increase the security of unused switch ports?

   a. shutdown

   b. switchport restrict

   c. switchport mac-secure

   d. firewall

9. What type of port is required for use with the port security feature on a switch?

   a. Dynamic

   b. Access

   c. Trunk

   d. STP Forwarding

10. An engineer enters the **no login** command under the line vty 0 4 ports. What is the effect?

   a. Access is permitted with a checking of the password.

   b. No access is permitted.

   c. Access is permitted with no password checking.

   d. None of these answers are correct.

Production Network Simulation Question 17-1

Provide your peer with a configuration for a Cisco switch that does the following:

- Configures an encrypted password of T3nn1sB@11 to protect privileged mode

- Configures a VTY password of V0113yB@11

- Places encryption on all unencrypted passwords in the configuration

- Enables switch port security in the default configuration on Fa0/12

Chapter 18

Managing Traffic with Access Control Lists

This chapter includes the following sections:

- Chapter Objectives

- Access Control List Operation

- Configuring ACLs

- Troubleshooting ACLs

- Chapter Summary

- Additional Resources

- Review Questions

- Production Network Simulation Question 18-1

Standard and extended Cisco IOS access control lists (ACL) can be used to classify IP packets. Using ACLs, you can apply a number of features, such as encryption, policy-based routing, quality of service (QoS), dial-on-demand routing (DDR), Network Address Translation (NAT), and Port Address Translation (PAT), to the classified packets.

You can also configure standard and extended Cisco IOS ACLs on router interfaces for access control (security) to control the type of traffic that is permitted through a given router. Cisco IOS features are applied on interfaces for specific directions (inbound versus outbound). This chapter describes the operation of different types of ACLs and shows you how to configure IP version 4 (IPv4) ACLs.

Chapter Objectives

Upon completing this chapter, you will be able to determine how to apply ACLs based on network requirements and configure, verify, and troubleshoot ACLs on a medium-sized network. This ability includes being able to meet these objectives:

- Describe the different types of IPv4 ACLs

- Configure and troubleshoot standard and extended, numbered and named IPv4 ACLs

Access Control List Operation

Understanding the uses of access control lists (ACL) enables you to determine how to implement them on your Cisco network. ACLs can provide an important network security feature and filter packets on inbound and outbound router interfaces.

This section describes some of the applications for ACLs on Cisco networks, identifies the different types of ACLs that can be implemented, and explains how Cisco IOS Software processes ACLs.

Understanding ACLs

To be able to configure and implement ACLs, you need to understand the capacity in which they are used. Cisco devices use ACLs in two primary functions: classification and filtering. The following explains each of these functions:

- **Classification:** Routers also use ACLs to identify particular traffic. After an ACL has identified and classified traffic, you can configure the router with instructions on how to handle that traffic. For example, you can use an ACL to identify the executive subnet as the traffic source and then give that traffic priority over other types of traffic on a congested WAN link.

- **Filtering:** As the number of router connections to outside networks increase and the use of the Internet increases, access control presents new challenges. Network administrators face the dilemma of how to deny unwanted traffic while allowing appropriate access. For example, you can use an ACL as a filter to keep the rest of your network from accessing sensitive data on the finance subnet.

Through classification and filtering, ACLs provide a powerful toolset in Cisco IOS. Consider the network diagram in Figure 18-1. Using ACLs, administrators have the tools to block traffic from the Internet, provide controlled access to manage Cisco IOS devices, and provide address translation for private addresses such as the 172.16.0.0 network.

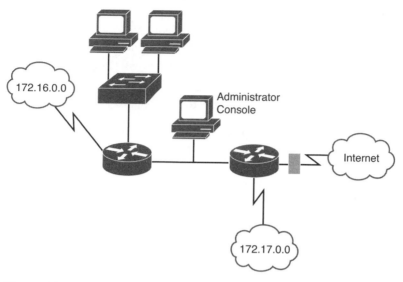

Figure 18-1   *ACLs Provide Control*

Filtering is the function of ACLs that people identify most readily. ACLs offer an important tool for controlling traffic on the network. Packet filtering helps control packet movement through the network. Figure 18-2 shows an example of ACLs filtering traffic transmission into and out of a physical interface or to the Telnet session of a Cisco IOS device.

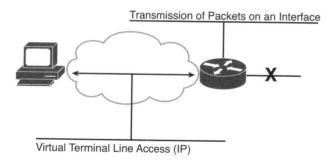

Figure 18-2   *ACL Filtering*

Cisco provides ACLs to permit or deny the following:

- The crossing of packets to or from specified router interfaces and traffic going through the router

- Telnet traffic into or out of the router vty ports for router administration

By default, all IP traffic is permitted into and out of all the router interfaces.

When the router discards packets, some protocols return a special packet to notify the sender that the destination is unreachable. For the IP protocol, an ACL discard results in a "Destination unreachable (U.U.U.)" response to a ping and an "Administratively prohibited (!A * !A)" response to a traceroute.

IP ACLs can classify and differentiate traffic. Classification enables you to assign special handling for traffic that is defined in an ACL, such as the following:

- Identify the type of traffic to be encrypted across a Virtual Private Network (VPN) connection.

- Identify the routes that are to be redistributed from one routing protocol to another.

- Use with route filtering to identify which routes are to be included in the routing updates between routers.

- Use with policy-based routing to identify the type of traffic that is to be routed across a designated link.

- Use with Network Address Translation (NAT) to identify which addresses are to be translated.

- Use with quality of service (QoS) to identify which packets should be scheduled in a given queue during times of congestion.

Figure 18-3 shows some examples of using ACLs for traffic classification, such as which traffic to encrypt across the VPN, which routes should be redistributed between Open Shortest Path First (OSPF) and Enhanced Interior Gateway Routing Protocol (EIGRP), and which addresses to translate using NAT.

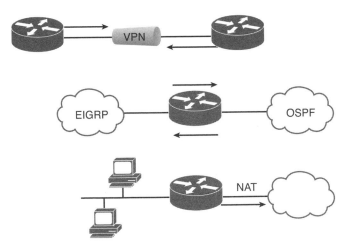

Figure 18-3   *ACLs Identify Traffic*

ACL Operation

ACLs express the set of rules that give added control for packets that enter inbound interfaces, packets that relay through the router, and packets that exit outbound interfaces of the router. ACLs do not act on packets that originate from the router. Instead, ACLs are statements that specify conditions of how the router handles the traffic flow through specified interfaces.

ACLs operate in two ways:

■ **Inbound ACLs:** Incoming packets are processed before they are routed to an outbound interface. An inbound ACL is efficient because it saves the overhead of routing lookups if the packet will be discarded after it is denied by the filtering tests. If the packet is permitted by the tests, it is processed for routing.

■ **Outbound ACLs:** Incoming packets are routed to the outbound interface and then processed through the outbound ACL.

Figure 18-4 shows an example of an outbound ACL.

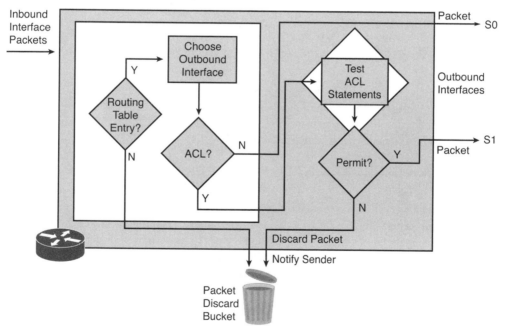

Figure 18-4   *Outbound ACL Operation*

When a packet enters an interface, the router checks the routing table to see whether the packet is routable. If the packet is not routable, it is dropped.

Next, the router checks to see whether the destination interface is grouped to an ACL. If the destination interface is not grouped to an ACL, the packet can be sent to the output buffer. Examples of outbound ACL operations are as follows:

■ If the outbound interface is S0, which has not been grouped to an outbound ACL, the packet is sent to S0 directly.

■ If the outbound interface is S1, which has been grouped to an outbound ACL, the packet is not sent out on S1 until it is tested by the combination of ACL statements that are associated with that interface. Based on the ACL tests, the packet is permitted or denied.

For outbound lists, "to permit" means to send the packet to the output buffer and "to deny" means to discard the packet.

With an inbound ACL, when a packet enters an interface, the router checks to see whether the source interface is grouped to an ACL. If the source interface is not grouped to an ACL, the router checks the routing table to see whether the packet is routable. If the packet is not routable, the router drops the packet. Examples of inbound ACL operations are as follows:

■ If the inbound interface is S0, which has not been grouped to an inbound ACL, the packet is processed normally, and the router checks to see whether the packet is routable.

■ If the inbound interface is S1, which has been grouped to an inbound ACL, the packet is not processed, and the routing table is not consulted until it is tested by the combination of ACL statements that are associated with that interface. Based on the ACL tests, the packet is permitted or denied.

For inbound lists, "to permit" means to continue to process the packet after receiving it on an inbound interface and "to deny" means to discard the packet.

ACL statements operate in sequential, logical order. They evaluate packets from the top down, one statement at a time. If a packet header and an ACL statement match, the rest of the statements in the list are skipped, and the packet is permitted or denied as determined by the matched statement. If a packet header does not match an ACL statement, the packet is tested against the next statement in the list. This matching process continues until the end of the list is reached. Figure 18-5 shows the logical flow of statement evaluation.

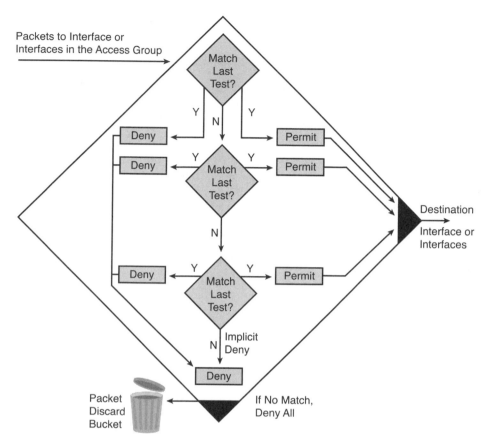

Figure 18-5 *ACL Evaluation*

A final implied statement covers all packets for which conditions did not test true. This final test condition matches all other packets and results in a "deny" instruction. Instead of proceeding into or out of an interface, the router drops all of these remaining packets. This final statement is often referred to as the "implicit deny any statement." Because of this statement, an ACL should have at least one permit statement in it; otherwise, the ACL blocks all traffic. This implicit deny all will not show up in the router configuration. In many of the examples in this text, it will be added as a reminder.

You can apply an ACL to multiple interfaces. However, only one ACL can exist per protocol, per direction, and per interface.

Types of ACLs

IPv4 ACLs come in various types. These differing ACLs are used depending on the functionality required. The types of ACLs can be classified as follows:

- **Standard ACLs:** Standard IP ACLs check the source addresses of packets that can be routed. The result either permits or denies the output for an entire protocol suite, based on the source network, subnet, or host IP address.

- **Extended ACLs:** Extended IP ACLs check both the source and destination IP addresses. They can also check for specific protocols, port numbers, and other parameters, which allow administrators more flexibility and control.

You can use two methods to identify standard and extended ACLs:

- Numbered ACLs use a number for identification.

- Named ACLs use a descriptive name or number for identification.

ACL Identification

When you create numbered ACLs, you enter an ACL number as the first argument of the global ACL statement. The test conditions for an ACL vary depending on whether the number identifies a standard or extended ACL.

You can create many ACLs for a protocol. Select a different ACL number for each new ACL within a given protocol. However, you can apply only one ACL per protocol, per direction, and per interface.

Specifying an ACL number from 1 to 99 or 1300 to 1999 instructs the router to accept numbered standard IPv4 ACL statements. Specifying an ACL number from 100 to 199 or 2000 to 2699 instructs the router to accept numbered extended IPv4 ACL statements.

Table 18-1 lists the different ACL number ranges for each protocol.

Table 18-1 *Protocol ACL Numbers*

Protocol	Range
IP	1–99
Extended IP	100–199
Ethernet type code	200–299
Ethernet address	700–799
Transparent bridging (protocol type)	200–299
Transparent bridging (vendor code)	700–799
Extended transparent bridging	1100–1199

Protocol	Range
DECnet and extended DECnet	300–399
XNS1	400–499
Extended XNS	500–599
AppleTalk	600–699
Source-route bridging (protocol type)	200–299
Source-route bridging (vendor code)	700–799
IPX2	800–899
Extended IPX	900–999
IPX SAP3	1000–1099
Standard Banyan VINES4	1–100
Extended Banyan VINES	101–200
Simple Banyan VINES	201–300
Standard IP (expanded)	1300–1999
Extended IP (expanded)	2000–2699

As of Cisco IOS Software Release 12.0, IPv4 ACLs have been expanded. The table shows that standard IPv4 ACLs have been expanded to include the numbers 1300 to 1999, and the extended IPv4 ACLs have been expanded to include the numbers 2000 to 2699.

The named ACL feature enables you to identify IP standard and extended ACLs with an alphanumeric string (name) instead of the numeric representations. Named IP ACLs give you more flexibility in working with the ACL entries.

IP access list entry sequence numbering has several benefits:

- You can edit the order of ACL statements.

- You can remove individual statements from an ACL.

Where additions are placed in an ACL depends on whether you use sequence numbers. There is no support for sequence numbering in software versions earlier than Cisco IOS Software Release 12.3; therefore, all the ACL additions for earlier software versions are placed at the end of the ACL.

IP access list entry sequence numbering is a new edition to Cisco IOS Software that enables you to use sequence numbers to easily add, remove, or reorder statements in an IP ACL. With Cisco IOS Software Release 12.3 and later, additions can be placed anywhere in the ACL based on the sequence number.

Earlier than Cisco IOS Software Release 12.3, only named ACLs enable the removal of individual statements from an ACL using the following command:

```
no {deny | permit} protocol source source-wildcard destination destination-
  wildcard
```

The *protocol source source-wildcard destination destination-wildcard* parameters match the line you are trying to remove. With Cisco IOS Software Release 12.3 and later, you can also use the **no** *sequence-number* command to delete a specific access list entry.

Well-designed and well-implemented ACLs add an important security component to your network. Follow these general principles to ensure that the ACLs you create have the intended results:

- Based on the test conditions, choose a standard or extended, numbered, or named ACL.

- Only one ACL per protocol, per direction, and per interface is allowed. Multiple ACLs are permitted per interface, but each must be for a different protocol or different direction.

- Your ACL should be organized to enable processing from the top down. Organize your ACL so that the more specific references to a network or subnet appear before ones that are more general. Place conditions that occur more frequently before conditions that occur less frequently.

- Your ACL contains an implicit deny any statement at the end:

  - Unless you end your ACL with an explicit permit any statement, by default, the ACL denies all traffic that fails to match any of the ACL lines.

  - Every ACL should have at least one permit statement. Otherwise, all traffic is denied.

- You should create the ACL before applying it to an interface. With most versions of Cisco IOS Software, an interface that has an empty ACL applied to it permits all traffic.

- Depending on how you apply the ACL, the ACL filters traffic either going through the router or going to and from the router, such as traffic to or from the vty lines.

- You should typically place extended ACLs as close as possible to the source of the traffic that you want to deny. Because standard ACLs do not specify destination addresses, you must put the standard ACL as close as possible to the destination of the traffic you want to deny so that the source can reach intermediary networks.

Additional Types of ACLs

Standard and extended ACLs can become the basis for other types of ACLs that provide additional functionality. These other types of ACLs include the following:

- Dynamic ACLs (lock-and-key)
- Reflexive ACLs
- Time-based ACLs

Dynamic ACLs

Dynamic ACLs depend on Telnet connectivity, authentication (local or remote), and extended ACLs. Lock-and-key configuration starts with the application of an extended ACL to block traffic through the router. Users who want to traverse the router are blocked by the extended ACL until they use Telnet to connect to the router and are authenticated. The Telnet connection is then dropped, and a single-entry dynamic ACL is added to the extended ACL. This permits traffic for a particular period; idle and absolute timeouts are possible. Figure 18-6 shows an example of dynamic access lists.

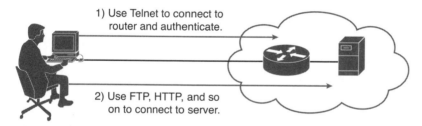

Figure 18-6   *Dynamic ACLs*

Some common reasons to use dynamic ACLs are as follows:

- Use dynamic ACLs when you want a specific remote user or group of remote users to access a host within your network, connecting from their remote hosts through the Internet. Lock-and-key authenticates the user and permits limited access through your firewall router for a host or subnet for a finite period.

- Use dynamic ACLs when you want a subset of hosts on a local network to access a host on a remote network that is protected by a firewall. With lock-and-key, you can enable access to the remote host only for the desired set of local hosts. Lock-and-key requires the users to authenticate through a TACACS+ server, or other security server, before it allows their hosts to access the remote hosts.

Dynamic ACLs have the following security benefits over standard and static extended ACLs:

- Use of a challenge mechanism to authenticate individual users
- Simpler management in large internetworks

- In many cases, reduction of the amount of router processing that is required for ACLs

- Reduction of the opportunity for network break-ins by network hackers

- Creation of dynamic user access through a firewall, without compromising other configured security restrictions

Although the entire configuration for a dynamic ACL is outside the scope of this course, the following example shows the steps that are required to configure a dynamic ACL. The goal of a dynamic ACL is to provide a means for some users on a network to have access through the router without knowing exactly what devices they will be connecting from. This type of list requires the end user to log in to the router from the device to set up a temporary access list to permit the traffic.

The following configuration creates a login name and password for authentication. The idle timeout is set to 10 minutes.

```
RouterX(config)# username test password test
RouterX(config)# username test autocommand access-enable host timeout 10
```

The following configuration enables users to open a Telnet connection to the router that is to be authenticated and blocks all other traffic:

```
RouterX(config)# access-list 101 permit tcp any host 10.1.1.1 eq telnet
RouterX(config)# interface Ethernet0/0
RouterX(config-if)# ip address 10.1.1.1 255.255.255.0
RouterX(config-if)# ip access-group 101 in
```

The following configuration creates the dynamic ACL that will be automatically applied to the existing access-list 101. The absolute timeout is set to 15 minutes.

```
RouterX(config)# access-list 101 dynamic testlist timeout 15 permit ip 10.1.1.0
    0.0.0.255 172.16.1.0 0.0.0.255
```

The following configuration forces users to authenticate when they open a Telnet connection to the router:

```
RouterX(config)# line vty 0 4
RouterX(config-line)# login local
```

After you have done these configurations, when the user at 10.1.1.2 successfully makes a Telnet connection to 10.1.1.1, the dynamic ACL is applied. The connection is then dropped, and the user can access the 172.16.1.x network.

Reflexive ACLs

Reflexive ACLs allow IP packets to be filtered based on upper-layer session information such as TCP port numbers. They are generally used to allow outbound traffic and limit inbound traffic in response to sessions that originate from a network inside the router. Reflexive ACLs contain only temporary entries. These entries are automatically created when a new IP session begins, for example, with an outbound packet, and the entries are automatically removed when the session ends. Reflexive ACLs are not applied directly to an interface but are "nested" in an extended named IP ACL that is applied to the interface. Figure 18-7 illustrates how the reflexive access list operates.

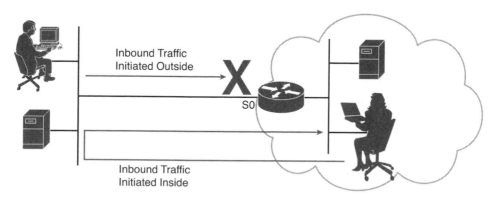

Figure 18-7 *Reflexive Access Lists*

Reflexive ACLs are an important part of securing your network against network hackers and can be included in a firewall defense. Reflexive ACLs provide a level of security against spoofing and certain denial of service (DoS) attacks. Reflexive ACLs are simple to use and, compared to basic ACLs, provide greater control over which packets enter your network.

Although the entire configuration for reflexive ACLs is outside the scope of this course, the following example shows the steps that are required to configure a reflexive ACL. The example is of a reflexive ACL that permits Internet Control Message Protocol (ICMP) outbound and inbound traffic, while it permits only TCP traffic that has initiated from inside. All other traffic is denied.

The following configuration causes the router to keep track of traffic that was initiated from inside:

```
RouterX(config)# ip access-list extended outboundfilters
RouterX(config-ext-nacl)# permit icmp 10.1.1.0 0.0.0.255 172.16.1.0 0.0.0.255
RouterX(config-ext-nacl)# permit tcp 10.1.1.0 0.0.0.255 172.16.1.0 0.0.0.255
reflect tcptraffic
```

The next configuration creates an inbound policy that requires the router to check incoming traffic to see whether it was initiated from inside and ties the reflexive ACL part of the outboundfilters ACL, called tcptraffic, to the inboundfilters ACL:

```
RouterX(config)# ip access-list extended inboundfilters
Router(config-ext-nacl)# permit icmp 172.16.1.0 0.0.0.255 10.1.1.0 0.0.0.255 eval-
uate tcptraffic
```

The configuration in Example 18-1 applies to both an inbound and an outbound ACL to the interface.

Example 18-1 *Applying Inbound and Outbound ACLs to an Interface*

```
RouterX(config)# interface Ethernet0/1
RouterX(config-if)# ip address 172.16.1.2 255.255.255.0
RouterX(config-if)# ip access-group inboundfilters in
RouterX(config-if)# ip access-group outboundfilters out
```

Reflexive ACLs can be defined only with extended named IP ACLs. They cannot be defined with numbered or standard named IP ACLs or with other protocol ACLs.

Time-Based ACLs

Time-based ACLs are similar to extended ACLs in function, but they allow for access control based on time. To implement time-based ACLs, you create a time range that defines specific times of the day and week. The time range is identified by a name and then referenced by a function. Therefore, the time restrictions are imposed on the function itself. For example, in Figure 18-8, a user is blocked from transmitting HTTP traffic after 7:00 p.m.

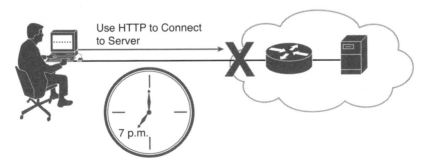

Figure 18-8 *Timed Access Lists*

Time-based ACLs have many benefits:

- The network administrator has more control over permitting or denying a user access to resources. These resources could be an application, identified by an IP address and mask pair and a port number; policy routing; or an on-demand link, identified as interesting traffic to the dialer.

- Network administrators can set time-based security policies such as the following:

  - Perimeter security using the Cisco IOS Firewall feature set or ACLs

  - Data confidentiality with Cisco Encryption Technology or IP security (IPsec)

- Policy-based routing and queuing functions are enhanced.

- When provider access rates vary by time of day, it is possible to automatically reroute traffic cost-effectively.

- Service providers can dynamically change a committed access rate (CAR) configuration to support the QoS service-level agreements (SLA) that are negotiated for certain times of day.

- Network administrators can control logging messages. ACL entries can log traffic at certain times of the day but not constantly. Therefore, administrators can simply deny access without analyzing the many logs that are generated during peak hours.

Although the entire configuration for time-based ACLs is outside the scope of this course, the following example shows the steps that are required to configure a time-based ACL. In the example, a Telnet connection is permitted from the inside network to the outside network on Monday, Wednesday, and Friday during business hours.

The following configuration defines the time range to implement the ACL and names it:

```
RouterX(config)# time-range EVERYOTHERDAY
RouterX(config-time-range)# periodic Monday Wednesday Friday 8:00 to 17:00
```

The following configuration applies the time range to the ACL:

```
RouterX(config)# access-list 101 permit tcp 10.1.1.0 0.0.0.255 172.16.1.0 0.0.0.255
  eq telnet time-range EVERYOTHERDAY
```

The following configuration applies the ACL to the interface:

```
RouterX(config)# interface Ethernet0/0
RouterX(config-if)# ip address 10.1.1.1 255.255.255.0
RouterX(config-if)# ip access-group 101 in
```

The time range relies on the router system clock. The router clock can be used, but the feature works best with Network Time Protocol (NTP) synchronization.

ACL Wildcard Masking

Address filtering occurs when you use ACL address wildcard masking to identify how to check or ignore corresponding IP address bits. Wildcard masking for IP address bits uses the numbers 1 and 0 to identify how to treat the corresponding IP address bits, as follows:

- **Wildcard mask bit 0:** Match the corresponding bit value in the address.

- **Wildcard mask bit 1:** Do not check (ignore) the corresponding bit value in the address.

Note   A wildcard mask is sometimes referred to as an *inverse mask*.

By carefully setting wildcard masks, you can permit or deny tests with one ACL statement. You can select a single IP address or many IP addresses. Figure 18-9 illustrates how to check corresponding address bits.

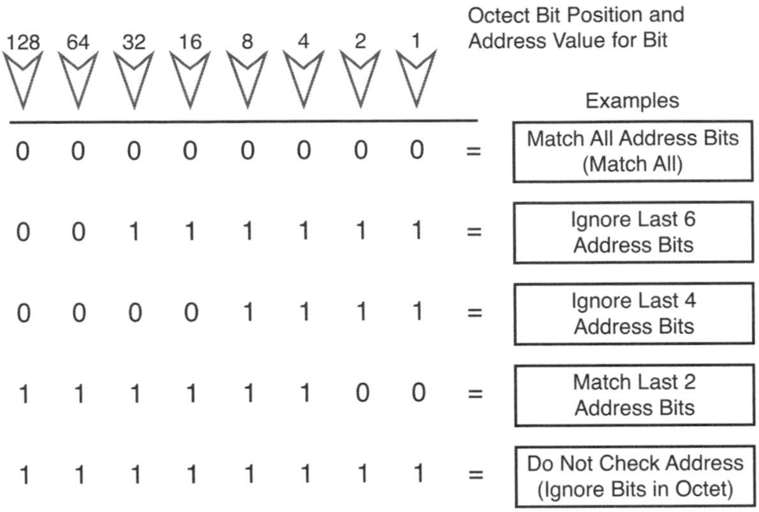

Figure 18-9 *Wildcard Mask*

Note Wildcard masking for ACLs operates differently from an IP subnet mask. A "0" in a bit position of the ACL mask indicates that the corresponding bit in the address must be matched. A "1" in a bit position of the ACL mask indicates that the corresponding bit in the address is not interesting and can be ignored.

In Figure 18-10, an administrator wants to test a range of IP subnets that is to be permitted or denied. Assume that the IP address is a Class B address (the first two octets are the network number), with 8 bits of subnetting. (The third octet is for subnets.) The administrator wants to use the IP wildcard masking bits to match subnets 172.30.16.0/24 to 172.30.31.0/24.

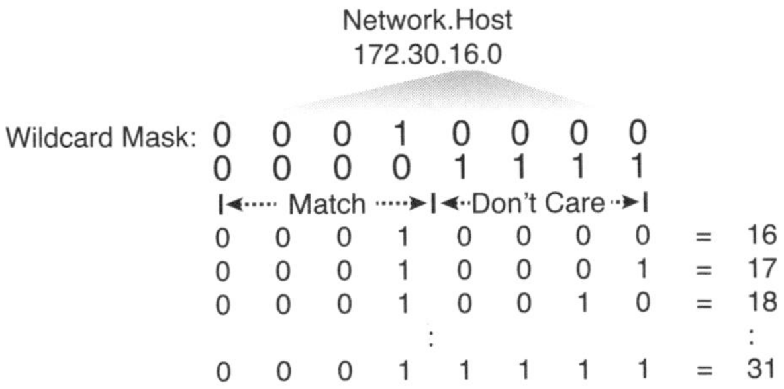

Figure 18-10 *Masking a Range of Addresses*

To use one ACL statement to match this range of subnets, use the IP address 172.30.16.0 in the ACL, which is the first subnet to be matched, followed by the required wildcard mask.

The wildcard mask matches the first two octets (172.30) of the IP address using corresponding 0 bits in the first two octets of the wildcard mask.

Because there is no interest in an individual host, the wildcard mask ignores the final octet by using the corresponding 1 bit in the wildcard mask. For example, the final octet of the wildcard mask is 255 in decimal.

In the third octet, where the subnet address occurs, the wildcard mask of decimal 15, or binary 00001111, matches the high-order 4 bits of the IP address. In this case, the wildcard mask matches subnets starting with the 172.30.16.0/24 subnet. For the final (low-end) 4 bits in this octet, the wildcard mask indicates that the bits can be ignored. In these positions, the address value can be binary 0 or binary 1. Thus, the wildcard mask matches subnet 16, 17, 18, and so on up to subnet 31. The wildcard mask does not match other subnets.

In the example, the address 172.30.16.0 with the wildcard mask 0.0.15.255 matches subnets 172.30.16.0/24 to 172.30.31.0/24.

In some cases, you must use more than one ACL statement to match a range of subnets; for example, to match 10.1.4.0/24 to 10.1.8.0/24, use 10.1.4.0 0.0.3.255 and 10.1.8.0 0.0.0.255.

The 0 and 1 bits in an ACL wildcard mask cause the ACL to either match or ignore the corresponding bit in the IP address. Working with decimal representations of binary wildcard mask bits can be tedious. For the most common uses of wildcard masking, you can use abbreviations. These abbreviations reduce how many numbers you are required to enter while configuring address test conditions. Figure 18-11 shows the wildcard masks used to match a specific host or to match all (any) host.

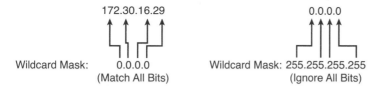

Figure 18-11   *Special Case Wildcard Masks*

Instead of entering **172.30.16.29 0.0.0.0**, you can use the string **host 172.30.16.29**. Using the abbreviation **host** communicates the same test condition to the Cisco IOS ACL Software.

Instead of entering **0.0.0.0 255.255.255.255**, you can use the word **any** by itself as the keyword. Using the abbreviation **any** communicates the same test condition to the Cisco IOS ACL Software.

Configuring ACLs

This section describes the steps to configure named and numbered, standard and extended ACLs. This section also explains how to verify that the ACLs function properly and discusses some common configuration errors to avoid.

Standard IPv4 ACLs, numbered 1 to 99 and 1300 to 1999 or named, filter packets based on a source address and mask, and they permit or deny the entire TCP/IP protocol suite. This standard ACL filtering might not provide the filtering control you require. You might need a more precise way to filter your network traffic. Figure 18-12 illustrates that standard access lists check only the source address in the IPv4 packet header.

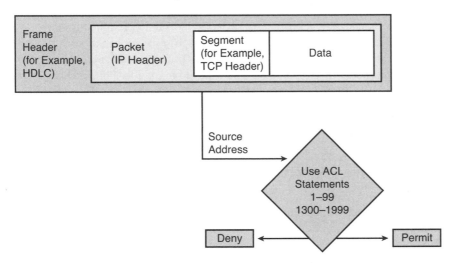

Figure 18-12 *Standard IPv4 Access Lists*

Configuring Numbered Standard IPv4 ACLs

To configure numbered standard IPv4 ACLs on a Cisco router, you must create a standard IPv4 ACL and activate an ACL on an interface. The **access-list** command creates an entry in a standard IPv4 traffic filter list.

The **ip access-group** command links an existing ACL to an interface. Only one ACL per protocol, per direction, and per interface is allowed.

Note To remove an IP ACL from an interface, first enter the **no ip access-group** *name/number* [**in|out**] command on the interface; then enter the global **no access-list** *name/number* command to remove the entire ACL.

The following provides an example of the steps that are required to configure and apply a numbered standard ACL on a router:

1. Use the **access-list** global configuration command to create an entry in a standard IPv4 ACL.

   `RouterX(config)# access-list 1 permit 172.16.0.0 0.0.255.255`

   Enter the global **no access-list** *access-list-number* command to remove the entire ACL. The example statement matches any address that starts with 172.16.x.x. You can use the **remark** option to add a description to your ACL.

2. Use the **interface** configuration command to select an interface to which to apply the ACL.

   `RouterX(config)# interface ethernet 1`

   After you enter the **interface** command, the command-line interface (CLI) prompt changes from (config)# to (config-if)#.

3. Use the **ip access-group** interface configuration command to activate the existing ACL on an interface.

   `RouterX(config-if)# ip access-group 1 out`

   To remove an IP ACL from an interface, enter the **no ip access-group** *access-list-number* command on the interface.

   This step activates the standard IPv4 ACL 1 on the interface as an outbound filter.

Example: Numbered Standard IPv4 ACL—Permit My Network Only

For the network shown in Figure 18-13, you want to create a list to prevent traffic that is not part of the internal networks (172.16.0.0/16) from traveling out either of the Ethernet interfaces.

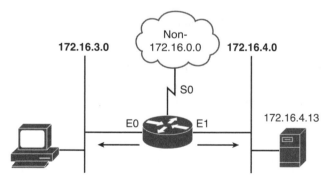

Figure 18-13 *Standard ACL Permitting a Specific Network*

The configuration in Example 18-2 provides a solution for this example.

Example 18-2   *Access List Preventing All Non-172.16.0.0 Traffic*

```
RouterX(config)# access-list 1 permit 172.16.0.0  0.0.255.255
(implicit deny all - not visible in the list)
(access-list 1 deny 0.0.0.0   255.255.255.255)
RouterX(config)# interface ethernet 0
RouterX(config-if)# ip access-group 1 out
RouterX(config)# interface ethernet 1
RouterX(config-if)# ip access-group 1 out
```

Table 18-2 describes the command syntax that is presented in Example 18-2.

Table 18-2   *Numbered Standard IPv4 ACL Example Permitting a Specific Network*

access-list Command Parameters	Description
1	ACL number that indicates that this ACL is a standard list
permit	Indicates that traffic that matches the selected parameters is forwarded
172.16.0.0	IP address that is used with the wildcard mask to identify the source network
0.0.255.255	Wildcard mask; 0s indicate positions that must match, and 1s indicate "don't care" positions
ip access-group 1 out	Links the ACL to the interface as an outbound filter

This ACL allows only traffic from source network 172.16.0.0 to be forwarded out on E0 and E1. Traffic from networks other than 172.16.0.0 is blocked.

Example: Numbered Standard IPv4 ACL—Deny a Specific Host

For the network shown in Figure 18-14, you want to create a list to prevent traffic that originates from host 172.16.4.13 from traveling out Ethernet interface E0.

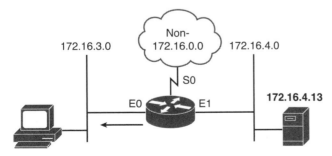

Figure 18-14   *Standard ACL Denying a Specific Host*

The configuration in Example 18-3 provides a solution for this example.

Example 18-3   *Access List Preventing Traffic Originating from a Specific Host*

```
RouterX(config)# access-list 1 deny 172.16.4.13 0.0.0.0
RouterX(config)# access-list 1 permit 0.0.0.0  255.255.255.255
(implicit deny all)
(access-list 1 deny 0.0.0.0   255.255.255.255)
RouterX(config)# interface ethernet 0
RouterX(config-if)# ip access-group 1 out
```

Table 18-3 describes the command syntax that is presented in Example 18-3.

Table 18-3   *Numbered Standard IPv4 ACL Example Denying a Specific Host*

access-list Command Parameters	Description
1	ACL number that indicates that this ACL is a standard list.
deny	Indicates that traffic that matches the selected parameters is not forwarded.
172.16.4.13	IP address of the source host.
0.0.0.0	A mask that requires the test to match all bits. (This is the default mask.)
permit	Indicates that traffic that matches the selected parameters is forwarded.
0.0.0.0	IP address of the source host; all 0s indicate a placeholder.
255.255.255.255	Wildcard mask; 0s indicate positions that must match, and 1s indicate "don't care" positions. All 1s in the mask indicate that all 32 bits are *not* checked in the source address. In other words, any address will match.

This ACL is designed to block traffic from a specific address, 172.16.4.13, and to allow all other traffic to be forwarded on interface Ethernet 0. The 0.0.0.0 255.255.255.255 IP address and wildcard mask combination permits traffic from any source. This combination can also be written using the keyword **any**.

Example: Numbered Standard IPv4 ACL—Deny a Specific Subnet

In Figure 18-15, the goal is to create a list to prevent traffic that originates from the subnet 172.16.4.0/24 from traveling out Ethernet interface E0.

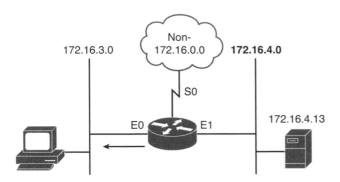

Figure 18-15   *Standard ACL Denying a Specific Subnet*

The configuration in Example 18-4 provides a solution for this example.

Example 18-4   *Access List Preventing Traffic Originating from a Specific Subnet*

```
RouterX(config)# access-list 1 deny 172.16.4.0 0.0.0.255
RouterX(config)# access-list 1 permit any
(implicit deny all)
(access-list 1 deny 0.0.0.0   255.255.255.255)
RouterX(config)# interface ethernet 0
RouterX(config-if)# ip access-group 1 out
```

Table 18-4 describes the command syntax that is presented in Example 18-4.

Table 18-4   *Numbered Standard IPv4 ACL Example Denying a Specific Subnet*

access-list Command Parameters	Description
1	ACL number indicating that this ACL is a standard list.
deny	Indicates that traffic that matches the selected parameters is not forwarded.
172.16.4.0	IP address of the source subnet.
0.0.0.255	Wildcard mask; 0s indicate positions that must match, and 1s indicate "don't care" positions. The mask with 0s in the first three octets indicates that those positions must match; the 255 in the last octet indicates a "don't care" condition.
permit	Indicates that traffic that matches the selected parameters is forwarded.
any	Abbreviation for the IP address of the source. The abbreviation **any** indicates a source address of 0.0.0.0 and a wildcard mask of 255.255.255.255; all source addresses will match.

This ACL is designed to block traffic from a specific subnet, 172.16.4.0, and to allow all other traffic to be forwarded out E0.

Controlling Access to the Router Using ACLs

To control traffic into and out of the router (not through the router), you will protect the router virtual ports. A virtual port is called a *vty*. By default, there are five such virtual terminal lines, numbered vty 0 through vty 4. When configured, Cisco IOS Software images can support more than five vty ports.

Restricting vty access is primarily a technique for increasing network security and defining which addresses are allowed remote terminal access to the router EXEC process.

Filtering Telnet traffic is typically considered an extended IP ACL function because it filters a higher-level protocol. Because you are filtering incoming or outgoing Telnet sessions by source addresses and applying the filter using the **access-class** command to the vty lines, you can use standard IP ACL statements to control vty access.

Example 18-5 demonstrates how to limit access to the Telnet process.

Example 18-5   *Access List Preventing Telnet Activity*

```
access-list 12 permit 192.168.1.0 0.0.0.255
(implicit deny any)
!
line vty 0 4
 access-class 12 in
```

In this example, you permit any device on network 192.168.1.0 0.0.0.255 to establish a virtual terminal (Telnet) session with the router. Of course, the user must know the appropriate passwords to enter user mode and privileged mode.

Notice that identical restrictions have been set on every vty line (0 to 4) because you cannot control on which vty line a user will connect. The implicit deny any statement still applies to the ACL when it is used as an access class entry.

Configuring Numbered Extended IPv4 ACLs

For more precise traffic-filtering control, use extended IPv4 ACLs, numbered 100 to 199 and 2000 to 2699 or named, which check for the source and destination IPv4 address. In addition, at the end of the extended ACL statement, you can specify the protocol and optional TCP or User Datagram Protocol (UDP) application to filter more precisely. Figure 18-16 illustrates the IP header fields that can be examined with an extended access list.

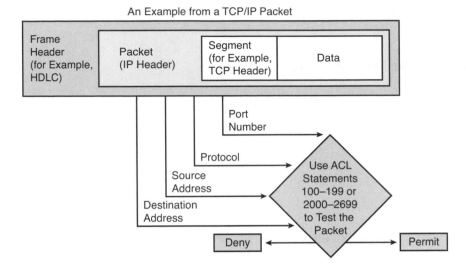

Figure 18-16   *Extended IPv4 Access Lists*

To specify an application, you can configure either the port number or the name of a well-known application. Table 18-5 shows an abbreviated list of some well-known port numbers of the various TCP applications.

Table 18-5   *Well-Known Port Numbers and IP Protocols*

Well-Known Port Number (Decimal)*	IP Protocol
20 (TCP)	FTP data
21 (TCP)	FTP control
23 (TCP)	Telnet
25 (TCP)	Simple Mail Transfer Protocol (SMTP)
53 (TCP/UDP)	Domain Name System (DNS)
69 (UDP)	TFTP
80 (TCP)	HTTP

* www.iani.org/assignments/port-numbers provides a more comprehensive list of well-known port numbers.

To configure numbered extended IPv4 ACLs on a Cisco router, create an extended IPv4 ACL and activate that ACL on an interface. Use the **access-list** command to create an entry to express a condition statement in a complex filter. The full command follows:

```
access-list access-list-number {permit | deny}
  protocol source source-wildcard [operator port]
  destination destination-wildcard [operator port]
  [established] [log]
```

Table 18-6 explains the syntax of the command.

Table 18-6   *Command Parameters for a Numbered Extended ACL*

access-list Command Parameters	Description
access-list-number	Identifies the list using a number in the ranges of 100–199 or 2000–2699.
permit | deny	Indicates whether this entry allows or blocks the specified address.
protocol	For example: `<0-255>` — An IP protocol number `ahp` — Authentication Header Protocol `eigrp` — Cisco EIGRP1 routing protocol `esp` — Encapsulation Security Payload `gre` — Cisco GRE2 tunneling `icmp` — Internet Control Message Protocol `igmp` — Internet Gateway Message Protocol `ip` — Any Internet Protocol `ipinip` — IP in IP tunneling `nos` — KA9Q NOS compatible IP over IP tunneling `object-group` — Service object group `ospf` — OSPF routing protocol `pcp` — Payload Compression Protocol `pim` — Protocol Independent Multicast `tcp` — Transmission Control Protocol `udp` — User Datagram Protocol
source and destination	Identifies the source and destination IP addresses.
source-wildcard and destination-wildcard	Wildcard mask; 0s indicate positions that must match, and 1s indicate "don't care" positions.
operator [port|app_name]	The operator can be **lt** (less than), **gt** (greater than), **eq** (equal to), or **neq** (not equal to). The port number referenced can be either the source port or the destination port, depending on where in the ACL the port number is configured. As an alternative to the port number, well-known application names can be used, such as Telnet, FTP, and SMTP.
established	For inbound TCP only. Allows TCP traffic to pass if the packet is a response to an outbound-initiated session. This type of traffic has the acknowledgment (ACK) bits set. (See the Extended ACL with the Established Parameter example.)
log	Sends a logging message to the console.

The syntax of the **access-list** command that is presented here is representative of the TCP protocol form. Not all parameters and options are given. For the complete syntax of all forms of the command, refer to the appropriate Cisco IOS Software documentation available at Cisco.com.

Extended ACL with the established Parameter

In Example 18-6, the **established** parameter of the extended ACL allows responses to traffic that originate from the mail host, 128.88.1.2, to return inbound on the serial 0 interface. A match occurs if the TCP datagram has the ACK or reset (RST) bits set, which indicates that the packet belongs to an existing connection. Without the **established** parameter in the ACL statement, the mail host could only receive SMTP traffic but not send it.

Example 18-6   *Access List Permitting Responses to an Originating Mail Host*

```
access-list 102 permit tcp any host 128.88.1.2 established
access-list 102 permit tcp any host 128.88.1.2 eq smtp


interface serial 0

 ip access-group 102 in
```

The **ip access-group** command links an existing extended ACL to an interface. Only one ACL per protocol, per direction, and per interface is allowed.

Table 18-7 defines the parameters of the **ip access-group** command.

Table 18-7   ip access-group *Command Parameters*

ip access-group Command Parameters	Description
access-list-number	Indicates the number of the ACL that is to be linked to an interface
in	out	Selects whether the ACL is applied as an input or output filter; out is the default

The following list shows the steps that are required to configure and apply an extended ACL on a router:

1. Define an extended IPv4 ACL. Use the **access-list** global configuration command.

```
RouterX(config)# access-list 101 permit tcp 172.16.4.0 0.0.0.255 172.16.3.0
   0.0.0.255 eq 21
```

Use the **show access-lists** command to display the contents of the ACL. In the example, access-list 101 denies TCP traffic from source 172.16.4.0, using the wildcard 0.0.0.255, to destination 172.16.3.0, using the wildcard 0.0.0.255 on port 21 (FTP control port).

2. Select a desired interface to be configured. Use the **interface** global configuration command.

```
RouterX(config)# interface gi0/0
```

After the **interface** command is entered, the CLI prompt changes from (config)# to (config-if)#.

3. Link the extended IPv4 ACL to an interface. Use the **ip access-group** interface configuration command.

```
RouterX(config-if)# ip access-group 101 in
```

Use the **show ip interfaces** command to verify that an IP ACL is applied to the interface.

Numbered Extended IP ACL: Deny FTP from Subnets

For the network in Figure 18-17, you want to create a list to prevent FTP traffic that originates from the subnet 172.16.4.0/24, going to the 172.16.3.0/24 subnet, from traveling out Ethernet interface E0.

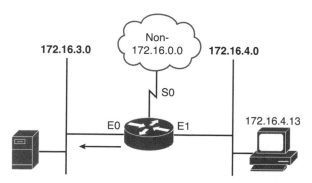

Figure 18-17   *Extended ACL Denying FTP from One Subnet to Another*

The configuration in Example 18-7 provides a solution for this example.

Example 18-7   *Access List Preventing FTP Traffic from Specific Subnets*

```
RouterX(config)# access-list 101 deny tcp 172.16.4.0 0.0.0.255 172.16.3.0 0.0.0.255
 eq 21
RouterX(config)# access-list 101 permit ip any any
(implicit deny all)
(access-list 101 deny ip 0.0.0.0 255.255.255.255 0.0.0.0 255.255.255.255)
RouterX(config)# interface ethernet 0
RouterX(config-if)# ip access-group 101 out
```

Table 18-8 describes the command syntax presented in Example 18-7.

Table 18-8   *Numbered Extended IPv4 ACL Example Denying FTP Between Subnets*

access-list Command Parameters	Description
101	ACL number; indicates an extended IPv4 ACL
deny	Indicates that traffic that matches the selected parameters is not forwarded
tcp	Transport layer protocol
172.16.4.0 0.0.0.255	Source IP address and mask; the first three octets must match but not the last octet
172.16.3.0 0.0.0.255	Destination IP address and mask; the first three octets must match but not the last octet
eq 21	Destination port; specifies the well-known port number for FTP control
out	Links ACL 101 to interface E0 as an output filter

The deny statements deny FTP traffic from subnet 172.16.4.0 to subnet 172.16.3.0. The permit statement allows all other IP traffic out interface E0.

Numbered Extended ACL: Deny Only Telnet from Subnet

For the network in Figure 18-18, you want to create a list to prevent Telnet traffic that originates from the subnet 172.16.4.0/24 from traveling out Ethernet interface E0.

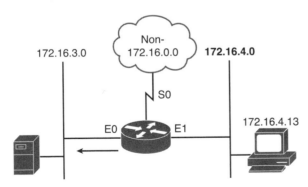

Figure 18-18   *Extended ACL Denying Telnet from a Given Subnet*

The configuration in Example 18-8 provides a solution for this example.

Example 18-8   *Access List Preventing Telnet Traffic from a Specific Subnet*

```
RouterX(config)# access-list 101 deny tcp 172.16.4.0  0.0.0.255  any eq 23
RouterX(config)# access-list 101 permit ip any any
(implicit deny all)
RouterX(config)# interface ethernet 0
RouterX(config-if)# ip access-group 101 out
```

This example denies Telnet traffic from 172.16.4.0 that is being sent out interface E0. All other IP traffic from any other source to any destination is permitted out E0.

Table 18-9 describes the command syntax that is presented in the example.

Table 18-9   *Numbered Extended IPv4 ACL Example Denying Telnet from a Subnet*

access-list Command Parameters	Description
101	ACL number; indicates an extended IPv4 ACL
deny	Indicates that traffic that matches the selected parameters is not forwarded
tcp	Transport layer protocol
172.16.4.0 0.0.0.255	Source IP address and mask; the first three octets must match but not the last octet
any	Match any destination IP address
eq 23 or eq telnet	Destination port or application; in this example, it specifies the well-known port number for Telnet, which is 23
permit	Indicates that traffic that matches the selected parameters is forwarded
ip	Any IP protocol
any	Keyword matching traffic from any source
any	Keyword matching traffic to any destination
out	Links ACL 101 to interface E0 as an output filter

Configuring Named ACLs

The named ACL feature allows you to identify standard and extended IP ACLs with an alphanumeric string (name) instead of the current numeric representations.

Named IP ACLs allow you to delete individual entries in a specific ACL. If you are using Cisco IOS Release 12.3, you can use sequence numbers to insert statements anywhere in the named ACL. If you are using a software version earlier than Cisco IOS Release 12.3, you can insert statements only at the bottom of the named ACL.

Because you can delete individual entries with named ACLs, you can modify your ACL without having to delete and then reconfigure the entire ACL. Use named IP ACLs when you want to intuitively identify ACLs.

Creating Named Standard IP ACLs

The following list shows the steps that are required to configure and apply a named standard IP ACL on a router:

1. Define a standard named IPv4 ACL. Use the **ip access-list standard** global configuration command:

   ```
   RouterX(config)# ip access-list standard name
   ```

   Define the list using a unique name. A descriptive name can be helpful when examining the configuration of the router.

2. Enter one of the following commands to establish test parameters:

   ```
   RouterX(config-std-nacl)# [sequence-number] deny {source [source-wildcard] | any}
   RouterX(config-std-nacl)# [sequence-number] permit {source [source-wildcard] | any}
   ```

   In access list configuration mode, specify one or more conditions permitted or denied. This determines whether the packet is passed or dropped. You can also use the sequence number to place the test parameter in a specific location within the list.

3. Exit from named access list configuration mode:

   ```
   RouterX(config-std-nacl)# exit
   RouterX(config)#
   ```

4. Select a desired interface to be configured. Use the **interface** global configuration command:

   ```
   RouterX(config)# interface ethernet 0
   ```

   After you enter the **interface** command, the CLI prompt changes from (config)# to (config-if)#.

5. Link the extended IPv4 ACL to an interface. Use the **ip access-group** interface configuration command:

   ```
   RouterX(config-if)# ip access-group 101 in
   ```

6. Use the **show ip interface** command to verify that an IP ACL is applied to the interface.

Creating Named Extended IP ACLs

The steps required to configure and apply a named extended IP ACL on a router are as follows:

1. Define a standard named IPv4 ACL. Use the **ip access-list extended** global configuration command:

   ```
   RouterX(config)# ip access-list extended name
   ```

   Define the list using a unique name. A descriptive name can be helpful when examining the configuration of the router.

2. Enter the following command syntax to establish test parameters:

   ```
   RouterX(config-ext-nacl)# [sequence-number] {deny | permit} protocol source
      source-wildcard destination destination-wildcard [option]
   ```

   In access list configuration mode, specify the conditions allowed or denied. You can use the keyword **any** to abbreviate an address of 0.0.0.0 with a wildcard mask of 255.255.255.255 for the source address, destination address, or both. You can use the keyword **host** to abbreviate a wildcard mask of 0.0.0.0 for the source address or destination address. Place the keyword **host** in front of the address.

3. Exit from named access list configuration mode:

   ```
   RouterX(config-ext-nacl)# exit
   RouterX(config)#
   ```

4. Select a desired interface to be configured. Use the **interface** global configuration command:

   ```
   RouterX(config)# interface ethernet 0
   ```

   After you enter the **interface** command, the CLI prompt changes from (config)# to (config-if)#.

5. Link the extended IPv4 ACL to an interface. Use the **ip access-group** interface configuration command:

   ```
   RouterX(config-if)# ip access-group 101 in
   ```

   Use the **show ip interfaces** command to verify that an IP ACL is applied to the interface.

You can take advantage of the sequence numbers in a named access list to add specific entries within an existing list. In Example 18-9, a new entry is added to a specified location within the access list.

Example 18-9 *Confirming Added Entries to an Existing Access List*

```
RouterX# show ip access-list

Standard IP access list MARKETING
2 permit 10.4.4.2, wildcard bits 0.0.255.255
5 permit 10.0.0.44, wildcard bits 0.0.0.255
10 permit 10.0.0.1, wildcard bits 0.0.0.255
20 permit 10.0.0.2, wildcard bits 0.0.0.255
RouterX(config)# ip access-list standard MARKETING
RouterX(config-std-nacl)# 15 permit 10.5.5.5 0.0.0.255
RouterX# show ip access-list
Standard IP access list MARKETING
2 permit 10.4.4.2, wildcard bits 0.0.255.255
5 permit 10.0.0.44, wildcard bits 0.0.0.255
10 permit 10.0.0.1, wildcard bits 0.0.0.255
15 permit 10.5.5.5, wildcard bits 0.0.0.255
20 permit 10.0.0.2, wildcard bits 0.0.0.255
```

Using the number of a standard access list as the name, you can also use this feature to place an entry in a specific location of a numbered access list. In Example 18-10, a new entry is added to a specified access list.

Example 18-10 *Placing an Entry in a Numbered List Using the Name Function*

```
RouterX# show ip access-list
Standard IP access list 1
2 permit 10.4.4.2, wildcard bits 0.0.255.255
5 permit 10.0.0.44, wildcard bits 0.0.0.255
10 permit 10.0.0.1, wildcard bits 0.0.0.255
20 permit 10.0.0.2, wildcard bits 0.0.0.255
RouterX(config)# ip access-list standard 1
RouterX(config-std-nacl)# 15 permit 10.5.5.5 0.0.0.255
RouterX(config-std-nacl)# end
RouterX# show ip access-list
Standard IP access list 1
2 permit 10.4.4.2, wildcard bits 0.0.255.255
5 permit 10.0.0.44, wildcard bits 0.0.0.255
10 permit 10.0.0.1, wildcard bits 0.0.0.255
15 permit 10.5.5.5, wildcard bits 0.0.0.255
20 permit 10.0.0.2, wildcard bits 0.0.0.255
```

Named Extended ACL: Deny a Single Host from a Given Subnet

For the network shown in Figure 18-19, you want to create a list named "troublemaker" to prevent traffic that originates from the host 172.16.4.13 from traveling out Ethernet interface E0.

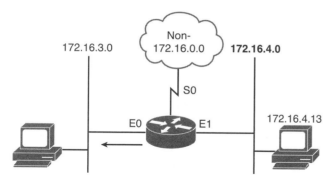

Figure 18-19 *Named Extended ACL Denying a Single Host*

The configuration in Example 18-11 provides a solution for this example.

Example 18-11 *Access List Preventing Traffic from a Specific Host*

```
RouterX(config)# ip access-list standard troublemaker
RouterX(config-std-nacl)# deny host 172.16.4.13
RouterX(config-std-nacl)# permit 172.16.4.0 0.0.0.255
RouterX(config-std-nacl)# interface e0
RouterX(config-if)# ip access-group troublemaker out
```

Table 18-10 describes the command syntax that is presented in Example 18-11.

Table 18-10 *Named Extended IPv4 ACL Example Denying a Single Host*

access-list Command Parameter	Description
standard	Indicates that the named ACL is a standard ACL
troublemaker	Name of the ACL
deny	Indicates that traffic that matches the selected parameters is not forwarded
host 172.16.4.13	Source IP address; "host" indicates a wildcard mask of 0.0.0.0
permit	Indicates that traffic that matches the selected parameters is forwarded
172.16.4.0 0.0.0.255	Source IP address and mask; the first three octets must match but not the last octet
ip access-group troublemaker out	Links ACL "troublemaker" to interface E0 as an output filter

Named Extended ACL—Deny a Telnet from a Subnet

Using Figure 18-19 again, this time you want to create a list named "badgroup" to prevent Telnet traffic that originates from the subnet 172.16.4.0/24 from traveling out Ethernet interface E0.

The configuration in Example 18-12 provides a solution.

Example 18-12   *Access List Preventing Telnet Traffic from a Specific Subnet*

```
RouterX(config)# ip access-list extended badgroup
RouterX(config-ext-nacl)# deny tcp 172.16.4.0 0.0.0.255 any eq 23
RouterX(config-ext-nacl)# permit ip any any
RouterX(config-ext-nacl)# interface e0
RouterX(config-if)# ip access-group badgroup out
```

Table 18-11 describes the command syntax that is presented in the figure.

Table 18-11   *Named Extended IPv4 ACL Example Denying Telnet from a Subnet*

access-list Command Parameter	Description
extended	Indicates that the named ACL is an extended ACL.
badgroup	Name of the ACL.
deny	Indicates that traffic that matches the selected parameters is not forwarded.
tcp	Transport layer protocol.
172.16.4.0 0.0.0.255	Source IP address and mask; the first three octets must match but not the last octet.
any	Match any destination IP address.
eq 23 or eq telnet	Destination port or application name. In this example, it specifies the well-known port number for Telnet, which is 23.
permit	Indicates that traffic that matches the selected parameters is forwarded.
ip	Network layer protocol.
any	Keyword matching traffic to any source and destination.
ip access-group badgroup out	Links ACL "badgroup" to interface E0 as an output filter.

Adding Comments to Named or Numbered ACLs

Comments, also known as *remarks*, are ACL statements that are not processed. They are simple descriptive statements you can use to better understand and troubleshoot either named or numbered ACLs.

Each remark line is limited to 100 characters. The remark can go before or after a permit or deny statement. You should be consistent about where you put the remark so that it is clear which remark describes which permit or deny statement. It would be confusing to have some remarks before the associated permit or deny statements and some remarks after the associated statements.

To add a comment to a named IP ACL, use the **remark** *remark* command in access list configuration mode. To add a comment to a numbered IP ACL, use the **access-list** *access-list-number* **remark** *remark* command.

The following is an example of adding a comment to a numbered ACL:

```
access-list 101 remark Permitting_John to Telnet to Server
access-list 101 permit tcp host 10.1.1.2 host 172.16.1.1 eq telnet
```

The following is an example of adding a comment to a named ACL:

```
ip access-list standard PREVENTION
remark Do not allow Jones subnet through
deny 171.69.0.0 0.0.255.255
```

Troubleshooting ACLs

When you finish the ACL configuration, use the **show** commands to verify the configuration. Use the **show access-lists** command to display the contents of all ACLs, as demonstrated in Example 18-13. By entering the ACL name or number as an option for this command, you can display a specific ACL. To display only the contents of all IP ACLs, use the **show ip access-list** command.

Example 18-13   *Verifying Access List Configuration*

```
RouterX# show access-lists
Standard IP access list SALES
    10 deny    10.1.1.0, wildcard bits 0.0.0.255
    20 permit 10.3.3.1
    30 permit 10.4.4.1
    40 permit 10.5.5.1
Extended IP access list ENG
    10 permit tcp host 10.22.22.1 any eq telnet (25 matches)
    20 permit tcp host 10.33.33.1 any eq ftp
    30 permit tcp host 10.44.44.1 any eq ftp-data
```

The **show ip interface** command displays IP interface information and indicates whether any IP ACLs are set on the interface. In the **show ip interface e0** command output shown in Example 18-14, IP ACL 1 has been configured on the E0 interface as an inbound ACL. No outbound IP ACL has been configured on the E0 interface.

Example 18-14   *Verifying Access List Configuration on a Specific Interface*

```
RouterX# show ip interface e0
Ethernet0 is up, line protocol is up
  Internet address is 10.1.1.11/24
  Broadcast address is 255.255.255.255
  Address determined by setup command
  MTU is 1500 bytes
  Helper address is not set
  Directed broadcast forwarding is disabled
  Outgoing access list is not set
  Inbound  access list is 1
  Proxy ARP is enabled
  Security level is default
  Split horizon is enabled
  ICMP redirects are always sent
  ICMP unreachables are always sent
  ICMP mask replies are never sent
  IP fast switching is enabled
  IP fast switching on the same interface is disabled
  IP Feature Fast switching turbo vector
  IP multicast fast switching is enabled
  IP multicast distributed fast switching is disabled
  <text ommitted>
```

Take a look at some examples of access list problems. For the following issues, refer to Figure 18-20.

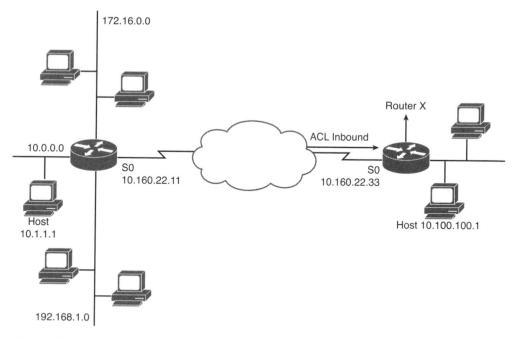

Figure 18-20 *ACL Troubleshooting Reference Network*

Each of the following problems assumes that an inbound access list is configured to S0 of RouterX, as shown in Figure 18-20. You will use the **show access-lists** command to determine information about the access list(s) in place to troubleshoot all these problems.

Problem: Host Connectivity

Host 10.1.1.1 has no connectivity with 10.100.100.1. The following output reveals information about the access list(s) in place to help determine the possible cause of the problem:

```
RouterX# show access-lists 10
Standard IP access list 10
    10 deny    10.1.1.0, wildcard bits 0.0.0.255
    20 permit 10.1.1.1
    30 permit ip any any
```

The cause of this problem is that Host 10.1.1.1 has no connectivity with 10.100.100.1 because of the order of the access list 10 rules. Because the router processes ACLs from the top down, statement 10 would deny host 10.1.1.1, and statement 20 would not be processed. The solution to this problem is to reverse statements 10 and 20.

The 192.168.1.0 network cannot use TFTP to connect to 10.100.100.1. The following output reveals information about the access list(s) in place to help determine the possible cause of the problem:

```
RouterX# show access-lists 120
Extended IP access list 120
    10 deny tcp 172.16.0.0 0.0.255.255 any eq telnet
    20 deny tcp 192.168.1.0 0.0.0.255 host 10.100.100.1 eq smtp
    30 permit tcp any any
```

The cause of this problem is that the 192.168.1.0 network cannot use TFTP to connect to 10.100.100.1 because TFTP uses the transport protocol UDP. Statement 30 in access list 120 allows all other TCP traffic, and because TFTP uses UDP, it is implicitly denied. The solution to this problem is to correct statement 30; it should be **ip any any**.

The 172.16.0.0 network can use Telnet to connect to 10.100.100.1, but this connection should not be allowed. The following output reveals information about the access list(s) in place to help determine the possible cause of the problem:

```
RouterX# show access-lists 130
Extended IP access list 130
    10 deny tcp any eq telnet any
    20 deny tcp 192.168.1.0 0.0.0.255 host 10.100.100.1 eq smtp
    30 permit ip any any
```

The cause of this problem is that the 172.16.0.0 network can use Telnet to connect to 10.100.100.1 because the Telnet port number in statement 10 of access list 130 is in the wrong position. Statement 10 currently denies any source with a port number that is equal to Telnet trying to establish a connection to any IP address. If you want to deny Telnet inbound on S0, the solution is to deny the destination port number that is equal to Telnet, for example, **deny tcp any any eq telnet**.

Host 10.1.1.1 can use Telnet to connect to 10.100.100.1, but this connection should not be allowed. The following output reveals information about the access list(s) in place to help determine the possible cause of the problem:

```
RouterX# show access-lists 140
Extended IP access list 140
    10 deny tcp host 10.160.22.11 10.100.100.0 0.0.0.255 eq telnet
    20 deny tcp 192.168.1.0 0.0.0.255 host 10.100.100.1 eq smtp
    30 permit ip any any
```

The cause of this problem is that the Host 10.1.1.1 can use Telnet to connect to 10.100.100.1 because there are no rules that deny host 10.1.1.1 or its network as the source. Statement 10 of access list 140 denies the router interface from which traffic would be departing. But as these packets depart the router, they have a source address of 10.1.1.1 and not the address of the router interface. The solution to this problem would be to modify entry 10 so that 10.1.0.0 subnet was denied instead of the address 10.160.22.11.

Problem: Host 10.100.100.1 can use Telnet to connect to 10.1.1.1, but this connection should not be allowed. The following output reveals information about the access list(s) in place to help determine the possible cause of the problem:

```
RouterX# show access-lists 150
Extended IP access list 150
    10 deny tcp host 10.100.100.1 any eq telnet
    20 permit ip any any
```

Access list 150 is applied to interface S0 in the inbound direction.

The cause of this problem is that the Host 10.100.100.1 can use Telnet to connect to 10.1.1.1 because of the direction in which access list 150 is applied to the S0 interface. Statement 10 denies the source address of 10.100.100.1, but that address would only be the source if the traffic were outbound on S0, not inbound. One solution would be to modify the direction in which the list was applied.

Host 10.1.1.1 can connect into RouterX using Telnet, but this connection should not be allowed. The following output reveals information about the access list(s) in place to help determine the possible cause of the problem:

```
RouterX# show access-lists 160
Extended IP access list 160
    10 deny tcp any host 10.160.22.33 eq telnet
    20 permit ip any any
```

The cause of this problem is that the Host 10.1.1.1 can connect into Router B using Telnet because using Telnet to connect *into* the router is different from using Telnet to connect *through* the router to another device. Statement 10 of access list 160 denies Telnet access to the address that is assigned to the S0 interface of Router B. Host 10.1.1.1 can still use Telnet to connect into Router B simply by using a different interface address, such as E0. The solution is recognizing which IOS command to use. When you want to block Telnet traffic into and out of the router, use the **access-class** command to apply access lists to the vty lines.

Chapter Summary

Standard and extended Cisco IOS access control lists (ACL) are used to classify IP packets. The many features of ACLs include security, encryption, policy-based routing, and quality of service (QoS). These features are applied on router and switch interfaces for specific directions (inbound versus outbound).

Numbered ACLs identify the type of ACL that is being created: standard or extended. They also allow administrators more flexibility when they are modifying the ACL entries.

The following list summarizes the key points that were discussed in this chapter:

- ACLs can be used to filter IP packets or identify traffic for special handling.

- ACLs perform top-down processing and can be configured for incoming or outgoing traffic.

- In a wildcard bit mask, 0 means to match the corresponding address bit, and 1 means to ignore the corresponding address bit.

- Standard IPv4 ACLs allow filtering based on source IP address.

- Extended IPv4 ACLs allow filtering based on source and destination IP addresses, as well as protocol and port number and message types.

- IP access list entry sequence numbering allows you to delete individual statements from an ACL to add statements anywhere in the ACL.

- The **show access-lists** and **show ip interface** commands are useful for troubleshooting common ACL configuration errors.

Additional Resource

- ACLs Video, AJS Networking: http://ajsnetworking.com/acls

Review Questions

Use the questions here to review what you learned in this chapter. The correct answers and solutions are found in Appendix A, "Answers to Chapter Review Questions."

1. What does a Cisco router do with a packet when it matches an ACL statement?
   a. Discards the packet
   b. Returns the packet to its originator
   c. Follows the instructions in that statement
   d. Holds the packet for further processing

2. You can apply an ACL to multiple interfaces. How many ACLs per protocol, per direction, and per interface can you apply?
   a. 1
   b. 2
   c. 4
   d. Any number, depending on the router model

3. What is the term for the final default statement at the end of every ACL?
   a. implicit deny all
   b. implicit deny host
   c. implicit permit any
   d. implicit permit host

4. Which statement best describes the difference between standard and extended IPv4 ACLs?

    a. Standard ACLs use the range 100 through 149, whereas extended ACLs use the range 150 through 199.

    b. Standard ACLs filter based on the source and destination addresses, whereas extended ACLs filter based on the source address.

    c. Standard ACLs permit or deny access to a specified well-known port, whereas extended ACLs filter based on the source address and mask.

    d. Standard ACLs permit or deny the entire TCP/IP protocol suite, whereas extended ACLs can choose a specific IP protocol and port number.

5. Which of the following ranges of numbers can you use to identify IPv4 extended ACLs on a Cisco router? (Choose two.)

    a. 1 to 99

    b. 51 to 151

    c. 100 to 199

    d. 200 to 299

    e. 1300 to 1999

    f. 2000 to 2699

6. A system administrator wants to configure an IPv4 standard ACL on a Cisco router to allow packets only from the hosts on subnet 10.1.1.0/24 to enter an interface on a router. Which ACL configuration accomplishes this goal?

    a. access-list 1 permit 10.1.1.0/8

    b. access-list 1 permit 10.1.1.0 host

    c. access-list 99 permit 10.1.1.0 0.0.0.255

    d. access-list 100 permit 10.1.1.0 0.0.0.255

7. Which Cisco IOS command links an extended IPv4 ACL to an interface?

    a. ip access-list 101 e0

    b. access-group 101 e0

    c. ip access-group 101 in

    d. access-list 101 permit tcp access-list 100 permit 10.1.1.0 0.0.0.255 eq 21

8. What is the complete command to create an ACL entry that has the following parameters?

Source IP address is 172.16.0.0

Source subnet mask is 255.255.0.0

Permit this entry

ACL number is 1

   a. access-list 1 deny 172.16.0.0 0.0.255.255

   b. access-list 1 permit 172.16.0.0 0.0.255.255

   c. access-list permit 1 172.16.0.0 255.255.0.0

   d. access-list 99 permit 172.16.0.0 0.0.255.255

9. Which command applies standard IP ACL filtering to vty lines for an incoming Telnet session?

   a. access-vty 1 in

   b. access-class 1 in

   c. ip access-list 1 in

   d. ip access-group 1 in

10. Which command is used on a Cisco router to determine whether IP ACLs are applied to an Ethernet interface?

   a. show interfaces

   b. show ACL

   c. show ip interface

   d. show ip access-list

Production Network Simulation Question 18-1

You must provide a router configuration that accomplishes the following:

■ Create an extended ACL named MYTEST.

■ This ACL must permit web server traffic from 172.16.1.100.

■ This ACL must deny all other traffic from this server.

■ All other IP traffic must be permitted.

■ This ACL must be assigned to the Gi0/1 interface in the inbound direction.

Chapter 19

Introducing WAN Technologies

This chapter includes the following sections:

- Chapter Objectives

- Introducing WANs

- Chapter Summary

- Additional Resources

- Review Questions

- Production Network Simulation Question 19-1

As an enterprise grows beyond a single location, it becomes necessary to interconnect LANs in various locations to form a wide-area network (WAN). Several technologies are involved in the functioning of WANs. This chapter describes the functions and characteristics of WANs.

Chapter Objectives

Upon completing this chapter, you will be able to discuss the importance of wide-area networking in today's networking environment. You will also be able to configure a simple WAN circuit. These abilities include meeting these objectives:

- Describe a WAN and explain the need for WANs

- Compare LANs and WANs

- Describe the role of routers for WAN access

- List the major options for WAN access communication links

- Describe Ethernet emulation for point-to-point connectivity

- Configure a WAN interface connection

Introducing WANs

A WAN is a data communications network that operates beyond the geographic scope of a LAN. Wide-area networks (WAN) use facilities that are provided by a service provider or carrier, such as a telephone or cable company. They connect the locations of an organization to each other, to locations of other organizations, to external services, and to remote users. WANs generally carry various traffic types, such as voice, data, and video.

Here are the three major characteristics of WANs:

- WANs connect devices that are located over wide geographical areas.

- WANs use the services of carriers, such as telephone companies, cable companies, satellite systems, and network providers.

- WANs use various connection types to provide access to bandwidth over large geographical areas.

There are several reasons why WANs are necessary in a communications environment. LAN technologies provide both speed and cost-effectiveness for transmission of data in organizations in relatively small geographic areas. However, there are other business needs that require communication among remote users:

- People in regional or branch offices of an organization need to be able to communicate and share data.

- Organizations often want to share information with other organizations across large distances. For example, software manufacturers routinely communicate product and promotion information to distributors that sell their products to end users.

- Employees who travel on company business or work from home frequently need to access information that resides on their corporate networks.

Because it is obviously not feasible to connect computers across a country or around the world with local-area network cables, various technologies have evolved to meet this need. WANs allow organizations and individuals to meet their wide-area communications needs.

In recent years, several new technologies, which use the Internet infrastructure to connect distant locations, matured to offer good alternatives to traditional WAN connectivity options. Figure 19-1 shows how a WAN fits into the overall networking structure of a typical organization.

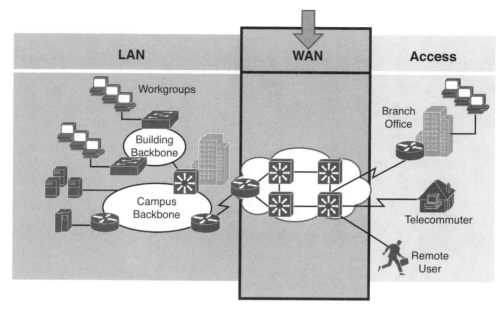

Figure 19-1 *Typical WAN*

WANs Versus LANs

WANs are different from LANs in several ways. The most significant differences are geographical area and ownership. A LAN connects computers, peripherals, and other devices in a single building or in a multicampus environment. A WAN allows the transmission of data across broad distances. In addition, a company or organization must subscribe to an outside WAN service provider to use WAN carrier network services. LANs are typically owned by the company or organization that uses them. This is reflected also in costs. While LANs usually require a one-time investment, WAN services normally involve a recurring monthly fee, which is paid to the service provider.

Some WANs are privately owned. However, because the development and maintenance of a private WAN is expensive, only very large organizations can afford to maintain a private WAN. Most companies purchase WAN connections from a service provider (SP) or ISP. The SP is then responsible for maintaining the back-end network connections and network services between the LANs.

When an organization has many global sites, establishing WAN connections and service can be complex. For example, the major SP for the organization might not offer service in every location or country in which the organization has an office. As a result, the organization must purchase services from multiple SPs. In many emerging countries, for example, network designers find differences in equipment availability, WAN services that are offered, and encryption technology for security. To support an enterprise network, it is important to have uniform standards for equipment, configuration, and services.

Figure 19-2 shows the variety of usage and connections for a WAN.

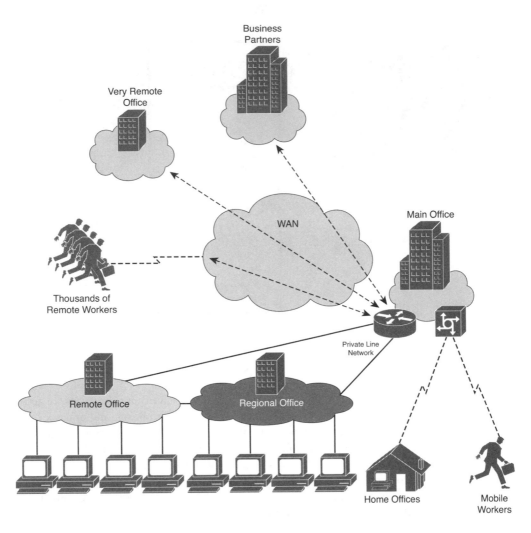

Figure 19-2 *WAN Connectivity*

Table 19-1 provides a summary of the differences between a WAN and a LAN.

Table 19-1 *Differences Between WANs and LANs*

	WANs	**LANs**
Area	Wide geographic area	Single building or multicampus
Ownership	Subscription to outside service provider	Owned by organization
Cost	Recurring	Fixed

The Role of Routers in the WAN

An enterprise WAN is a collection of separate but connected LANs. Routers play a central role in transmitting data through this interconnected network. Routers have both LAN and WAN interfaces. While a router is used to segment LANs, it is also used as the WAN access connection device. The functions and role of a router in accessing the WAN can be best understood by looking at the types of connections that are available on the router. There are three basic types: LAN interfaces, WAN interfaces, and management ports. LAN interfaces allow the router to connect to the LAN media through Ethernet or some other LAN technology.

WAN connections are made through a WAN interface on a router to a service provider to a distant site or to the Internet. These can be serial connections or any number of other WAN interfaces. With some types of WAN interfaces, an external device such as a channel service unit / data service unit (CSU/DSU) or modem (such as an analog modem, cable modem, or DSL modem) is required to connect the router to the local point of presence (POP) of the service provider, unless the port on the router has a built-in CSU/DSU. The physical demarcation point is the place where the responsibility for the connection changes from the user to the service provider. It is very important, because when problems arise, both sides of the link need to know which side the problem resides on.

WAN Communication Link Options

Options for implementing WAN solutions differ in technology, speed, and cost. WAN connections can be carried over a private infrastructure or over a public infrastructure, such as the Internet.

Private connections include dedicated and switched communication link options:

- **Dedicated communication links:** When permanent dedicated connections are required, point-to-point lines are used with various capacities that are limited only by the underlying physical capabilities and the willingness of users to pay for these dedicated lines. A point-to-point link provides an established WAN communications path from the customer premises through the provider network to a remote destination. Point-to-point lines are usually leased from a carrier and are also called leased lines.

- **Switched communication links:** Many WAN users do not make efficient use of the fixed bandwidth that is available with dedicated communication links, because the data flow fluctuates. Service providers have data networks available to more appropriately service these users. In packet-switched networks, the data is transmitted in labeled cells, frames, or packets over a common infrastructure, which is utilized by several customers at once. Different technologies can be used to ensure privacy and isolation of different customers and to provide desired bandwidth requirements and service-level agreements.

Public connections use the global Internet infrastructure. Until recently, the Internet was not a viable networking option for many businesses because of the significant security risks and lack of adequate performance guarantees in an end-to-end Internet connection. With the development of Virtual Private Network (VPN) technology, however, the Internet is now an inexpensive and secure option for connecting to teleworkers and remote offices when performance guarantees are not critical. Internet WAN connection links are through broadband services such as DSL, cable modem, and broadband wireless and are combined with VPN technology to provide privacy across the Internet. Broadband connection options are typically used to connect telecommuting employees to a corporate site over the Internet.

Point-to-Point Connectivity

A point-to-point communication link provides a single, established WAN communication path from the customer premises through a service provider infrastructure to a remote network. Different technologies can be used to provide point-to-point connectivity.

When permanent connections are required, a point-to-point link is used to provide an established WAN communication path from the customer premises through the provider network to a remote destination. A point-to-point link can connect two geographically distant sites, such as a corporate office in New York and a regional office in London. Point-to-point links are usually leased from a service provider.

Service providers can use different technologies to provide point-to-point connectivity. In recent years, different solutions based on Ethernet emulation became popular.

The advantages of Ethernet emulation services include the following:

- **Simplicity:** Although different technologies are used in SP networks, customers always get an Ethernet link that is simply plugged into their equipment. What technology is used beyond the demarcation point is transparent for end customers.

- **Cost:** Ethernet ports on customer equipment are the cheapest connectivity option compared to other solutions like optical or serial interfaces.

- **Flexibility:** Service providers are able to offer different link capabilities depending on the technology used. Different bandwidth arrangements, bandwidth guarantees, and service-level agreements can be offered to define the appropriate service that fits customers' needs.

Configuring a Point-to-Point Link

Example 19-1 demonstrates the configuration of a typical point-to-point link.

Example 19-1 *Configuring a Typical Point-to-Point WAN Link*

```
Branch(config)# interface GigabitEthernet0/1
Branch(config-if)# ip address 192.168.1.1 255.255.255.252
Branch(config-if)# description WAN Link to HQ
Branch(config-if)# no shutdown
```

Notice how these commands are familiar to you and how simple this link is to configure. There are various WAN encapsulations that are available, and Example 19-1 would use the default encapsulation on a Cisco router of High-Level Data Link Control (HDLC). To choose another form of WAN encapsulation (such as the Point-to-Point Protocol [PPP]), use the **encapsulation** command in interface configuration mode.

To perform verification, you can use the **show interfaces** command. Because the local interface is connected to the service provider equipment, the status of the interface and line protocol does not always reflect the status of the WAN connection. You can use ping to verify end-to-end connectivity over WAN link.

Chapter Summary

A WAN allows the transmission of data across broad geographic distances. A WAN is actually a collection of LANs, and routers play a central role in the creation of the WANs. There are three main WAN communication link options: dedicated communication links, switched communication links, and public connections. A common type of WAN connectivity is the point-to-point connection that emulates Ethernet. Configuring an interface for emulated Ethernet WAN connectivity consists of setting the IP address and enabling the interface.

Additional Resource

- Wide Area Networking Video, AJS Networking: http://ajsnetworking.com/wan

Review Questions

Use the questions here to review what you learned in this chapter. The correct answers and solutions are found in Appendix A, "Answers to Chapter Review Questions."

1. Which network type is used to connect resources over the widest possible geographic distances?

   a. MAN

   b. WAN

   c. LAN

   d. PAN

2. What is a common feature of a WAN?

   a. It features fixed costs.

   b. It features equipment that is owned by the organization.

   c. It features equipment located in a single geographic area.

   d. It features subscription to equipment that the organization does not own.

3. What is the demarcation point in the WAN?

   a. The point at which transport for data is no longer counted toward the bill of the organization

   b. The largest bottleneck for bandwidth in the WAN

   c. The point at which packets are converted to frames in the WAN

   d. The point at which the responsibility for a problem changes between the organization and the service provider

4. A point-to-point link is an example of what type of a WAN connection?

   a. Private—circuit-switched

   b. Private—dedicated connection

   c. Public connection

   d. Private—switched connection

5. What command would you use to verify the status and Layer 2 encapsulation used by a WAN circuit in your organization?

   a. show ip interface

   b. show interface

   c. show wan interface

   d. show serial interface

Production Network Simulation Question 19-1

Your supervisor wants you to give the junior IT team a presentation about the differences between a LAN and a WAN. Prepare a short statement to provide an overview of this topic.

Chapter 20

Introducing IPv6

This chapter includes the following sections:

- Chapter Objectives
- An Overview of IPv6
- Other IPv6 Features
- IPv6 Routing
- Chapter Summary
- Additional Resources
- Review Questions
- Production Network Simulation Question 20-1

The growth of the Internet and the adoption of networking over the past 20 years are pushing the IP version 4 (IPv4) to the limits of its addressing capacity and its ability for continued growth. To sustain the evolution of the Internet, the Internet Engineering Task Force (IETF) developed a next-generation protocol, IP version 6 (IPv6). This chapter describes the factors leading toward IPv6 development and compares IPv4 with IPv6.

Chapter Objectives

Upon completing this chapter, you will be able to discuss the importance of IPv6 and the many improved features this suite of protocols brings. You will also be able to configure a basic IPv6 network. These abilities include meeting these objectives:

- Describe IPv6 main features, addresses, and basic configuration
- Describe IPv6 operations
- Identify routing protocols for IPv6
- Configure an IPv6 basic routed network

Overview of IPv6

The ability to scale networks for future demands requires a limitless supply of IP addresses and improved mobility. To cope with the depletion of IP addresses, several short-term solutions were developed.

IPv6 satisfies the increasingly complex requirements of hierarchical addressing that IPv4 does not satisfy. With a 128-bit address length, the IPv6 address space is significantly larger and more diverse, and thus is more complicated to manage. Figure 20-1 compares the IPv4 and IPv6 address.

IPv4:	4 Octets
11000000.10101000.11001001.0111000	
192.168.201.113	
4,294,467,295 IP Addresses	

IPv6:	16 Octets
11010001.11011100.11001001.01110001.11010001.11011100. 11001100.01110001.11010001.11011100.11001001.01110001. 11010001.11011100.11001001.01110001	
A524:72D3:2C80:DD02:0029:EC7A:002B:EA73	
3.4 x 10^{38} IP Addresses	

Figure 20-1   *IPv4 Versus IPv6 Addresses*

In an effort to allocate IPv4 addresses efficiently, classless interdomain routing (CIDR) was developed, which allowed the address space to be divided into smaller blocks.

Variable-length subnet masks (VLSM) allow more efficient use of IP addresses, specifically on small segments such as point-to-point serial links. VLSM usage was recommended in RFC 1817.

Network Address Translation (NAT) introduced a model in which a device facing outward to the Internet would have a globally routable IPv4 address, while the internal network would be configured with private addresses. These private addresses could never leave the site, so they could be identical in many different enterprise networks. In this way, even large enterprises with thousands of systems could hide behind a small number of routable public networks.

DHCP is used by a client to acquire configuration information, such as an IP address, a default route, and Domain Name System (DNS) setup from a server.

One of the arguments against deploying IPv6 is that NAT will solve the problems of limited address space in IPv4. The use of NAT merely delays the exhaustion of the IPv4 address space by using global addresses for large internal networks. In fact, we have indeed reached the point where NAT can no longer serve as a long-term solution—IPv4 addresses are indeed at the point of exhaustion.

There are several negative implications of using NAT, some of which are identified in RFC 2775 and RFC 2993, as follows:

- NAT breaks the end-to-end model of IP. IP was defined so that underlying layers do not process the connection; only the endpoints process the connection.

- NAT inhibits end-to-end network security. To protect the integrity of the IP header by some cryptographic functions, the IP header cannot be changed between the origin of the packet (to protect the integrity of the header) and the final destination (to check the integrity of the received packet). Any translation of parts of a header on the path will break the integrity check.

- When applications are not "NAT-friendly"—which means that, for a specific application, more than just port and address mapping are necessary to forward the packet through the NAT device—NAT has to embed complete knowledge of all the applications to perform correctly. This is especially the case for dynamically allocated ports with rendezvous ports, embedded IP addresses in application protocols, security associations, and so on. Therefore, the NAT device needs to be upgraded each time a new non-NAT-friendly application is deployed—for example, peer-to-peer. An example of a non-NAT-friendly application is TFTP.

- When different networks use the same private address space and they have to merge or connect, there is an address-space collision. Different hosts have the same address, and routing disables reaching the other network. This can be resolved by techniques such as renumbering or Twice NAT. (Twice NAT is the practice of changing both the source and destination address of a packet.) However, these techniques are costly and, later on, increase NAT complications.

IPv6 Features and Addresses

IPv6 includes a number of features that make it attractive for building global-scale, highly effective networks. The larger address space, strict aggregation, and autoconfiguration provide important capabilities.

Streamlined header structures make processing IPv6 packets faster and more efficient for intermediate routers within the network. This is especially true when large numbers of packets are routed in the core of the IPv6 Internet.

Features that were not part of the original IPv4 specification, such as security and mobility, are now built into IPv6.

IPv6 also includes a rich set of transition tools to allow an easy, nondisruptive transition over time to IPv6-dominant networks.

IPv6 addresses are represented as a series of eight 16-bit hexadecimal fields that are separated by colons. The A, B, C, D, E, and F in hexadecimal fields are case insensitive.

These are some ways to shorten the writing of IPv6 addresses:

- The leading 0s in a field are optional, so 010F can be written as 10F and 0000 can be written as 0.

- Successive fields of 0s can be represented as a double colon (::), but only once in an address. An address parser can identify the number of missing 0s by separating the two parts and filling in 0s until the 128 bits are completed. However, if two double colons are placed in the address, there is no way to identify the size of each block of 0s. Therefore, only one double colon is possible in a valid IPv6 address.

The use of the double-colon technique makes many addresses very small; for example, FF01:0:0:0:0:0:0:1 becomes FF01::1. The unspecified address is written as a double colon because it contains only 0s.

IPv6 Address Types

IPv6 supports three types of addresses:

- **Unicast:** Unicast addresses are used in a one-to-one context.

- **Multicast:** A multicast address identifies a group of interfaces. Traffic that is sent to a multicast address is sent to multiple destinations at the same time. An interface can belong to any number of multicast groups.

- **Anycast:** An IPv6 anycast address is assigned to an interface on more than one node. When a packet is sent to an anycast address, it is routed to the nearest interface that has that address. The nearest interface is found according to the measure of distance of the particular routing protocol. All nodes that share the same address should behave the same way so that the service is offered similarly regardless of the node that services the request.

Each address type has specific rules regarding its construction and use. IPv6 has no support for broadcast addresses in the way that they are used in IPv4. Instead, specific multicast addresses (such as the all nodes multicast address) are used.

There are several basic types of IPv6 unicast addresses: global, reserved, private (link-local), loopback, and unspecified.

RFC 4291 specifies 2000::/3 to be the global unicast address space that the Internet Assigned Numbers Authority (IANA) can allocate to the Regional Internet Registries (RIR). A global unicast address is an IPv6 address from the global unicast prefix. The structure of global unicast addresses enables the aggregation of routing prefixes, which limits the number of routing table entries in the global routing table. Global unicast addresses that are used on links are aggregated upward through organizations and eventually to the ISPs. Figure 20-2 demonstrates the global unicast address space.

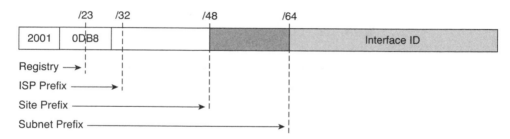

Figure 20-2 *Global Unicast Address Space*

Link-local addresses are new to the concept of addressing with IP in the network layer. These addresses refer only to a particular physical link. Link-local addresses typically begin with FE80. The next digits can be defined manually. If you do not define them manually, the interface MAC address is used based on the EUI-64 format.

Just as in IPv4, a provision has been made for a special loopback IPv6 address for testing; datagrams that are sent to this address "loop back" to the sending device. However, in IPv6, there is just one address, not an entire block, for this function. The loopback address is 0:0:0:0:0:0:0:1, which is normally expressed as ::1.

In IPv4, an IP address of all 0s has a special meaning; it refers to the host itself and is used when a device does not know its own address. In IPv6, this concept has been formalized, and the all-0s address is named the "unspecified" address. It is typically used in the source field of a datagram that is sent by a device that seeks to have its IP address configured. You can apply address compression to this address; because the address is all 0s, the address becomes just ::.

The IETF reserved a portion of the IPv6 address space for various uses, both present and future. Reserved addresses represent 1/256th of the total IPv6 address space:

■ The lowest address within each subnet prefix (the interface identifier set to all 0s) is reserved as the "subnet-router" anycast address.

■ The 128 highest addresses within each /64 subnet prefix are reserved to be used as anycast addresses.

The EUI-64 standard explains how to stretch IEEE 802 MAC addresses from 48 to 64 bits by inserting the 16-bit 0xFFFE in the middle (at the 24th bit) of the MAC address to create a 64-bit, unique interface identifier. This is what we consider the host portion of an address. In the first byte of the vendor's Organizational Unique Identifier (OUI), bit 7 indicates the scope: 0 or global and 1 for local. As most burned-in addresses are globally scoped, bit 7 will usually be 0. The EUI-64 standard also specifies that the value of the seventh bit be inverted. So for example, MAC address 00-90-27-17-FC-0F becomes 02-90-27-17-FC-0F. The resulting EUI-64 address on network 2001:0DB8:0:1::/64 would be 2001:0DB8:0:1:0290:27FF:FE17:FC0F. Figure 20-3 demonstrates this EUI-64 standard process.

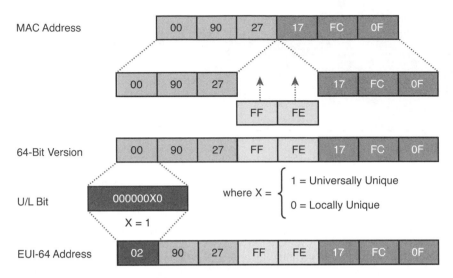

Figure 20-3   *EUI-64 Address Process*

IPv6 Address Allocation Options

The IPv6 address can be completely specified, or the host identifier (the rightmost 64 bits) can be computed from the extended unique identifier (EUI)-64 of the interface.

Having a much larger address space available, IPv6 engineers designed a way to enable autoconfiguration of the addresses while still keeping the global uniqueness. A router on the local link will send network-type information, such as the prefix of the local link and the default route, to all the nodes on the local link. A host can autoconfigure itself by appending its data link layer address (in a special 64-bit EUI-64 format) to the local link prefix (64 bits). This autoconfiguration results in a complete 128-bit IPv6 address that is usable on the local link and is, most likely, globally unique. To avoid the rare event of address collision, a process is enabled to detect duplicate addresses.

Autoconfiguration enables "plug and play," which connects devices to the network without any configuration and without any stateful servers (such as DHCP servers). Autoconfiguration is an important feature for enabling deployment of new devices on the Internet, such as cell phones, wireless devices, home appliances and networks, and so on.

Autoconfiguration can be accomplished in two ways: stateless—through neighbor discovery and router advertisements—as described earlier, and stateful, using a DHCPv6 server. The difference between the two is that with the stateful method, a record is kept of which hosts are assigned which addresses. The stateless method maintains no such records.

Router announcement can indicate to hosts whether additional configuration parameters are available through stateful configuration (DHCPv6), such as DNS, IP options, and so on. Figure 20-4 reviews these address allocation options.

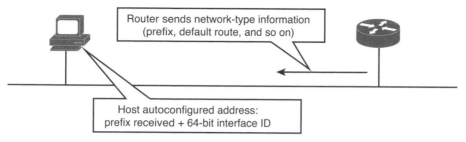

- Manual assignment with or without EUI-64

- Stateless autoconfiguration: Uses neighbor discovery mechansims to find routers and dynamically create IPv6 addresses

- Stateful autoconfiguration: Uses a DHCP version 6 (DHCPv6) server to assign IPv6 addresses and additional parameters to nodes

Figure 20-4   *IPv6 Address Allocation Options*

DNS is a distributed Internet directory service that is used to translate between domain names and IP addresses, and between IP addresses and domain names. The DNS protocol had to be updated to support IPv6 in addition to IPv4. Using Dynamic DNS, DHCPv6 clients can dynamically update their records in DNS.

IPv6 Header Changes and Benefits

The IPv4 header contains 12 fields. Following those fields is an Options field of variable length, and a data portion, which is usually the transport layer segment. The basic IPv4 header has a size of 20 octets. The Options field increases the size of the IP header.

Of these 12 header fields, six are removed in IPv6. The main reasons for removing these fields in IPv6 are as follows:

- The Internet Header Length (Hd Len) field was removed because all IPv6 headers are a fixed, 40-byte length, unlike IPv4, in which the header length is variable.

- Fragmentation is now processed differently and does not need the fields in the basic IP header. In IPv6, routers no longer process fragmentation, a change that removes the processing issues that result when routers process IPv4 fragmentation. The related, removed fields appear in the Fragmentation Extension Header in IPv6, which is attached only to a packet that is actually fragmented.

- The Header Checksum field at the IP layer was removed because most data link layer technologies already perform checksum and error control and because the relative reliability of the data link layer is very good. However, this removal forces the upper-layer optional checksums, such as User Datagram Protocol (UDP), to become mandatory.

The Options field is changed in IPv6 and is now processed by an extension header chain. Most other fields were either unchanged or changed only slightly. Figure 20-5 shows the new IPv6 header format.

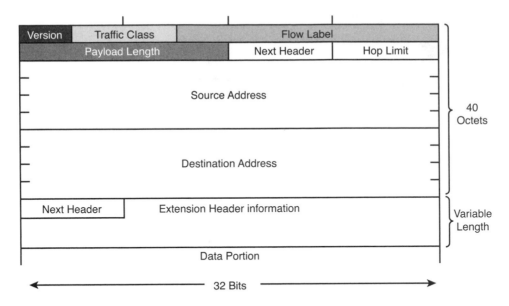

Figure 20-5 *IPv6 Header*

The IPv6 header has 40 octets, instead of the 20 octets in IPv4. The IPv6 header has fewer fields, and the header is aligned on 64-bit boundaries to enable fast processing by current and next-generation processors. Address fields are four times larger than in IPv4.

The IPv6 header contains eight fields:

- **Version:** This 4-bit field contains the number 6, instead of the number 4 as in IPv4.

- **Traffic Class:** This 8-bit field is like the type of service (ToS) field in IPv4.

- **Flow Label:** This new field has a length of 20 bits and is used to mark individual traffic flows with unique values, which routers can use to provide per-flow nondefault treatment.

- **Payload Length:** This field is like the Total Length field of IPv4, but because the IPv6 base header is a fixed size, this field describes the length of the payload only, not of the entire packet.

- **Next Header:** The value of this field determines the type of information that follows the basic IPv6 header.

- **Hop Limit:** This field specifies the maximum number of hops that an IP packet can traverse.

- **Source Address:** This field of 16 octets or 128 bits identifies the source of the packet.

- **Destination Address:** This field of 16 octets or 128 bits identifies the destination of the packet.

Following these eight fields are the extension headers, if any. The number of extension headers is not fixed, so the total length of the extension header chain is variable.

Other IPv6 Features

While the amazing increase in the available address space is often what engineers think of first regarding IPv6, there are also numerous other enhancements to the protocol suite. This section describes just some of them.

ICMPv6

Internet Control Message Protocol version 6 (ICMPv6) is like ICMP version 4 (ICMPv4). ICMPv6 enables nodes to make diagnostic tests and report problems. Like ICMPv4, ICMPv6 implements two kinds of messages: (a) error messages, such as Destination Unreachable, Packet Too Big, or Time Exceeded and (b) informational messages, such as Echo Request and Echo Reply.

The ICMPv6 packet is identified as 58 in the Next Header field. Inside the ICMPv6 packet, the Type field identifies the type of ICMP message. The Code field further details the specifics of this type of message. The Data field contains information that is sent to the receiver for diagnostics or information purposes.

ICMPv6 is used on-link for various purposes including neighbor dicovery.

Neighbor Discovery

Neighbor discovery is used on-link for router solicitation and advertisement, for neighbor solicitation and advertisement, and for the redirection of nodes to the best gateway.

Neighbor discovery is a process that enables these functions:

- Determine the data link layer address of a neighbor on the same link, like the Address Resolution Protocol (ARP) does in IPv4.

- Find neighbor routers.

- Keep track of neighbors.

Neighbor discovery achieves these results by using ICMP with multicast addresses.

Stateless Autoconfiguration

Stateless autoconfiguration uses neighbor discovery mechanisms to find routers and dynamically create IPv6 addresses. Router advertisements are sent periodically and on request, by routers on all their configured interfaces. A router advertisement is sent to the all-nodes multicast address. This information that might be contained in the message is as follows:

- One or more prefixes that can be used on the link. This information enables stateless autoconfiguration of the hosts. These prefixes must be /64 for stateless autoconfiguration.

- Lifetime of the prefixes. By default, in Cisco IOS Software, the lifetime is very long: The default valid lifetime is 30 days, and the default preferred lifetime is seven days.

- Flags that indicate the kind of autoconfiguration that the hosts can perform – also default router information, such as its existence and lifetime.

- Other types of information for hosts, including default maximum transmission unit (MTU) and hop count.

By sending prefixes, a router advertisement enables the autoconfiguration of hosts. By assigning lifetimes to prefixes, a router advertisement enables the renumbering of hosts. An old, deprecated prefix has a lifetime that is decreased to zero, and a new prefix will have a normal lifetime.

Router advertisement timing and other parameters can be configured on the routers.

A router advertisement is sent immediately following a router solicitation. Router solicitations are sent by hosts at boot time, to ask routers to send an immediate router advertisement on the local link so that the host can receive the autoconfiguration information without waiting for the next scheduled router advertisement.

The router solicitation message is defined as follows: The ICMP type is 133.

The source address is the unspecified address (or the IP address that is assigned to the sending interface when the IP address is known, which is not usually the case).

The destination address is the all-routers multicast address with the link-local scope.

When an answer to a router solicitation is sent, the destination address of the router advertisement is the unicast address of the requestor.

To avoid flooding, router solicitation should be sent only at boot time and only three times. This practice avoids flooding of router solicitation packets in the absence of a router on the network.

The configuration command that enables stateless autoconfiguration on the router interface is simple and is shown in Example 20-1.

Example 20-1   *Configuring IPv6*

```
TampaR1(config)# interface GigabitEthernet0/1
TampaR1(config-if)# ipv6 address autoconfig
```

IPv6 Routing

Many of the common routing protocols have been modified to handle longer IPv6 addresses and different header structures. Figure 20-6 shows some of the routing options for IPv6.

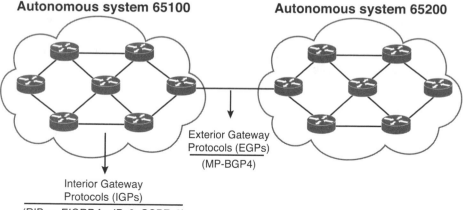

Figure 20-6   *IPv6 Routing Options*

You can use and configure IPv6 static routing in the same way that you would with IPv4. There is an IPv6-specific requirement per RFC 2461 that a router must be able to determine the link-local address of each of its neighboring routers to ensure that the target address of a redirect message identifies the neighbor router by its link-local address. This requirement means that using a global unicast address as a next-hop address with IPv6 routing is not recommended.

Basic IPv6 Connectivity

While you have learned about the dramatic new enhancements and features of IPv6, you will be happy to learn that its configuration at the command-line interface is not that difficult, especially after you have mastered IPv4 configurations.

Examine Example 20-2, where we configure an IPv6 address in the EUI-64 format, and then on another router, manually configure the network and host portion.

Example 20-2   *Configuring IPv6 Addresses*

```
TampaR1(config)# interface GigabitEthernet0/1
TampaR1(config-if)# ipv6 address 2001:db8:d1a5:c900::/64 eui-64


NewYorkR2(config)# interface GigabitEthernet0/1
NewYorkR2(config-if)# ipv6 address 2001:db8:d1a5:c900::2/64
```

How would you perform verifications of the these configurations? Just think of how you would do it in an IPv4 environment. The same commands apply; we just substitute the **ip** keyword with the **ipv6** keyword. For example, we can use **show ipv6 interface GigabitEthernet0/1**, **show ipv6 interface brief**, or even **ping 2001:db8:d1a5:c900::2** and **traceroute 2001:db8:d1a5:c900::2**.

Configuring IPv6 Routing

While the configuration of routing protocols in IPv6 is certainly new for students of this latest version of the CCNA, it is certainly not that difficult. In fact, because you can leverage the knowledge you have obtained regarding version 4 protocols, you should find it fun!

Static Routing

As you might guess, the configuration of IPv6 static routing is very straightforward as it follows the configuration of IPv4 static routing. Example 20-3 demonstrates a static route and a default route configuration.

Example 20-3 *Static and Default Routing Configurations*

```
HQ(config)# ipv6 route 2001:DB8:A01::/48 Gi0/1 2001:DB8:D1A5:C900::1
Branch(config)# ipv6 route ::/0 Gi0/1 2001:DB8:D1A5:C900::2
```

How would you verify the static routing? Use **show ipv6 route**, of course.

OSPFv3

These Open Shortest Path First (OSPF) features have been updated for IPv6:

- The OSPFv3 process no longer requires an IPv4 address for the router ID, but it does require a 32-bit number to be set. This 32-bit identifier is provided in dotted-decimal notation and has the exact structure of an IPv4 address. Yes, this is painful irony.

- OSPFv3 adjacencies use link-local addresses to communicate. Router next-hop attributes are neighboring router link-local addresses. Because link-local addresses have the same prefix, OSPF needs to store the information about the outgoing interface.

- OSPFv3 uses IPv6 for transport of link-state advertisements (LSA). IPv6 protocol number 89 is used.

- OSPFv3 is enabled per-link and identifies which networks (prefixes) are attached to that link for determining prefix reachability propagation and OSPF area.

Example 20-4 demonstrates the OSPF version 3 configuration.

Example 20-4 *OSPFv3 Configuration*

```
HQ(config)# interface GigabitEthernet0/0
HQ(config-if)# ipv6 ospf 1 area 0
HQ(config-if)# exit
HQ(config)# interface GigabitEthernet0/1
HQ(config-if)# ipv6 ospf 1 area 0
HQ(config-if)# exit
HQ(config)# ipv6 router ospf 1
HQ(config-rtr)# router-id 0.0.0.1
```

Notice in this configuration how the **network** command is no longer used. As described earlier, OSPF is enabled under interfaces now. There is still router configuration mode of course, but this is reserved for the setting of global parameters for the process. In Example 20-4, this means setting the router ID on the device.

As you would guess at this point, verification commands include IPv6 versions of the commands that we know and love from OPSFv2. These include

- show ipv6 ospf
- show ipv6 route ospf
- show ipv6 ospf neighbor

Chapter Summary

IPv6 includes a number of features that make it attractive for building global-scale, highly effective networks. The larger address space and autoconfiguration provide important capabilities. Neighbor discovery is used on-link for router solicitation and advertisement, for neighbor solicitation and advertisement, and for the redirection of nodes to the best gateway. You can use and configure IPv6 static routing in the same way you would with IPv4. The OSPFv3 is an upgraded OSPFv2 routing protocol.

Additional Resource

- IPv6 Video, AJS Networking: http://ajsnetworking.com/ipv6

Review Questions

Use the questions here to review what you learned in this chapter. The correct answers and solutions are found in Appendix A, "Answers to Chapter Review Questions."

1. What is the shortest way to represent IPv6 address 2001:0DB8:0000:300F:0000:000
   0:A87C:040B?

   a. 2001:DB8:0:300F:0:A87C:40B

   b. 2001:DB8:0:300F::A87C:40B

   c. 2001:DB8::300F::A87C:40B

   d. 2001:0DB8:0:300F::A87C:040B

2. Which of the following IPv4 header fields are not in the IPv6 header? (Choose three.)

   a. IHL

   b. Type of Service

   c. Header Checksum

   d. Flags

   e. Flow Label

3. The extension headers serve which important function in IPv6 networks?

   a. Identify optional processes that can be run on each IPv6 packet

   b. Allow IPv6 nodes to manipulate routers

   c. Identify processes that manipulate the routers in the path of a packet

   d. Replace the traditional role of TCP and UDP in a network

4. What interface command causes the IPv6 interface address to be obtained using
   stateless autoconfiguration?

   a. autoconfig ipv6 address

   b. ipv6 address autoconfig

   c. ipv6 address enable

   d. ipv6 address dhcp

5. What command is used to configure a static IPv6 default route?

   a. ipv6 route ::/0 interface next_hop

   b. ipv6 route default interface next_hop

   c. ipv6 route 0.0.0.0/0 interface next_hop

   d. ip route 0.0.0.0/0 interface next_hop

6. What is the main difference between OSPF version 2 and version 3?

   a. One is distance vector and the other is link state.

   b. Version 3 can be used for IPv4 or IPv6, but version 2 is for IPv4 only.

   c. Version 3 is enabled under an interface only.

   d. Version 3 requires a 128-bit router ID.

Production Network Simulation Question 20-1

Your boss requires you to provide him with an IPv6 OPSF configuration for a key router in your organization. Ensure that this configuration accomplishes the following:

- Configures OSPF version 3 process ID 1 area 0 on GigabitEthernet0/0

- Configures OSPF version 3 process ID 1 area 1 on GigabitEthernet0/1

- Configures the device with the router ID 4.4.4.4

Answers to Chapter Review Questions

Chapter 1

Answers to Review Questions

1. A, B, and C
2. A
3. D
4. C
5. A, B, and D
6. 1. D
   2. G
   3. C
   4. A
   5. E
   6. B
   7. F

7. C
8. C
9. 1. B
   2. A
   3. D
   4. C
   5. E
   6. F
10. C

Answers to the Production Network Simulation Questions

Production Network Simulation Question 1-1: Solution

You will need a router and a switch. The purpose of the switch will be to provide ports for the sixteen devices to access the network. The purpose of the router is to connect to the switch and to route packets from these devices to the Internet. The router can also provide basic security functions and can supplement the security functions provided by the switch. You can also consider a multilayer switch. This device can route and switch traffic.

Chapter 2

Answers to Review Questions

1. A and B

2. 1. E
   2. C
   3. A
   4. D
   5. G
   6. B
   7. F

3. 1. F
   2. C
   3. A
   4. B
   5. E
   6. D
   7. G
   8. H

4. B

5. 1. B
   2. A
   3. C

6. C

7. 1. D
   2. C
   3. A
   4. B

8. B

9. D

10. C

Answers to the Production Network Simulation Questions

Production Network Simulation Question 2-1: Solution

The network layer is also known as simply Layer 3. This is the layer where routers function. Routers forward PDUs called packets. These packets are moved by routers from network to network. The addressing used at this layer is called IP addressing. This layer in the TCP/IP model is known as the Internet layer.

Chapter 3

Answers to Review Questions

1. B

2. A, C, and E

3. D

4. A

5. B

6. D

7. 1. D
   2. F
   3. G
   5. E
   6. A
   7. B
   8. C
   9. H

8. B

9. B

10. B

Answers to the Production Network Simulation Questions

Production Network Simulation Question 3-1: Solution

1. Straight-through

2. Crossover

3. Straight-through

4. Crossover

Chapter 4

Answers to Review Questions

1.	C	6.	B
2.	B	7.	A
3.	C	8.	A
4.	D	9.	A
5.	D	10.	C

Answers to the Production Network Simulation Questions

Production Network Simulation Question 4-1: Solution

```
hostname BO1
!
interface fastethernet0/0
ip address 10.10.10.1 255.255.255.0
no shutdown
!
interface fastethernet0/1
ip address 172.16.1.101 255.255.255.0
no shutdown
!
interface serial0/0
ip address 192.168.1.1 255.255.255.0
no shutdown
```

Chapter 5

Answers to Review Questions

1. A and C
2. B
3. D
4. B
5. D

6. C
7. A
8. C
9. A
10. D

Answers to the Production Network Simulation Questions

Production Network Simulation Question 5-1: Solution

```
enable
!
configure terminal
!
hostname Lindfield2
!
ip default-gateway 10.10.10.1
!
interface vlan 1
ip address 10.10.10.100 255.255.255.0
no shutdown
!
interface range fa0/1 - 24
shutdown
!
copy run star
```

Chapter 6

Answers to Review Questions

1. A
2. C and E
3. D
4. B, C, and E
5. C

6. C
7. A
8. B
9. B and D
10. D

Answers to the Production Network Simulation Questions

Production Network Simulation Question 6-1: Solution

```
vlan 10, 20
!
interface fastethernet 0/10
switchport mode trunk
!
interface fastethernet 0/5
switchport access vlan 10
```

Chapter 7

Answers to Review Questions

1.	B	**6.**	A, E, and F
2.	D	**7.**	A
3.	B	**8.**	B
4.	C	**9.**	D
5.	A and B	**10.**	C

Answers to the Production Network Simulation Questions

Production Network Simulation Question 7-1: Solution

If 27 bits are used for network identification, 5 bits are left for host address assignment. 2 raised to the 5th power is 32 minus 2 equals 30. There are 30 host addresses available per subnet.

Production Network Simulation Question 7-2: Solution

The correct ranges are as follows:

10.0.0.0 to 10.255.255.255

172.16.0.0 to 172.31.255.255

192.168.0.0 to 192.168.255.255

Production Network Simulation Question 7-3: Solution

The correct process at the command line is as follows:

```
ipconfig /release
ipconfig /renew
```

Chapter 8

Answers to Review Questions

1. B
2. C
3. B
4. B
5. A
6. C
7. B
8. C
9. D
10. A

Answers to the Production Network Simulation Questions

Production Network Simulation Question 8-1: Solution

The subnet address is 192.168.1.64.

The first usable host address is 192.168.1.65.

The last usable host address is 192.168.1.78.

The broadcast address for the subnet is 192.168.1.79.

Chapter 9

Answers to Review Questions

1. B, D, and F
2. B
3. A and C
4. A, C, and D
5. C and D
6. C
7. A
8. D
9. B
10. C

Answers to the Production Network Simulation Questions

Production Network Simulation Question 9-1: Solution

TCP is called connection-oriented because of the reliability features that are built in to the protocol. Some of these features are segment sequencing, flow control, windowing, and the TCP three-way handshake. When your application wants to use less overhead in the communications, it can be programmed to use UDP at the transport layer. UDP is referred to as connectionless, and it does not use any of the reliability-type mechanisms that TCP uses. Another layer of the OSI model needs to ensure to provide the reliability.

Production Network Simulation Question 9-2: Solution

FTP: TCP, 21

TFTP: UDP, 69

Telnet: TCP, 23

SMTP: TCP, 25

SNMP: UDP, 161

RIP: UDP, 520

DNS: TCP and UDP, 53

WWW: TCP, 80

Chapter 10

Answers to Review Questions

1.	A	**6.**	A, C, and D
2.	A and B	**7.**	1. D
3.	A, B, and D		2. C
			3. A
4.	1. E		4. B
	2. A		
	3. C	**8.**	A, B, and C
	4. B	**9.**	A and C
	5. D		
		10.	B, D, and E
5.	B		

Answers to the Production Network Simulation Questions

Production Network Simulation Question 10-1: Solution

The metric used by a routing protocol is the criterion that is used to judge one path from the next. Different routing protocols will use different metrics. For example, OSPF will base its decision solely on bandwidth, while EIGRP will use bandwidth and delay. While metrics are used within the routing protocol to determine the best path, administrative distance is used by a router to choose between different routing protocols. The routing protocols use their metric to present a best path to the router, and then the router needs to use administrative distance to choose which routing protocol it will "believe."

Chapter 11

Answers to Review Questions

1. D
2. B and D
3. B
4. D
5. D
6. A
7. B
8. D
9. A
10. A

Answers to the Production Network Simulation Questions

Production Network Simulation Question 11–1: Solution

1. arp -a
2. ipconfig /all
3. ping 10.10.10.1
4. tracert www.cisco.com

Chapter 12

Answers to Review Questions

1. C
2. C
3. A
4. C
5. A
6. A
7. 1. B
   2. D
   3. A
   4. E
   5. C
8. B
9. A
10. A and D

Answers to the Production Network Simulation Questions

Production Network Simulation Question 12-1: Solution

```
hostname Branch
!
line console 0
exec-timeout 1 45
logging synchronous
!
interface serial 0/0
ip address 192.168.0.126 255.255.255.192
no shutdown
```

Chapter 13

Answers to Review Questions

1. B
2. D
3. C
4. D

Answers to the Production Network Simulation Questions

Production Network Simulation Question 13-1: Solution

```
ip route 192.168.2.0 255.255.255.240 10.10.10.1
```

Production Network Simulation Question 13-2: Solution

```
ip route 0.0.0.0 0.0.0.0 10.20.20.1
```

Chapter 14

Answers to Review Questions

1. B
2. C
3. A
4. B
5. A
6. D
7. A
8. A
9. B
10. D

Answers to the Production Network Simulation Questions

Production Network Simulation Question 14-1: Solution

This production router is termed an ABR (area border router). It maintains two link-state databases: one for Area 0 and one for Area 2.

Chapter 15

Answers to Review Questions

1. A and C
2. D
3. B
4. A
5. A

6. A
7. D
8. A and C
9. D
10. D

Answers to the Production Network Simulation Questions

Production Network Simulation Question 15-1: Solution

```
hostname Tampa1
!
interface gi0/0
ip address 10.10.10.1 255.255.255.0
no shutdown
!
interface gi0/1
ip address 10.20.20.1 255.255.255.0
no shutdown
!
interface gi0/2
ip address 192.168.1.1 255.255.255.0
no shutdown
!
router ospf 1
router-id 1.1.1.1
network 10.0.0.0 0.255.255.255 area 0
network 192.168.1.1 0.0.0.0 area 1
!
```

Chapter 16

Answers to Review Questions

1. C

2. B

3. 1. C
   2. D
   3. A
   4. B

4. A

5. D

6. 1. A
   2. B
   3. E
   4. D
   5. C

7. A

8. B

9. A, D, and E

10. B

Answers to the Production Network Simulation Questions

Production Network Simulation Question 16-1: Solution

```
!
ip dhcp pool MYPOOL
network 10.1.50.0 /24
default-router 10.1.50.1
dns-server 10.1.50.2
domain-name ciscopress.com
lease 0 12
exit
!
ip dhcp excluded-address 10.1.50.1 10.1.50.50
```

Production Network Simulation Question 16-2: Solution

```
access-list 1 permit 10.10.10.0 0.0.0.255
!
ip nat inside source list 1 interface gi0/0 overload
!
interface gi0/1
ip nat inside
!
interface gi0/0
ip nat outside
```

Chapter 17

Answers to Review Questions

1.	B	6.	C
2.	B and D	7.	B
3.	D	8.	A
4.	D	9.	B
5.	A	10.	C

Answers to the Production Network Simulation Questions

Production Network Simulation Question 17-1: Solution

```
!
enable secret T3nn1sB@11
!
line vty 0 4
password V0113yB@11
login
!
service password-encryption
!
interface fa0/12
switchport mode access
switchport port-security
```

Chapter 18

Answers to Review Questions

1.	C	6.	C
2.	A	7.	C
3.	A	8.	B
4.	D	9.	B
5.	C and F	10.	C

Answers to the Production Network Simulation Questions

Production Network Simulation Question 18-1: Solution

```
!
ip access-list extended MYTEST
permit tcp host 172.16.1.100 eq www any
deny ip host 172.16.1.100 any
permit ip any any
!
interface gi0/1
ip access-group MYTEST in
```

Chapter 19

Answers to Review Questions

1. B
2. D
3. D
4. B
5. B

Answers to the Production Network Simulation Questions

Production Network Simulation Question 19-1: Solution

Local-area networks are known for several qualities:

- The equipment is relatively close in proximity.
- Bandwidth tends to be very fast.
- Companies tend to own all the LAN equipment.

Wide-area networks are known for the following:

- The equipment can be separated by vast geographic distances.
- Bandwidth tends to be slower.
- Companies do not always own all the WAN equipment.

Chapter 20

Answers to Review Questions

1. B

2. A, C, and D

3. A

4. B

5. A

6. C

Answers to the Production Network Simulation Questions

Production Network Simulation Question 20-1: Solution

```
interface GigabitEthernet0/0
ipv6 ospf 1 area 0
!
interface GigabitEthernet0/1
ipv6 ospf 1 area 1
!
ipv6 router ospf 1
router-id 4.4.4.4
```

Appendix B

Acronyms and Abbreviations

AAA (authentication, authorization, and accounting)

ABR (area border routers)

ARP (Address Resolution Protocol)

AS (autonomous system)

ASBR (autonomous system boundary router)

ASCII (American Standard Code for Information Interchange)

Auto-MDIX (automatic medium-dependent interface crossover)

AUX (auxiliary)

BDR (backup DR)

BGP (Border Gateway Protocol)

BOOTP (Bootstrap Protocol)

BYOD (Bring Your Own Device)

CBAC (Context-Based Access Control)

CCENT (Cisco Certified Entry Network Technician)

CCNA (Cisco Certified Network Associate)

CCNP (Cisco Certified Networking Professional)

CDP (Cisco Discovery Protocol)

CLI (command-line interface)

CON (console)

CPE (customer premises equipment)

CPU (central processing unit)

CRC (cyclic redundancy check)

CSI (Computer Security Institute)

CSMA/CD (Carrier Sense Multiple Access/Collision Detection)

CSU (channel service unit)

CWS (congestion window size)

DB (D-subminiature)

DC (data center)

DEC (Digital Equipment Corporation)

DHCP (Dynamic Host Configuration Protocol)

DoS (denial of service)

DR (designated router)

DSL (Digital subscriber line)

DSU (digital service unit)

DTP (Dynamic Trunking Protocol)

EBCDIC (extended binary coded decimal interchange code)

EGP (Exterior gateway protocol)

EIA/TIA (Electronic Industries Alliance/Telecommunications Industry Association)

EIGRP (Enhanced Interior Gateway Routing Protocol)

EMI (electromagnetic interference)

ERP (Enterprise Resource Planning)

ESD (electrostatic discharge)

FBI (Federal Bureau of Investigation)

FCS (frame check sequence)

FDDI (Fiber Distributed Data Interface)

FTP (File Transfer Protocol)

GARP (Gratuitous Address Resolution Protocol)

GBIC (Gigabit Interface Converter)

Gbps (gigabits per second)

HDLC (High-Level Data Link Control)

HTTP (Hypertext Transfer Protocol)

I/O (input/output)

IANA (Internet Assigned Numbers Authority)

ICMP (Internet Control Message Protocol)

ICND (Interconnecting Cisco Network Devices)

IEEE (Institute of Electrical and Electronics Engineers)

IETF (Internet Engineering Task Force)

IGP (Interior gateway protocols)

IGRP (Interior Gateway Routing Protocol)

IOS (Internetwork Operating System)

IP (Internet Protocol)

IPv6 (Internet Protocol version 6)

IRQ (interrupt request line)

IS-IS (Intermediate System–to–Intermediate System)

ISL (Inter-Switch Link)

ISO (International Organization for Standardization)

ISP (Internet service provider)

kbps (kilobits-per-second)

LAN (local-area network)

LEDs: (light-emitting diodes)

LLC (logical link control)

LLDP (Link Layer Discovery Protocol)

LLS (link-local signaling)

LSA (link-state advertisements)

LSB (least significant bit)

LSP (link-state packets)

MAC (Media Access Control)

MAN (metropolitan-area network)

Mbps (megabits per second)

MD5 (message digest algorithm 5)

Microsoft WINS (Microsoft Windows Internet Name Service)

MMF (multimode fiber)

MOP (Maintenance Operation Protocol)

MSB (most significant bit)

MTBF (mean time between failures)

MTU (maximum transmission unit)

NAT (Network Address Translation)

NIC (Network interface cards)

NOS (network operating systems)

NSAP (network service access point)

NSF (nonstop forwarding)

NSSA (not-so-stubby area)

NTP (Network Time Protocol)

NVRAM (nonvolatile random-access memory)

NX-OS (Next Generation Operating System)

OOB (out-of-band)

OSI (Open Systems Interconnection)

OSPF (Open Shortest Path First)

OTP (one-time password)

OUI (Organizational Unique Identifier)

PAD (Packet assembler/disassembler)

PAT (Port Address Translation)

PC (personal computer)

PDU (protocol data units)

POP (point of presence)

POST (power-on self-test)

PPP (Point-to-Point Protocol)

QoS (quality of service)

RADIUS (Remote Authentication Dial-In User Service)

RAM (random-access memory)

RARP (Reverse Address Resolution Protocol)

RBAC (Role-Based Access Control)

RFC (Request for Comments)

RFI (radio frequency interference)

RIP (Routing Information Protocol]

RIPv1 (Routing Information Protocol version 1)

RIPv2 (Routing Information Protocol version 2)

RJ (Registered Jack)

ROM (read-only memory)

RTT (round-trip time)

SAID (security association ID)

SAN (storage-area network)

SCP (Secure Copy Protocol)

SFP (Small Form-Factor Pluggable)

SMF (single-mode fiber)

SMTP (Simple Mail Transfer Protocol)

SNMP (Simple Network Management Protocol)

SOF (start-of-frame)

SOHO (small office/home office)

SPD (security policy database)

SPF (shortest path first)

SQL (Structured Query Language)

SSH (Secure Shell)

SSHv1 (Secure Shell version 1)

SSHv2 (Secure Shell version 2)

STP (shielded twisted-pair)

SVI (Switched Virtual Interface)

TACACS+ (Terminal Access Controller Access Control System Plus)

TCP (Transmission Control Protocol)

TCP/IP (Transmission Control Protocol/Internet Protocol)

TFTP (Trivial File Transfer Protocol)

UDP (User Datagram Protocol)

UNIX (Uniplexed Information and Computing System)

UPS (uninterruptible power supply)

URL (Uniform Resource Locator)

USB (Universal Serial Bus)

UTP (unshielded twisted-pair)

VID (VLAN ID)

VLAN (virtual local-area network)

VLSM (variable-length subnet masking)

VoIP (Voice over IP)

VPN (Virtual Private Network)

VTP (VLAN Trunking Protocol)

VTY (Virtual Terminal Line)

WAN (wide-area network)

Glossary of Key Terms

This glossary defines many of the terms and abbreviations related to networking. It includes all the key terms used throughout the book. As with any growing technical field, some terms evolve and take on several meanings. Where necessary, multiple definitions and abbreviation expansions are presented. We also included some terms here that were not covered in the book, but that you may find interesting and useful.

A

access control list (ACL)   A list kept by Cisco routers to control access to or from the router for a number of services. For example, ACLs prevent packets with a certain IP address from leaving a particular interface on the router.

access layer   The access layer in the three-layer hierarchical network model describes the portion of the network where devices connect to the network and includes controls for allowing devices to communicate on the network.

access server   A communications processor that connects asynchronous devices to a LAN or WAN through network and terminal emulation software. Performs both synchronous and asynchronous routing of supported protocols. Sometimes called a network access server.

Advanced Encryption Standard (AES)   The National Institute of Standards and Technology (NIST) adopted AES to replace the existing DES encryption in cryptographic devices. AES provides stronger security than DES and is computationally more efficient than 3DES. AES offers three different key lengths: 128-, 192-, and 256-bit keys.

application-specific integrated circuit (ASIC)   A development process for implementing integrated circuit designs that are specific to the intended application, as opposed to designs for general-purpose use.

asymmetric encryption   Uses different keys for encryption and decryption. Knowing one of the keys does not allow a hacker to deduce the second key and decode the information. One key encrypts the message, and a second key decrypts it. It is impossible to encrypt and decrypt with the same key.

Asynchronous Transfer Mode (ATM)   An international standard for cell relay in which multiple service types (such as voice, video, or data) are conveyed in fixed-length (53-byte) cells. Fixed-length cells allow cell processing to occur in hardware, thereby reducing transit delays. ATM is designed to take advantage of high-speed transmission media such as E3, T3, and SONET.

attenuation   Loss of communication signal energy.

Authentication Header (AH)   Provides data authentication and integrity for IP packets passed between two systems. It verifies that any message passed between two systems has not been modified during transit. It also verifies the origin of the data. AH does not provide data confidentiality (encryption) of packets. Used alone, the AH protocol provides weak protection.

auto-MDIX   An optional feature of Catalyst switches. When the auto-MDIX feature is enabled, the switch detects the required cable type for copper Ethernet connections and configures the interface pin-outs accordingly, enabling the use of either a crossover cable or a straight-through cable for connections to a 10/100/1000 port on the switch, regardless of the type of device on the other end of the connection.

Automatic Private IP Addressing (APIPA)   Certain Windows clients have this feature, with which a Windows computer can automatically assign itself an IP address in the 169.254.x.x range if a DHCP server is unavailable or does not exist on the network.

AutoSecure   Uses a single command to disable nonessential system processes and services, eliminating potential security threats.

B

backbone   The part of a network that acts as the primary path for traffic that is most often sourced from and destined for other networks.

Backward Explicit Congestion Notification (BECN)   A bit set by a Frame Relay network in frames traveling in the opposite direction of frames encountering a congested path. The DTE receiving frames with the BECN bit set can request that higher-level protocols take flow control action as appropriate.

Basic Rate Interface (BRI)   An ISDN interface composed of two B channels and one D channel for circuit-switched communication of voice, video, and data.

bearer (B) channel   In ISDN, a full-duplex, 64-kbps channel used to send user data.

bit-oriented   A class of data link layer communication protocols that can transmit frames regardless of frame content. Compared with byte-oriented protocols, bit-oriented protocols provide full-duplex operation and are more efficient and reliable.

black hat   Someone who uses his knowledge of computer systems to break into systems or networks that he is not authorized to use, usually for personal or financial gain. A cracker is an example of a black hat.

Bootstrap Protocol (BOOTP)   A protocol used by a network node to determine the IP address of its Ethernet interfaces to affect network booting.

bot   An application that runs automated tasks.

bottom-up troubleshooting   You start with the physical components of the network and move up through the layers of the OSI model until you find the cause of the problem. Bottom-up troubleshooting is a good approach to use when you suspect a physical problem.

BPDU (Bridge Protocol Data Unit)   A frame used by spanning tree protocol to communicate key infromation about the avoidance of Layer 2 loops in the network topology

broadband   A transmission system that multiplexes multiple independent signals onto one cable. In telecommunications terminology, any channel having bandwidth greater than a voice-grade channel (4 kHz). In LAN terminology, a coaxial cable on which analog signaling is used. Also called wideband.

buffer   A storage area used to handle data in transit. Buffers are used in internetworking to compensate for differences in process speed between network devices. Bursts of data can be stored in buffers until they can be handled by slower processing devices. Also known as a packet buffer.

C

cable   A transmission medium of copper wire or optical fiber wrapped in a protective cover.

cable analyzer   A multifunctional handheld device that is used to test and certify copper and fiber cables for different services and standards. The more sophisticated tools include advanced troubleshooting diagnostics that measure distance to performance defect (NEXT, RL), identify corrective actions, and graphically display crosstalk and impedance behavior.

cable modem (CM)   Enables you to receive data at high speeds. Typically, the cable modem attaches to a standard 10BASE-T Ethernet card in the computer.

cable modem termination system (CMTS)   A component that exchanges digital signals with cable modems on a cable network. A headend CMTS communicates with cable modems that are located in the subscriber homes.

cable television   A communication system in which multiple channels of programming are transmitted to homes using broadband coaxial cable. Formerly called community antenna television (CATV).

cable tester   A specialized handheld device designed to test the various types of data communication cabling. Cabling testers can be used to detect broken wires, crossed-over wiring, shorted connections, and improperly paired connections.

call setup time   The time required to establish a switched call between DTE devices.

Carrier Sense Multiple Access with Collision Avoidance (CSMA/CA)   This media access method requires WLAN devices to sense the medium for energy levels and wait until the medium is free before sending.

cell   1) The basic unit for ATM switching and multiplexing. Cells contain identifiers that specify the data stream to which they belong. Each cell consists of a 5-byte header and 48 bytes of payload. 2) In wireless technology, a cell is the area of radio range or coverage in which the wireless devices can communicate with the base station. The cell's size depends on the speed of the transmission, the type of antenna used, and the physical environment, as well as other factors.

cell relay   A network technology based on the use of small, fixed-size packets, or cells. Because cells are fixed length, they can be processed and switched in hardware at high speeds. Cell relay is the basis of many high-speed network protocols, including ATM, IEEE 802.6, and SMDS.

central office (CO)   A local telephone company office to which all local loops in a given area connect and in which circuit switching of subscriber lines occurs.

Challenge Handshake Authentication Protocol (CHAP)   A security feature supported on lines using PPP encapsulation that prevents unauthorized access. CHAP does not itself prevent unauthorized access; it merely identifies the remote end. The router or access server then determines whether that user is allowed access.

channel   1) A communication path. Multiple channels can be multiplexed over a single cable in certain environments. 2) In IBM, the specific path between large computers (such as mainframes) and attached peripheral devices.

channel service unit (CSU)   A digital interface device that connects end-user equipment to the local digital telephone loop. Often mentioned with DSU as CSU/DSU.

circuit   A communications path between two or more points.

circuit switching   A switching system in which a dedicated physical circuit path must exist between sender and receiver for the duration of the "call." Used heavily in the telephone company network. Circuit switching can be contrasted with contention and token passing as a channel access method, and with message switching and packet switching as a switching technique.

Cisco 7000   Any of the Cisco 7000 Series of routers. A high-end router platform that supports a wide range of network interface and media types and is designed for use in enterprise networks.

Cisco Discovery Protocol (CDP)   A media- and protocol-independent device-discovery protocol that runs on all Cisco-manufactured equipment, including routers, access servers, bridges, and switches. Using CDP, a device can advertise its existence to other devices and receive information about other devices on the same LAN or on the remote side of a WAN.

Cisco IOS helper address   An address configured on an interface to which broadcasts received on that interface are sent.

Cisco Router and Security Device Manager (SDM)   An easy-to-use, web-based device-management tool designed for configuring LAN, WAN, and security features on Cisco IOS Software–based routers.

classless interdomain routing (CIDR)   A technique supported by BGP4 and based on route aggregation. CIDR allows routers to group routes to reduce the quantity of routing information carried by the core routers. With CIDR, several IP networks appear to networks outside the group as a single, larger entity. With CIDR, IP addresses and their subnet masks are written as four octets, separated by periods, followed by a slash and a two-digit number that represents the subnet mask.

Clear to Send (CTS)   A circuit in the EIA/TIA-232 specification that is activated when the DCE is ready to accept data from the DTE.

clock skew   A clock's frequency difference, or the first derivative of its offset with respect to time.

coaxial cable   A cable consisting of a hollow cylindrical conductor that surrounds a single inner wire conductor. Two types of coaxial cable are currently used in LANs: 50-ohm cable, which is used for digital signaling, and 75-ohm cable, which is used for analog signal and high-speed digital signaling.

Committed Information Rate (CIR)   The rate at which a Frame Relay network agrees to transfer information under normal conditions, averaged over a minimum increment of time. CIR, measured in bits per second, is one of the key negotiated tariff metrics.

communications line   The physical link (such as a wire or telephone circuit) that connects one or more devices to one or more other devices.

community antenna television (CATV)   A communication system in which multiple channels of programming are transmitted to homes using broadband coaxial cable.

community string   A text string that acts as a password and is used to authenticate messages sent between a management station and a router containing an SNMP agent. The community string is sent in every packet between the manager and the agent.

configuration register   In Cisco routers, a 16-bit user-configurable value that determines how the router functions during initialization. The configuration register can be stored in hardware or software. In hardware, you set the bit position by specifying a hexadecimal value using configuration commands.

congestion   Traffic in excess of network capacity.

connectionless   A term used to describe data transfer without the existence of a virtual circuit.

connection-oriented   A term used to describe data transfer that requires the establishment of a virtual circuit.

control plane   Handles the interaction of the router with the other network elements, providing the information needed to make decisions and control the overall router operation. This plane runs processes such as routing protocols and network management.

convergence   The speed and capability of a group of switches running STP to agree on a loop-free Layer 2 topology for a switched LAN.

core layer   The backbone of a switched LAN. All traffic to and from peripheral networks must pass through the core layer. It includes high-speed switching devices that can handle relatively large amounts of traffic.

core router   In a packet-switched star topology, a router that is part of the backbone and that serves as the single pipe through which all traffic from peripheral networks must pass on its way to other peripheral networks.

cracker   Someone who tries to gain unauthorized access to network resources with malicious intent.

Customer Premises Equipment (CPE)   Terminating equipment, such as terminals, telephones, and modems, supplied by the telephone company, installed at customer sites, and connected to the telephone company network.

cut-through switching   An Ethernet frame switching approach that streams data through a switch so that the leading edge of a packet exits the switch at the egress port before the packet finishes entering the ingress port. A device using cut-through packet switching reads, processes, and forwards packets as soon as the destination address is read and the egress port determined.

cycles per second   A measure of frequency.

D

data communications   The sending and receiving of data between two endpoints. Data communications require a combination of hardware (CSU/DSUs, modems, multiplexers, and other hardware) and software.

Data Communications Equipment (DCE)   Data communications equipment is the EIA expansion. Data circuit–terminating equipment is the ITU-T expansion. The devices and connections of a communications network that comprise the network end of the user-to-network interface. The DCE provides a physical connection to the network, forwards traffic, and provides a clocking signal used to synchronize data transmission between DCE and DTE devices. Modems and interface cards are examples of DCE.

Data Encryption Standard (DES)   Developed by IBM, DES uses a 56-bit key, ensuring high-performance encryption. DES is a symmetric key cryptosystem.

Data Link Connection Identifier (DLCI)   A value that specifies a PVC or SVC in a Frame Relay network. In the basic Frame Relay specification, DLCIs are locally significant (connected devices might use different values to specify the same connection). In the LMI extended specification, DLCIs are globally significant (DLCIs specify individual end devices).

data plane   Handles packet forwarding from one physical or logical interface to another. It involves different switching mechanisms such as process switching and Cisco Express Forwarding (CEF) on Cisco IOS Software routers.

data service unit (DSU)   A device used in digital transmission that adapts the physical interface on a DTE device to a transmission facility such as T1 or E1. The DSU is also responsible for such functions as signal timing. Often mentioned with CSU as CSU/DSU.

data VLAN   A VLAN that is configured to carry only user-generated traffic. In particular, a data VLAN does not carry voice-based traffic or traffic used to manage a switch.

decryption   The reverse application of an encryption algorithm to encrypted data, thereby restoring that data to its original, unencrypted state.

dedicated line   A communications line that is indefinitely reserved for transmissions, rather than switched as transmission is required.

default gateway   The route that the device uses when it has no other explicitly defined route to the destination network. The router interface on the local subnet acts as the default gateway for the sending device.

default VLAN   The VLAN that all the ports on a switch are members of when a switch is reset to factory defaults. All switch ports are members of the default VLAN after the initial boot of the switch. On a Catalyst switch, VLAN 1 is the default VLAN.

delta (D) channel   A full-duplex 16-kbps (BRI) or 64-kbps (PRI) ISDN channel.

demarcation point   The point where the service provider or telephone company network ends and connects with the customer's equipment at the customer's site.

demilitarized zone (DMZ)   The interface of a firewall where the publicly accessible segment exists. The host on the outside might be able to reach the host on the public services segment, the DMZ, but not the host on the inside part of the network.

DHCPACK   Unicast message sent by a DHCP server in response to a device sending a DHCPREQUEST. This message is used by the DHCP server to complete the DHCP process.

DHCPDISCOVER   Broadcast messages sent by a client device to discover a DHCP server.

DHCP for IPv6 (DHCPv6)   Dynamic Host Configuration Protocol for IPv6.

DHCPOFFER   Unicast message returned by the DHCP server in response to a client device sending a DHCPDISCOVER broadcast message. This message typically contains an IP address, subnet mask, default gateway address, and other information.

DHCP relay agent   A component that relays DHCP messages between DHCP clients and DHCP servers on different IP networks.

DHCPREQUEST   Broadcast message sent by a client device in response to a DHCP server's DHCPOFFER message. This message is used by the device to accept the DHCP server's offer.

Diffie-Hellman (DH)   An algorithm to securely derive shared keys across an untrusted network infrastructure. Diffie-Hellman is used to generate keys to be used in the ciphers specified in IPsec transforms. IPsec uses these transforms in conjunction with Diffie-Hellman keys to encrypt and decrypt data as it passes through the VPN tunnel.

digital multimeter (DMM)   A test instrument that directly measures electrical values of voltage, current, and resistance. In network troubleshooting, most multimedia tests involve checking power-supply voltage levels and verifying that network devices are receiving power.

digital subscriber line (DSL)   An always-on connection technology that uses existing twisted-pair telephone lines to transport high-bandwidth data and that provides IP services to subscribers. A DSL modem converts an Ethernet signal from the user device into a DSL signal, which is transmitted to the central office.

Discard Eligible (DE)   Also known as tagged traffic. If the network is congested, tagged traffic can be dropped to ensure delivery of higher-priority traffic.

distributed DoS (DDoS) attack   Designed to saturate network links with illegitimate data. This data can overwhelm an Internet link, causing legitimate traffic to be dropped. DDoS uses attack methods similar to standard DoS attacks, but it operates on a much larger scale. Typically, hundreds or thousands of attack points attempt to overwhelm a target.

distribution layer   In the three-layer hierarchical network design model, the distribution layer is the layer that invokes policy and routing control. Typically, VLANs are defined at this layer.

divide-and-conquer troubleshooting   You start by collecting users' experiences with the problem and document the symptoms. Then, using that information, you make an informed guess about the OSI layer at which to start your investigation. After you verify that a layer is functioning properly, assume that the layers below it are functioning, and work up the OSI layers. If an OSI layer is not functioning properly, work your way down the OSI layer model.

DoS attack   A denial of service (DoS) attack is designed to saturate network links with illegitimate data. This data can overwhelm an Internet link, causing legitimate traffic to be dropped.

drop cable   Generally, a cable that connects a network device (such as a computer) to a physical medium. A type of attachment user interface (AUI).

DS0 (digital signal level zero)   A framing specification used to transmit digital signals over a single channel at 64 kbps in a T1 facility.

DSL access multiplexer (DSLAM)   The device located at the provider's central office (CO). Concentrates connections from multiple DSL subscribers.

dual stacking   A common transition mechanism to enable the smooth integration of IPv4 to IPv6.

dynamic 6to4 tunneling   Automatically establishes the connection of IPv6 islands through an IPv4 network, typically the Internet. It dynamically applies a valid, unique IPv6 prefix to each IPv6 island, which enables the fast deployment of IPv6 in a corporate network without address retrieval from the ISPs or registries.

dynamic auto   A DTP setting whereby the local switch port advertises to the remote switch port that it is able to trunk but does not request to go to the trunking state. After a negotiation, the local port ends up in trunking state only if the remote port trunk mode has been configured to be on or desirable. If both ports on the switches are set to auto, they do not negotiate to be in the trunking state; they negotiate to be in the access (nontrunk) mode state. This is the default setting on Catalyst 2960 and 3560 switches.

dynamic desirable   A DTP setting whereby the local switch port advertises to the remote switch port that it is able to trunk and asks the remote switch port to go to the trunking state. If the local port detects that the remote has been configured in on, desirable, or auto mode, the local port ends up in the trunking state. If the remote switch port is in the nonegotiate mode, the local switch port remains a nontrunking port. This is the default setting on Catalyst 2950 and 3550 switches.

Dynamic Host Configuration Protocol (DHCP)   Makes the process of assigning new IP addresses almost transparent. DHCP assigns IP addresses and other important network configuration information dynamically.

dynamic NAT   Uses a pool of public addresses and assigns them on a first-come, first-served basis. When a host with a private IP address requests access to the Internet, dynamic NAT chooses an IP address from the pool that is not already in use by another host.

Dynamic Trunking Protocol (DTP)   A Cisco-proprietary protocol that negotiates both the status and encapsulation of trunk ports.

dynamic VLAN   VLAN port membership modes are either static or dynamic. Dynamic VLANs are not widely used in production networks. Dynamic port VLAN membership is configured using a special server called a VLAN Membership Policy Server (VMPS).

E

E1   A wide-area digital transmission scheme used predominantly in Europe that carries data at a rate of 2.048 Mbps. E1 lines can be leased for private use from common carriers.

E3   A wide-area digital transmission scheme used predominantly in Europe that carries data at a rate of 34.368 Mbps. E3 lines can be leased for private use from common carriers.

Encapsulating Security Payload (ESP)   Provides a combination of security services for IPsec-processed IP packets. Examples of the services offered by ESP include data confidentiality, data origin authentication, data integrity, and data confidentiality.

encryption   Applying a specific algorithm to data to alter its appearance, making it incomprehensible to those who are not authorized to see the information.

end-system configuration table   Contains baseline records of the hardware and software used in end-system devices such as servers, network management consoles, and desktop workstations. An incorrectly configured end system can have a negative impact on a network's overall performance.

enterprise network   A large and diverse network connecting most major points in a company or other organization. Differs from a WAN in that it is privately owned and maintained.

Ethernet   The main media used in local-area networking. There are many varieties of this media implementation at various speeds.

EUI-64 (Extended Universal Identifier 64)   An IPv6 address format created by taking an interface's MAC address (which is 48 bits long) and inserting another 16-bit hexadecimal string (FFFE) in the OUI (first 24 bits) of the MAC address. To ensure that the chosen 48-bit address is a unique Ethernet address, the seventh bit in the high-order byte is set to 1 (equivalent to the IEEE U/L, Universal/Local bit).

Excess Burst Size (BE)   A negotiated tariff metric in Frame Relay internetworks. The number of bits that a Frame Relay internetwork attempts to transmit after the committed burst (BC) is accommodated. In general, BE data is delivered with a lower probability than BC data, because BE data can be marked as DE by the network.

exchange identification (XID)   Request and response packets exchanged before a session between a router and a Token Ring host. If the parameters of the serial device contained in the XID packet do not match the host's configuration, the session is dropped.

F

firewall   A router or access server designated as a buffer between any connected public network and a private network. A firewall router uses access lists and other methods to ensure the security of the private network.

firmware   Software instructions set permanently or semipermanently in ROM. On Cisco Catalyst switches, the firmware provides a means of booting the switch with these instructions, which are unaffected by a power loss.

Flash   Technology developed by Intel and licensed to other semiconductor companies. Flash memory is nonvolatile storage that can be electrically erased and reprogrammed. Flash allows software images to be stored, booted, and rewritten as necessary.

fragmentation   The process of breaking a packet into smaller units when transmitting over a network medium that cannot support the packet's original size.

Frame Relay   An industry-standard switched data link layer protocol that handles multiple virtual circuits using HDLC encapsulation between connected devices. Frame Relay is more efficient than X.25, the protocol for which it is generally considered a replacement.

Frame Relay access device (FRAD)   Any network device that provides a connection between a LAN and a Frame Relay WAN.

frequency   The number of cycles, measured in hertz, of an alternating current signal per unit of time.

full duplex   The capability of a port for simultaneous data transmission and reception.

full-mesh topology   A network in which each network node has either a physical circuit or a virtual circuit connecting it to every other network node. A full mesh provides a great deal of redundancy, but because it can be prohibitively expensive to implement, it is usually reserved for network backbones.

G

gateway   A special-purpose device that performs an application layer conversion of information from one protocol stack to another. The term gateway also is used to refer to a router or an interface on a router that enables users in an organization to connect to the Internet.

Generic Route Encapsulation (GRE)   A tunneling protocol developed by Cisco that can encapsulate a wide variety of protocol packet types inside IP tunnels. This creates a virtual point-to-point link to Cisco routers at remote points over an IP internetwork. By connecting multiprotocol subnetworks in a single-protocol backbone environment, IP tunneling using GRE allows network expansion across a single-protocol backbone environment.

global routing prefix   Part of the IPv6 address that is a hierarchically structured value assigned to a site.

H

hacker   A general term that has historically been used to describe a computer programming expert. More recently, this term is often used in a negative way to describe an individual who attempts to gain unauthorized access to network resources with malicious intent.

half duplex   Refers to the transmission of data in just one direction at a time. At any given instant, the device can transmit or receive, but not both simultaneously.

hash   Contributes to data integrity and authentication by ensuring that unauthorized persons do not tamper with transmitted messages. A hash, also called a message digest, is a number generated from a string of text. The hash is smaller than the text itself. It is generated using a formula in such a way that it is extremely unlikely that some other text will produce the same hash value.

hashed message authentication code (HMAC)   A data integrity algorithm that guarantees the message's integrity.

headend   The endpoint of a broadband network. All stations transmit toward the headend; the headend then transmits toward the destination stations.

High-Level Data Link Control (HDLC)   A bit-oriented synchronous data link layer protocol developed by ISO. Derived from SDLC, HDLC specifies a data encapsulation method on synchronous serial links using frame characters and checksums.

High-Speed Serial Interface (HSSI)   A network standard for high-speed (up to 52-Mbps) serial connections over WAN links.

hub   Generally, a term used to describe a device that serves as the center of a star topology network.

I

IANA (Internet Assigned Numbers Authority)   An organization operated under the auspices of the ISOC as part of the IAB. IANA delegates authority for IP address-space allocation and domain-name assignment to the NIC and other organizations. IANA also maintains a database of assigned protocol identifiers used in the TCP/IP stack, including autonomous system numbers.

IEEE 802.11   An IEEE specification developed to eliminate problems inherent in the proprietary WLAN technologies. It began with a 1-Mbps standard and has evolved into several other standards, including 802.11a, 802.11b, and 802.11g.

IEEE 802.11b   The IEEE WLAN standard for 11 Mbps at 2.4 GHz.

IEEE 802.11g   The IEEE WLAN standard for 54 Mbps at 2.4 GHz.

IEEE 802.11n   The IEEE WLAN standard for 248 Mbps at 2.4 or 5 GHz. As the latest standard, 802.11n is a proposed amendment that builds on the previous 802.11 standards by adding multiple input, multiple output (MIMO).

IEEE 802.16   The WiMAX standard. It allows transmissions of up to 70 Mbps and has a range of up to 30 miles (50 km). It can operate in licensed or unlicensed bands of the spectrum from 2 to 6 GHz.

inside global address   Used with NAT, a valid public address that the inside host is given when it exits the NAT router.

inside local address   Used with NAT, this usually is not an IP address assigned by an RIR or service provider and is most likely an RFC 1918 private address.

Integrated Services Digital Network (ISDN)   A communication protocol, offered by telephone companies, that permits telephone networks to carry data, voice, and other source traffic.

Internet Control Message Protocol (ICMP)   Chiefly used by TCP/IP network operating systems to send error messages indicating, for example, that a requested service is not available or that a host or router could not be reached.

Internetwork Packet Exchange (IPX)   A NetWare network layer (Layer 3) protocol for transferring data from servers to workstations. IPX is similar to IP and XNS.

inter-switch link (ISL)   A Cisco-proprietary protocol that maintains VLAN information as traffic flows between switches and routers, or switches and switches. ISL is used by trunk ports to encapsulate Ethernet frames between network devices.

inter-VLAN routing   The process of routing data between VLANs within a switched LAN.

intrusion detection system (IDS)   Detects attacks against a network and send logs to a management console.

intrusion prevention system (IPS)   Prevents attacks against the network and should provide active defense mechanisms in addition to detection, including prevention and reaction. Prevention stops the detected attack from executing. Reaction immunizes the system from future attacks from a malicious source.

Inverse Address Resolution Protocol (ARP)   A method of building dynamic routes in a network. Allows an access server to discover the network address of a device associated with a virtual circuit.

IP multicast   Enables single packets to be copied by the network and sent to a specific subset of network addresses. These receivers subscribe to the multicast group, which correlates to the destination multicast address in the transmission from the source.

IP Next Generation (IPng)   Now known as IPv6, a network layer IP standard used by electronic devices to exchange data across a packet-switched internetwork. It follows IPv4 as the second version of the Internet Protocol to be formally adopted for general use. IPv6 includes support for flow ID in the packet header, which can be used to identify flows.

IP Security (IPsec)   A protocol suite for securing IP communications that provides encryption, integrity, and authentication. IPsec spells out the messaging necessary to secure VPN communications, but it relies on existing algorithms.

IPv6 global unicast address   A globally unique address that can be routed globally with no modification. It shares the same address format as an IPv6 anycast address. The IANA assigns global unicast addresses.

J

J1   A wide-area digital transmission scheme used predominantly in Japan that carries data at a rate of 1.544 Mbps. J1 lines can be leased for private use from common carriers.

jabber   The condition in which a network device continually transmits random, meaningless data onto the network.

K

keepalive interval   The amount of time between each keepalive message sent by a network device.

knowledge base   An information database used to assist in the use or troubleshooting of a product. Online network device vendor knowledge bases have become indispensable sources of information. When vendor-based knowledge bases are combined with Internet search engines such as Google, a network administrator has access to a vast pool of experience-based information.

L

LACNIC (Latin America and Caribbean Internet Addresses Registry)   One of five Regional Internet Registries. LACNIC is a not-for-profit membership organization that is responsible for distributing and registering Internet address resources throughout the Latin America and Caribbean region.

Layer 2 switch   These devices operate at the data link layer of the OSI model. They transparently forward and filter frames based on destination MAC address.

leased line   A transmission line reserved by a communications carrier for a customer's private use. A leased line is a type of dedicated line.

Link Access Procedure, Balanced (LAPB)   A data link layer protocol in the X.25 protocol stack. LAPB is a bit-oriented protocol derived from HDLC.

Link Access Procedure for Frame Relay (LAPF)   As defined in the ITU Q.922, specifies Frame Mode Services in the Frame Relay network.

Link Control Protocol (LCP)   A protocol that establishes, configures, and tests data-link connections for use by PPP.

local-area network (LAN)   A high-speed network for connecting equipment that is in close proximity to each other. This equipment is typically owned by the organization hosting it.

local loop   A line from the premises of a telephone subscriber to the telephone company CO.

Local Management Interface (LMI)   A keepalive mechanism that provides status information about Frame Relay connections between the router (DTE) and the Frame Relay switch (DCE).

logical topology   Describes the arrangement of devices on a network and how they communicate with one another.

M

man-in-the-middle (MITM) attack   Carried out by an attacker who positions himself between two legitimate hosts. The attacker might allow the normal transactions between hosts to occur, and only periodically manipulate the conversation between the two.

mesh   A network topology in which devices are organized in a manageable, segmented manner with many, often redundant, interconnections strategically placed between network nodes.

Message Digest 5 (MD5)   An algorithm used for message authentication. MD5 verifies the integrity of the communication, authenticates the origin, and checks for timeliness.

metropolitan-area network (MAN)   A network that spans a metropolitan area. Generally, a MAN spans a larger geographic area than a LAN but a smaller geographic area than a WAN.

microfilter   A device that prevents certain router frequencies from traveling over the telephone line and interfering with telephone calls.

microwave   Electromagnetic waves in the range of 1 to 30 GHz. Microwave-based networks are an evolving technology gaining favor due to high bandwidth and relatively low cost.

modem   A device that converts digital and analog signals. At the source, a modem coverts digital signals to a form suitable for transmission over analog communication facilities. At the destination, the analog signals are returned to their digital form. Modems allow data to be transmitted over voice-grade telephone lines.

multilayer switch   This is a switch that has the ability to also route packets, in addition to switching Layer 2 frames.

N

NAT overloading   Sometimes called Port Address Translation (PAT). Maps multiple private IP addresses to a single public IP address or a few addresses.

NAT pool   A list of public IP addresses used in NAT.

native VLAN   A native VLAN is assigned to an IEEE 802.1Q trunk port. An IEEE 802.1Q trunk port supports tagged and untagged traffic coming from many VLANs. The 802.1Q trunk port places untagged traffic on the native VLAN. Native VLANs are set out in the IEEE 802.1Q specification to maintain backward compatibility with untagged traffic common to legacy LAN scenarios. A native VLAN serves as a common identifier on opposing ends of a trunk link. It is a security best practice to define a native VLAN to be a dummy VLAN distinct from all other VLANs defined in the switched LAN. The native VLAN is not used for any traffic in the switched network.

Network Address Translation (NAT)   Only globally unique in terms of the public Internet. A mechanism for translating private addresses into publicly usable addresses to be used within the public Internet. An effective means of hiding actual device addressing within a private network.

network analysis module (NAM)   Can be installed in Cisco Catalyst 6500 Series switches and Cisco 7600 Series routers to provide a graphical representation of traffic from local and remote switches and routers. The NAM is an embedded browser-based interface that generates reports on the traffic that consumes critical network resources. In addition, the NAM can capture and decode packets and track response times to pinpoint an application problem to the network or server.

network baseline   Used to efficiently diagnose and correct network problems. A network baseline documents what the network's expected performance should be under normal operating conditions. This information is captured in documentation such as configuration tables and topology diagrams.

network configuration table   Contains accurate, up-to-date records of the hardware and software used in a network. The network configuration table should provide the network engineer with all the information necessary to identify and correct the network fault.

Network Control Protocol (NCP)   Used to establish and configure different network layer protocols.

network documentation   Provides a logical diagram of the network and detailed information about each component. This information should be kept in a single location, either as hard copy or on the network on a protected website. Network documentation should include a network configuration table, an end-system configuration table, and a network topology diagram.

network interface device (NID)   Connects the customer premises to the local loop at the demarcation point.

network management system (NMS)   Responsible for managing at least part of a network. An NMS is generally a reasonably powerful and well-equipped computer, such as an engineering workstation. NMSs communicate with agents to help keep track of network statistics and resources.

Network Security Wheel   Helps you comply with a security policy. The Security Wheel, a continuous process, promotes retesting and reapplying updated security measures on a continuous basis.

network topology diagram   A graphical representation of a network that illustrates how each device is connected and its logical architecture. A topology diagram has many of the same components as the network configuration table. Each network device should be represented on the diagram with consistent notation or a graphical symbol. Also, each logical and physical connection should be represented using a simple line or other appropriate symbol. Routing protocols also can be shown.

nonbroadcast multiaccess (NBMA)   A term describing a multiaccess network that does not support broadcasting (such as X.25) or in which broadcasting is not feasible (for example, an SMDS broadcast group or an extended Ethernet that is too large).

nonvolatile RAM (NVRAM)   RAM that retains its contents when a device is powered off. In Cisco products, NVRAM is used to store configuration information.

Novell IPX   See Internetwork Packet Exchange (IPX).

null modem   A small box or cable used to join computing devices directly, rather than over a network.

O

one-step lockdown wizard   Tests your router configuration for potential security problems and automatically makes any necessary configuration changes to correct any problems found.

optical time-domain reflectometer (OTDR)   Pinpoints the distance to a break in a fiber-optic cable. This device sends signals along the cable and waits for them to be reflected. The time between sending the signal and getting it back is converted into a distance measurement. The TDR function normally is packaged with data cabling testers.

OSI model   The Open Systems Interconnection model is a seven-layer model for describing the functions of computer networking. This model is used to teach and troubleshoot networks.

OSPF   Open Shortest Path First is a scalable, link-state routing protocol used by many networks inside companies.

outside global address   A reachable IP address used in NAT and assigned to hosts on the Internet.

P

packet-switched network   Uses packet-switching technology to transfer data.

packet switching   A networking method in which nodes share bandwidth with each other by sending packets.

partial mesh topology   A network in which some network nodes are organized in a full mesh and others are connected to only one or two other nodes in the network. A partial mesh does not provide the level of redundancy of a full-mesh topology, but it is less expensive to implement. Partial-mesh topologies generally are used in the peripheral networks that connect to a fully meshed backbone.

passphrase   A sentence or phrase that translates into a more secure password. Make sure that the phrase is long enough to be hard to guess but easy to remember and type accurately.

Password Authentication Protocol (PAP)   An authentication protocol that allows PPP peers to authenticate one another. The remote router attempting to connect to the local router is required to send an authentication request. Unlike CHAP, PAP passes the password and username in the clear (unencrypted). PAP does not itself prevent unauthorized access, but merely identifies the remote end. The router or access server then determines whether that user is allowed access. PAP is supported only on PPP lines.

password recovery   The process of legitimately accessing a device when the password is unknown.

permanent virtual circuit (PVC)   A virtual circuit that is permanently established. PVCs save bandwidth associated with circuit establishment and are torn down in situations where certain virtual circuits must exist all the time.

Per-VLAN Spanning Tree (PVST)   A Cisco-proprietary STP implementation that maintains a spanning-tree instance for each VLAN configured in the network. PVST relies on ISL for VLAN trunk encapsulation.

Per-VLAN Spanning Tree Plus (PVST+)   PVST+ provides the same functionality as PVST, including PortFast, and adds support for IEEE 802.1Q. PVST+ is not supported on non-Cisco devices.

phisher   Someone who uses e-mail or other means to trick others into providing sensitive information, such as credit card numbers or passwords. A phisher masquerades as a trusted party that has a legitimate need for the sensitive information.

physical topology   The mapping of a network that shows the physical layout of equipment, cables, and interconnections.

ping   A command used to verify Layer 3 connectivity. Ping sends an ICMP echo request to the destination address. When a host receives an ICMP echo request, it responds with an ICMP echo reply to confirm that it received the request.

point of presence (POP)   A point of interconnection between the communications facilities provided by the telephone company and the building's main distribution facility.

point-to-point connection   A connection used to connect LANs to service provider WANs and to connect LAN segments within an enterprise network.

Point-to-Point Protocol (PPP)   A successor to SLIP. Provides router-to-router and host-to-network connections over synchronous and asynchronous circuits.

Port Address Translation (PAT)   Sometimes called NAT overloading. Maps multiple private IP addresses to a single public IP address or a few addresses.

portable network analyzer   A portable device that is used to troubleshoot switched networks and VLANs. By plugging in the network analyzer anywhere on the network, a network engineer can see the switch port to which the device is connected and the average and peak utilization.

port forwarding   Sometimes called tunneling. The act of forwarding a network port from one network node to another. This technique can allow an external user to reach a port on a private IP address (inside a LAN) from the outside through a NAT-enabled router.

preshared key (PSK)   A secret key that is shared between the two parties using a secure channel before it needs to be used. PSKs use symmetric key cryptographic algorithms. A PSK is entered into each peer manually and is used to authenticate the peer. At each end, the PSK is combined with other information to form the authentication key.

Primary Rate Interface (PRI)   An ISDN interface to primary rate access. Primary rate access consists of a single 64-kbps D channel plus 23 (T1) or 30 (E1) B channels for voice or data.

primary station   In bit-synchronous data link layer protocols such as HDLC and SDLC, a station that controls the transmission activity of secondary stations. Also performs other management functions such as error control through polling or other means. Primary stations send commands to secondary stations and receive responses.

protocol analyzer   Decodes the various protocol layers in a recorded frame and presents this information in a relatively easy-to-use format.

public switched telephone network (PSTN)   A general term referring to the variety of telephone networks and services in place worldwide. Also called the plain old telephone service (POTS).

Q

quality of service (QoS)   A measure of performance for a transmission system that reflects its transmission quality and service available.

R

radio frequency (RF)   A generic term referring to frequencies that correspond to radio transmissions. Cable TV and broadband networks use RF technology.

Rapid Per-VLAN Spanning Tree Plus (Rapid PVST+)   A Cisco implementation of RSTP. It supports one instance of RSTP for each VLAN.

Rapid Spanning Tree Protocol (RSTP)   RSTP, specified by IEEE 802.1w, is a dramatic improvement to IEEE 802.1D, providing very fast spanning-tree convergence on a link-by-link basis using a proposal and agreement process independent of timers.

read-only memory (ROM)   Nonvolatile memory that can be read, but not written to, by the microprocessor.

reassembly   The putting back together of an IP datagram at the destination after it has been fragmented at either the source or the intermediate node.

Regional Internet Registry (RIR)   An organization overseeing the allocation and registration of Internet number resources in a particular region of the world. There are currently five RIRs.

RFC 1918, Address Allocation for Private Internets   Private IP addresses that are a reserved block of numbers that can be used by anyone. ISPs typically configure their border routers to prevent privately addressed traffic from being forwarded over the Internet.

RIPE (Réseaux IP Européens) Network Coordination Centre   One of five Regional Internet Registries. RIPE is a not-for-profit membership organization that is responsible for distributing and registering Internet address resources throughout Europe, the Middle East, and parts of Central Asia.

Rivest, Shamir, and Adleman (RSA)   An asymmetric key cryptosystem. The keys use a bit length of 512, 768, 1024, or larger.

router   A device used to route packets between TCP/IP subnets.

router-on-a-stick   A term used to describe the topology of a Layer 2 switch trunked to an interface on a router for the purposes of inter-VLAN routing. In this topology, the router interface is configured with one logical subinterface for each VLAN.

Routing Information Protocol next generation (RIPng)   RIP for IPv6.

routing table   The table, stored in a router or other internetworking device, that keeps track of routes of network destinations and metrics associated with those routes.

RSA signature   Uses the exchange of digital certificates to authenticate the peers. The local device derives a hash and encrypts it with its private key. The encrypted hash (digital signature) is attached to the message and is forwarded to the remote end. At the remote end, the encrypted hash is decrypted using the public key of the local end. If the decrypted hash matches the recomputed hash, the signature is genuine.

S

Secure Hash Algorithm 1 (SHA-1)   Uses a 160-bit secret key. The variable-length message and the 160-bit shared secret key are combined and are run through the HMAC-SHA-1 hash algorithm. The output is a 160-bit hash. The hash is appended to the original message and is forwarded to the remote end.

Secure Shell (SSH)   A protocol that allows data to be exchanged over a secure channel between two computers. A secure form of Telnet.

security policy   A policy for an organization that informs users, staff, and managers of their obligations for protecting technology and information assets.

Serial Line Internet Protocol (SLIP)   A standard protocol for point-to-point serial connections using a variation of TCP/IP. A predecessor of PPP.

signaling   The process of sending a transmission signal over a physical medium for purposes of communication.

SNA Control Protocol   Part of the family of Network Control Protocols (NCP), specifically for Systems Network Architecture (SNA). Used to establish and configure different network layer protocols.

SONET   A high-speed (up to 2.5-Gbps) synchronous network specification developed by Bellcore and designed to run on optical fiber. STS-1 is the basic building block of Synchronous Optical Network (SONET). Approved as an international standard in 1988.

spammer   An individual who sends large quantities of unsolicited e-mail messages. Spammers often use viruses to take control of home computers and use them to send bulk messages.

spanning-tree algorithm (STA)   Used by STP to create a spanning tree.

Spanning Tree Protocol (STP)   A bridge protocol that utilizes the spanning-tree algorithm, enabling a learning bridge to dynamically work around loops in a network topology by creating a spanning tree. Bridges exchange BPDU messages with other bridges to detect loops, and then remove the loops by shutting down selected bridge interfaces. Refers to both the IEEE 802.1 Spanning Tree Protocol standard and the earlier Digital Equipment Corporation Spanning Tree Protocol, on which it is based. The IEEE version supports bridge domains and allows the bridge to construct a loop-free topology across an extended LAN. The IEEE version is generally preferred over the Digital Equipment Corporation version. Sometimes abbreviated as STP. *See also* BPDU and spanning-tree algorithm.

star topology   A LAN topology in which endpoints on a network are connected to a common central switch by point-to-point links.

stateless autoconfiguration   A plug-and-play IPv6 feature that enables devices to connect themselves to the network without any configuration and without any servers (such as DHCP servers). This key feature enables the deployment of new devices on the Internet, such as cell phones, wireless devices, home appliances, and home networks.

static NAT   Uses a one-to-one mapping of local and global addresses, and these mappings remain constant. Static NAT is particularly useful for web servers or hosts that must have a consistent address that is accessible from the Internet. These internal hosts can be enterprise servers or networking devices.

statistical time-division multiplexing (STDM)   A technique whereby information from multiple logical channels can be transmitted across a single physical channel. Statistical multiplexing dynamically allocates bandwidth only to active input channels, making better use of available bandwidth and allowing more devices to be connected than with other multiplexing techniques.

subnet ID   Individual organizations can use a 16-bit subnet field to create their own local addressing hierarchy. This field allows an organization to use up to 65,535 individual subnets.

switched virtual circuit (SVC)   A virtual circuit that is dynamically established on demand and that is torn down when transmission is complete. SVCs are used in situations where data transmission is sporadic.

symmetric encryption   Encryption algorithms, such as DES and 3DES, require a shared secret key to perform encryption and decryption. Each of the two computers must know the key to decode the information. With symmetric key encryption, also called secret key encryption, each computer encrypts the information before sending it over the network to the other computer. Symmetric key encryption requires knowledge of which computers will be talking to each other so that the same key can be configured on each computer.

synchronization   The establishment of common timing between sender and receiver.

Synchronous Data Link Control (SDLC)   An SNA data link layer communications protocol. A bit-oriented, full-duplex protocol that has spawned numerous similar protocols, including HDLC and LAPB.

systematic approach   A troubleshooting method that analyzes the network as a whole rather than in a piecemeal fashion. A systematic approach minimizes confusion and cuts down on time that would be wasted with trial and error.

T

T1   A digital WAN carrier facility. T1 transmits DS-1-formatted data at 1.544 Mbps through the telephone switching network, using AMI or B8ZS coding.

T3   A digital WAN carrier facility. T3 transmits DS-3-formatted data at 44.736 Mbps through the telephone switching network.

TACACS/TACACS+   Short for Terminal Access Controller Access Control System (Plus). An authentication protocol, developed by the Defense Data Network (DDN) community, that provides remote-access authentication and related services, such as event logging. User passwords are administered in a central database rather than in individual routers, providing an easily scalable network security solution.

T-carrier   A TDM transmission method that usually refers to a line or cable carrying a DS-1 signal.

TCP/IP model   This model predates the OSI model and describes the technologies used to allow TCP/IP to function for internetworking.

telephony   The science of converting sound to electrical signals and transmitting it between widely removed points.

teleworker   An employee who enjoys some flexibility in working location and hours. The daily commute to an office is replaced by telecommunication links.

TFTP server   Trivial File Transfer Protocol is a simplified version of FTP that allows files to be transferred from one computer to another over a network. The TFTP server stores and receives the uploaded files for download at the user's request.

time-division multiplexing (TDM)   A technique in which information from multiple channels can be allocated bandwidth on a single wire based on preassigned time slots. Bandwidth is allocated to each channel regardless of whether the station has data to transmit.

time-to-live (TTL)   The field in an IP header that indicates how long a packet is considered valid; each routing device that an IP packet passes through decrements the TTL by 1.

top-down troubleshooting   You start with the end-user applications and move down through the layers of the OSI model until you find the cause of the problem. You test end-user applications of an end system before tackling the more specific networking pieces. Use this approach for simpler problems or when you think the problem is with a piece of software.

transaction   A result-oriented unit of communication processing.

transmission link   A network communications channel consisting of a circuit or transmission path and all related equipment between a sender and a receiver. Most often used to refer to a WAN connection.

Triple DES (3DES)   A newer variant of DES that encrypts with one key, decrypts with a different key, and then encrypts a final time with another key. 3DES provides significantly more strength to the encryption process.

Trivial File Transfer Protocol (TFTP)   A simplified version of FTP that allows files to be transferred from one computer to another over a network in clear text without authentication.

Trojan horse   A type of virus in which the application is written to look like something else, when in fact it is an attack tool. An example of a Trojan horse is a software application that runs a simple game on a workstation. While the user is occupied with the game, the Trojan horse mails a copy of itself to every address in the user's address book. The other users receive the game and play it, thereby spreading the Trojan horse to the addresses in each address book.

trunk   Used to create multiple network cables or ports in parallel to increase the link speed beyond the limits of any single cable or port.

tunneling   An architecture that is designed to provide the services necessary to implement any standard point-to-point encapsulation scheme.

U–V

Universal Asynchronous Receiver/Transmitter (UART)   An integrated circuit, attached to a computer's parallel bus, used for serial communications. The UART translates between serial and parallel signals, provides transmission clocking, and buffers data sent to or from the computer.

virtual circuit (VC)   A logical circuit created to ensure reliable communication between two network devices. A virtual circuit is defined by a VPI/VCI pair, and it can be either permanent (a PVC) or switched (an SVC). Virtual circuits are used in Frame Relay and X.25. In ATM, a virtual circuit is called a virtual channel.

virtual LAN (VLAN)   A group of hosts with a common set of requirements that communicate as if they were attached to the same wire, regardless of their physical location. A VLAN has the same attributes as a physical LAN, but it allows end stations to be grouped together even if they are not located on the same LAN segment. Network reconfiguration can be done through software instead of physically relocating devices.

Virtual Private Network (VPN)   A means to securely and privately transmit data over an unsecured and shared network infrastructure.

virus   Malicious software that is attached to another program to execute a particular unwanted function on a workstation.

VLAN ID (VID)   The parameter in the IEEE 802.1Q tag that indicates the VLAN the frame is associated with. A Catalyst 2960 switch supports up to 4096 VLAN IDs.

VLAN trunk   An Ethernet point-to-point link between an Ethernet switch interface and an Ethernet interface on another networking device, such as a router or a switch, carrying the traffic of multiple VLANs over the singular link. A VLAN trunk allows you to extend the VLANs across an entire switched LAN.

VLAN Trunking Protocol (VTP)   A Cisco-proprietary Layer 2 protocol that enables a network manager to configure a single switch so that it propagates VLAN configuration information to other switches in the network, as well as synchronizes the information with the switches in the VTP domain.

Voice over IP (VoIP)   The capability to carry normal telephony-style voice over an IP-based Internet with POTS-like functionality.

voice VLAN   A specialized Catalyst switch VLAN with an accompanying Catalyst CLI command set. Voice VLANs are designed for and dedicated to the transmission of voice traffic involving Cisco IP phones or Cisco softphones. QoS configurations are applied to voice VLANs to prioritize voice traffic.

VTP advertisements   VTP advertisements are messages transmitted between Catalyst switches to share and synchronize VLAN configuration details in the switched LAN.

VTP client   VTP clients participate in VTP operation, but do not permit creating, changing, or deleting of VLANs on the client itself. A VTP client stores VLAN information for the VTP domain only while the switch is powered on. A switch reset deletes the VLAN information. A switch must be manually configured to change its mode from VTP server to VTP client.

VTP configuration revision number   A number that indicates the current state of the VLAN information on the switch. The number enables the synchronization of VLAN information within the VTP domain.

VTP domain   A set of Catalyst switches with the same VTP domain name; all switches in a VTP domain share the same synchronized VLAN information.

VTP modes   VTP has three operating modes: server, client, and transparent. The operating mode determines how the switch uses and shares VLAN information within the VTP domain.

VTP password   The VTP password must match on all switches in a VTP domain. The password secures the information in the VTP domain and prevents a rogue switch added to a network from compromising VLAN information.

VTP pruning   Prevents unnecessary transmission of VLAN information from one VLAN across all trunks in a VTP domain. VTP pruning permits switches to negotiate which VLANs have active associations with ports on the portion of the network connected to the opposing end of a trunk link and, hence, prune the VLANs that are not actively associated with ports on that portion of the network. VTP pruning is disabled by default.

VTP server   VTP servers advertise the VTP domain VLAN information to other VTP-enabled switches in the same VTP domain. VTP servers store the VLAN information for the entire domain in NVRAM. The server is where VLANs can be created, deleted, or renamed for the domain. It might take multiple subset advertisements to fully update the VLAN information.

VTP transparent   VTP transparent mode switches forward VTP advertisements to VTP clients and VTP servers, but does not originate or otherwise process VTP advertisements. VLANs that are created, renamed, or deleted on a VTP transparent mode switch are local to that switch only.

VTP version   VTP has three versions: version 1, version 2, and version 3. Catalyst 2960 and 3560 switches support versions 1 and 2.

W–Z

white hat   Someone who looks for vulnerabilities in systems or networks and then reports them to the system's owners so that they can be fixed. This person is ethically opposed to the abuse of computer systems. A white hat generally focuses on securing IT systems, whereas a black hat (the opposite) wants to break into them.

wide-area network (WAN)   A data communications network that serves users across a broad geographic area and often uses transmission devices provided by common carriers. Frame Relay, SMDS, and X.25 are examples of WANs.

Wi-Fi Alliance   Offers certification for interoperability between vendors of 802.11 products. It helps market a WLAN technology by promoting interoperability between vendors. Certification includes all three 802.11 RF technologies and Wi-Fi Protected Access (WPA).

wildcard mask   A 32-bit quantity used in conjunction with an IP address to determine which bits in an IP address should be ignored when comparing that address to another IP address. A wildcard mask is specified when setting up access lists.

WiMAX (Worldwide Interoperability for Microwave Access)   Described in the IEEE standard 802.16. WiMAX offers high-speed broadband service with wireless access. It provides broad coverage like a cell phone network rather than using small Wi-Fi hotspots.

wiring closet   A specially designed room used to wire a data or voice network. Wiring closets serve as a central junction point for the wiring and wiring equipment that is used to interconnect network devices.

worm   Executes code and installs copies of itself in the memory of the infected computer, which can, in turn, infect other hosts.

X.25   An ITU-T standard that defines how connections between the DTE and DCE are maintained for remote terminal access and computer communications in packet data networks (PDN). X.25 specifies LAPB, a data link layer protocol, and Packet Level Protocol (PLP), a network layer protocol. Frame Relay has to some degree superseded X.25.

Index

Symbols

A

E

F

J-K

L

M

O

P

U

V

FREE
Online Edition

Your purchase of *Interconnecting Cisco Network Devices, Part 1 (ICND1) Foundation Learning Guide* includes access to a free online edition for 45 days through the **Safari Books Online** subscription service. Nearly every Cisco Press book is available online through **Safari Books Online**, along with thousands of books and videos from publishers such as Addison-Wesley Professional, Exam Cram, IBM Press, O'Reilly Media, Prentice Hall, Que, Sams, and VMware Press.

Safari Books Online is a digital library providing searchable, on-demand access to thousands of technology, digital media, and professional development books and videos from leading publishers. With one monthly or yearly subscription price, you get unlimited access to learning tools and information on topics including mobile app and software development, tips and tricks on using your favorite gadgets, networking, project management, graphic design, and much more.